THIRD EDITION

CONTEMPORARY URBAN PLANNING

JOHN M. LEVY
Virginia Polytechnic Institute and State University

Prentice Hall, Englewood Cliffs, New Jersey 07632

Library of Congress Cataloging-in-Publication Data

LEVY, JOHN M.
Contemporary urban planning/John M. Levy.—3rd ed.
p. cm.
Includes bibliographical references and index.
ISBN 0-13-146614-3
1. City planning—United States. 2. Urban policy—United States.
3. Urbanization—United States. 4. Sociology, Urban—United States.
I. Title.
HT167.L38 1994
307.1'216'0973—dc20 93-24560

Acquisitions editor: *Maria DiVencenzo*
Editorial/production supervision: *Edie Riker*
Cover design: *Design Solutions*
Cover photo: *Courtesy of Battery Park City Authority*
Production Coordinator: *Mary Ann Gloriande*
Editorial assistant: *Nicole Signoretti*

To LUCIE, RACHEL, BERNIE, and KARA

Printed in the United States of America

10 9 8 7 6 5 4 3

ISBN 0-13-146614-3

Prentice-Hall International (UK) Limited, *London*
Prentice-Hall of Australia Pty. Limited, *Sydney*
Prentice-Hall Canada Inc., *Toronto*
Prentice-Hall Hispanoamericana, S.A., *Mexico*
Prentice-Hall of India Private Limited, *New Delhi*
Prentice-Hall of Japan, Inc., *Tokyo*
Simon & Schuster Asia Pte. Ltd., *Singapore*
Editora Prentice-Hall do Brasil, Ltda., *Rio de Janeiro*

Contents

Preface *xiii*

A Note on Further Readings, *xv*

Illustration Credits, *xv*

Acknowledgments, *xvi*

PART ONE THE BACKGROUND AND DEVELOPMENT OF CONTEMPORARY PLANNING

1 An Overview *1*

The Need for Planning, *1*

The Specific Concerns of Planning, *3*

Who Are the Planners? *4*

Satisfactions and Discontents, *5*

The Plan of This Book, *5*

2 The Urbanization of America *7*

Urbanization in the Nineteenth Century, *7*

- The Forces Behind Urban Growth, *9*
- Urban Concentration and Density, *10*
- The Beginnings of Decentralization, *13*

Urban Trends in the Twentieth Century, *15*

- Urban Growth and the Great Depression, *16*
- The Rush to the Suburbs, *18*
- The Age of Central-City Shrinkage, *19*
- The Decentralization of Employment, *21*
- Cities and the Poor, *21*
- Urban Fiscal Problems, *23*

Central-City Decline in Perspective, *24*

Summary, 25

Notes, 25

Selected Bibliography, 26

3 THE HISTORY OF PLANNING: PART I 27

Colonial America, 27

Limited Means and Growing Problems, 29

The Pressure for Reform, 30

Sanitary: Reform, 31
Urban Open Space, 32
Housing Reform, 33
The Tradition of Municipal Improvement, 34
The Municipal Art Movement, 35
The City Beautiful Movement, 36

The Birth of Modern City Planning, 38

The Public Control of Private Property, 39

The Rush to Zone, 40
The Growth of Community Master Planning, 41

The Emergence of Regional and State Planning, 42

Grander Visions, 46

Summary, 49

Notes, 50

Selected Bibliography, 51

4 THE HISTORY OF PLANNING: PART II 52

Planning and the Great Depression, 53

The Postwar Period, 55

The Expansion of Municipal Planning, 56
Urban Renewal, 56
The Age of Highway Planning, 56
Environmental Planning, 57
Growth Control and Growth Management, 58
The Growth of Statewide Planning, 59
Economic Development Planning, 59

Summary, 60

Notes, *60*

Selected Bibliography, *61*

PART TWO THE STRUCTURE AND PRACTICE OF CONTEMPORARY PLANNING

5 THE LEGAL BASIS OF PLANNING *62*

The Constitutional Framework, *62*

Powers and Limitations, *63*

Public Control Over Private Property, *64*

State Enabling Legislation, *69*

The Legal Link to State Planning, *70*

The Federal Role, *71*

Political Ideology and Federal Grants, *73*
Mandated Responsibilities, *74*

Summary, *75*

Notes, *75*

Selected Bibliography, *76*

6 PLANNING AND POLITICS *77*

Why Is Planning Political? *77*

Planners and Power, *78*

The Fragmentation of Power, *80*

Styles of Planning, *81*

How Planning Agencies Are Organized, *84*

Reaching Out to the Public, *85*

Summary, *86*

Notes, *86*

Selected Bibliography, *87*

7 THE SOCIAL ISSUES *88*

What Are the Issues? *89*

Who Does Social Planning? *94*

Summary, *94*

Notes, *94*

Selected Bibliography, *95*

8 THE COMPREHENSIVE PLAN *96*

The Goals of Comprehensive Planning, *96*

The Comprehensive Planning Process, *98*

Planning Research, *99*
Formulating Community Goals, *102*
Formulating the Plan, *102*
Implementing the Plan, *103*
Review and Updating, *104*

Summary, *104*

Notes, *105*

Selected Bibliography, *106*

9 THE TOOLS OF LAND-USE PLANNING *107*

Public Capital Investment, *108*

Land-Use Controls, *110*

Subdivision Regulations, *110*
Zoning Ordinances, *111*
Recent Developments in Zoning, *121*
Other Types of Local Land-Use Controls, *128*
State, Regional, and Federal Controls on Land Use, *129*

Combining Capital Investment and Land-Use Controls, *130*

Summary, *131*

Notes, *132*

Selected Bibliography, *133*

PART THREE FIELDS OF PLANNING

10 URBAN DESIGN *134*

What Is Urban Design? *136*

The Urban Design Process, *139*

Analysis, 140
Synthesis, 141
Evaluation, 145
Implementation, 145

What Is Good Urban Design? 145

The Neighborhood Concept, 149

Replanning Suburbia: Andres Duany and Neotraditional Planning, 150

Visions of the City of the Future, 154

Summary, 157

Notes, 158

Selected Bibliography, 158

11 CAPITAL FACILITIES PLANNING 159

The Need for Capital Facilities Planning, 159

Components of Capital Facilities Planning, 160

The Planning Phase, 160

Forecasting Community Growth and Change, 161
The Computer in Capital Facilities Planning, 162

The Financing Phase, 162

Revenue Analysis, 163
Expenditure Analysis, 164
Methods of Financing, 165
Evaluation Criteria, 170

The Programming Phase, 174

Summary, 174

Notes, 175

Selected Bibliography, 175

12 URBAN RENEWAL AND COMMUNITY DEVELOPMENT 176

Urban Renewal, 177

The Origins of Urban Renewal, 178
Intention and Reality, 179
Urban Renewal in Retrospect, 182

Community Development, *185*

Community Development versus the Urban Renewal Approach, *186*

The Housing Question, *188*

Planning for Housing, *189*

Federal Requirements, *190*
A More Comprehensive Approach to Planning for Housing, *191*
How Effective Are Housing Plans? *192*

Summary, *192*

Notes, *193*

Selected Bibliography, *194*

13 TRANSPORTATION PLANNING *195*

Recent Trends in Urban Transportation, *195*

Paying for Transportation, *196*

Transportation Planning and Use, *197*

The Transportation Planning Process, *198*

Modeling Metropolitan Area Transportation, *198*
The Policy Decision, *202*
Planning for Public Transportation, *204*
Transportation Management Systems, *205*
A Look Ahead, *205*

Summary, *207*

Notes, *208*

Selected Bibliography, *208*

14 ECONOMIC DEVELOPMENT PLANNING *209*

Historic Roots, *209*

Perspectives on Local Economic Development, *210*

The Federal Presence in Local Economic Development, *210*

State Economic Development Efforts, *213*

Local Economic Development Efforts, *215*

A Crucial Difference, *216*
What a Community Can Do to Promote Economic Growth, *216*
A Systematic Approach to Economic Development Planning, *218*

A Look Ahead, 221
Summary, 222
Notes, 223
Selected Bibliography, 223

15 GROWTH MANAGEMENT PLANNING 224

The Origins of Growth Management, 225
The Mechanics of Growth Management, 226
Winners and Losers in Growth Management, 230
The "Defense of Privilege" Issue, 231
A Sampling of Growth Management Programs, 232
State-Level Growth Management, 236
Growth Management—Pro or Con? 239
Summary, 240
Notes, 240
Selected Bibliography, 241

16 ENVIRONMENTAL AND ENERGY PLANNING 242

The Environmental Planning Problem, 243
Environmental Progress at the National Level, 243
The Intergovernment Context of Environmental Planning, 246
The NEPA Process, 247
Economic and Political Issues in Environmental Planning, 249
Local Environmental Planning, 250
Analyzing the Physical Environment, 250
Two Examples of Environmental Planning, 253
Water Quality Planning, 253
Solid Waste Management Planning, 255
Energy Planning, 258
An Energy Planning Process, 260
Federal Environmental Policy During the Bush Administration, 261
Summary, 263

Notes, *264*

Selected Bibliography, *265*

17 PLANNING FOR METROPOLITAN REGIONS *266*

The Evolution of Urban Regional Planning, *267*

The Basic Functions of Regional Planning Agencies, *268*

Implementing the Regional Plan, *269*

Regional Planning in Practice—A Tale of Two Cities, *270*

The Rise of the Twin Cities Metropolitan Planning Commission, *271*
Enter the Twin Cities Metropolitan Council, *274*
What Has Been Accomplished? *276*

A Look Ahead, *276*

Summary, *277*

Notes, *277*

Selected Bibliography, *277*

PART FOUR LARGER QUESTIONS

18 NATIONAL PLANNING IN THE UNITED STATES *279*

Is There National Planning in the U.S.? *279*

The Pattern of Land Settlement, *280*

Establishing the Rail Network, *281*

Water and the West, *283*

Western Water Policy in Retrospect, *287*

Systematic Regional Planning, *288*

The Interstate Highway System, *290*

Financing the Suburbs, *294*

Suburbanization and Tax Policy, *295*
But Is it Planning, *295*

Other Areas, *296*

Summary, *296*

Notes, 297

Selected Bibliography, 298

19 PLANNING THEORY 299

Is Theory Necessary? 299

A Distinction Between Public and Private Planning, 300

The Process of Planning, 301

The Rational Model, 301
Disjointed Incrementalism, 305
Middle-Range Models, 306

Planning and Ideology, 308

The View from the Right, 309
The View from the Left, 311

Summary, 314

Notes, 314

Selected Bibliography, 315

INDEX 316

PREFACE

The term *planning* is a very general one. There are city and town planners and also corporate planners. The Pentagon employs numerous military planners. The launching of a space shuttle is the culmination of a tremendously complex and sophisticated planning process. Wealthy individuals who prefer to leave as much as possible of their wealth to their heirs and as little as possible to the Internal Revenue Service employ the services of estate planners. And so on.

Planning in its generic meaning, then, is a ubiquitous activity. Cutting across all types of planning is a certain common denominator. All have in common a conscious effort to define systematically and think through a problem to improve the quality of decision making. The planning discussed in this book represents a very small part of the total planning activity in the United States. Specifically, this book focuses on public planning at the substate level, that which is done by and for cities, counties, towns, and other units of local governments. We will also examine, much more briefly, planning for metropolitan regions, the states, and the question of national planning.

The reader who has at least sampled other books on planning will notice that this book has some particular emphases, specifically on politics, economics, ideology, law, and the question of who benefits and who loses by particular decisions. These emphases stem from my experience as a working planner. I entered planning in 1969 with a background in economics and journalism but with no specific training in planning. In my ignorance of the field I assumed that if engineers planned bridges and architects planned buildings, then city and town planners planned cities and towns in an essentially similar way. In effect, I thought of planning as engineering or architecture writ large.

It did not take me long to learn that planning is a highly political activity. Not only is it immersed in politics, but also it is inseparable from the law. The ultimate arbiter of many a planning dispute is the court. And for every case that comes to court, some dozens of planning decisions have been conditioned by what the participants in the process think would be the decision if the matter were to come to court.

Planning decisions very often involve large sums of money. In some cases large sums of public money are involved in the form of capital investments. But even when little in the way of public expenditure is involved, planning decisions can deliver large benefits to some and large losses to others. Thus to understand planning, one must understand something of the economic and financial issues at stake.

The study of planning quickly takes one into ideology. Planning issues and controversy inevitably raise questions about the proper role of government and the line between public needs and private rights. What properly is to be a matter of political decision and what properly should be left to the market? Planning can raise issues that are not easily resolved. Planners are a fairly idealistic lot and often enter the field to serve the public interest. After immersion in a few public controversies, the beginning planner may wonder if there *is* such a thing as the public interest. For if there is, there ought to be some general agreement among the public on what it is. But one can spend a long time in some areas of planning without seeing a single instance of this agreement.

In this book I have tried to convey something of the reality of planning practice and something of what goes on under the surface of events. I hope that the reader will not find this reality disillusioning, for planning in an open and democratic society cannot be smooth and simple. Planning as it is—involved in political controversy, hedged about by the trends of judicial decisions, inextricably tied to economic questions, and connected to issues of ideology—is far more interesting than it would be if it were simply architecture or engineering writ large.

The book contains a certain amount of material on history and technology because the issues that planning focuses on are largely ones that political, social, and economic change bring to the forefront. For example, it can be argued that one of the biggest influences on American cities in the 1960s and 1970s was the massive acceleration in the mechanization of agriculture that began after the end of World War II. That event, the result of both economic and technological forces, set in motion a huge migration of population. The effects of this migration are still being felt in America's cities. I hope the book will help readers make some connections of that sort and develop the habit of looking for other such connections on their own.

Though the book is about planning, it is assumed that most of its readers will not become planners. Therefore I have tried to write a book that would be of some value in the course of a liberal education, quite apart from imparting information on planning. I have gone somewhat more lightly over matters like the enumeration of federal programs (information that tends to age rapidly in any case) and placed an emphasis on connecting planning with ideas and with main currents of events in the larger society.

The best and most effective planners are those with good peripheral vision—those who not only have mastered the technical side of planning but also understand the relationships between planning issues and the major forces in the society around them. I have endeavored to write a text consistent with that view.

The basic structure of this book is similar to that of the second edition. The most important change is the addition of Chapter 18, National Planning. Though there is no national plan, nor has there ever been one, the federal government has, through legislation and policy, engaged in nation-shaping acts that have had a major effect on the pattern of settlement of 3 million square miles. The chapter takes a historical look at these acts beginning with the Ordinance of 1785 and ending with federal tax policy and the development of the suburbs. Chapter 10, Urban Design, contains a new block of material on Neotraditional Planning and, specifically, the work of Andres Duany. Chapter 16, Environmental and Energy Planning, includes substantial new material on the measurement of environmental quality, the Bush environmental record, recent legislation and the Rio Earth Summit. Beyond the above, other chapters have been updated in regard to statistics, legislation, court cases, and political events.

A NOTE ON FURTHER READINGS

Each chapter contains footnotes and a brief selected bibliography. But beyond these readings, I would like to suggest a few general sources on planning and related matters.

The foremost scholarly journal in the field in the United States is the *Journal of the American Planning Association,* published quarterly. A newer and somewhat less well-known American scholarly publication is the *Journal of Planning Education and Research,* published three times a year. A practitioner-oriented publication, *Planning,* is published monthly by the American Planning Association (APA). Its short, nonacademic articles will give the student a quick overview of current issues and techniques. For trends in real estate and urban development I recommend *Urban Land,* published monthly by the Urban Land Institute (ULI).

Several widely used general references to planning have been published by the International City Managers Association. These include *The Practice of Local Government Planning, 1988;* and *The Practice of State and Regional Planning, 1986.* Generally referred to in the profession as "the big green books," they are well worth looking into.

Planning and data are inseparable. For the student interested in looking up a statistic dealing with demography, housing, economics, or many other areas, the best place to start is usually the *Statistical Abstract of the United States,* an annual series published by the Bureau of the Census. Very likely, the statistic will be there. If it is not, the table footnotes or the "Guide to Sources" at the end of the volume will tell you where it can be found.

ILLUSTRATION CREDITS

p. 12 The Bettmann Archive, New York City

p. 28 Plan of Savannah from Harold M. Lewis, *Planning the Modern City,* John Wiley & Sons, 1949. View of Savannah, Georgia, courtesy of the New York Historical Society, New York City. Map of Philadelphia courtesy of Cornell University Library.

p. 33 Courtesy of Map Division of The New York Public Library, Astor, Lennox, and Tilden Foundations.

p. 38 From the Avery Architectural and Fine Arts Library, Columbia University, New York.

p. 43 Plans from Clarence Stein, *Towards New Towns for America,* MIT Press, Cambridge, MA., 1951.

p. 45 Regional Plan Association, *Regional Plan of New York and Its Environs,* New York, 1929.

p. 48 Courtesy of MIT Press, Cambridge, MA.

p. 92 Mark Vergari, Gannett Suburban Newspapers.

p. 135 Map courtesy of Virginia Polytechnic Institute and State University Architectural School Library. Photograph from Robert W. Cameron, *Above Paris,* Cameron and Co., San Francisco, 1984, p. 51.

p. 137 Lawrence Halprin, *Cities*, copyright © 1963 Van Nostrand Reinhold, New York. p. 19. All rights reserved.
p. 138 Courtesy of Battery Park City Authority.
p. 144 Spatial analysis and plan courtesy of Greater London Council. Photograph by Charles W. Steger.
p. 149 Regional Plan Association, *Regional Plan of New York and Its Environs*, New York, 1929.
p. 152 Drawing courtesy of Andres Duany and Elizabeth Plater-Zyberk, Architects.
p. 155 Illustration from *The Radiant City* by Le Corbusier. Translation © 1967 by Grossman Publishers, Inc. and Faber and Faber, Ltd. All rights reserved. Reprinted by permission of Viking Penguin Inc. Photograph by Charles W. Steger.
p. 156 Paolo Soleri, *Arcology: The City in the Image of Man*, MIT Press, Cambridge, MA., 1969, p. 62.
p. 184 Courtesy of F.D. Rich Realty, Stamford, CT.; photograph by Santi Visalli.
p. 199 Maps by Ramen De.

ACKNOWLEDGMENTS

It is not possible to thank everyone who assisted in the writing of a book. However, I would like to express gratitude to three of my colleagues at Virginia Polytechnic Institute and State University (Virginia Tech), College of Architecture and Urban Studies—C. David Loeks, professor; Charles W. Steger, dean; and Alan W. Steiss, associate provost for research—for taking time out of their busy schedules to contribute guest chapters in the areas of their special expertise. I would also like to thank Professor Loeks and two other colleagues here at Tech, Larz Anderson and Robert Stuart, for reviewing and making many helpful suggestions on earlier drafts of this book. A rough draft of this book was also reviewed for Prentice Hall by Edward Kaiser, University of North Carolina; David J. Forkenbrock, The University of Iowa; and William A. Howard, California Polytechnic State University. The present draft bears their imprint on many points. The second edition incorporated many suggestions made by Dennis E. Gale, University of Southern Maine, and Harvey M. Jacobs, University of Wisconsin–Madison. For ten years before I became an academic I was employed in various capacities by the Westchester County, New York, Department of Planning, where I had fine opportunity to learn some of the realities of planning. I am thus indebted to a number of my former colleagues there, in particular Commissioner Peter Q. Eschweiler and Planning Board Chairman Dr. William Cassella. When all is said and done, however, the viewpoints expressed here and any mistakes made are my own.

CHAPTER 1

AN OVERVIEW

THE NEED FOR PLANNING

Perhaps the first question that has to be answered in a book about planning is simply "why do we need planning?" The need for planning comes down to two words, *interconnectedness* and *complexity*. If there were few of us and the technologies by which we lived were relatively simple, there would be little need for planning as described in this book. We could each go our own way and would gain little from common planning efforts. However, the fact is that we are numerous enough and our technologies complicated enough that this is not the case.

Consider a simple illustration of interconnectedness, the use of a few acres of urban land. The amount and character of development on that land will determine the amount of traffic it generates. Developing it with single-family houses will produce a different traffic flow than developing it with apartments, which will generate a different traffic flow than developing it with a neighborhood shopping center. Thus a land development decision is a traffic decision as well. That, potentially, affects everyone in the area. How much of the site is paved, and even what material is used for paving, affects how fast rainwater runs off from the property. Runoff may affect flooding and stream flow conditions miles down-stream from the property. The types and quantities of commercial or residential activity on the property may affect air quality, noise levels, water quality, and the visual and social qualities of the area.

Decisions about the residential uses of land will affect housing prices, rents, and vacancies—in short, who can live in the community. Those decisions, in turn, will have effects on the economy of the community and the demands that are placed on the community for educational, social, and other services.

The land-use decisions made by a community shape its very character—what it is like to walk through, what it is like to drive through, who lives in it, what kinds of jobs and businesses exist in it, how well the natural environment survives, and whether the community is an attractive one or an ugly one. In some cases such decisions may directly affect human life and health, for example, whether traffic patterns are safe or hazardous.

Land-use decisions affect the fiscal health of the community. Every property that is developed burdens the community with obligations such as education, police and fire protection, recreational services, and social services. Conversely, every development contributes, directly or indirectly, to municipal revenues through property taxes, sales taxes, or charges and fees. Thus the pattern of land development will affect how heavily the community must tax its residents and the level of public services the community can provide.

The land in question may be privately owned, in which case public control is exercised through a regulatory process. It may be owned publicly, in which case direct public investment will determine its use. But in either case there is a distinct public interest in what happens on the land. To generalize, it is the fact of interconnectedness, whether we are discussing land use or other questions, which helps to justify public planning efforts.

Complexity is the condition that justifies planning as a separate profession and as a separate activity of government. If all of the sorts of relationships suggested were simple, they could be dealt with simply and informally. If the community were tiny, perhaps direct negotiations between private parties would suffice. If the community were somewhat larger, perhaps they could be easily dealt with along with the general flow of municipal business. But the complexity of a modern community renders such simple and direct approaches inadequate.

The complexity of the community also means that many things that in a simpler place could be done privately must be done publicly. In an agricultural area with a population of perhaps a few dozen people per square mile, water supply and waste disposal are handled on site by the individual household. No common decision making or investment is necessary. In a large metropolitan area, these functions are likely to involve systems that span many communities and may involve billions of dollars of capital investment. Comparable comments could be made about transportation, education, public safety, recreation, and the like.

Thus in thousands of communities in the United States planning is a formalized and distinct process of government. In relatively small communities the planning function may be lodged in an unpaid part-time planning board with the technical work done by a planning consultant. In larger communities the planning function is generally located within a planning department. Depending on community size, that department may have a staff ranging from one to several hundred individuals. In a very small department the planner(s) may be a jack-of-all-trades handling land-use questions one day, capital budgeting another day, and economic development a third day. In a larger agency there may be considerable specialization of labor. One section of the agency may specialize in zoning issues, another in master planning, a third in planning-related research, another in environmental issues, and so on.

THE SPECIFIC CONCERNS OF PLANNING

What might a community seek to achieve through planning? In a growing community, planners might be concerned with shaping the pattern of growth to achieve a sensible and attractive land-use pattern. That means avoiding both oppressively dense development or overly scattered and fragmentary development. It means encouraging a pattern of development that gives residents ready access to recreational, cultural, school, shopping, and other facilities. It means having a street pattern that is convenient to use and through which traffic flows without excessive congestion. It means separating incompatible land uses and activities, for example, high-intensity commercial activity from residential areas. In a modern planned community it might mean providing a system of pathways so that pedestrian and bicycle traffic is separated from automobile traffic.

The community's planners will also be concerned with the location of public facilities like schools and social service centers, both for the convenience of the people served and to reinforce the development of a desirable land-use pattern. If the community anticipates or desires significant industrial or commercial development, its planners will be concerned with seeing that sufficient conveniently located blocks of land are available and that they are served with adequate roads, water, and sewer facilities.

In an older community that is not growing and that does not anticipate growth, planners may be concerned primarily with preserving or improving that which now exists. Thus planners may focus on measures to preserve the quality of the housing stock. In many communities planners will also be concerned with housing cost questions, specifically, how to provide housing for the community's lower-income residents. In many older communities planners devote much effort to preserving historic buildings and other landmarks. If the community is concerned (as many are) about the health of its downtown, planners may be involved in implementing street improvements and other changes designed to help downtown businesses compete successfully with establishments in outlying areas.

In a community that faces a serious unemployment problem, economic development may be a major task of the planners. Much of their effort may be devoted to creating conditions that encourage existing industry to remain and expand and new firms to locate within the community.

In recent years much planning effort has focused on environmental issues: how to guide and manage development to minimize environmental damage. For example, a planner might be concerned with evaluating the relative environmental merits and financial costs of landfill disposal versus incineration for a municipality's solid wastes and then with helping to select the best site.

Planners employed by regional planning organizations may be concerned with improving the regionwide road network, with acquiring or developing land for a regionwide park and open space system, or with improving regionwide sewage disposal and water systems. They will also be concerned with encouraging coordination between the planning efforts of the various municipalities in the region to avoid duplication of capital facilities and interference effects (for example, community A siting its landfill operation at a point where it borders a residential area in community B).

This is far from a complete listing. It is simply meant to give some feeling for the range of planning issues.

WHO ARE THE PLANNERS?

Planners come from a variety of backgrounds. The single most common educational background is formal training in planning, most often a master's degree. But the field, and particularly larger agencies and consultants, absorb people with many other backgrounds. Agencies that are large enough to have a separate research operation are likely to hire people with training in economics or statistics. Agencies that do transportation planning are likely to hire people with training in civil engineering and, particularly, transportation engineering. Large agencies often do a substantial amount of data handling and are likely to have on staff a few people with background in programming and data processing. Agencies that do significant amounts of environmental planning are likely to hire people with backgrounds in biology, chemistry, environmental science, and remote sensing. Planning inevitably involves mapping and spatially organized data, so that a certain number of geographers and cartographers find their way into the profession. Planning involves many issues of law, particularly in regard to land use and environmental considerations. Thus many attorneys and people with joint training in law and planning have entered the field. In fact, several universities have joint law and planning degree programs.

The majority of planners are employed by government. Of these, the larger share are employed by local governments, that is, by cities, towns, counties, and other substate jurisdictions. Smaller numbers are employed by state governments, by intergovernment organizations like councils of governments (COGs), and by a variety of authorities and special-purpose agencies. Some planners are employed by the federal government, particularly in departments like Housing and Urban Development (HUD), which fund and regulate planning-related activities of local governments. Most planners employed by government are civil servants, but a certain number are political appointees chosen outside the civil service process. Over the years many planners have found their way into municipal administration, where the sort of "big picture" view that planning tends to develop seems to be useful.

A substantial minority of all planners are employed within the private sector of the economy. Many work for planning consultants and in that capacity serve both government and a variety of private clients. A certain number of planners are employed directly by private organizations like land developers and corporations with substantial real property holdings. Some planners work for particular groups in society which feel they need the planners' skills to make their own case in the public forum. These may be neighborhood or community groups, environmental organizations, and citizens' groups of one type or another.

SATISFACTIONS AND DISCONTENTS

Planning is both anticipatory and reactive. At times planning will be devoted to anticipating and developing responses to problems that have not yet presented themselves. At other times planning will be devoted to responding to problems that are here and demand solutions. In either case planning is about trying to serve that elusive and controversial but very important item known as "the public interest." It can be a profoundly satisfying field when one feels that one has succeeded in making a contribution to the public good. Because much of planning is concerned with the physical environment, the planner can be often have the satisfaction of seeing the results of his or her efforts on the ground.

However, the field can also be very frustrating, for planners are basically advisors with little or no power. Sometimes they are heeded and sometimes they are not. And sometimes the planner's brainchild gets more than a little altered during that long trip from drawing board to reality. In general, it is not a good field for someone with a short time horizon or very low frustration tolerance. It is also not a good field for someone who cannot tolerate ambiguity, for many issues that appear black or white at a distance have the dismaying quality of becoming grey as one gets close to them.

THE PLAN OF THIS BOOK

The main body of the book begins with a chapter on the history of urbanization of the United States. To a large extent, the history of planning in the United States is a series of responses to problems that have flowed from the process of urbanization. Thus that chapter serves as background for the rest of the book. Chapters 3 and 4 trace the history of planning in the United States in the historical context established by Chapter 2. Planning is conditioned and limited by the law and takes place within a political process. Ultimately, planning is a political act. Chapters 5 and 6 establish the legal and political framework in which planning takes place. All important planning decisions have social implications. They deliver gains to some and losses to some, and they often get to the root of questions about what we consider to be a good and a just society. Chapter 7 lays out some of the main social issues in planning. The concept of the community master plan or comprehensive plan occupies a central place in the development of planning, and the development and implementation of such a plan is often a major task of the planning agency. Chapter 8 presents the master planning process. Chapter 9 follows with a presentation on the tools of land-use planning to give the reader a feeling for how the community can implement the comprehensive plan.

Part III of the book, from Chapter 10 "Urban Design," to Chapter 17, "Planning for Metropolitan Regions," covers a variety of fields in contemporary planning practice. If the book is used as the text for a short course, the instructor might select among these chapters on the basis of student interest. Once the material in Parts I and II has been assimilated, each chapter in Part III will stand on its own.

Chapter 18, "National Planning in the United States," addresses the extent to which we have had de facto national planning. If the course has a purely local focus it can readily be omitted. If there is time to include it, the chapter will help to place local planning in an historic and national context.

Chapter 19, "Planning Theory," serves as a wrap-up and expansion of many ideas suggested earlier in the book. It contains two major components, a discussion of planning as a process and a discussion of the relationship of planning and political ideology. It is intentionally left to the end so that the reader can approach it with some background and thus be able to put some meat on the bare theoretical and ideological bones.

CHAPTER 2

THE URBANIZATION OF AMERICA

The history of planning in the United States is largely one of response to urbanization and the problems it has brought. To understand that history it is necessary to have some sense of the main currents of U.S. urban history. This chapter will emphasize economic, technological, and demographic trends, for these, over the long term, have far more effect than discrete events like elections.

There is something of a break in the trend of U.S. urbanization around the end of the nineteenth century. For convenience, then, we will divide the discussion into two parts: an account of urbanization in the nineteenth century and another from the turn of the century to the present.

URBANIZATION IN THE NINETEENTH CENTURY

In the year 1800 the urbanized population of the United States was roughly 300,000 and the total population was 5 million. Thus perhaps 6 percent of the U.S. population lived in urbanized areas. By 1900 the U.S. urbanized population was 30 million and total population was 76 million. Approximately 40 percent of the population lived in urbanized areas.[1] From 1800 to 1900 the U.S. population increased by a factor of 15, an annual compounded rate of about 2.4 percent. However, urban populations increased by a factor of 100, an annual compounded rate of about 5 percent. In 1800 the largest city in the United States, New York, had a population of well under 100,000. By 1900 its population was over 3 million.

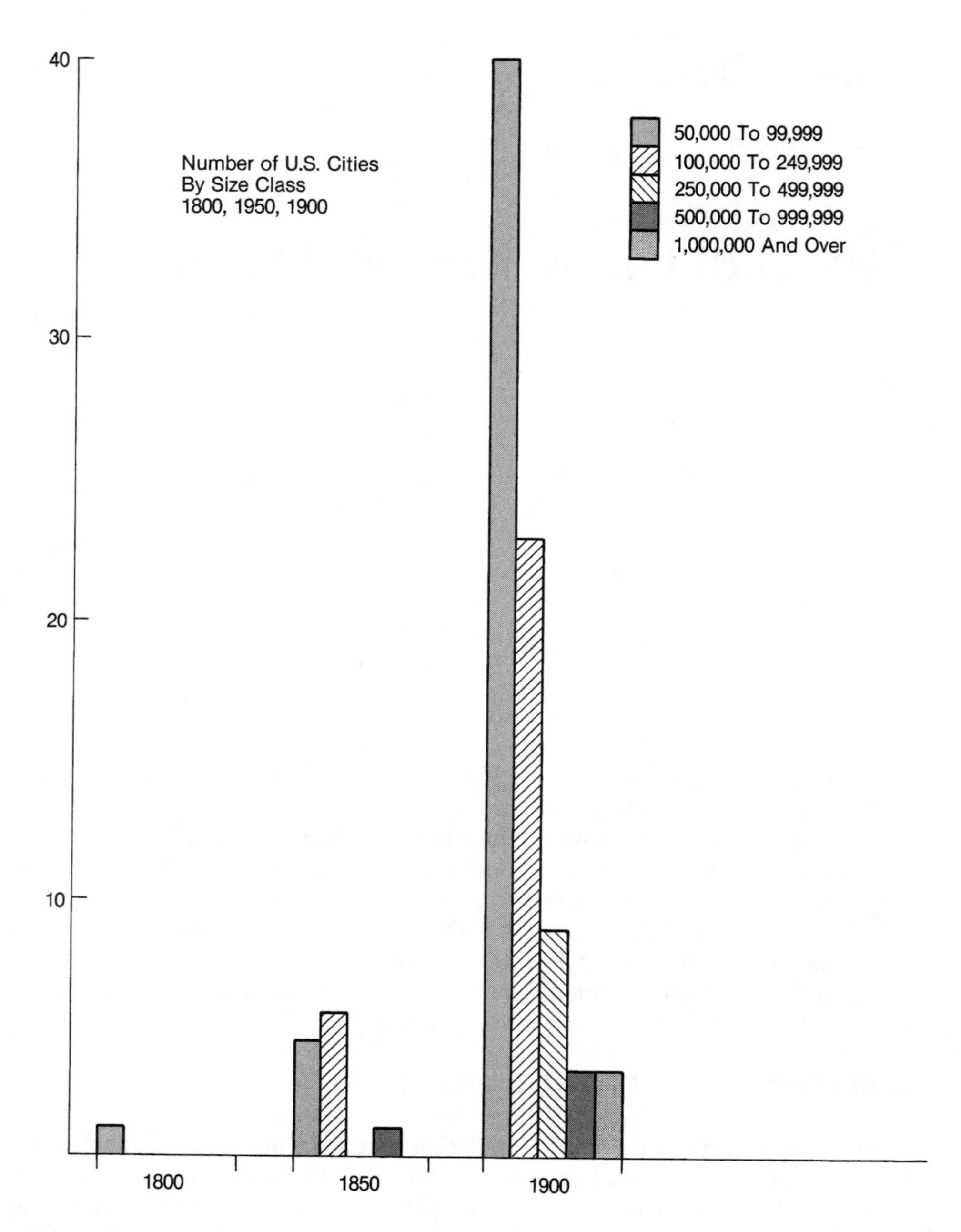

From 1800 to 1900 the urbanized population of the United States increased one hundredfold. The population of the nation's largest city, New York, went from under 100,000 to 3 million. Source: *The Statistical History of the United States: from Colonial Times to the Present*, prepared by the Bureau of the Census with introduction and *User's Guide* by Ben Wattenberg, Basic Books, New York, 1976.

The Forces Behind Urban Growth

One force behind urban growth was simply national population growth. The U.S. rate of natural increase (births minus deaths) was extremely rapid and was augmented by immigration, particularly after the inauguration of transatlantic steam service in the 1840s. But this does not answer the question of why urban growth proceeded so much more rapidly than did total population growth.

Part of the explanation was a side effect of the industrial revolution. As agricultural machinery made farmers more productive, workers were freed to take other employment, much of it in the cities. In 1800 perhaps 85 or 90 percent of the U.S. labor force was engaged in farming. By 1880 that figure was down to about 50 percent.

Another consequence of the industrial revolution was the shift from cottage industries to factory production, creating the need for mass labor forces at specific points. That, in turn, created the need for massed housing nearby. The growth of large-scale manufacturing also brought into being the modern corporation, with a large administrative force concentrated at a single point. Finally, factory production and the enormous increase in consumer goods it created brought into being the department store, which also concentrated a large labor force at a single point.

The growth of large cities was also promoted by the development of low-cost transportation. The coming of railroad and steamboat technology around 1830 gave cities a long reach into their hinterlands to obtain raw materials and agricultural products and also to market the products they produced. In the absence of such transportation, cities would necessarily be small, for the market areas that sustained their commercial and manufacturing sectors would have been small.

The rapid settling of the country and the opening of new lands demanded the creation in short order of a system of cities to perform the commercial and manufacturing processes that the new industrial technology was making possible. Thus a number of U.S. cities such as New York and Chicago grew at spectacular rates. Writing in 1899 Adna Weber noted,

> In a new country the rapid growth of cities is both natural and necessary, for no efficient industrial organization of a new settlement is possible without industrial centres to carry on the necessary work of assembling and distributing goods. A Mississippi Valley empire rising suddenly into being without its Chicago and its smaller centers of distribution is almost inconceivable to the nineteenth-century economist. That America is the "land of mushroom cities" is therefore not at all surprising.[2]

Although the four forces noted—population growth, increased agricultural productivity, factory production, and low-cost transportation—are sufficient to explain the rapid growth of urban populations, they do not entirely explain the form of nineteenth-century cities.

Urban Concentration and Density

The distinguishing feature of many nineteenth-century cities was concentration and density. As the century progressed the more gracious and open pattern of the colonial city disappeared. The spaces between buildings vanished and buildings grew higher. Streets became increasingly congested and the natural world was replaced by a none-too-attractive manmade world.

Population densities which have never again been seen in the United States were built up in the late nineteenth and very early twentieth century. For example, Manhattan island in 1900 had about 2.2 million residents on 22 square miles for an average density of 100,000 people per square mile. In the most densely populated part of the island, the Lower East Side, densities in some wards were several times that high.[3] Since the turn of the century Manhattan's population has fallen to slightly under 1.5 million in 1990, a drop of over 700,000. Some of the decline in population has been due to the replacement of residential with commercial uses. Most of it, however, is simply because people will no longer tolerate the degree of crowding which prevailed a few generations ago.

What made nineteenth-century cities so concentrated? Much of the answer lies in the transportation technology of the age. At the opening of the nineteenth century water transportation was cheap and land transportation was expensive. The ton/mile cost of transporting freight by canal boat was about one-tenth that of transporting it by horse and wagon. The cost of transporting freight by sailing vessel was still lower than for canal boat. One effect of these cost differences was to favor the growth of port cities.[4] But another effect was to concentrate economic activity in those areas of the city with direct water access. Since most people got to work by walking, concentration of workplaces inevitably meant concentration of residences as well.

The coming of railroad technology beginning in the 1820s continued the concentrating effect. Over long distances railroad ton/mile rates were a very small fraction of the ton/mile rates for horse and wagon. Thus rail-served sites permitted manufacturers and wholesalers very large cost savings. But achieving these savings meant tremendous concentrations around rail terminals and sidings.

In port cities an ideal industrial location was one between rail lines and docks. The remains of such a configuration can be seen on the Lower West Side of Manhattan today. Old loft buildings once occupied by manufacturers lie immediately to the east of the Hudson shore and up against the former rail lines which connected Manhattan to the rest of the nation. Today the rail lines are gone and cargo handling has ceased along the Manhattan waterfront. But in the nineteenth century, the port was busy and lower Manhattan was a major manufacturing and goods-handling center. Goods could move between Europe and the Midwest through Manhattan and make all but a few hundred yards of the trip entirely by low-cost modes.

The desirability of rail- and water-served sites made centrally located land very valuable. That, in turn, caused the builders of industrial, commercial, and residential structures to use the minimum amount of land for a given amount of structure. Manufacturing and commercial uses were located in multi-story loft buildings constructed side to side. For residences, the same desire to crowd a maximum amount of structure on a given amount of land led to the tenement, with conditions of crowding that seem appalling by modern standards.

> The residence of the worker in New York City and other large industrial cities in 1850 was frequently the "railroad flat," a walk-up structure that was generally 5 to 7 stories high, 25 feet wide and 75 feet long on a 25 by 100 foot lot. Constructed solidly in rows across entire block faces, these units had four apartments on each floor surrounding a common staircase. The rooms in these apartments were constructed in tandem, with just one room in each apartment provided with a window or two for light and air. No sanitary facilities or water supply were provided for in these structures. The small rear yard contained a multi-seat outhouse and often a well, resulting in deplorable conditions of sanitation and public health.[5]

Thus a population of well over 100 people might be housed on a plot not much more than one-twentieth of an acre in size.

Several other features of emerging nineteenth-century technology also contributed to very dense patterns of development. In contrast to a modern factory, where power to run individual pieces of machinery is supplied electrically, power was generally supplied by a steam engine and transmitted through a system of belts, pulleys, and shafts. The distance power could be sent in this manner was limited. This further contributed to the use of compact loft buildings with transmission belts taking power from one floor to another. Shortly after the end of the Civil War there emerged two other technologies which contributed to higher urban densities: the elevator and steel-frame construction. Together they made the skyscraper economically and structurally possible.

For most of the nineteenth century cities became both more populous and more dense. Industry was concentrated in cities and, most often, in the more central areas. There is some evidence that in the post-Civil War period not only did manufacturing become more urbanized but also it grew faster in the larger cities. In 1899 Adna Weber noted,

> In 1860 the annual production of manufacturers per capita was $60 for the United States as a whole, $193.50 for 10 cities having a population of 50,000 or more, $424 for 10 cities under 50,000, and $44 for the rural districts. Thus per capita production was at that time largest in the smaller cities. In 1890, however, the per capita product of manufacturers was $455 in the 28 great cities, $335 in 137 cities of 20,000–100,000 population, and $58 for the remainder of the country. The superiority of the smaller cities in 1860 had in 1890 given way to that of the great.[6]

Congestion had more than just esthetic or psychological consequences. In an age before treatment of water supplies, before modern sewage disposal, and before antibiotics—an age when communicable diseases were the major threat—the congestion of the city exacted a huge cost in life and health. In fact, for much of the nineteenth century most large cities experienced natural decrease (more

Tenements on New York's Lower East Side (right) at the turn of the century. Note the narrow building width and side-by-side construction.
The four windows across the building front represent two narrow apartments side by side. Behind them are two more apartments whose windows open onto the rear yard. Photos like that of the mens' sleeping quarters (below) in a New York tenement about 1905 helped to put housing conditions on the top of the reformers' agenda .

deaths than births). They grew only because of in-migration. The situation was well understood at the time, and decongestion of the city was a major goal of reform-minded citizens and planners.

> Few municipalities have planned intelligently for this rapid urban growth. Buildings have been crowded upon land and people have been crowded within buildings. Urban living has become in many ways inconvenient, unsafe and unhealthful. . . . Transit facilities fail to develop much in advance of demonstrable need, so the population becomes crowded within a limited area. . . . It becomes used to living a life quite divorced from nature. The responsibilities of homeownership are felt only by a few. The sense of citizenship and the sense of moral responsibility for evils suffered by neighbors become weak.
>
> In the interests of both hygiene and public morality, the cottage home is much to be preferred to the tenement dwelling. . . . Tuberculosis is responsible for nearly one-tenth of all deaths in the United States. . . . The tubercule bacillus can live for weeks outside the human body in a sunless, damp room, hall or cellar. The tenement house may thus at once reduce vitality, through absence of sunlight and fresh air, and may provide abundant opportunity for transmission of prevalent and dangerous diseases.[7]

This widely held view helped to shape the agenda and direction of the planning profession in the nineteenth and early twentieth centuries.

The Beginnings of Decentralization

Late in the nineteenth century the first forces for decentralization appeared on the urban scene. These forces have grown in strength to the present time. In the 1880s electric motor and power transmission technology advanced far enough to make possible the electric streetcar. Faster and cheaper than the horse-drawn trolleys it supplanted, the electric streetcar was a powerful decentralizing force. In a few years the effective radius of the city was doubled. Three miles, a distance the average person can comfortably walk in an hour, had been something of a limit for the population that worked in the urban core. With the streetcar, tendrils of urban growth extended from the city and the process of suburbanization was begun. In an aptly titled book, *Streetcar Suburbs*, Warner describes how in a few years the streetcar effectively doubled the radius of Boston and converted the old "walking city" into a modern metropolis.[8] The decentralizing power of rail-based transportation was not lost on the more prophetic writers of the times. In 1902 H.G. Wells wrote,

> Many of our railway-begotten giants are destined to such a process of dissection and diffusion as to amount almost to obliteration. . . . The social history of the middle and later thirds of the nineteenth century . . . has been the history of a gigantic rush of population into the magic radius—for most people—of four miles, to suffer there physical and moral disaster . . . far more appalling than any pestilence that ever swept the world. . . . But new forces . . . may finally be equal to the complete reduction of all our present congestions. . . . What will be the forces acting upon the prosperous household? The passion for nature . . . and that craving for a little private imperium are the chief centrifugal inducements. The city will

> diffuse itself until it has taken many of the characteristics of what is now country. . . . We may call . . . these coming town provinces "urban regions."[9]

Wells was writing about England, but the same forces of national population growth, the growth of manufacturing, and urbanization were operative in the United States.

In common with most nineteenth- and early twentieth-century reformers, Wells viewed the congestion of the city as a profound evil and the coming decentralization as an obviously desirable event. To the nineteenth-century reformer what we now contemptuously refer to as "urban sprawl" or, sometimes, "suburban sprawl" would have looked like an improvement almost too good to be imagined.

By the end of the nineteenth century manufacturing was beginning to decentralize though it was still a predominantly urban phenomenon. In larger urban areas firms began to move out along rail lines toward the suburbs. These more

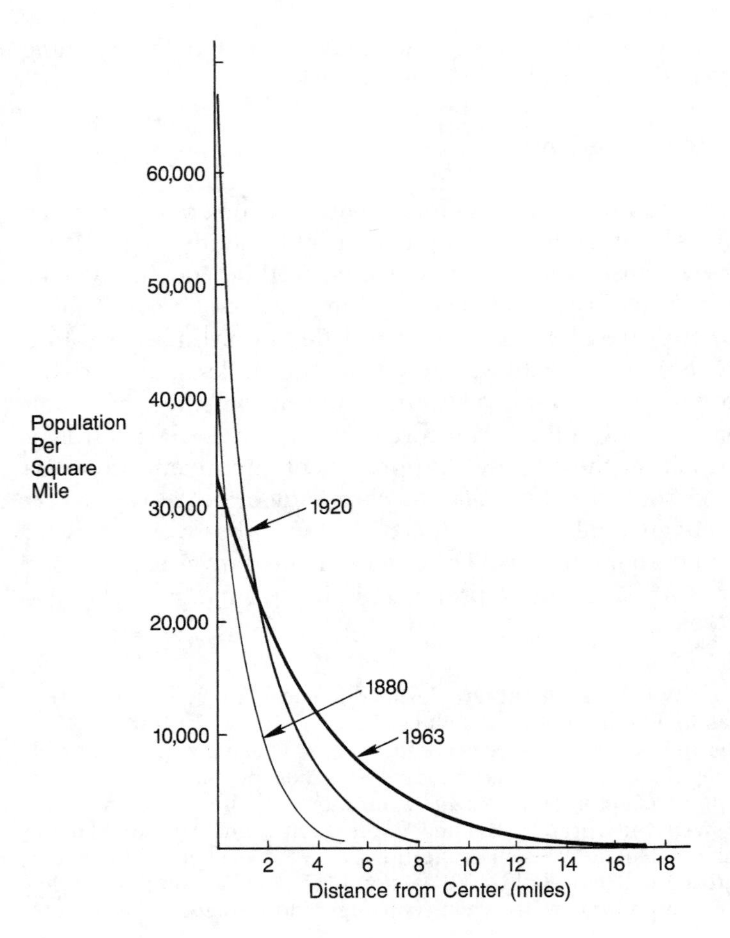

Population density at various distances from the center, Milwaukee 1880 to 1963. Note that the density gradient fell during the entire period and that from 1920 to 1963 the density at the center fell by about 50 percent. Plotted from data in Edwin S. Mills, *Studies in the Structure of the Urban Economy*, Johns Hopkins University Press, Baltimore, 1972.

suburban locations (many of which have since become urban with continued growth) offered lower land costs, often lower taxes, and the advantages of being able to locate heavy machinery on ground level rather than higher up. To some extent, the decentralizing of population by the streetcar provided the labor force for suburbanizing industry.

Population densities (people per square mile) at the center grew more slowly or actually began to decline, while population densities many miles out from the center increased rapidly.[10] The graph on page 14 shows the population density of Milwaukee as a function of distance from the city center over the period 1880 to 1963. From 1880 to 1920 population density continued to increase at the center, but in percentage terms the growth in the periphery was much more rapid. From 1920 to 1963 population density in the center fell drastically while growth in the periphery continued at a rapid pace. In fact, in 1963, population density in the center was actually lower than it had been in 1880, in spite of the fact that the total population of the metropolitan area was vastly larger.

There appear to be two main reasons for the change in population distribution in the last years of the nineteenth century. One, we noted, was the emergence of the streetcar. In a few metropolitan areas steam railroads also stimulated some long-distance commuting. A more general cause of decentralization was simply the rise in incomes. People were able to spend more on land, more on transportation, and more on housing to escape the slums and tenements. Then, too, rising productivity permitted the shortening of working hours, which in turn permitted additional time to be spent on travel.

URBAN TRENDS IN THE TWENTIETH CENTURY

Just as nineteenth-century technology proved to be centralizing and to promote very great population densities, twentieth-century technology proved to be exactly the reverse. One decentralizing technology after another appeared on the scene, a process that continues to the present time. For perhaps roughly the first half of the twentieth century, technology favored decentralization within metropolitan areas but did not favor smaller over larger areas. Thus many large metropolitan areas grew rapidly, usually with the major share of growth occurring in their suburban areas. In the last several decades technological changes continued to favor decentralization within most if not all metropolitan areas. But they have also apparently increased the strength of small- and medium-sized areas relative to large areas. Since the early 1970s there is evidence that technological and economic trends may also be favoring the growth of nonmetropolitan areas.[11]

For population, the big decentralizing force was the automobile. Its speed and flexibility of route and schedule were preconditions for large-scale suburbanization. The first vehicles appeared in the 1890s but their numbers grew slowly, reaching about 5 million by 1915. About this time mass production of Henry Ford's Model T began, and the number of autos in the United States increased rapidly, reaching about 25 million by 1930. It is no coincidence that the 1920s were the first great period of suburbanization in the United States. The truck bore very much the same relationship to retailing, wholesaling, and light manufacturing as did the automobile to population. It permitted wide-scale decentralization by freeing firms from the necessity of being near rail lines. Retailers could follow their customers and manufacturers could follow the labor force with far more freedom than would have been possible a few years earlier. The decentralization of wholesaling followed naturally from the decentralization of retailing, which in turn followed naturally from the decentralization of population.

Other forces also accelerated the process of suburbanization. As noted before, rising incomes were inherently decentralizing because they permitted people to spend more on transportation and more on housing and other forms of construction. Improved telephone communications made possible some decentralization of economic activity by reducing the need for face-to-face contact. The development of motion pictures and commercial radio broke the monopoly of central places on entertainment and thus increased the relative attractiveness of outlying residential areas. The invention of the limited-access highway in the 1920s proved also to be decentralizing. The first limited-access divided highway in the United States, and possibly the world, was the Bronx River Parkway in Westchester County, NY, completed in 1926. Parkways were originally envisioned as giving the urban middle class, with its newly acquired automobiles, access to the countryside. Their unanticipated, but more profound, effect was to make it easier to live in suburbia while working in the central city.

Although metropolitan area populations were clearly decentralizing ("suburbanizing" and "experiencing falling density gradients" would be synonyms) in the first three decades of the twentieth century, metropolitan areas grew rapidly both in absolute population and as a percentage of total population. The nation's population was growing; farm employment, though steady in absolute terms, was shrinking as a percentage of total population; and employment in manufacturing, trade, and services was rising. All of this added up to an increasingly urbanized nation.

Urban Growth and the Great Depression

The 1930s temporarily halted the rural-to-urban shift. Population growth slowed nationally because of immigration restrictions enacted in the mid-1920s and falling birthrates. Rising unemployment reduced rural-to-urban migration, and some of the surplus agricultural workers who might have migrated to the cities a decade before now stayed in the countryside. Thus during the 1930s, Standard Metropolitan Statistical Area (SMSA) populations as a percentage of total U.S. population increased by very little. However, as Table 2–1 indicates, the suburbanizing trend continued.

One Depression-era innovation, a change in the way housing was financed, set loose tremendous suburbanizing forces, though most of the effect was not felt until after World War II. This change merits a brief digression.

Prior to the Great Depression there was little public presence in mortgage lending. Banks protected themselves against the risk of nonpayment in two ways. First, they required very large down payments, generally one-half to one-third the price of the house. Second, banks tended to lend short term on mortgages, typi-

TABLE 2–1 Population in metropolitan areas, 1900–1980 (in millions)

Year[1]	*Total U.S.*	*Total SMSA*	*Central City*	*Ring*[5]	*Metropolitan Population as Percentage of Total Population*	*Central City Population as Percentage of Metropolitan Population*
1900	76.0	24.1	16.0	8.1	31.7	66.4
1910	92.0	34.5	22.9	11.6	37.5	66.4
1920	105.7	46.1	30.5	15.6	43.6	66.2
1930	122.8	61.0	39.0	22.0	49.7	63.9
1940	131.7	67.1	41.5	25.6	50.9	61.8
1950[2]	151.3	84.9	49.7	35.2	56.1	58.5
1960	179.3	112.9	58.0	54.9	63.0	51.4
1970	203.2	139.4	63.8	75.6	68.6	45.8
1970[3]	203.2	153.9	67.9	85.8	75.7	44.1
1980	226.5	169.4	67.9	101.5	74.8	40.1
1980[4]	226.5	172.7	73.0	99.7	75.6	42.3
1990	248.7	192.7	77.8	114.9	77.4	40.3

[1] Figures for 1900 through 1940 are estimates based on 1950 SMSA boundaries.
[2] Alaska and Hawaii included from 1950 on.
[3] Two sets of 1970 figures are shown. The upper set is that actually recorded after the 1970 census. The lower set is the 1970 population applied to SMSA boundaries as they existed in 1980. Thus comparison of the second set of 1970 figures with 1980 figures shows change within the same set of boundaries.
[4] Two sets of 1980 figures are shown. The upper set is the data actually recorded by the 1980 census. The lower set is the 1980 population as it would have appeared had the 1990 boundaries been in place.
[5] The term *ring* means all of the metropolitan area outside of its central city or cities.
[6] Through the 1980 census the Bureau of the Census used the term Standard Metropolitan Statistical Area (SMSA) for metropolitan areas. For the 1990 census the bureau uses the term Metropolitan Statistical Area (MSA) and Consolidated Metropolitan Area (CMSA) for larger metropolitan areas. The definition of central city was broadened somewhat after the 1980 census. Thus some of the central city population increases from 1980 to 1990 is simply definitional.

Sources: For 1950 and earlier, Donald J. Bogue, *Population Growth in Standard Metropolitan Areas 1900–1950,* Housing and Home Finance Agency, Washington, D.C. pp. 11 and 13. For 1960 and subsequent years the *Statistical Abstract of the U.S.*, 112th and earlier editions and direct communication with the Population Division, Bureau of the Census.

cally three to five years. At this point the entire unpaid balance would come due. The homeowner then had to refinance or face loss of the property. The old-fashioned melodrama scene with the villain about to foreclose on the hapless widow had a certain basis in fact. But the point of interest for U.S. urban history is that the large down payment and the uncertainty regarding refinance kept many people from home ownership.

With the Great Depression of the 1930s, construction activity slowed and the federal government saw restoration of construction employment as a way to stimulate the nation's economy. One way to increase the demand for housing was to expand the opportunity for home ownership. The technique invented was mortgage insurance. The Federal Housing Administration (FHA) began to guarantee mortgages. The recipient of an FHA mortgage paid a small premium, which went into a fund that reimbursed banks should the borrowers default. At this point, mortgage lending became essentially riskless for banks. Banks were willing to lend 90 to 95 percent of the purchase price and to lend at long term, typically 20 to 30 years. The financial instrument which built much of America's suburbs, the low-down-payment, long-term, fixed-interest mortgage thus came into being.

Over the years the federal presence in mortgage markets expanded. The general thrust of federal policy then was twofold: First, as noted, the direct risk in mortgage lending was reduced. Second, so-called secondary mortgage markets were created. This made banks much more willing to lend long term because they could sell the mortgages they held if better uses for their money came along.[12]

The intention of Congress was to stimulate residential construction and open up home ownership to more families. Ultimately both of these effects were achieved on a massive scale. The implications for the reshaping of urban and metropolitan areas discussed in chapter 18 were not anticipated. Yet federal intervention in mortgage markets probably had more effect on the shape and fate of cities than any specifically urban federal policy in the nation's history.

The Rush to the Suburbs

America's participation in World War II between 1941 and 1945 represented a brief break in the suburbanizing process. Residential construction, other than for war workers, was halted; civilian automobile production was suspended; and gasoline was rationed. When the war ended, the country entered into a sustained suburban housing boom. In the first decade or so after the war, part of the force behind suburbanization probably came simply from accumulated demand from the low construction years between 1930 and 1945. But the process continued unabated for many years beyond the period which could be explained in terms of pent-up demand from the 1930s and 1940s. Table 2–1 makes this clear.

The forces behind this sustained growth of the suburbs were numerous. Mortgage finance was readily available on attractive terms. Employment was high and incomes were rising rapidly. The nation thus had more wealth to spend on land development, on housing, and on the additional personal transportation that suburbanization required. Automobile ownership rose from 25 million in 1945 to about 40 million in 1950 to 62 million in 1960, 89 million in 1970, and 122 million in 1980. At the end of World War II there was one automobile for every five Americans. By 1980 there was one automobile for every two Americans.

Paralleling the increase in automobile ownership was a great expansion of the nation's highway system. Shortly after the war there began a major surge of highway building by the states, powerfully encouraged by federal subsidies. Practical commuting distances increased and suburban residence for city workers became much more feasible. Then the National Defense Highway Act of 1956 funded the beginning of the interstate highway system. The suburbanizing effect of the Interstate Highway System on both population and economic activity were enormous. This matter is discussed in detail in Chapter 18.

Decentralization has also been promoted by improvements in electronic communications. Long-distance direct dialing, facsimile transmission, common carrier links between computers, closed-circuit television and electronic message systems like Telex and fax all reduce the need for face-to-face communication. Having the capacity for interaction at a distance does not cause decentralization. But it permits it if economic or social forces favor it.

For example, stock and commodity brokerages involve a tremendous amount of communication. In fact, they involve little physical movement of anything other than paper. Twenty or 30 years ago such activities were inevitably bound to a few downtowns because of the need for face-to-face communications. This is no longer true. In the 1970s New York City, desperate for revenues, decided that a "stock transfer tax" would be a good revenue raiser, given all the transfer activity that occurred on Wall Street. City officials were surprised and distressed when a sizable piece of the brokerage industry threatened to move across the Hudson River to Jersey City, and the stock transfer tax idea was quickly dropped. It was recently developed electronic communications that gave the brokerage industry that option. In many industries like brokerage and insurance, which still maintain a large central-city presence for the highest interaction activities, much "back office" work like data processing has moved to the suburbs. This is possible only because electronic technology provides sufficient links to the downtown office. In its way, the transistor may be as decentralizing as the automobile.

The baby boom, a phenomenon that began in the late 1940s, peaked in 1957, and lasted into the mid-1960s, further fueled the suburban housing boom. The attraction of the suburbs for couples in the family-formation state was an enormous decentralizing force.

The Age of Central-City Shrinkage

As Table 2–1 indicates, the first decades following World War II saw metropolitan areas grow rapidly in absolute terms and also as a percentage of total population. Within metropolitan areas most growth occurred outside the central cities. However, the picture is a mixed one. Much growth occurred in a number of sunbelt and western cities. Some of this was genuine urban growth. But in many western cities, the city limits extend well beyond the urbanized area. Therefore much growth that is suburban in character occurs within the city boundaries and appears as part of the central city total. Then, too, if the city is not surrounded by incorporated municipalities that resist annexation the city may grow substantially in land area. This was and is the case for many western cities. In the older and larger cities, particularly in the east and north central parts of the nation the general rule was shrinkage. From 1950 to 1990 the population of Buffalo shrank from 580,000 to 328,000; St. Louis from 857,000 to 397,000; Cleveland from 915,000 to 506,000; Chicago from 3,621,000 to 2,784,000; and Boston from from 801,000 to 574,000. New York City declined only slightly in percentage terms, from 7,891,000 to 7,323,000.[13] In general the declines were largest, in percentage terms, in inland cities. In the case of New York the decline was cushioned by immigration. Miami grew from 249,000 to 359,000. It swam against the general tide of big city shrinkage largely because of massive Cuban immigration following the coming to power of Fidel Castro in Cuba about 1960.

The losses of population by many of the larger and older cities took place within the context of the sunbelt-frostbelt shift. In the last several decades there have been large population movements from the northeastern and north central states to southern and western states.

The reasons for the shifts shown in Table 2–2 are numerous. In part the movement may simply be a continuation of a historic trend. The nation was settled from the eastern seaboard, particularly the Northeast, and some diffusion away from the original centers should be expected. A preference for warm climates is also considered to be a a significant factor. As the population becomes more affluent it is free to give more weight to its climatological preferences. The interstate highway system and electronic communications have made many southern and western locations more accessible than previously. The development of air conditioning undoubtedly accelerated the growth of some parts of the South by making life there far more comfortable. It has also been argued that there are factors relating to politics and the pattern of expenditures of federal funds which may explain part of the shift. These and other possibilities are discussed in some detail in a number of works on urban and regional economics.[14]

Regardless of the cause of the movement, the facts of massive shifts in population and employment are not in doubt. The city in a lagging region is, all other things being equal, more likely to lose population than a city in a growing region. Thus for cities like Cleveland or Detroit, internal forces predisposing them to population and job loss are augmented by regional trends. Conversely, some of the growth of cities like Ft. Myers, Houston, or Phoenix is explained by their location in growing regions.

TABLE 2–2 Regional population, 1940–1980 (in thousands)

*Region**	*1940*	*1950*	*1960*	*1970*	*1980*	*1990*	*Percent Change 1980–90*
Northeast	35,977	39,478	44,678	49,061	49,139	50,976	3.7
New England	8,437	9,314	10,509	11,848	12,348	13,197	4.2
Mid-Atlantic	27,539	30,164	34,168	37,213	36,788	37,779	2.7
North-Central	40,143	44,461	51,619	56,589	58,854	60,225	2.3
East North-Central	26,626	30,399	36,225	40,262	41,670	42,414	1.8
West North-Central	13,517	14,061	15,394	16,327	17,184	17,811	3.6
South	41,666	47,197	54,973	62,812	75,349	86,916	15.4
South Atlantic	17,823	21,182	25,972	30,678	36,943	44,421	20.2
East South-Central	10,778	11,477	12,050	12,808	14,663	15,347	4.7
West South-Central	13,065	14,538	16,951	19,326	23,743	27,148	14.3
West	14,379	20,190	28,053	34,838	43,165	54,060	25.2
Mountain	4,150	5,075	6,855	8,289	11,368	14,035	23.5
Pacific	10,229	15,115	21,198	26,549	31,797	40,025	25.9

*These regions are standard Bureau of the Census groupings, as follows: New England: Maine, New Hampshire, Vermont, Massachusetts, Rhode Island, Connecticut; Mid-Atlantic: New York, New Jersey, Pennsylvania; East North-Central: Ohio, Indiana, Illinios, Michigan, Wisconsin; West North-Central: Minnesota, Iowa, Missouri, North Dakota, South Dakota, Nebraska, Kansas; South Atlantic: Delaware, Maryland, District of Columbia, Virginia, West Virginia, North Carolina, Georgia, Florida: East South-Central: Kentucky, Tennessee, Alabama, Mississippi; West South-Central: Arkansas, Louisiana, Oklahoma, Texas; Mountain: Montana, Idaho, Wyoming, Colorado, New Mexico, Arizona, Utah, Nevada; Pacific: Washington, Oregon, California, Alaska, Hawaii.

Source: U.S. Bureau of the Census, Census of the Population, 1940, 1950, 1960, 1970, 1980, 1990.

The Decentralization of Employment

Although data on the decentralization of employment is not as comprehensive as that for population, it appears that jobs decentralized about as rapidly as population. For example, in 1970 51 percent of all employment in the Philadelphia SMSA was in the city itself and 49 percent was in the suburban ring. By 1977 the central city percentage had dropped to 41 percent, with a corresponding increase for the suburban ring. Comparable drops for central-city percentage shares for the same time period were 61 to 47 for Baltimore, 73 to 58 for New Orleans, 48 to 35 for St. Louis, and 46 to 34 for Washington, D.C.[15] In general, these trends have continued since then with little or no sign of reversal.

Cities and the Poor

Relative to the rest of the nation, central cities have become substantially poorer since the end of World War II. In 1959 central cities had only 83 percent of their proportionate share of the nation's poor. In 1985 they had 136 percent of their proportionate share. In 1958, on a per capita basis, central cities had 1.5 times as many poor people as did their suburbs. By 1985 that figure had risen to 2.3. Even the 2.3 figure understates the real difference. The "suburbs" referred to here are the entirety of the metropolitan area outside of the central city. But that part outside includes many cities (such as the city of Yonkers, discussed in Chapter 7). If one compared central cities with the part outside that is actually "suburban" in the ordinary meaning of the term, the disparity would be much greater. In 1959 central cities had about half as many poor people per capita as nonmetropolitan areas. By 1985 per capita poverty rates were higher in central cities than in nonmetropolitan areas. In brief, poverty became much more of an urban phenomenon than it had been two decades earlier.[16] Note, however, that these statistics are relative ones. In absolute terms real personal income in the United States has been rising for many decades. Thus it is possible for an area to experience both an absolute increase in average personal income and yet lose ground in relative terms. And this is exactly what has happened in a great many cities.

If one considers the nonpoor population, one sees trends complementary to those just described. Good statistics on the geographic distribution of personal income are available back to the 1940s. From then until the present, the ratio of personal income in suburban areas relative to central cities rose steadily. The loss of population from central cities to suburbs was a selective one, with the more affluent central-city residents the ones most likely to make the move.[17]

Increasingly, central cities became the home of minorities and lost their white residents. From 1970 to 1980 central-city population totals remained unchanged, but central-city white populations fell by almost 6 million. Given the large disparity between white and nonwhite incomes this change was actually as much or more an economic than a racial phenomenon. Whites as a group were using their higher incomes to move to suburbia and beyond, leaving the central cities to less affluent ethnic groups.[18]

Knowing what to do about the relative impoverishment of central cities is an enormously difficult problem. But understanding why the cities became relatively poorer is not difficult. The out-migration from city to suburb drained off the more prosperous members of the urban population, simply because they were the households which could afford new, largely single-family suburban housing. The movement of population, particularly of a prosperous population, pulled out retailing activity, for retailers have no choice but to follow their customers. Wholesaling activity, given an increased choice of location by improved regional highway networks, followed naturally. A variety of business and personal services also followed, in some cases to follow their customers and in other cases to follow their employees. Manufacturing activity departed for several reasons. Improved highway systems made suburban locations more attractive for truck-served industries. Vacant suburban land permitted the building of single-story plants, which tend to be more efficient than multistory buildings. Finally, the decentralization of population enriched the suburban labor force, and the availability and quality of labor is one of the most important determinants of industrial location.

At the same time that cities were losing their grip on much of the blue-collar employment, they were, as a result of the vast rural-to-urban migration, gaining a population that needed such employment. The migration was due to one of the most important economic events in post-World War II America, a startlingly rapid mechanization of agriculture. In 1945 agricultural employment was about 10 million and the farm population about 25 million. By 1970 agricultural employment was under 4 million and total farm population under 10 million even though the population of the nation had grown by about 65 million people during those 25 years. The decline has continued somewhat more slowly since 1970. By 1990 the agricultural labor force was down to 2.5 million and total farm population was approximately 4.6 million. One might define degree of urbanization by the percentage of a group that lives in central cities. Using this definition, American blacks went from being a predominantly rural population in the immediately postwar period to being considerably more urbanized than the nation's white population by 1980—a vast internal migration accomplished in the space of two or three decades.

A rural population, both black and white and also Hispanic in some parts of the United States, often having few nonagricultural skills, arrived in American cities just at a time when the demand for relatively unskilled labor was shrinking. Nor could rural migrants to the city readily follow job opportunities to the suburbs because they did not have the income to afford suburban housing.[19] In most metropolitan areas the largest supply of low-cost housing is older housing in the central cities. The oldest housing tends to be centrally located simply because most metropolitan areas have grown from the center outward. This natural difference in housing prices was increased in many cases by the resistance of suburban areas to the construction of multifamily housing, a point discussed in subsequent chapters.

The loss of blue-collar jobs at the same time as the cities received a mass migration from rural America proved to be a social disaster. The formation of a large urban "underclass" appears to be caused, in large measure, by a lack of jobs that can be filled by the population from which the underclass comes.[20] The links between chronic unemployment (particularly of males), welfare dependency, family dissolution, and a host of ills that necessarily follow are not hard to discern. In turn, the formation of a large underclass hastens the flight of population and jobs. Nothing is likely to drive out working-class and middle-class residents faster than concerns about crime and the quality of the school system. And when consumers and workers leave, firms soon follow.

Urban Fiscal Problems

The fiscal situation of cities in the United States varies greatly from one to another and, to some extent, from one region to another. In recent years many growing cities enjoyed relatively good fiscal health. Expenses rose, but a growing population, rising personal incomes, and an increasing economic base enabled revenues to keep up with expenses. However, a number of larger old cities experienced severe distress.

In the 1970s both New York and Cleveland verged on bankruptcy. At one point in the 1970s expectations of New York's bankruptcy became so great that city bonds were selling for not much more than 60 cents on the dollar. The city was pulled back from the brink of bankruptcy by loans from the federal government. But a condition for that assistance was that much of the power to make financial decisions was removed from the city government and placed in the Emergency Financial Control Board (EFCB). Ultimately, through substantial layoffs of city workers and some cutbacks in services, the city skated away from disaster and by the mid-1980s seemed to be in reasonably good financial health. However, even now, there is much concern about how the city, along with many other older cities, will fund the huge amount of work needed by its aging infrastructure (roads, bridges, water and sewer lines and mass transit system). Its newly elected mayor in 1989, David Dinkins, found that he had to recommend against much needed expenditures in police protection, education, and social services because the tax revenues to support them simply were not there. As of 1993 the City's financial situation was still precarious.

The fiscal problems of many urban areas are largely the consequence of trends discussed earlier. The selective out-migration of more affluent residents represents a major loss of revenue-raising capacity. Sales tax receipts fall because of the loss of buying power. In the long term, tax collections from residential properties fall because property values fall and it is these values that are the basis of tax-paying ability. Simultaneously, the loss of firms to the suburbs or other regions of the nation chips away at the nonresidential side of the municipal tax base. At the same time that revenues decline the in-migration of poor people adds a population that costs more in the way of many types of municipal services.

The revenue problem may feed on itself. Declining revenue reduces the ability of the city to provide adequate services, and this accelerates the out-migration of residents and jobs, which, of course, further shrinks the tax base.

For the city in fiscal distress the options are limited. In many cases cities are legally restrained by state-enacted taxing and borrowing limits. But even in the absence of such limits, the mobility of people and jobs puts a cap on revenue-raising efforts. The city that tries to tax too heavily is likely to find that those it seeks to tax begin to relocate. The ill-fated stock transfer tax noted earlier is a case in point. Few cities avail themselves of corporate and personal income taxes for fear of driving out residents and firms. Although no one can move a building because property taxes are too high, high property taxes can reduce the rate of new construction. Raising taxes on properties that are only marginally profitable may cause abandonment.[21] It may provide a motivation for arson, wherein the unscrupulous property owner converts an unprofitable structure into a check from an insurance company. When taxes on a structure are more than the structure can earn, the owner may demolish the structure to escape the burden of taxation—a perfectly legal maneuver that is not unheard of. Ultimately, new structures may be erected, but in the interval the municipality has lost whatever tax revenues the demolished structures had yielded. In these senses even real property can be regarded as being mobile in the face of overly steep taxation.

CENTRAL-CITY DECLINE IN PERSPECTIVE

The last several pages of this chapter may present a rather pessimistic picture of the recent situation of many older central cities and their residents. We see losses of jobs, losses of population, relative decline in personal income, and relative increases in the number of poor people.

But the picture is not as grim as it might at first seem. First, as noted, the income declines are relative and thus it is possible to move forward in absolute terms and yet slip backward in relative terms. Similarly, most statistics will show a decrease in the quality of central-city housing relative to suburban and nonmetropolitan housing. Yet the same statistics will also show that in the last several decades there has been an absolute increase in the quality of central-city housing.[22]

Then, too, one should not confuse the welfare of places and the welfare of people. Consider an urban neighborhood that was once a thriving middle-class area but is now somewhat poorer, more rundown physically, and perhaps, not as safe as it once was. The place, in some senses, has "suffered." That does not necessarily imply that any individual has suffered. Many of the former residents are now, by their own choices, relocated in the suburbs of the metropolitan area. Many of the new residents may be immigrants from overseas, who presumably prefer it to the places from which they came. A number of other residents of the neighborhood may be former slum dwellers from the most deteriorated neighborhoods of the city's core. It is likely that they too prefer it to their former locations. In short, the fact that a place has "suffered" does not necessarily imply that we can find an individual who has also suffered.

Finally, the statistical trends cited are aggregates. They do not describe the situation in every city. Boston, San Francisco, Phoenix, and many other cities are doing very well.

Cities have gone through enormous social and economic change in the last several decades, and change can be painful. But that need not imply pessimism about the ultimate outcome.

SUMMARY

The forces that produced a hundredfold increase in urban population in the United States between 1800 and 1900 included national population growth, increased agricultural productivity, the growth of factory production and the development of low-cost modes of transportation. The nature of nineteenth-century transportation contributed to an extremely dense pattern of urban development.

In the late nineteenth century the first signs of suburbanization became visible as the electric streetcar began expanding the old "walking city." In the twentieth century, automotive transportation, electronic communications, and increased income promoted massive suburbanization of population and economic activity, which continue to the present time.

We noted the complete cessation of central-city population growth in recent years and declines in the population of many of the largest cities, particularly inland industrial cities such as Cleveland and St. Louis. But at the same time that central-city growth has halted, the total population of metropolitan areas continues to grow.

In the post-World War II period central cities have grown poorer relative to both the suburbs and to nonmetropolitan areas. The selective out-migration of more prosperous households and the loss of employment to suburbs, nonmetropolitan areas, and overseas competitors have contributed to this trend. Another factor was the migration to the cities of a large, generally poor population pushed off the land by the rapid mechanization of agriculture in the decades after World War II. The fiscal problems of many cities are clearly related to these economic and demographic trends.

NOTES

1. For urban data going back many decades see *Historical Statistics of the United States*, Bureau of the Census, Department of Commerce, Washington, D.C.
2. Adna Weber, *The Growth of Cities in the Nineteenth Century*, The Macmillan Company, New York, 1899. Reprinted by Cornell University Press, Ithaca, NY, 1963, p. 20.
3. Ibid., p. 460.
4. For discussion of the relationship between transportation costs and the growth of cities in the late eighteenth and early nineteenth centuries, see Alan Pred, *City Systems in Advanced Economies*, John Wiley, New York, 1977.
5. Frank S. So et al. (eds.), *The Practice of Local Government Planning*, International City Managers Association, Washington, D.C. 1979, p. 27.
6. Weber, op. cit., p. 208.
7. James Ford, "Residential and Industrial Decentralization," In *City Planning*, 2nd ed., John Nolen, ed., D. Appleton & Co., New York, 1929, pp. 334 and 335. The first edition was printed in 1916, and the article appears to have been written between 1910 and 1916.
8. Sam Bass Warner, *Steetcar Suburbs: A Process of Growth in Boston*, Atheneum, New York, 1968.
9. H.G. Wells, *Anticipation. The Reaction of Mechanical and Scientific Progress on Human Life and Thought*, London, Harper & Row, 1902, quoted in *Post Industrial America: Metropolitan Decline and Inter-Regional Job Shifts*, George Sternlieb and James W. Hughes, eds., Rutgers University Center for Urban Policy Research, New Brunswick, NJ, 1975, p. 176.
10. For a discussion of population density gradients, see John M. Levy, *Urban and Metropolitan Economics*, McGraw-Hill Book Co., New York, 1985, pp. 24–26.

11. John D. Kasarda, "The Implications of Contemporary Redistribution Trends for National Urban Policy," *Social Science Quarterly* , vol. 61, nos. 3 and 4, December 1980, p. 380. For statistics on metropolitan/nonmetropolitan residence, see *Statistical Abstract of the United States*, Bureau of the Census, Department of Commerce, Washington, D.C. section 1, various years.
12. Carter M. McFarland, *Federal Government and Urban Problems*, Westview, Boulder, CO, 1978, p. 117. See, also, Levy, op. cit., pp. 208–10.
13. Statistical Abstract of the United States, 1992, 112th ed., Table 38.
14. For a detailed discussion of factors involved in regional growth, see Edgar M. Hoover and Frank Giarranti, *An Introduction to Regional Economics*, 3rd ed., Alfred A. Knopf, New York, 1984.
15. Peter Muller, *Contemporary Suburban America*, Prentice Hall, Englewood Cliffs, NJ, 1981, p. 132.
16. For statistics on poverty, see *Statistical Abstract of the United States*, section on "Income, Expenditures and Wealth," various years, which will provide some statistics and references to Bureau of the Census reports. See also, Bureau of the Census, *Current Population Reports*, Series P. 60, nos. 115 and 124.
17. See Levy, op. cit., pp. 41–42, for a brief discussion on this point. For a more detailed presentation, see George Sternlieb, "Is the Urban Crisis Over," Report by the Subcommittee on Fiscal and Intergovernmental Policy, Joint Economic Committee, 95th Congress of the United States, March 20, 1979.
18. A similar comparison in the movement of population between 1980 and 1990 is not possible at this writing because the Bureau of the Census made major changes in the definition of the term "central city" prior to the 1990 census. These changes had the effect of reclassifying many suburban subcenters as central cities. It will be possible to make a valid comparison if at some time 1990 population data is recalculated in terms of 1980 central city definitions or if 1980 population data is recalculated in terms of the 1990 definition.
19. For a statistical study of the effect of location within the metropolitan area on employment, see John F. Kain, "Housing Segregation, Negro Employment and Metropolitan Decentralization," *Quarterly Journal of Economics*, May 1968, p. 176. This is an old article and the data in it are now obsolete, but the ideas are still valid and it has been cited many times in the urban economic literature.
20. For a detailed and convincing development of this argument, see William J. Wilson, *The Truly Disadvantaged*, University of Chicago Press, 1987.
21. This simply means that the owner, in effect, disappears and ceases to pay taxes, to repay debt, and to do repairs and maintenance. In some cities it is illegal to abandon a building, but that does not stop the event from occurring.
22. Judging housing quality from statistical measures is difficult. Among the common measures used are percentage of units with complete kitchen facilities, percentage of units with complete plumbing facilities, and percentage of overcrowded units. A unit is said to be overcrowded if the number of occupants exceeds the number of rooms, that is, more than 1.00 occupant per room. Data on these and other housing items are gathered by the Bureau of the Census in both the decennial census and the annual Survey of Housing. In regard to all three items mentioned, urban housing has improved in each decade since the end of World War II.

SELECTED BIBLIOGRAPHY

CALLOW, ALEXANDER B., *American Urban History*, Oxford University Press, 1973.

GLAAB, CHARLES N., AND BROWN, THEODORE A., *A History of Urban American*, The Macmillan Company, New York, 1973.

MCKELVEY, BLAKE, *The Urbanization of America*, Rutgers University Press, New Brunswick, NJ, 1963.

WEBER, ADNA, *The Growth of Cities in the Nineteenth Century*, first printed in 1899, reprinted by Cornell University Press, Ithaca, NY, 1967.

CHAPTER 3

THE HISTORY OF PLANNING: PART I

The history of city and town planning, in its full sense, goes back many centuries. The logical and orderly arrangement of streets and public spaces in Roman towns, for instance, indicates the existence of a high level of city planning before the birth of Christ. However, since the focus of this book is present-day planning, we do not present a full history of the subject. This chapter begins with a brief note on the prerevolutionary period in the United States and proceeds through the first great age of suburbanization, the 1920s. The following chapter picks up the story from the start of the Great Depression and carries it through to the present time.

The focus of this chapter, as of the book as a whole, is on events in the United States. However, the chapter does contain some discussion of planning in Europe as well, as for the development of planning in the United States was and is closely tied to events across the ocean. In fact, today, the American planner who observes the practice of planning in Europe—whether by visiting new towns in Scandinavia, France, or the Netherlands; by observing the preservation of historic districts in any one of a number of countries; or simply by observing the sensitivity and wisdom with which the Swiss have treated a beautiful but potentially fragile natural heritage—will realize that there is still much that we can learn from the Europeans.

COLONIAL AMERICA

Prior to the American Revolution municipalities had strong powers to control the use of land and thus shape their own form. These powers came out of a European tradition that treated the town or village as an independent corporation, which

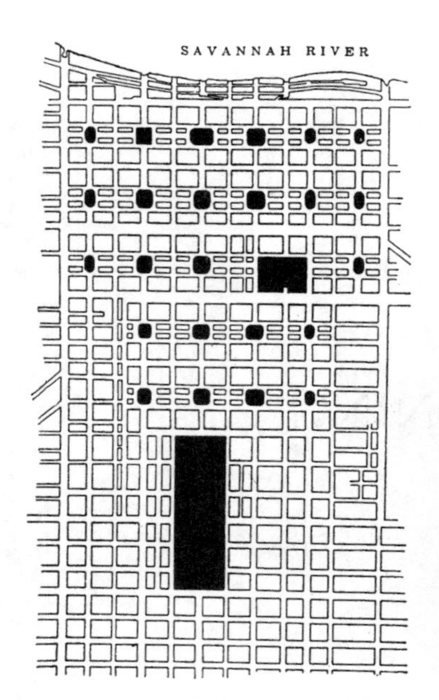

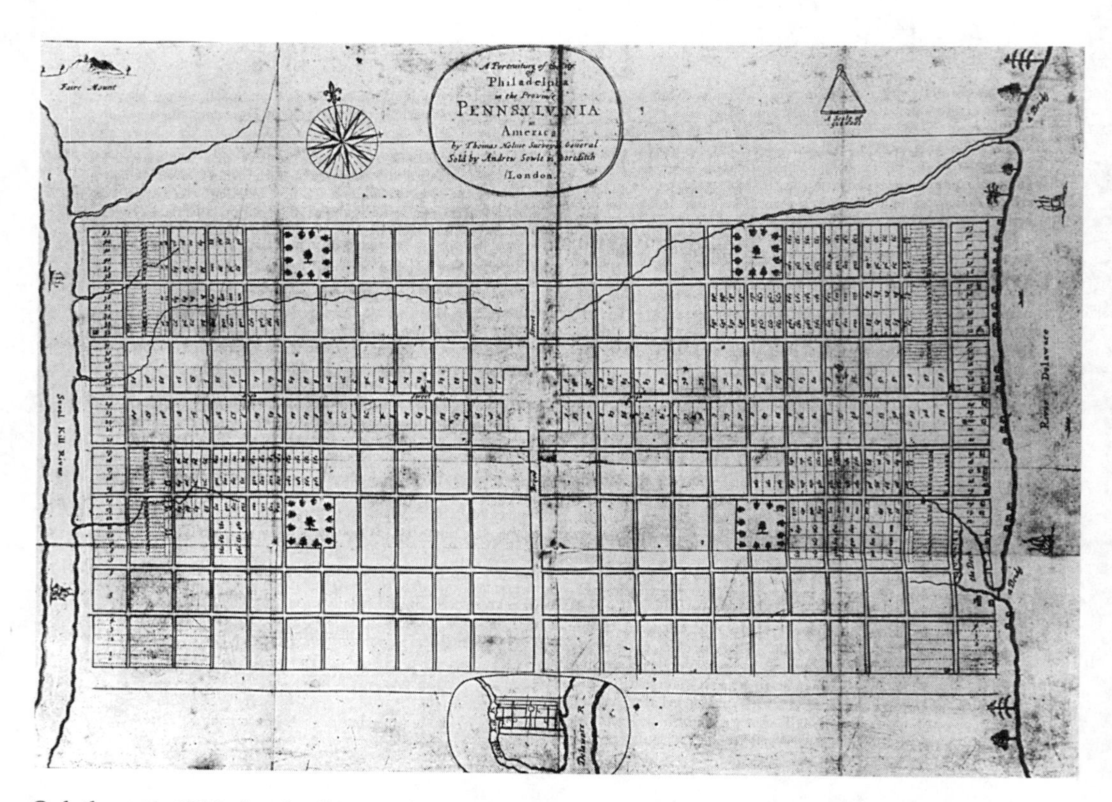

Oglethorpe's 1733 plan for Savannah (top left) and the gracious and open results from an 1855 drawing (top right). William Penn's 1682 plan for Philadelphia is shown at bottom. In both plans note the symmetry, the differentiation between primary and secondary streets, and the provision of public open space.

might own, control, or dispose of most of the land within its boundaries. Then, too, many U.S. communities started as grants to individuals or groups, which then, by virtue of the grant, had the power to dispose of and control land within their borders. Communities had broad powers to control economic activities within their borders. For example, municipal governments frequently had the power to decide whether an individual was to be allowed to practice a particular trade or set up a business establishment. Thus colonial towns had formidable powers to shape their pattern of development. In that preindustrial age, they also faced much weaker growth pressures than was later to be the case.

Today, one can see the results of prerevolutionary town planning in various communities where subsequent growth pressures were not so overwhelming as to sweep away all traces of earlier times.[1] Prerevolutionary planning survives well in parts of New England away from major metropolitan areas, including much of New Hampshire, Vermont, parts of Maine, parts of western Massachusetts, and parts of Connecticut and Rhode Island. In fact, much of the charm of these areas comes from the fact that so much of the past does survive. The gracious urban pattern that characterizes such towns—the town square, the reasonable amounts of space between buildings, the simple rectangular street pattern—are all legacies of the town planning of the period. The regular pattern of development and open areas in Savannah are also an example of prerevolutionary town planning. The land for the city was a grant to a single individual, James Oglethorpe, who as grantee had the power to plan and to impose an orderly and gracious pattern on subsequent development.

The Revolution changed much of this. To some extent a certain amount of disorder was the price to be paid for political and personal freedom—a small price for what was gained, but still a price. Quite obviously, the Revolution ended the practice of creating municipalities through the mechanism of royal grants to individuals. More important, it placed the bulk of political power in the hands of the states and made substate units of government "creatures of the state," possessing only those powers granted them by the states. Municipal powers to control the use and disposition of land were thus greatly diminished. Finally, the Constitution contained numerous safeguards for the rights of private property. (See, for example, the quotation from the Fifth Amendment in Chapter 5.) The protection of private property rights limits the capacity of a municipality to control development on privately owned land.

LIMITED MEANS AND GROWING PROBLEMS

The reductions in the powers of municipalities occasioned by the Revolution preceded by only a very few decades the emergence of enormous growth pressures discussed in Chapter 2. Many municipalities grew rapidly, with little public control over the pattern of growth. In most cases municipal planning was in the hands of the commercial elite of the city.[2] Planning thus often focused on the commercial heart of the city and ignored residential areas, particularly the less than prosperous ones. Often, planning was concentrated on steps that would facilitate the commercial and industrial growth of the city, such as inducing a railroad to extend a branch line to the city or improving the docks and the waterfront. Street patterns were often laid out in such a manner as to facilitate land subdivision and speculation.

The rectangular "gridiron" pattern became commonplace for exactly these reasons. It was easy to lay out and it facilitated subdivision and speculation. More imaginative plans and plans adapted to particular terrain and topographic features were relatively rare. As land values rose with the growth of urban populations, pressures on remaining open space increased. Few municipalities were willing to accept the costs of acquiring land to protect it from development. Rapid growth, a strong regard for the sanctity of private property, the lure of quick profits from land development and speculation, and a feeling that promoting commercial growth was the number one function of municipal government were dominant motifs of the early nineteenth-century urban scene.

There were a few exceptions to the picture just presented. For example, L'Enfant's plan for Washington, D.C. was a unified vision of how street pattern, public spaces, and structures should form a grand design. And the motivation behind it was essentially civic, not commercial. In Savannah, Georgia, Oglethorpe's original plan continued to guide the development of the city into the mid-nineteenth century. But more often than not, the forces of growth ran rampant over plans made in the prerevolutionary period. For example, William Penn's plan for Philadelphia, formulated in the 1680s, called for a system of broad streets, public open spaces, and setbacks around individual structures. But under the growth pressures that began in the late eighteenth century the plan was simply overwhelmed. The side yard setbacks disappeared as houses were built wall to wall in block-long rows. Alleys were cut through blocks from one face to the other and then filled with row housing. Many of the public open spaces disappeared into commercial or residential use. There was no shortage of gracious and attractive city plans in eighteenth-century America, but most of them, like Philadelphia's, did not survive the growth pressures of the nineteenth century. By and large, Calvin Coolidge's famous aphorism, "the business of America is business," though uttered a century later, described the early nineteenth-century urban scene quite well.

THE PRESSURE FOR REFORM

As urban populations and the density of urban development increased, pressures for reform mounted. U.S. planning history and tradition to a large extent mirror concern with the problems arising from urban growth. Over the years these problems have included sanitation and public health, housing quality and overcrowding, the disappearance of urban open space, the ugliness and grimness of the nineteenth-century industrial city, traffic congestion, and the problem of providing urban populations with adequate mobility. In recent years planning effort has also been directed to problems of urban unemployment, to urban fiscal problems, to a variety of issues that might be lumped under the heading of social justice, and to issues of environmental preservation and quality. And this listing is far from complete.

Sanitary Reform

In the mid-nineteenth century sanitary conditions in most cities were appalling by modern standards. Human wastes were generally disposed of on site in a backyard septic tank or cesspool—a situation that is acceptable at low population densities but a major menace to public health at high densities. The menace was compounded by the fact that most water for household use came from wells and streams. Thus contamination of drinking water sources was common. In an age before antibiotics and vaccinations, water-borne diseases like cholera and typhoid fever were major killers. So, too, were insect-borne diseases like malaria, yellow fever, and typhus. The mechanics of disease transmission were not known in the mid-1800s, for understanding of the relationship between bacteria and disease was still several decades in the future. However, it was widely understood that environments with large amounts of decaying material or stagnant water bred disease, perhaps because of "vapors" given off by putrifying materials or perhaps for some other reason.

Sewers, where they existed, served not to carry away organic wastes but to carry off storm water and prevent flooding. Very often they were constructed large enough for a man to go inside to make repairs. Water flow was too slow and too intermittent to carry off wastes, and so sewers themselves often became "elongated cesspools."[3]

Clearly the situation cried for reform. About 1840 a simple but very important invention was made in England that promised to be the agent of reform. This was the "water carriage" sewer. The insight behind the invention was remarkably simple. If a sewer pipe was made with a relatively small diameter and with a cross section somewhat like an egg sliced through the long way and provided with a sufficient source of water, it would be essentially self-cleansing. The water velocity would be sufficient to carry off animal carcasses, fecal matter, and so on. In this case household wastes, instead of being dumped in on-site cesspools, could be piped into a common sewer and transported for miles before being released into the environment. The prospect for improvement in public health was enormous.

But building a water carriage sewer system for a city required planning on a major scale. Since the system was operated by gravity, the topography of the city had to be taken into account in the layout of streets. Because the system depended on a necessary volume of flow, streets had to be built with crowns so that rain water would be diverted into the sewer. Deciding where to install sewer lines meant that some data on population distribution and present health conditions were needed. The "sanitary survey" of the late nineteenth century—a mapping of houses, cases of contagious disease, and presence of outhouses and cesspools and the like—was perhaps the first systematic data collection and mapping effort to be seen in many cities. The amount of planning required to provide sewers to a city did not constitute a comprehensive planning effort. But it did require that at least one aspect of the city be considered as a whole.

Planning for adequate waste disposal was only a part of the larger goal of a generally healthful environment. It was understood that dark, damp, crowded places were associated with higher rates of disease and death. Thus a more complete planning effort would include provision of open space, consideration of sunlight and ventilation, and some contractual arrangements (see Chapter 9) to prevent excessive density of development. In densely developed urban areas, little could be done about these latter considerations. Providing sewers was largely a matter of fitting, however it could be done, a system to an existing pattern of development. However, in developing new areas a more comprehensive approach could be taken.

Sanitation and Integrated Design Frederick Law Olmsted, probably the outstanding U.S. planner/urban designer of the second half of the nineteenth century, designed a number of new communities in which all of these elements were part of an integrated design. The design was carefully keyed to the contour of the land for adequate drainage of both sewage and storm water. The location of swampy areas, brooks, streams, and other physical features were taken into account for health as well as aesthetic reasons. For example, it was known that malaria, which was widespread in the United States in the mid-nineteenth century, was somehow associated with swampy and poorly drained areas. Thus, design that was sensitive to drainage patterns could minimize the incidence of the disease. The fact that it did so because it eliminated the breeding area for malaria-carrying mosquitoes was not to be understood for several more decades, but the beneficial effect could be achieved nonetheless. The location of open spaces and plantings were also considered for their effects on the adequacy of light and ventilation. In fact, in Olmsted's mind, planning was largely to be judged by the extent to which it reduced disease. Sunlight, good air circulation, and an adequate amount of vegetation were, in his view, the most effective preventives of disease.

Urban Open Space

The interest in sanitation dovetailed with another preoccupation of nineteenth-century planners, the provision of urban parkland. In an analogy that was used at the time, just as good ventilation would make a house a healthier house, so too would parkland serve to ventilate a city. Many splendid examples of municipal park design date from the mid-nineteenth century. New York's Central Park, designed by Frederick Law Olmsted and Calvin Vaux in 1857, furnished inspiration for parks in many cities. The park covers a rectangle in Manhattan roughly two-and-one-half miles long by one-half mile wide. Bordered on all sides by dense urban development, it provides the Manhattanite with a beautifully landscaped piece of countryside in town. Across the East River in Brooklyn is a much less well-known but equally fine piece of Olmsted's design work, Prospect Park. A splendid system of meadows, wooded areas, connecting paths, and two artificial lakes provide an idyllic relief from mile upon mile of dense urbanization. In the case of both parks, as was true for the parks of many other cities, there is no doubt that had these areas not been acquired for public use they would have soon been covered with a dense carpeting of residences, stores, and other commercial

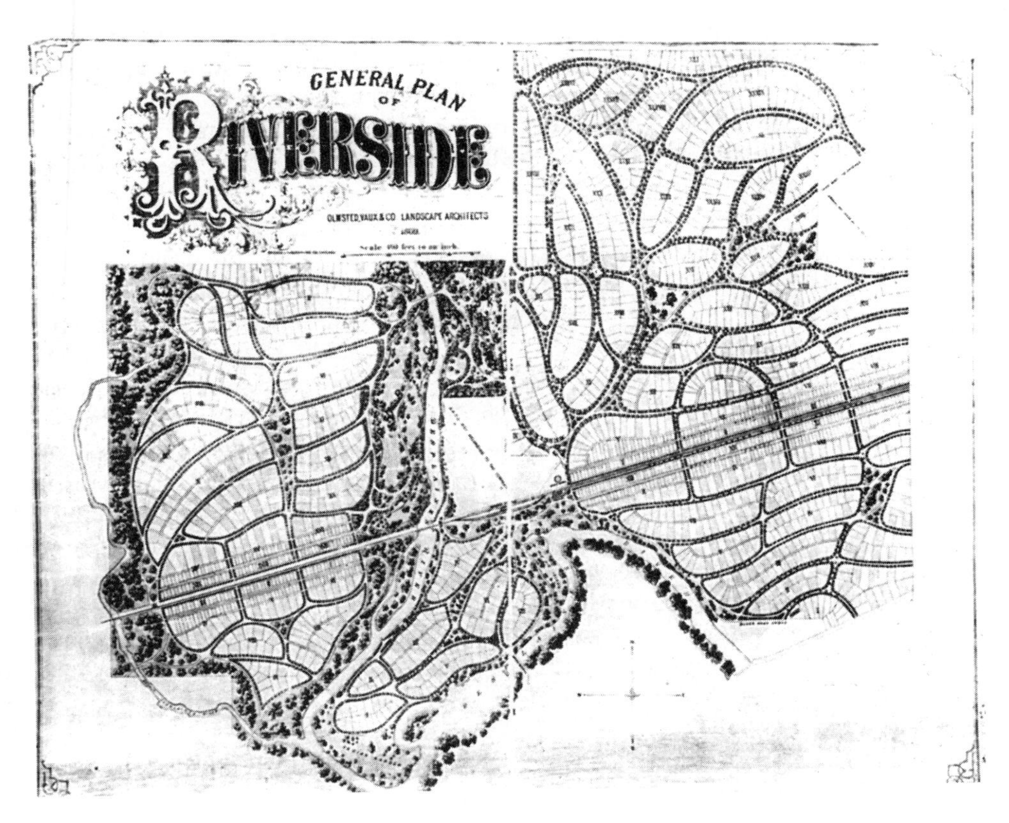

Riverside, a Chicago suburb, was planned by Olmstead and Vaux shortly after the Civil War. The curvilinear street pattern, close attention to fitting the street pattern to the topography, preservation of green areas, and separation of through-traffic from local traffic are all commonly used design techniques today.

activities. Other examples of Olmsted's work in park design can be seen today in Buffalo, Chicago, Montreal, Detroit, Boston, Bridgeport, Rochester, Knoxville, and Louisville.

Housing Reform

A major item on the agenda of nineteenth-century urban reformers was the condition of housing for the urban poor.[4] In one form or another the issue of housing for those who do not have enough income to obtain on the private market what society deems to be adequate housing has been on the planning agenda ever since. In the nineteenth century housing reform largely took the form of pressing for legislation that mandated minimum standards for housing quality.

In New York City the first legislation regulating tenement construction was passed in 1867, and other legislation followed at intervals thereafter. The city's 1901 Tenement House Act is considered a landmark in this tradition. It cut lot coverage back to 70 percent and required a separate bathroom for each apartment, courtyards (for light and ventilation) whose width was determined by building height, and improved fire safety measures. It also set up a Tenement House Commission, with a staff of inspectors and enforcement powers. By 1920 at least 40 other cities had enacted building codes backed by some enforcement machinery.[5]

Although much was accomplished through housing regulation, we must also note what was not done. Housing reform in the United States took a conservative direction. The more far-reaching housing policies that had been adopted in some European countries were rejected here, much to the disappointment of the more radical reformers. In Europe much public money was invested in building housing for workers of modest means. Municipal governments often played the roles of landowner, developer, and financier. Local and national governments took the view that it was a responsibility of government to provide adequate housing at acceptable cost. The sort of policy that appealed to the more radical housing reformers was exemplified by the city of Ulm, Germany. The city acquired 1,400 acres of suburban land, planned the area, built housing, and sold it at cost to working-class families. The city had also subsidized the building of cooperative apartments along with related community facilities.[6] But the view that prevailed in the United States was that housing is to be provided by the market and that the most government should do is to regulate the market. Government was not to be a landowner, a developer, or a source of housing capital. Even Lawrence Veiller, the moving force behind the 1901 Tenement House Act, believed that only local government should concern itself with housing and such concern should be limited to regulatory matters and general planning issues such as street layout. He opposed the idea that public monies should be spent on housing.

The United States subsequently did move toward public housing and housing subsidies (see Chapter 4) but, in contrast to Great Britain, Germany, France, the Netherlands, and other European nations, has never gone very far in that direction. The great majority of Americans live in housing that has been built for profit by the private market. Whether the United States would have been wise to follow the European approach is arguable. What the divergence between them does clearly indicate, however, is that one cannot separate major planning questions from matters of political ideology. The European approach, regardless of its technical merits or demerits, looked too much like socialism to be accepted in the United States.

The Tradition of Municipal Improvement

Another part of the planning tradition that emerged in the second half of the nineteenth century was what might loosely be called municipal improvement. Its origins are generally traced to the founding of an improvement society in Stockbridge, Massachusetts, in 1853.[7] The civic improvement movement grew rapidly, at first largely in New England and then nationally. In 1900 the National League of Improvement Associations was founded, to be supplanted two years later by the American League for Civic Improvement. The agenda for the hundreds of civic improvement organizations included diverse items like tree plantings, antibillboard campaigns, paved streets and sidewalks, provision of drinking fountains and public baths, provision of parks and recreational facilities, and numerous other public matters. The movement initiated a tradition of public concern with planning issues and helped build a climate of opinion receptive to municipal and regional planning.

The Municipal Art Movement

Toward the end of the nineteenth century there formed an interest in municipal aesthetics that is generally referred to as municipal or civic art. A fusion of art, architecture, and planning, it attempted to transcend the mere utilitarianism of the late nineteenth century and make the city a place of beauty as well. Though later criticized for attending to the cosmetic aspects of urban life rather than the most pressing problems, the movement had a strong component of idealism.

> The darkness rolls away, and the buildings that had been shadows stand forth distinctly in the grey air. The tall facades glow as the sun rises; their windows shine as topaz; their pennants of steam, tugging flutteringly from high chimneys, are changed to silvery plumes. Whatever was dingy, coarse, and ugly, is either transformed or hidden in shadow. The streets, bathed in the fresh morning light, fairly sparkle, their pavements from upper windows appearing smooth and clean. There seems to be a new city for the work of a new day. . . . There are born a new dream and a new hope. And of such is the impulse to civic art.

Distinguishing between "civic art" and "art" in its usual meaning, the same writer stated.

> It is municipal first of all. If men seek it they seek it not for art's sake, but for the city's; they are first citizens and then, in their own way, artists jealous of the city's looks because they are citizens . . . they so band themselves together and so commission sculptors, painters, artists, and landscape designers for the glorifying of civic art—not just because it is art, but because it is civic.[8]

The results of the movement are still visible all over America in the form of arches, fountains, statues, and other works of urban design and decoration. The inspiration for the movement came largely from Europe. One has only to look at the photographic plates of Robinson's classic work to see his inspiration: St. Pauls and the Thames embankment in London, the Arc de Triomphe in Paris, and other public areas in European cities. The motivation to catch up with the Europeans stemmed in part from the economic growth of nineteenth-century America. For it was wealth and leisure that gave us the feeling that we could afford that which was not purely functional.

The City Beautiful Movement

The City Beautiful movement brought together the ideas of municipal art, civic improvement, and landscape design. The event that is generally considered to mark the beginning of the movement is the 1893 Columbian Exposition in Chicago. Intended to celebrate the 400th anniversary of the discovery of America, though it opened a year later, it had been the object of a major competition between a number of cities.

Two examples of the fruits of the Municipal Art–City Beautiful movement three quarters of a century later. Above, Grand Army Plaza in Brooklyn, NY, and, below, the Pulitzer Fountain at Fifty-ninth Street and Fifth Avenue in Manhattan.

The Columbian Fountain at the 1893 Columbian Exposition in Chicago.

Designed by Daniel Burnham, possibly the most prominent architect and urban designer of the day, and Frederick Law Olmsted, Jr. (the son of the designer of Central Park), the fairgrounds presented the visitor with a carefully integrated combination of landscaped areas, promenades, exposition halls, and other buildings. By the time the exposition closed some 26 million people had seen it. By itself, the exposition opened the nation's eyes to what the planner, the architect, and the landscape architect, working in concert, could do.

> In this "White City" of almost 700 acres Chicagoans and millions of visitors, accustomed to urban ugliness, saw for the first time a splendid example of civic design and beauty in the classic pattern and on a grand scale, and they liked it. Indeed it marked the beginning in this country of orderly arrangement of extensive buildings and grounds.[9]

One effect was to set off a wave of a particular type of planning activity in American cities. Plans coming out of the City Beautiful movement tended to focus on those things over which municipal government had clear control—streets, municipal art, public buildings, and public spaces. The results can be seen today in dozens of cities, particularly in civic centers, municipal buildings, and the like.

Probably the best-known example of City Beautiful planning is the Mall and its immediate surroundings in Washington, D.C. The carefully designed vistas, the symmetry and axial layout (i.e., the Washington Monument placed at the end of the reflecting pool), the formality, the classicism, and the scale and magnificence of the whole conception are hallmarks of city beautiful era design. The City Beautiful movement has obviously close links to the municipal art movement, and to argue about whether a particular turn-of-the-century city hall and adjacent public spaces are products of one movement rather than the other is unimportant. Perhaps what distinguishes the two movements is more a matter of scale than intent. The municipal art movement tended to focus on particular points in the city: an arch, a plaza, a traffic circle, a fountain. The City Beautiful movement sought to create or remake a part of the city: a civic center, a boulevard, a parkway.

THE BIRTH OF MODERN CITY PLANNING

The single most important offshoot of the City Beautiful movement, as far as the development of an American planning tradition is concerned, was the *Plan of Chicago*. Interest in citywide planning, particularly within the business community, had been growing since the exposition. In 1906 the Merchants Club, essentially a chamber of commerce, commissioned Burnham to develop a plan. The work of planning was funded by the Commercial Club, another business organization, with $85,000, and the finished plan was presented to the city as a gift in 1909. The plan was remarkable for its scope. It laid out a system of radial and circumferential highways, some extending as far as 60 miles from the city center. Thus in its transportation elements it was a regional as well as a city plan. It laid out an integrated public transportation system and suggested the unification of rail freight terminals. Chicago's Union Station is one outgrowth of the plan. Within the city, extensive plans for street widening and overpasses at critical points were suggested. A system of parks and wildlife preserves both within and proximate to the city was suggested.

In a remarkable act of foresight the plan's sponsors appreciated that the political and public relations side of planning was just as important as the technical side, and set about fostering the public will to accomplish the plan. The original plan was a lavishly printed and expensive document that could have only a limited circulation. To make the concept of the plan known to the populace at large, a summary version was printed with private funds and given to every property owner in the city and to every renter who paid more than $25 per month. Shortly thereafter a version of the plan was done as a textbook and widely used in the eighth grade of the city schools. Not only did this reach many students as they were about to leave school—for many students ended their education with primary school at that time—but the plan also found its way into many households by this route. The plan was also promoted by means of illustrated lectures, a popular form of entertainment in that pre-electronic age, and also by a short motion picture, *A Tale of One City*.

The city responded with the creation of a Planning Commission charged with the responsibility for carrying out the plan. As a strategy, the planners decided that one concrete accomplishment was needed to demonstrate that the plan was not simply an idle dream. The particular project was to carry Twelfth Street across the railroad yards south of the Loop on a viaduct and thus facilitate the flow of traffic within the city's downtown. When this was accomplished, skepticism about the practicality of the plan was greatly reduced and one project after another was funded by bond issues. By 1931 close to $300 million had been raised by bond issues and special assessments to finance various elements of the plan. Wrigley lists the following as some of its accomplishments:

> . . . The doubled decked Wacker Drive and several large bridges were major improvements along the main stem of the Chicago River . . . . The South Branch of the Chicago River was straightened, and harbor facilities were enlarged in the downtown area and at Lake Calumet. The famous Navy Pier was built far out into Lake Michigan. Now land was slowly built up as the Lake was pushed back and over 20 miles of lake-front park and beaches resulted . . . . And within these lake-front parks notable museums and other institutions were developed, much as Burnham and his associates had suggested. The outlying forest preserves were vastly extended until by 1933 they included 32,400 acres.[10]

By its very impressiveness, both as a document and as real accomplishment, the Plan of Chicago defined for a long time the planner's and perhaps also the informed citizen's view of what a plan should be. In particular, a plan should be comprehensive and it should have a relatively long time horizon. The plan was to be effectuated largely through public capital investment on publicly owned land. Support by the citizenry was essential to provide the political will for making the necessary investment.

Some modern concepts of planning were absent from the Plan of Chicago. Among these were a concern with social issues, the notion of frequent plan revision and updating, and the view that the public should participate in the making of the plan rather than just receive and approve it as a finished document. The plan has sometimes been criticized for its emphasis on land and structures and its slighting of social issues. But judging the plan by the standards of a later day is not entirely fair. As a product of its time, it is a remarkable accomplishment.

THE PUBLIC CONTROL OF PRIVATE PROPERTY

The reader may have noticed that all the elements discussed in connection with the Plan of Chicago essentially pertained to public land, whether it was actually in public ownership at the time or was to be acquired at some later time. This focus on public-owned land was not accidental, for at the turn of the century the public had little control over the uses to which privately owned land might be put.

One important part of the history of planning has been the evolution of public control over privately owned land. Beginning in the very late nineteenth century a series of laws and court cases began to establish the right of local government to control the use of land that it did not own. The capacity of government to zone land for different uses was fairly well established by 1920 or so, though the definitive Supreme Court decision did not come until a few years later. The zoning process is one in which a municipal government can exercise control over the density with which land is developed, the types of uses permitted, and the physical configuration (heights of buildings, setbacks from property lines, etc.) of development. Typically, the community is divided into a number of zones displayed on a zoning map, and the permitted uses, densities, and design for each zone are specified in the zoning ordinance. The zoning process, as well as some related types of land-use controls, is described in detail in Chapter 9.

The Rush to Zone

The 1920s saw zoning ordinances appear across the nation with remarkable speed. The causes are not difficult to see. The legal precedents had been or were being established and a very complex but legally defensible zoning ordinance in New York City gave some notion of what might be done. Automobile ownership was climbing at roughly 2 million vehicles per year. Within built-up areas, congestion, particularly in commercial districts, was mounting. Beyond that, widespread automobile ownership was promoting a vast wave of suburbanization. One way to control congestion in commercial areas and prevent the invasion of residential areas by commercial development was through zoning. To many communities, both in older urban areas and on the suburbanizing fringe, the power to zone looked like the best way to protect what was desirable in the status quo against the vagaries of rapid economic and social change. Perhaps a single-family neighborhood was threatened with invasion by filling stations, used car lots, and hamburger stands. Zoning it so that only single-family houses could be built seemed like an effective and costless way to protect it from the undesirable side effects of progress.

Then, as now, zoning was not only a tool of planning and a technique for shaping the future but also a device for defense of an existing order. And though no court would accept this as a legitimate purpose of zoning, the act of zoning might raise property values. Zone a pasture on the edge of town for manufacturing and dreams of a prosperous retirement would glimmer in the eyes of the farmer who owned it. In fact, overzoning for commerce and industry was one of the hallmarks of the early age of zoning. For—aside from the pleas of expectant property owners—what municipality did not need more jobs for its people and more tax dollars for its coffers?

As we shall see, most planners regard zoning as only one aspect of planning and, particularly, as one tool for implementing the master plan. In the early 1920s zoning often preceded planning and, in the minds of many, became almost synonymous with planning (a confusion that is much less common but not unheard of today). That is not terribly surprising, nor is it meant as a critical statement. A new technique with apparently substantial power to alter events had appeared on the scene, and it would take a while before its limits and its potential for abuse would become evident.

In 1921 it was estimated that there were 48 municipalities with a combined population of 11 million that had zoning. By 1923 the figures had risen to 218 municipalities and 22 million people.[11] The move toward zoning was further accelerated in 1924 when the Department of Commerce headed by Herbert Hoover came out with a model state zoning enabling act. Drafted by Edward M. Bassett, the attorney who had drawn up New York City's zoning ordinance a few years earlier, the Standard Enabling Act encouraged many states to adopt their own enabling acts. These acts, which specifically authorized local zoning laws, encouraged many more municipalities to enact zoning laws because it reassured them that their new laws would be able to withstand court challenge.

The Growth of Community Master Planning

Although the single most important trend in planning in the 1920s was the spread and acceptance of land-use controls, other events were occurring as well. In city after city, planning was institutionalized with the establishment of a planning commission. In some cases commissions had paid staffs that did the actual planmaking. More frequently, plans and zoning ordinances were drawn up by planning consultants. Roughly two dozen planning consultant firms were active in the United States in the 1920s.

Community plans of the period typically covered the following:[12]

Land use (often considered synonymous with zoning)
Street pattern
Transit
Rail (and where appropriate, water) transportation
Public recreation
Civic art

The goals of these plans typically included a number of items. One was an orderly and attractive pattern of land use. Related to this was avoiding the juxtaposition of incompatible land uses, for example, a factory in a residential area. Another goal was achieving a well-functioning system for both private and public transportation. Still another was to achieve an adequate system of parks and recreational areas. Goals of municipal beautification and attractive design for public spaces, for example, the area around the city hall, were common. Safeguarding property values and making the community attractive for business were very common general motivations behind the more specific goals already noted. The imprint of the City Beautiful movement and the Plan for Chicago are clear.

By modern standards these plans were less than complete. They neglected housing, except in the sense that zoning specified what housing types were permissible in the various zones. They generally neglected to plan for public capital investments, which in the view of most contemporary planners, are often more powerful shapers of land use than are land-use controls. Citizen participation as we know it today was still beyond the horizon. Then, too, many planners of the time thought of the plan as something to be laid down once and then followed, much as an architect's drawings are to be followed as the building is erected. A more modern view, as we shall see, is that the plan is to be periodically monitored and revised as events take development in directions not anticipated in the plan or as community goals change.

But these limitations having been noted, it must be said that the typical plan for the 1920s was a major step forward in comprehensiveness from the focus on public places and public spaces that dominated the City Beautiful movement of a decade or two earlier. It covered the entire municipality and it addressed a number of matters of municipality-wide concern.

As is the case today, most planning took place in established places where the planner worked within the constraints inherited from earlier periods. But a certain number of planners did have the ultimate design opportunity, the chance to plan a community *de novo*. Mariemont near Cincinnati; Palos Verdes in California; Longview, Washington; Chicopee, Massachusetts; Kingsport, Tennessee; Venice, Florida; and Radburn, New Jersey, are among the new communities planned in this period. Some, like Mariemont, were essentially residential and very often ended as expensive residences for the upper middle class. Others, like Chicopee, were developed as industrial towns and contained places of employment and residences for the working class as well. Some were completed in the 1920s and some were stopped short of full development by events beyond the planners' control.

For example, Radburn, New Jersey, billed as a suburb "for the motor age," was roughly half built when the Great Depression began. It was never completed and today stands surrounded by conventional post-World War II suburban development. But the part that was completed is, in the eyes of many, a fine residential area. Planners and students of urban design still make field trips to Radburn. Large blocks of internal open space, a system of internal pathways, and a street pattern that keeps the automobile from intruding make it a very attractive living environment. House prices are high, vacancies are low, waiting lists are long, and many residents seem to take special pride in being Radburnites. By that ultimate arbiter, the marketplace, it is a very successful community. In general, many of the communities planned in the 1920s have stood the test of time quite well. When the planners had a clean slate, they often did very well. The more difficult feat was, and still is, to do well in an existing community, where one is stuck with the decisions (and mistakes) of the past and where one is quickly adrift in a sea of special interests and local politics.

THE EMERGENCE OF REGIONAL AND STATE PLANNING

The 1920's also saw a growing interest in planning for an entire urban region, an idea that had been foreshadowed by the Burnham Plan of Chicago. Suburbanization and the emergence of widespread automobile ownership rapidly made city boundaries obsolete as the functional city—the economic and social city—often sprawled across dozens of political jurisdictions.

Perhaps the most comprehensive regional plan was one drawn up for the New York City region. The area then contained a population of 10 million, since grown to over 18 million. The plan covered 5,528 square miles, of which only 300 were New York City itself. The remainder consisted of nearby counties in New

Master plan for Radburn, NJ, done in 1920s, at left. At lower right is detail for a court showing the separation of vehicular from pedestrian traffic. The housefronts face the walkway rather than street. At lower left is an internal pathway for pedestrian use.

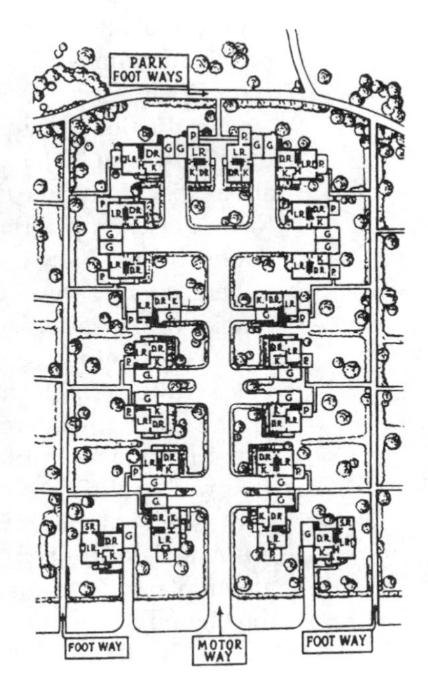

York State, Fairfield County in Connecticut, and about 2,000 square miles in adjacent parts of New Jersey.

The plan was drawn up by a nonprofit, nongovernment group, the Committee on a Regional Plan, which later metamorphosed into the Regional Plan Association (RPA), a group that exists to the present time. Funding for the plan, roughly $500,000, was provided by a philanthropy, the Russell Sage foundation.[13] The Committee had no political power or status whatsoever. Thus whatever influence it had came purely from the force of its ideas and whatever public and political support those ideas could garner. Yet over the years the plan has had considerable effect on the physical shape of the region. Not only did it help guide the development of the New York region, but also it served as a model for many other metropolitan area planning efforts in decades to come.

The first task of the planners was simply to define the region. The criteria they used, and which are still hard to improve upon, were described in this way: (1) "they [the region's boundaries] embraced an area within which the population can and does travel in a reasonable time from home to place of work"; (2) "they included the large outlying recreational areas within easy reach of the metropolitan center"; (3) "they followed the boundaries of cities and counties at the periphery"; and (4) "they had regard to the physical characteristics, such as watersheds and waterways."[14]

The transportation sections covered highway, rail, water, and perhaps surprisingly for the period, air transportation. The highway portions envisioned a complex of radial and circumferential routes, many of which have since been built. In a few cases routes that were envisioned originally as rail routes have subsequently been built as highways. By modern standards the plan was perhaps overly focused on physical features and capital investment and underemphasized some social and economic issues. But it was still a remarkable document in that it provided a unified vision of a three-state region containing hundreds of separate municipalities.

Regional plans appeared in numerous other parts of the country during the 1920s. John Nolen, a prominent planner and landscape architect, in 1929 listed about 15.[15] Many, like the plan for the New York region, were entirely private ventures. For example, the Tri-State District plan for the Philadelphia area (parts of Pennsylvania, New Jersey, and Delaware) was paid for by private subscription. Others, such as that done by the Boston Metropolitan Planning Commission, an official organization created by legislative act, were publicly funded. In several cases large counties engaged in regional planning even though the planning took place within a single political jurisdiction. On the East Coast, Westchester County, New York, with an area of about 450 square miles, engaged in extensive regional planning activity through the mechanism of the county parks commission. The results of that effort are visible today in the form of parkways and a splendid county park system of some 15,000 acres. On the West Coast, the largest county effort was Los Angeles County, with an area of about 4,000 square miles. Unlike the other regional plans of the era, it included a county zoning plan, believed to be the first in the United States.

In all cases other than counties, regional planning efforts had to be carried

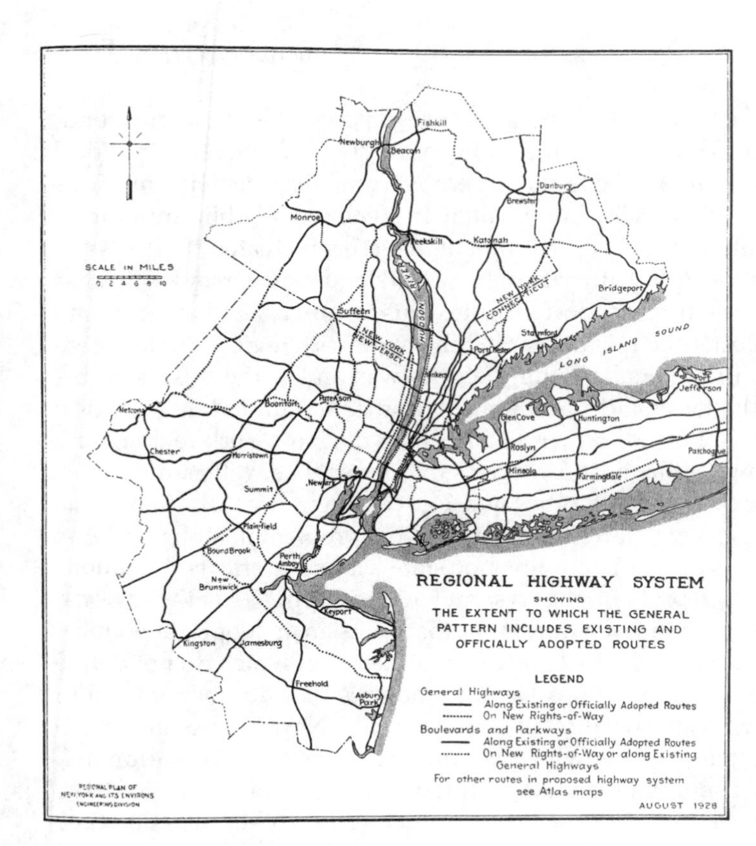

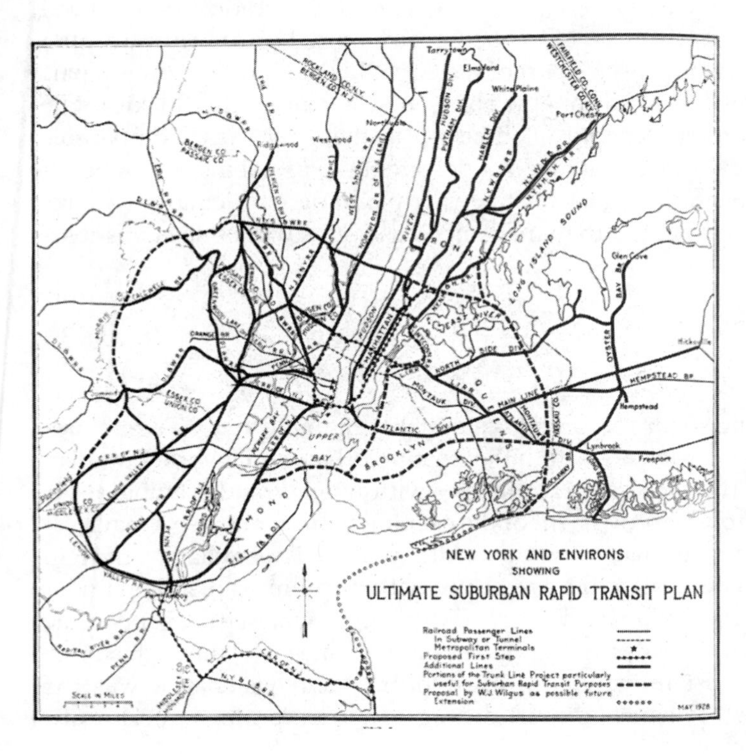

Transportation plans done for the New York Regional Plan in the 1920s. A very large part of what was planned has subsequently been built, though some of the transit links have been built as highways. The highway map covers about 10,000 square miles and the transit map about 2,500 square miles.

out in the face of the fact that there is no appropriate political entity corresponding to an urban region. Thus there is inevitably a question of where the political power to carry out the plan will be found. Intergovernment agreements may create some political basis for carrying out the plan. In some cases public authorities, which have some of the powers of government, have been created. Perhaps the best known of these is the Port Authority of New York and New Jersey, which has built or operated bridges, tunnels, port facilities, bus terminals, and airports and which has played a substantial role in shaping the New York region. But as a generality, the weakness in regional planning efforts was and is the mismatch between the nature of the tasks and the fragmentation of the underlying political structure. In the 1960s Robert Wood wrote a book on the New York region, with its complex of city, town, village, and county governments as well as numerous school districts, sewer districts, and other quasi-government organizations.[16] The book's title, *1400 Governments*, states the essence of the problem in a phrase.

The 1920s also saw the beginnings of state planning efforts. Statewide planning is bedeviled by a problem that is somewhat the opposite of the regional planning problem. The region is a natural unit that lacks an appropriate political structure. The state is a political structure, the boundaries of which do not define a "natural" planning unit. Most states have boundaries that do not conform to any geographic, economic, or social reality. For example, New York State, which was the first state to attempt a statewide planning effort, extends from Montauk point on Long Island, roughly due south of Rhode Island, to the shores of Lake Erie. The residents have little in the way of common interests other than that they are subject to the same state government. The state of Colorado has a natural break where the Rockies rise up out of the Great Plains. The eastern part, in a topographic and economic sense, is part of the Great Plains. But the western part of the state, in an economic and topographic sense, is part of the Rockies. The state's rectangular borders bear no relationship to these realities. Comparable comments can be made for most states. Yet despite these problems, a number of states have made substantial strides in statewide planning, particularly with regard to environmental and growth management issues, as will be seen in subsequent chapters.

GRANDER VISIONS

The history of planning so far recounted is a largely pragmatic one, that of a profession seeking to solve problems within the existing urban framework. But there has also been within the profession a minority with much grander ambitions—one that seeks not simply improvement of the existing pattern but also a major restructuring of the form of human settlement. Although the issues change, the tension between those who see planning as an activity that optimizes planning under the existing rules and those who hold a more radical view, who see the proper role of planning as rewriting the rules, is one of the central themes of planning history.[17]

Perhaps the most influential of all reformers and visionaries was the Englishman Ebenezer Howard. A court stenographer by profession, Howard conceived a vision of the city of the future and of a system of such cities. He set it forth in a short and very simply written book, *Garden Cities of Tomorrow*, published in 1902.[18] Howard observed the congestion and pollution of the late nineteenth-century London and concluded that hope for the future lay in diverting population growth to new urban centers. People moved from the countryside to the congestion of the city for compelling economic and social reasons, but they paid a great price. The solution to the problem was to create new towns ("garden cities" in his terminology), which would offer the economic and social advantages of the city combined with the tranquility, healthful environment, and closeness to nature that had been lost in the nineteenth-century city.

Howard proposed the following general design. The total development would have an area of about 6,000 acres (there are 640 acres in a square mile). The urbanized area itself would have an area of about 1,000 acres and be laid out in a circle about 1½ miles in diameter. A garden and a grouping of public buildings would constitute the core and would be accessible by radial boulevards. The core would be ringed by residential areas divided into neighborhoods by the boulevards. The residential ring would be ringed by commercial and industrial establishments. The commercial and industrial ring would be enclosed in a circular rail spur, which would connect the city to other garden cities and to the central city of the region. Around the urban area would be agricultural and institutional uses. The dimensions of the city would be such that any resident would be within a few minutes' walk of both the city core and the places of work on the periphery. Yet he or she would live in an area from which industrial uses and heavy traffic were excluded.

The city, by virtue of quick rail access would have close economic links to other cities, but it would have enough economic activity within its boundaries so that the great majority of its residents would not have to commute. Total population in the city would be about 30,000 and there might be another 2,000 or so people in the 5,000 acres surrounding the city. In the words of Lewis Mumford, perhaps the best known U.S. writer on architecture and urbanization, the garden city as conceived by Howard was more than just a bucolic retreat.

> [It should] . . . be large enough to sustain a varied industrial, commercial, and social life. It should not be solely an industrial hive, solely an overgrown market, or solely a dormitory; instead, all these and many other functions, including rural ones, should be contained in a new kind of urbanization to which he applied the slightly misleading name of garden city. Howard had no thought of a return to the "simple life" or to a more primitive economy; on the contrary, he was seeking higher levels of both production and living. He believed that a city should be big enough to achieve social cooperation of a complex kind based on the necessary division of labor, but not so big as to frustrate these functions—as the big city tended to do even when viewed solely as an economic unit.[19]

Howard perceived that no matter how well designed and well balanced the garden city might be, it could not exist in isolation. He envisioned a system of cities, all at a modest scale, as illustrated schematically in the accompanying figure. As Mumford characterized Howard's view,

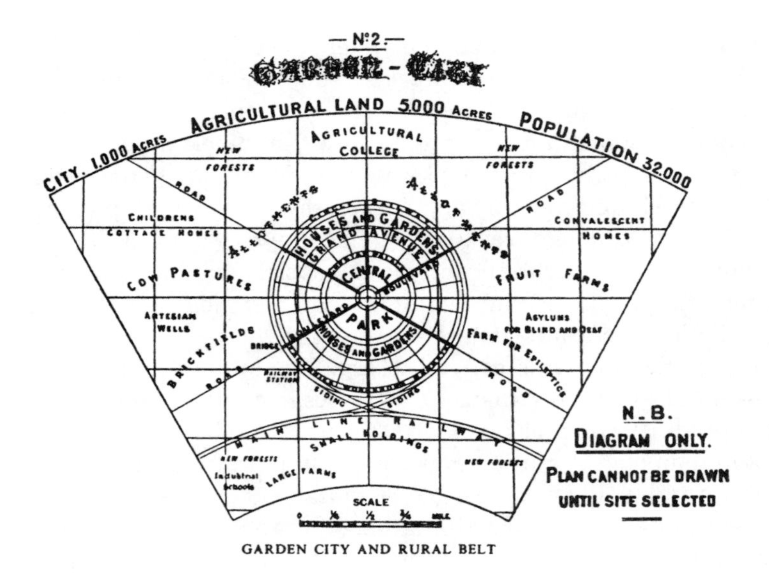

GARDEN CITY AND RURAL BELT

The plan for the entire 6,000 acres is shown at upper left. Note the radial routes dividing the city into sectors and the circumferential rail line. One sector is shown at lower left. Note the Grand Avenue and school. At lower right is a schematic illustration of the system of garden cities. Replace the intermunicipal railway with modern beltway and the garden cities with suburban subcenters like Tyson's Corner, and the design looks relatively modern.

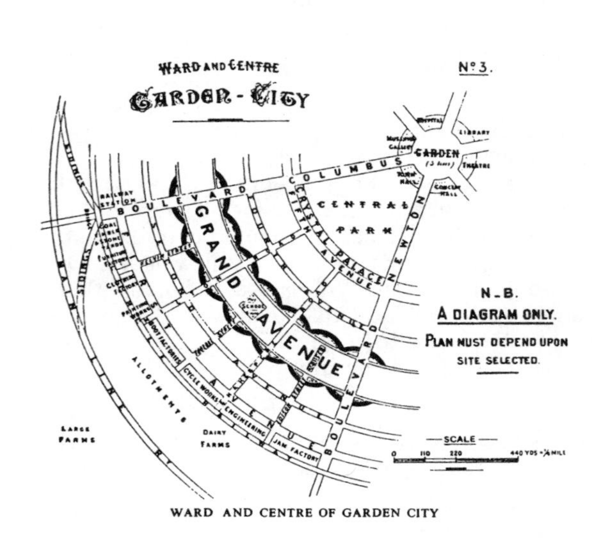

WARD AND CENTRE OF GARDEN CITY

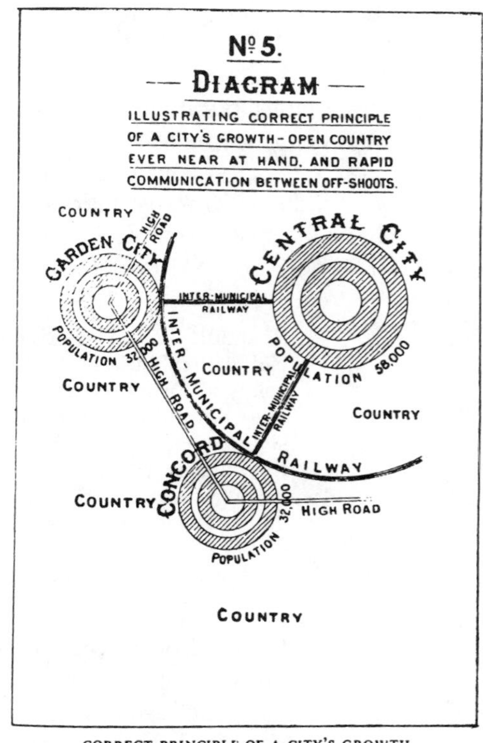

CORRECT PRINCIPLE OF A CITY'S GROWTH

> . . . a city, no matter how well balanced, can never be completely self-contained. He pointed out that in a group of garden cities united by rapid transportation each would have facilities and resources that would supplement those of the others; so grouped, these "social cities" would in fact be the functional equivalent of the congested metropolis.[20]

Howard, as did many nineteenth-century reformers and planners, saw the fragmented private ownership of land as an impediment to good urban form because each property owner would be motivated to develop his or her land as intensely as possible and with no regard to its effect on the rest of the community. Thus one feature of his plan was common ownership of land, with profits from land development reverting to the municipal treasury.

The plan is a remarkable mixture of vision and practicality. Howard was a doer and an organizer as well as a visionary. In 1903 a company he organized purchased a site of 3,818 acres 35 miles from the center of London and proceeded to build the Garden City of Letchworth. Writing about it in 1945, F.J. Osborn stated,

> For Letchworth was, and remains, a faithful fulfillment of Howard's essential ideas. It has today a wide range of prosperous industries, it is a town of homes and gardens with ample spaces and a spirited community life, virtually all its people find employment locally, it is girdled by an inviolate agricultural belt, and the principles of single ownership, limited profit, and the earmarking of any surplus revenue for the benefit of the town have been fully maintained.[21]

A second planned community in the greater London area, Welwyn Garden City, was begun by Howard in 1919 with quite successful results.

Ultimately, Howard's work influenced urban development in dozens if not hundreds of communities from Radburn in the United States to Chandigarh in India. Radburn, for example, is very much an outgrowth of the garden city movement begun by Howard, as are Columbia, Maryland, and Reston, Virginia. In western Europe numerous new communities were built after World War II to deal with a desperate shortage of housing resulting from the low rates of construction during the Great Depression and the destruction of housing during the war. These communities, too, are an outgrowth or extension of Howard's garden city vision.

SUMMARY

This chapter covered the history of planning in the United States from the colonial period to the end of the 1920s and the onset of the Great Depression. The Constitution made no direct mention of substate units of government. Thus municipalities became "creatures of the state," exercising only those powers granted them by the states. The Constitution also expanded the rights of individuals with regard to property rights and due process. The combined effect was to reduce greatly the power of municipalities to control the use and development of land within their boundaries. Early nineteenth-century urban growth thus often occurred with a minimum of planning and public control. The crowding, ugliness, and haphazard development of many nineteenth-century cities gave birth to a series of reform movements, which shape to the present day much of the agenda of planning in the United States.

Among the movements discussed were sanitary reform, the movement to secure urban open space, the movement for housing reform, the municipal improvement movement, the municipal art movement, and the City Beautiful movement. The Columbian Exposition of 1893, which brought to millions of visitors a vision of what urban design and planning could accomplish, is often considered to mark the birth of the City Beautiful movement. The 1909 Plan of Chicago marked the beginning of the age of modern city planning and shaped the ideas of planners, politicians, and citizens about what a comprehensive plan should be and how it should be implemented.

The tradition of public control of the use of privately owned land evolved slowly, in part because of constitutional issues involved in the "taking" issue. However, roughly by the time of World War I, the right of local governments to exercise substantial control over the use of private property was reasonably well established. Post-World War I suburbanization, facilitated by a rapid expansion in automobile ownership, propelled hundreds of communities into zoning and master planning. The same period also saw the beginnings of regional planning as the automobile dispersed jobs and residences, creating vast urban regions.

NOTES

1. For a detailed account of prerevolutionary planning, see John W. Reps, *The Making of Urban America*, Princeton University Press, Princeton, NJ, 1965.
2. For a discussion of urban government in the United States during the nineteenth century, see Charles N. Glabb and A. Theodore Brown, *A History of Urban America*, 2nd ed., Macmillan Publishing Company, New York, 1976.
3. See John A. Peterson, "The Impact of Sanitary Reform upon American Urban Planning," in *Introduction to Planning History in the United States.* Donald A. Krueckeberg, ed., Rutgers University Center for Urban Policy Research, New Brunswick, NJ, 1983, pp. 13–39.
4. For an example of reformist literature on urban housing and living conditions in the nineteenth century, see Jacob Riis, *How the Other Half Lives: Studies Among the Tenements of New York.* Dover, New York, 1971, (first published by Scribner & Sons, New York, 1890).
5. Blake McKelvey, *The Urbanization of America*, Rutgers University Press, New Brunswick, NJ, 1963, p. 120.
6. Mel Scott, *American City Planning Since 1890*, University of California Press, Berkeley, 1971, p. 131.
7. For an account of the civic improvement movement, see John A. Peterson, "The City Beautiful Movement: Forgotten Origins and Lost Meanings," in Krueckeberg, op. cit.
8. Charles Mulford Robinson, *Modern Civic Art or The City Made Beautiful*, 4th ed., G. P. Putnam's Sons, New York and London, 1917, p. 1. First edition published in 1903.
9. Robert L. Wrigley, Jr., "The Plan of Chicago" in Kruckelberg, op. cit., p. 58.
10. Ibid., p. 70.
11. Scott, op. cit., p. 194.
12. Ibid., p. 228.
13. Ibid., p. 261.
14. *Regional Plan of New York and Its Environs*, vol. I, Committee on the Regional Plan of New York and its Environs, William F. Fell Co., Printers, Philadelphia, 1929, p. 133.
15. For a contemporary description of regional planning efforts in the 1920s, see John Nolen, "Regional Planning," in *City Planning*, 2nd ed., John Nolen, ed., D. Appleton & Co., New York, 1929, pp. 472–95.
16. Robert C. Wood, *1400 Governments: The Political Economy of the New York Metropolitan Region*, Harvard Uni-

versity Press, Cambridge, MA, 1961. By *quasi-government* is meant a public body having some of the powers of government. For example, a school district has the power to collect taxes and to issue tax-exempt bonds.

17. See William H. Wilson, "Moles and Skylarks," in Kruckeberg, op. cit., pp. 88–121. Reprinted from William H. Wilson, *Coming of Age: Urban America 1915–1945.* John Wiley, New York, 1974.
18. Ebenezer Howard, *Tomorrow: A Peaceful Path to Real Reform* in 1988; republished with revisions as *Garden Cities of Tomorrow* in 1902; reissued by MIT Press, Cambridge, MA, 1970.
19. Lewis Mumford, "The Ideal Form of the Modern City,"in *The Lewis Mumford Reader*, Donald L. Miller, ed., Random House, New York, 1986, p.166.
20. Ibid., p. 169.
21. Howard, op. cit., p. 13.

SELECTED BIBLIOGRAPHY

See Selected Bibliography, Chapter 4.

CHAPTER 4

THE HISTORY OF PLANNING: PART II

This chapter covers a six-decade period from the beginning of the Great Depression to the present time. The Depression years stand as an isolated decade sandwiched between the prosperous 1920s and the beginning of World War II. The period from the end of the war to the present is very different. Although marked by enormous social, political, and technological changes, it is a more or less continuous period. The 1930s was a period in which capitalism functioned very poorly and in which the enemy abroad, fascism, was on the political right. In the postwar period, capitalism in the United States, by and large, functioned well and the enemy abroad, communism, was on the political left. Our former enemies had been defeated and were now our allies. Our former ally was now our mortal enemy. Then, in a series of remarkable events beginning in 1989 the Soviet empire in Eastern Europe and the the Soviet Union itself broke up and the Cold War appeared to be over. These events will undoubtedly have major effects on the political tone and worldview of the United States and will affect the background against which planning issues of the last decade of the twentieth century and beyond are decided.

One theme of this book is that one cannot understand the history of planning by itself. One must see planning in a historic and ideological context. This brief contrast between the 1930s and the postwar era is here to remind the reader to view the last six decades of planning history against a changing ideological background.

PLANNING AND THE GREAT DEPRESSION

The 1930s were a peculiar time in the history of planning. They awakened great optimism about planning, and indeed, several new areas of planning were opened up. Yet on balance, for those who had great hopes for planning, they were something of a disappointment. To those planners who would wish to see the scope of planning greatly enlarged—and this does not include all planners—the Depression years still have something of the bittersweet taste of a tantalizing opportunity nearly grasped. What happened?

The country began to slide into depression with the stock market crash of 1929, and economic conditions gradually worsened for the next several years. By the time President Roosevelt was inaugurated in March 1933, the unemployment rate was in the 25 percent range and the cash value of goods and services produced had fallen by almost half since 1929. The fact that the free enterprise system was clearly malfunctioning and was unable to connect idle workers with idle machinery created an intellectual climate that favored planning in a way that the prosperous 1920s had not.

Planning is an ambiguous term. It may include everything from the most minor control over land use in a small town to Soviet style centralized economic planning. But political moods and movements can be intellectually fuzzy. In general, the economic distress and disillusion of the Great Depression tended to favor more *planning*, whatever the word might mean.

There was relatively little consensus about what ought to be planned or by what principles. Within the Roosevelt administration there was a wide ideological spectrum. Roosevelt, himself, was not at all radical. He was a pragmatist who would adjust and tune the system as required but who had no agenda for large-scale restructuring. Some in his administration, such as the secretary of the interior, Harold Ickes, were relatively conservative. Others, like Rexford Tugwell and Henry Wallace, who were well to Roosevelt's left, favored major change and a major shift of economic power from private to public hands.

Apart from the administration there was a Congress, which although much more willing to experiment than it had been in better times, was hardly radical. Finally, there was the Supreme Court, then a relatively conservative body, which in modern terms might be described as "strict constructionist."[1] It turned out to be a major limitation on the amount of social and economic experimentation in which the national government might engage.

A number of planning initiatives began during the Great Depression.[2] Some persist to the present time. Others have sunk without leaving much trace.[3] One initiative was the federal funding of local and state planning efforts. Federal funding was provided for planning staffs, both as a job creation measure and as a commitment to planning. Numerous communities used federal funds to build and staff planning departments, to develop maps and data bases, and to formulate plans, including many community master plans. In the slow-growing, fiscally strained environment of the 1930s, many plans simply sat on the shelf. But the federal funding did help build the size and technical competence of the profession.

Federal funding and increased state interest in planning accelerated a trend that had begun in the late 1920s, namely, the creation of state planning agencies. By 1936 every state except one had a state planning board. The focus of these boards varied greatly. In many, particularly those in which agriculture was a dominant part of the economy, the focus was on conservation and farmland preservation. In others the primary focus was on urban issues, including housing quality, sewage treatment, water pollution, the provision of adequate recreational facilities, and issues of public finance and urban governance. Much of the work of state planning agencies simply focused on finding the facts, whether that meant mapping areas of soil erosion in a rural area or studying public finance and the structure of government in a metropolitan area.

The federal government moved into the provision of low-cost housing, an area in which it has remained in one way or another ever since. The motivation was twofold. First was the obvious goal of improving the housing of the poor. The second goal was expansion of construction as a way of stimulating the economy. At first the federal government built public housing directly. Then a Supreme Court decision forced a change in the program and the federal government switched to providing financial support, both capital and operating, for local public housing authorities. There are today somewhat over 1 million units of public housing in the United States and several million units of privately owned but publicly assisted units. That public presence in the housing market had its origins in the Great Depression.

In the mid-1930s, the Resettlement Administration embarked on a program of new town building. The program lost favor with Congress after a time and was discontinued in 1938. However, three new communities, Greenbelt, Maryland; Green Hills, Ohio; and Greendale, Wisconsin, were constructed.

The housing initiative of the federal government that had the most far-reaching effects was not one that fell in the realm of planning but rather in the realm of finance. That was the provision of mortgage insurance by the Federal Housing Administration (FHA) noted briefly in in Chapter 2 and discussed in more detail in Chapter 18. Few, if any, acts of the federal government have had more effect on the pattern of settlement than did FHA mortgage insurance.

The conceptual basis for Urban Renewal was also a Depression-era development. Economists and others within the federal government foresaw the difficulty central cities would have in competing with suburban areas for development capital, largely because of differences in site acquisition costs (see Chapter 12). The solution proposed was the City Realty Corporation, an organization that would use federal subsidy monies plus the power of eminent domain to produce marketable development sites at below cost.[4] World War II swept the City Realty Corporation off the national agenda, but the idea, under a different name, became one of the bases of the Housing Act of 1949, which established Urban Renewal.

Still another Depression-era initiative was the first planning for what was to become the interstate highway system. World War II shelved the idea for a time, but it reappeared as the National Defense Highway Act of 1956. This initiated the building of the interstate highway system, the largest single construction project in U.S. history.

The Depression also saw the creation of the National Resources Planning Board (NRPB) under the leadership of Rexford Tugwell, a member of FDR's so-called "brain trust." Though the board never fulfilled the dreams of those who favored the major move to the left, it did do a certain amount of useful work. One contribution was the support of local and state planning efforts. Another was the making of an inventory of natural resources on a national scale. In the conflicting political currents of the time, noted earlier, the board did not make much of a mark on the nation and in 1943 was dissolved by Congress. The war and national preoccupation with war-related matters was one cause for its demise. Another cause was that any organization that seeks to plan on a broad canvas will naturally step on toes and make enemies.

Whether the NRPB's dissolution is a cause for sorrow or rejoicing is largely a matter of ideology. From the left its dissolution looks like a major missed opportunity. From the right its dissolution looks like a slaying of the socialist monster before it could grow to maturity and do any damage.

Finally, the Depression era saw the start of a number of regional planning efforts, the best known of which was the Tennessee Valley Authority (TVA). Established in 1933 to provide a combined approach to flood control, power generation, and natural resource conservation, the TVA was planned on a major scale. Dams that served for flood control also produced power, which facilitated rural electrification and brought industry into the valley. The creation of lakes behind dams naturally led the agency into recreation planning. Among those who favored a much larger role for government, the TVA occasioned much enthusiasm as a prototype for what large-scale regional planning could accomplish.

Other regional initiatives included the New England Regional Commission, the Colorado River Basin Compact, and the Pacific Northwest Regional Planning Commission. The latter two ultimately resulted in the construction of the Boulder, Bonneville, and Grand Coulee dams.

THE POSTWAR PERIOD

The war provided a sharp break with the Depression and Depression-era issues. The conversion to a war economy quickly ended the unemployment of the 1930s, and political and military events abroad shifted the nation's political focus from internal to external. From the end of the war to this writing the country followed a generally successful economic course. It is true that there were several recessions, several brief inflationary episodes, and some slowdown in productivity growth beginning in the 1970s. But on the whole, the U.S. economy has flourished. There was thus much less willingness to contemplate radical changes than there had been during the Depression. Perhaps this was just a matter of heeding that bit of folk wisdom, "If it ain't broke, don't fix it." Then, too, the success of capitalist economies in Europe and Japan, contrasted with the poor performance of centrally planned economies in the Soviet Union and eastern Europe, militated against major moves toward national planning.

Postwar planning initiatives took place in a relatively conservative framework. Where possible, they involved a heavy reliance on private initiative and private capital. Typically, the major planning initiatives also involved a combination of federal, state, and local effort. A share of the funding and some legislative guidelines were provided by the federal government, but much of the initiative, detailed planning, and implementation came from state and local governments.

The Expansion of Municipal Planning

The postwar period saw a large expansion of planning activity at the city, town, and county level. The causes of this expansion were numerous. The prosperity of the postwar period gave municipal governments more funds to spend on planning. The satisfaction of private wants with the growth of the postwar economy naturally turned people's attention to public needs. It is easier to be concerned about the quality of one's community when one is well fed, well housed, and financially secure than when one is not. Postwar suburbanization, as it did after World War I, stimulated planning activity in thousands of suburban cities and towns by thrusting on them the problems of growth. The difference was that this time there was no Depression to cut short the suburbanization process. The growth of local planning activity was also powerfully stimulated by the federal government. Federal grants, Urban Renewal, and other programs discussed in this chapter stimulated the expansion of planning agencies. Beyond that, federal funds were made available to local agencies for general planning purposes under section 701 of the Housing Act of 1954 and subsequent legislation.

Urban Renewal

The first major initiative to appear after the war was Urban Renewal or, as it was called in its early days, Urban Redevelopment. As noted, the difficulties that cities faced in competing with suburban areas for investment capital had been perceived during the later years of the Depression. In the Housing Act of 1949 Congress set up the mechanism by which cities might be enabled to compete more effectively with outlying areas. At the time the biggest need of the cities appeared to be for investment in housing, both to clear away many acres of slum housing and also to alleviate the severe housing shortage that many cities faced because of low rates of construction during the Great Depression and World War II. Thus Urban Renewal started as a slum clearance and housing program. It soon added a major commercial thrust as well. By the time the program was ended in 1973 some $13 billion of federal funds had been expended, making it the largest urban program in U.S. history. A great deal had been accomplished, but there were also some very high human costs in the form of neighborhood disruption and the forced relocation of hundreds of thousands of households. The program is discussed in detail in Chapter 12.

The Age of Highway Planning

Another major theme of the postwar period was highway planning and highway building. The period after the war witnessed an enormous amount of suburbanization accompanied by massive increases in automobile ownership, as noted in Chapter 1. Coincident with the suburbanization of population was the suburbanization of economic activity. As a consequence of the changing distribution of economic activity there was also a significant increase in the importance of truck transportation relative to rail transportation in the carriage of both intra- and intermetropolitan freight.

As a result of these pressures one metropolitan region after another moved into large-scale highway planning. The first and possibly best known of these was the Chicago Area Transportation Study (CATS).

The postwar period also saw the building of the interstate highway system, which, measured in physical terms, is the largest engineering project in the history of the nation. The idea, as noted, is of Depression-era vintage, but work did not begin until after the passage of the National Defense Highway Act of 1956. Most of the system was constructed in the 1960s and 1970s. By the end of the 1980s only a few links remained to be completed. The system, about 40,000 miles in length, has been a major force in reshaping the nation, largely, one suspects, in ways unanticipated by its planners. The transportation planning process is described in Chapter 13.

Environmental Planning

Environmental planning, a term that would have been virtually unrecognizable 30 years ago, emerged as a field at the end of the 1960s. Its emergence can be traced to two separate background forces. First, with the growth of population and prosperity, humanity had acquired more ability to damage the environment. More people, more kilowatt hours of electricity generated, more vehicle miles driven, more acres covered with paving and structures—all meant that the natural environment was at greater risk. Second, and more important according to some, were changes in what we produced and the way we produced it. Around 1940 there began a revolution in the types of materials we produced and used. Up to that time most of our materials were naturally occurring substances, though often processed and modified in some way. Since then we have increasingly relied on substances that have never before existed, which often have some degree of toxicity, and for which natural pathways of degradation do not exist. For example, in a very influential book, *Silent Spring*, Rachel Carson argued that DDT (a compound that had been known for some decades but only came into use about the time of World War II) was entering the food chain, with all sorts of dire consequences both to the ecosystem in general and to humans—who eat fairly high up on the food chain—in particular.[5] Barry Commoner in *The Closing Circle* (a title whose ominous ring fitted the tone of the book very well) cited a long list of changes in products and processes with adverse environmental consequences: for example, pesticides, chemical rather than natural fertilizers, and the increasing use of plastics like polyethylene for which natural degradative pathways do not exist.[6]

By the end of the 1960s mounting concern with the effect of our impact on the environment resulted in the passage of the National Environmental Protection

Act (NEPA), which created the Environmental Protection Agency (EPA). The act also required the filing of an environmental impact statement (EIS) for a project involving substantial amounts of federal funding, a stipulation that more than any other single event brought the field of environmental planning into being. Simply complying with the requirement that an EIS accompany a request for federal funding created employment for large numbers of environmental planners. In the following years many states passed laws analogous to NEPA, often referred to as "little NEPA" acts. Congress passed numerous other pieces of environmental legislation such as the CleanAir Act and the Toxic Substances Control Act. In each case, the studies and planning required to comply with the requirements of the law expanded the field of environmental planning. Increasing consciousness of environmental issues has also prompted agencies doing traditional land-use planning to consider environmental aspects that a few years ago were often ignored in the planning process. The subject is pursued further in Chapter 14.

For a time a subfield of environmental planning—energy planning—flourished. After the rise in oil prices following the Arab-Israeli War of 1973 there was much interest in reducing U.S. energy consumption. One path to that goal appeared to be community energy planning. For example, a community design that reduced the length of the average work or shopping trip would reduce automotive fuel consumption. A community land-use pattern that could be served by public transportation would be more fuel efficient than one that could be served only by private transportation. Planning for these and other measures made up the substance of energy planning. Interest in the field was strong until the early 1980s. At that time the real cost (dollar cost adjusted for inflation) of oil began to decline. By 1990 the real cost of a barrel of oil was lower than it had been in 1973. Perhaps unfortunately, interest in energy planning declined sharply as the oil shortage of the 1970s was replaced by the oil glut of the 1980s. The Iraqi invasion of Kuwait in August, 1990 pushed petroleum prices upward and and for a time it appeared that another "energy crisis" was in the making. But other oil producers quickly compensated for the loss of Kuwati production and oil prices dropped. As of 1993 the real cost of gasoline is still lower than it was in 1973. Whether the gasoline tax enacted in 1993 or concern with the "greenhouse effect" will cause a major renewal of interest in energy planning remains to be seen.

Growth Control and Growth Management

In the 1960s growth control and growth management emerged as a distinct area of planning and also as an area of legal and moral controversy. Two separate trends in the postwar period combined to create this field. The first was the growth of population and the movement of population from central cities into suburban and exurban areas. Many communities felt themselves threatened by growth and thus saw a need to develop a means to prevent growth entirely or to limit and control it. The second factor was the growing environmental consciousness of the 1960s. Concern with the natural environment in general easily translated into concern with the natural environment of a particular city or town or county and furnished motivation and rationale for local growth-control efforts. One movement of the 1960s, spawned by global environmental concerns, was zero population growth (ZPG), whose slogan for would-be parents was "stop at two."[7] Concern with population control at the global or national level spilled over into concern with population control at the local level.

The growth-control movement raised legal and moral issues that have not been easy to resolve. In fact, there is now a substantial record of litigation pertaining to the subject. One question at issue is exactly what rights communities have to exclude potential residents. The subject is pursued in Chapter 15.

The Growth of Statewide Planning

Beginning in the late 1960s the nation began to witness an increase in statewide planning efforts. This development was closely related to growing concern over environmental issues. In general, state planning efforts do not supersede local planning efforts but rather add another layer of control. State planning may address a variety of environmental or growth-management goals, which because they transcend municipal boundary lines, cannot be adequately handled at the local level. A number of state planning processes are described in Chapter 15.

Economic Development Planning

In the period immediately after World War II it was generally thought that the economic function of government was simply to ensure that the national economy functioned well. Specifically, the main problem was to employ suitable fiscal and monetary policies to maintain a high level of employment and a reasonable degree of cyclical stability. To the extent that there was poverty stemming from unemployment, the way out was thought to be economic growth in order to bring more people into the work force and exert upward pressure on wages.

After a time, however, it became apparent that prosperous as the nation was, there were parts of the country in which poverty and unemployment were rampant. The first geographic area so recognized was the Appalachian region, sandwiched between the much more prosperous East Coast and the then thriving Midwest. The terms *pockets of poverty* and *structural unemployment* came into use.

At the beginning of the 1960s the federal government began to fund local economic development programs through a series of agencies and programs discussed in Chapter 14. Briefly, its intention was to promote by means of planning and subsidies the flow of capital into distressed areas. Initially, most of the federal effort regarding structural unemployment had a rural and small-town focus, for in the early 1960s that was where the problem was most acute. Gradually, with the urbanization of poverty discussed in Chapter 2, the focus of these efforts became more urban.

For reasons of political ideology the Reagan administration was opposed to such programs, and the federal government largely withdrew from the field during the 1980s. However, thousands of local governments still pour much effort and billions of dollars into economic development. The structural unemployment issue is one of the prime motivations for such efforts. The other major motivation is property tax relief, a point discussed in Chapter 9. The property tax relief motivation was greatly strengthened in the late 1970s by increasing citizens' resistance to further increases in local taxes, as exemplified by California's Proposition 13. For municipal governments trapped between citizens' resistance to taxation on one hand and rising costs of providing services on the other, expansion of the tax base through economic development seemed like the best way out. Thus, despite the federal withdrawal, economic development planning was one of the growth areas in planning in the 1980s and early 1990s.

SUMMARY

This chapter noted the increased interest in planning during the Great Depression, in part as a result of the poor performance of American capitalism during this period. Though the hopes of those such as Rexford Tugwell, who favored a major swing toward national planning, were disappointed, some planning initiatives that lasted well into the postwar period did have their origins in the 1930s. Urban Renewal and the interstate highway system were conceived during the Great Depression, though not enacted into law and funded until after the war. Federal subsidization of housing and federal financial support of local planning efforts began during the Great Depression. Statewide planning, though seen to a limited extent in the 1920s, became widespread during the Great Depression. World War II quickly ended the unemployment of the Depression years and shifted the nation's political focus from internal to international affairs.

The political climate of the postwar period was very different from that of the Great Depression and there was little support for national planning. In fact, the National Resources Planning Board had been abolished during World War II and was never reconstituted. Nonetheless, there was a major expansion of planning activity, in large measure fueled by federal grants and pushed forward by national legislation. Among new or expanded activities were Urban Renewal, highway planning (including planning for the interstate highway system), environmental planning, community development, planning for growth management, and local economic development planning.

Among the forces behind the increase in planning activity were the growth in population and wealth, the rapid suburbanization and increased automobile ownership that followed World War II, the weakened competitive position of many central cities vis à vis the suburbs, and increasing concern with the effects of human activity on the natural environment.

NOTES

1. Meaning a relatively literal interpretation of the Constitution based on the "original intent" of its authors and relatively little willingness to define new individual rights or new obligations of government that are not clearly implied by the wording of the Constitution. The reader who wants to pursue the debate over whether the Constitution should be interpreted strictly or flexibly might see Robert Bork, *The Tempting of America: The Political Seduction of the Law*, Free Press, New York, 1990.

2. For a general account of the New Deal, see William E. Leuchtenburg, *Franklin Delano Roosevelt and the New Deal*, Harper & Row, New York, 1963; or Arthur M. Schlesinger, *The Coming of the New Deal*, Houghton Mifflin, Boston, 1958.
3. For a general account of Depression-era planning initiatives see Mel Scott, *American City Planning Since 1890*, University of California Press, Berkeley, 1965, chap. 5.
4. Guy Greer and Alvin Hansen, "Urban Redevelopment and Housing," a pamphlet published by the National Planning Association, 1941. For additional references to Urban Renewal, see Chapter 12.
5. Rachel Carson, *Silent Spring*, Houghton Mifflin, Boston, 1962. (Note: DDT was subsequently banned in the United States but is in use in parts of the Third World.)
6. Barry Commoner, *The Closing Circle*, Alfred A. Knopf, New York, 1971.
7. For a statement of the ZPG view, which was widely read and quoted at the time, see Paul Ehrlich, *The Population Bomb*, Ballantine Books, New York, 1971.

SELECTED BIBLIOGRAPHY

KRUECKEBERG, DONALD, A., ed., *Introduction to Planning History in the United States.* Rutgers University Center for Urban Policy Research, New Brunswick, NJ, 1983.

REPS, JOHN W., *The Making of Urban America*, Princeton University Press, Princeton, NJ, 1965.

SCOTT, MEL, *American City Planning Since 1890*, University of California Press, Berkeley, 1965.

For references to particular fields of planning mentioned in this chapter see the Selected Bibliography for the chapter that treats that field in detail.

CHAPTER 5

THE LEGAL BASIS OF PLANNING

Planning, as discussed in this book, is an activity of government. It involves the exercise of powers vested in the government and the expenditure of public funds. It is limited by, among other things, the limitations of the powers of government. In this chapter we describe the legal framework and the legal limitations within which local and state governments act. In Chapter 6 we turn to the political framework.

THE CONSTITUTIONAL FRAMEWORK

The Constitution, although it has much to say about which powers and responsibilities are assigned to the federal government and which powers and responsibilities are delegated to state governments, is silent on the issue of how the powers of government are to be divided between state and substate units of government. In fact, a literal reading of the Constitution gives no indication that there are to be substate units of government at all: Words like *city, town, township, village, parish,* or *county* are totally absent.

As a result it has become an accepted principle of law that substate units of government are "creatures of the state" and have no powers other than those assigned to them by state governments. This is referred to as Dillon's Rule, after Judge John F. Dillon.[1] Obviously a state government cannot assign to a substate government powers that it itself does not have. But of those that it has, some will be assigned to substate units of government. In general, the structure of local governments and the powers and responsibilities of local governments are specified in charters, laws, and state constitutions.

Powers and Limitations

Local governments have those powers, and only those powers, granted to them by state governments. Just as state governments grant powers to local governments, they also can and do impose obligations on them. Local governments are also guided and limited in their actions by rights guaranteed individuals by the U.S. Constitution or by state constitutions. When there is disagreement over issues of individual rights or the extent of government power, the ultimate arbiter is the court system. Local planning efforts are thus limited by what the courts will allow or what local officials believe they might allow were the issue at hand put to a legal test. In many cases, local planning efforts are also influenced by what the courts require local governments to do.

With this introduction, let us look briefly at the evolution of the legal framework of planning. Early planning efforts such as the Chicago Plan often took place in the absence of any specific planning framework. In the Chicago case the plan was formulated by a group that had no legal mandate or authority and which, in essence, delivered the plan as a gift to the city. The plan was implemented by the city through exercise of the normal powers of government. Specifically, the city used its powers to levy taxes and to issue bonds to raise funds, which were used to finance projects called for in the plan. The power of the city to enter into contracts was used to acquire properties in voluntary transactions. Where that did not avail, the city's powers of eminent domain were used to acquire property through condemnation.

The power of *eminent domain* is important and deserves a brief explanation. The phrase means that government has the right to take property for public purposes. The building of roads, for example, generally involves taking of private property for the right of way. When government takes property it must compensate the owner for the value of what is taken. If agreement cannot be reached between government and property owner, the matter goes to court. After hearing expert testimony the court then determines the value of the loss imposed on the property owner by the act of taking. That value, the condemnation award, must then be paid to the property owner by the government. The eminent domain process is an example of the exercise of government power subject to limitation by the constitutional rights of individuals. Specifically, the "taking" clause of the Fifth Amendment states, ". . . nor shall private property be taken for public use, without just compensation"—hence the necessity for the condemnation award. The Fourteenth Amendment states that no person shall be deprived of "life, liberty, *or property* without due process of law"—hence the requirement for a judicial procedure should voluntary agreement not be reached. The Fourth Amendment guarantees "the right of the people to be secure in their persons, houses, papers and effects against *unreasonable* searches and seizures." Thus the taking of property for a trivial purpose would not be sustainable in court.

PUBLIC CONTROL OVER PRIVATE PROPERTY

Public control over the use of private property is a very different matter than the public taking (with "just compensation") of private property. The evolution, over several decades, of the right of government to exercise some control over the use of privately owned property is one of the central stories in the history of modern planning. Were local governments unable to exercise control over the use of privately owned land, the practice of planning in the United States would be vastly different and more limited.

Public control of the use of private property involves the imposition of uncompensated losses on property owners. This point requires a word of explanation. Consider someone who owns a building lot in a downtown area. Market forces such as the demand for office space and the cost of construction create a situation in which the most profitable use for the site is a 12-story office building. If the municipality, however, limits the height of structures on the site to 6 stories, the difference in profit between the 12- and the 6-story building is a loss imposed on the owner of the site. This is true whether the owner would develop the site, sell the site to another party who would develop it, or lease the site to someone else who would build on it. In the first case the owner would take the loss directly in the form of reduced operating profits. In the latter two cases the loss would be manifest as a lower selling price or lower rental fee for the site.

The land-use control technique that has evolved over the years, zoning (see Chapter 9 for details), does exactly what is alluded to. It limits the uses to which land can be put. If the most profitable use is not among the permitted uses, a loss is necessarily imposed on the owner. However, no compensation need be paid to the owner, nor is a judicial procedure required for the community to exercise control and thereby impose the loss. The community's zoning law stands unless the property owner brings a successful law suit against the community. This capacity to obtain the benefits of limiting an owner's use of his or her property without having to pay compensation clearly accounts for the popularity of zoning. The community obtains partial rights of ownership—some control over the use of the property—without having to go to the expense of becoming an owner.

Given the apparent conflict between such community powers and constitutional guarantees regarding property rights—most particularly the taking clause of the Fifth Amendment's requirement of "just compensation"—it is not surprising that it took many years and many court cases to establish the zoning rights of communities. Even today, the legal structure of zoning is still evolving, and many an attorney earns his or her living in zoning-related litigation and negotiation. Some on the political right view all zoning as fundamentally illegitimate because it represents an uncompensated taking and hence a violation of constitutionally guaranteed property rights.[2]

The legitimacy of zoning rests on the legal concept of the *police power*. That perhaps misleading term refers to the right of the community to regulate the activities of private parties to protect the interests of the public. Very often a phrase like *health, safety, and public welfare* will be used to indicate the range of public interests that may be safeguarded through exercise of the police power. Thus a law that limited the height of buildings so that they not cast the street below into a permanent shadow might be justified as an exercise in the police power. So too, might a law that prevented certain industrial or commercial operations in a residential neighborhood. So, too, might laws that prevented property owners from developing their lands so intensely that undue congestion resulted in nearby streets.

The rights of the community under the concept of the police power and the rights of the property owner under constitutional and other safeguards push in opposite directions. Exactly where the equilibrium point is located is a matter to be decided by the courts. The question of how much and for what purposes government can take some of the value of privately owned property, as in the building height example, is generally referred to as the "taking issue" and is the subject of a very large literature.[3]

The process by which municipalities acquired some control over the use of private land began in the late nineteenth century. It typically started with the passage of legislation that limited the use of, and hence reduced or "took" some of the value of, privately owned property. The legislation was then appealed in court by the property owner because of the loss it imposed. Very often the loser of the first trial appealed to a higher court. Through this process of litigation and appeal the extent and the limitations of the public power to control private land use has been and continues to be defined.

A very early case in this long history was *Mugler* v *Kansas* in 1887. The U.S. Supreme Court sustained a Kansas prohibition law that forced the closing of a brewery without compensation. The owners of the brewery argued that compensation was due, but the court held that a loss imposed through exercise of the police power to protect the health or safety of the community required no compensation. Note the distinction between "police power" and "eminent domain" here. Had the brewery been taken under eminent domain, compensation would clearly have been required. In 1899 a bill passed by Congress limited the heights of buildings in residential sections of Washington, D.C. to 90 feet and heights of buildings on some of the widest streets to 130 feet. Light, air, and traffic congestion in the streets were the considerations behind the ordinance. In 1904 the Massachusetts legislature passed somewhat similar legislation for Boston. Structures in the business district were limited to 125 feet and structures elsewhere to 80 feet. Several years later the Boston ordinance was challenged by a property owner, but the Massachusetts courts sustained the law as a valid exercise of the police power.

In 1909 the city of Los Angeles carried the idea of public control over the private use of land further by dividing the city into a number of commercial districts plus a residential district. In the latter, commercial uses were permitted only as exceptions. In what became a landmark case the city compelled a brickyard in a residential area to cease operations. The item of "public welfare" being protected was the interest of residents in having an environment not subject to undue noise, dust, and traffic. The owner sued the city, a series of appeals followed, and the case ultimately went to the U.S. Supreme Court. In *Hadacheck* v *Sebastian* the Court sustained the city. Though this was, literally, a nuisance abatement rather than a zoning case, the effect of the decision was clearly a strengthening of municipal rights under the police power.[4]

The city that enacted what might be considered the first modern zoning ordinance—though it left much to be desired by present standards—was New York. In the early twentieth century lower Manhattan was growing rapidly as a commercial center. Steel-frame construction and the elevator were making it practical to build to unprecedented heights of 40, 50, or even 60 stories. The horizontal expansion of the business district was limited by the fact that Manhattan is an island. In fact, at the latitude of Wall Street—then, as now, the center of the financial district—one can walk across the island from the East River to the Hudson River in perhaps 15 minutes. To add to the congestion the city was in the process of building a subway system, which permitted employers in the business district to reach far out into the other boroughs for their labor forces. Thus the same rapid transit that permitted central residential densities to fall was, paradoxically, permitting increased employment densities downtown.

With downtown space at a premium, builders tended to cover the entire lot and to build without any setbacks. The result was a building shaped like a child's building block set on end. Such buildings darkened the streets below and cast shadows several blocks long. By being allowed to build straight up from the property line, builders could accidentally or otherwise impose major losses on adjacent property owners by casting the facing wall of an adjacent structure in a perpetual shadow.

At the same time that concern over skyscraper development was growing, merchants in the fashionable Fifth Avenue retailing area were concerned that the invasion by manufacturing firms displaced from lower Manhattan would lower the tone of the area and drive away customers. They thus put pressure on the city government for some sort of relief.

Prompted by these concerns, the city in 1916 enacted a comprehensive zoning ordinance covering all five boroughs. The city was divided into three districts on the basis of land use: residential, commercial, and mixed. Overlaid on these use districts were five height districts, where the heights were expressed as multiples of street widths, ratios justified on considerations of congestion and sunlight. Also overlying the entire city were five districts that specified ground coverage requirements such as minimum lot sizes. Beyond that, the ordinance also specified a building "envelope" for skyscrapers, which mandated that there had to be setbacks from the street at higher levels. The stepped-back design that can be seen today in dozens of Manhattan office buildings comes from this ordinance and has been caricatured by some as a modern ziggurat (from a Babylonian temple built as a series of stepped-back terraces). But regardless of the aesthetic merits (or lack thereof) of many of these stepped-back structures, they were a major improvement over structures that rise straight up from the lot lines.[5]

The ordinance was designed by an attorney, Edward M. Bassett, who is generally regarded as the father of zoning in the United States. Bassett designed it in such a way as to ground every facet in some matter of public health, safety, or welfare. Thus he produced an ordinance that proved invulnerable to the inevitable court challenges. Again, the fact that the provisions of the ordinance

Stepped-back configuration of old-style office building in foreground shows the effect of New York's 1916 zoning law. Modern structure at rear rises without distinct setbacks but has gradual taper in lower floors and does not cover the entire lot.

rested on the police power further established the principle that compensation need not be paid for any loss of property value that the zoning might impose. This point is critical, for if compensation had to be paid, public control of land use would be far more expensive, far more cumbersome, and far less widespread than is now the case. A theoretical argument can be made that there are some disadvantages to the fact that municipalities can essentially treat the zoning power as a free good, but we reserve this more modern view to Chapter 9.

In 1926 any lingering doubts about the constitutionality of zoning were relieved when a zoning case finally reached the U.S. Supreme Court. In the case of *The Village of Euclid* v *Ambler Realty Co.*, the court sustained a village zoning ordinance that prevented Ambler Realty from building a commercial structure in a residential zone.[6] The point that a municipality could impose an uncompensated loss upon a property owner through the mechanism of land use controls was now firmly established. In effect, the court had ruled that such a loss need not constitute a "taking" of property for a "taking" of property would require compensa-

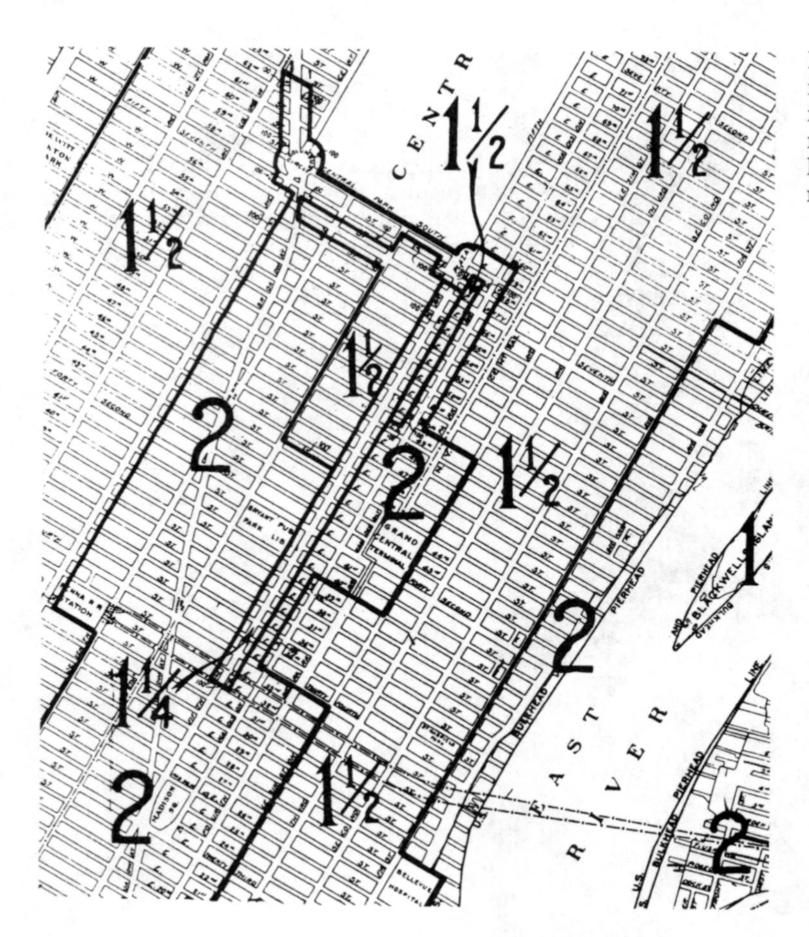

Midtown Manhattan zoning districts as designated in the 1916 plan. The numbers are building height limits expressed as multiples of street width.

tion as in the "taking" clause of the Fifth Amendment quoted earlier. The term *Euclidian Zoning* named for the town of Euclid is now used to refer to conventional zoning ordinances rather than some of the more modern and flexible types discussed in Chapter 9.

Since the 1920s zoning as a planning tool has continued to evolve, and a number of new techniques have been developed. That somewhat fuzzy boundary between the interests of the property owner and the interests of the public has been much clarified by litigation and legislation. Some issues that would not have occurred to even the most sophisticated planner or attorney of the 1920s—for example, the community's obligations to consider the interests of nonresidents when enacting and implementing zoning legislation—are also being gradually clarified in the same way. It is enough to say here that in the first three decades of this century, the right of the public to exercise substantial control over the use of private property—without having to make compensation—was clearly established. Zoning is not the only form of public control over the use of private property, though it is the best-known form and, perhaps, from the standpoint of law and political philosophy, the most interesting form. Some of the other types of controls, particularly those over the subdividing of land into building lots, are discussed in Chapter 9.

STATE ENABLING LEGISLATION

Another change in the legal framework of planning since the days of the Plan of Chicago has been the passage of state legislation that defines in broad terms the local planning function. Legislation varies greatly from state to state. In most cases legislation merely permits localities to engage in particular planning activities. But in other cases the legislation requires that communities perform certain planning acts. Note, incidentally, that state enabling legislation also defines municipal obligations and powers with regard to taxation, borrowing, the judicial system, the provision of police protection, and many other matters.

As an example of state enabling legislation with regard to planning, consider the state of Virginia.[7] Legislation requires that all cities, towns, and counties establish a planning commission and adopt a master plan. The intent of the state's local planning legislation is given as follows:

> To encourage local governments to improve public health, safety, convenience and welfare of its citizens and to plan for the future development of communities to the end that transportation systems be carefully planned; that new community centers be developed with adequate highway, utility, health, educational and recreational facilities; that the needs of agriculture, industry and business be recognized in future growth; that residential areas be provided with healthy surroundings for family life; and that the growth of the community be consonant with efficient and economical use of public funds.

Having laid out the general reasons for requiring communities to plan, the law then goes on to state,

> The governing body of every county and municipality shall by resolution or ordinance create a local planning commission. . . . In accomplishing the objectives . . . such planning commissions shall serve primarily in an advisory capacity to the governing bodies.

The law requires that each city, county, or town draw up a master plan and then, in a general way, it suggests the areas the plan is to cover.

> The local commission shall prepare and recommend a comprehensive plan for the physical development of the territory within its jurisdiction. Every governing body in this state shall adopt a comprehensive plan by July one, nineteen hundred eighty.

Note the requirement for adoption as well as for plan preparation. The reason for this wording is that plans themselves are not laws. They become law and acquire force when the legislative body of a community passes a resolution stating that the attached document (the plan) is adopted as the master plan of the municipality.

The legislation stipulates that the plan and accompanying maps, plats,[8] and so on "may include, but need to be limited to" the following:

1. The designation of areas for various types of public and private development and use, such as different kinds of residential, business, industrial, agricultural, conservation, recreation, public service, flood plain and drainage, and other areas
2. The designation of a system of transportation facilities such as streets, roads, highways, parkways, railways, bridges, viaducts, waterways, airports, ports, terminals, and other like facilities
3. The designation of a system of community service facilities such as parks, forests, schools, playgrounds, public buildings and institutions, hospitals, community centers, waterworks, sewage disposal or waste disposal areas, and the like
4. The designation of historical areas and areas for urban renewal and other treatment
5. An official map, a capital improvements program, a subdivision ordinance (this term is explained in Chapter 9), and a zoning ordinance and zoning district maps

Where state laws or state constitutions permit municipalities to engage in certain acts of planning, it could be said that they are merely granting permission for municipalities to do that which is implicit under the concept of the police power. There is some truth in this. However, planning enabling acts and zoning enabling acts are useful in that they encourage municipalities to plan, define the scope of planning, and furnish legal support for the municipality should its actions in the realm of planning be challenged in court. As noted, many planning enabling acts go beyond simply permitting communities to plan and *require* them to plan. These laws thus establish a minimum planning effort that every community must make.

The Legal Link to State Planning

Many states, as noted in Chapter 4, engage in some statewide planning. Such planning efforts generally impose legal requirements on local governments to ensure that they act in conformity with state plans or planning requirements. For example, if a state engages in planning designed to preserve wetlands, it may require that local governments not grant permits for development in or near wetlands until certain types of studies have been made or hearings conducted. These requirements will prevent local governments from permitting actions that contravene the intent of state plans. Since local governments are "creatures of the state," it is clearly within the power of the state to bind local governments so that they act in conformity to state-established guidelines.

THE FEDERAL ROLE

The 1930s saw the beginnings of a federal presence in local planning. The federal government funded local and state planning agencies, provided funds for public housing, and actually built a few planned communities such as Greenbelt, Maryland. In the years after World War II the federal presence in local planning expanded enormously. Even in the early 1980s, when the Reagan administration consciously sought to reduce the role of the federal government in local and state affairs, the federal presence was still vastly larger than it had been during the prewar period.

Perhaps the single most important way that the federal government influences local behavior is through the giving of money and the conditions it attaches thereto. The monies the federal government takes in through taxes and borrowing substantially exceed what it spends on goods and services or on transfers to individuals. The excess is used to make transfers from the federal government to state and local governments. Note the substantial flow of funds from the federal government to state and local governments shown in the accompanying chart. State government make large transfers to local governments, but in the year shown, 1990, they received about two-thirds as much from the federal government as they transferred to local governments.

Essentially, the intergovernment flows go only one way, downward. In 1990, local governments were thus able to spend on goods, services, transfers to individuals, and the like roughly $190 billion more than they took in from taxes, user charges, and borrowing.[9] This massive downward transfer of funds has not always been part of the American political picture. In 1960 federal aid to state and local governments totaled about $7 billion.[10] Adjusting that figure for inflation would convert it to roughly $31 billion in 1990. Thus in real terms federal aid to state and local governments increased by a factor of almost 4 between 1960 and 1990.

Why this pattern of transfers evolved can be explained in various ways. Sometimes it is said that the federal government can raise monies more easily than state and local governments because it has "the best revenue sources." This is largely a reference to the personal income tax, which over the years has proven to be highly income elastic.[11] A more general explanation, and one that I find more convincing, is simply that state and local governments are restrained in their taxing behavior by fear of losing residents and economic activity to other jurisdictions that tax more lightly. The federal government is not nearly so restrained in this regard.

Regardless of the reasons for the present pattern of intergovernment transfers, the existence of the pattern gives the federal government enormous influence over localities, both directly and also indirectly through the states. Making certain types of behavior a prerequisite for receiving grants is one way. For example, the federal government has no literal power to compel a community to adopt certain procedures to take citizens into its planning processes. However, if the implementation of the plans, or even the formulating of the plans, will be done

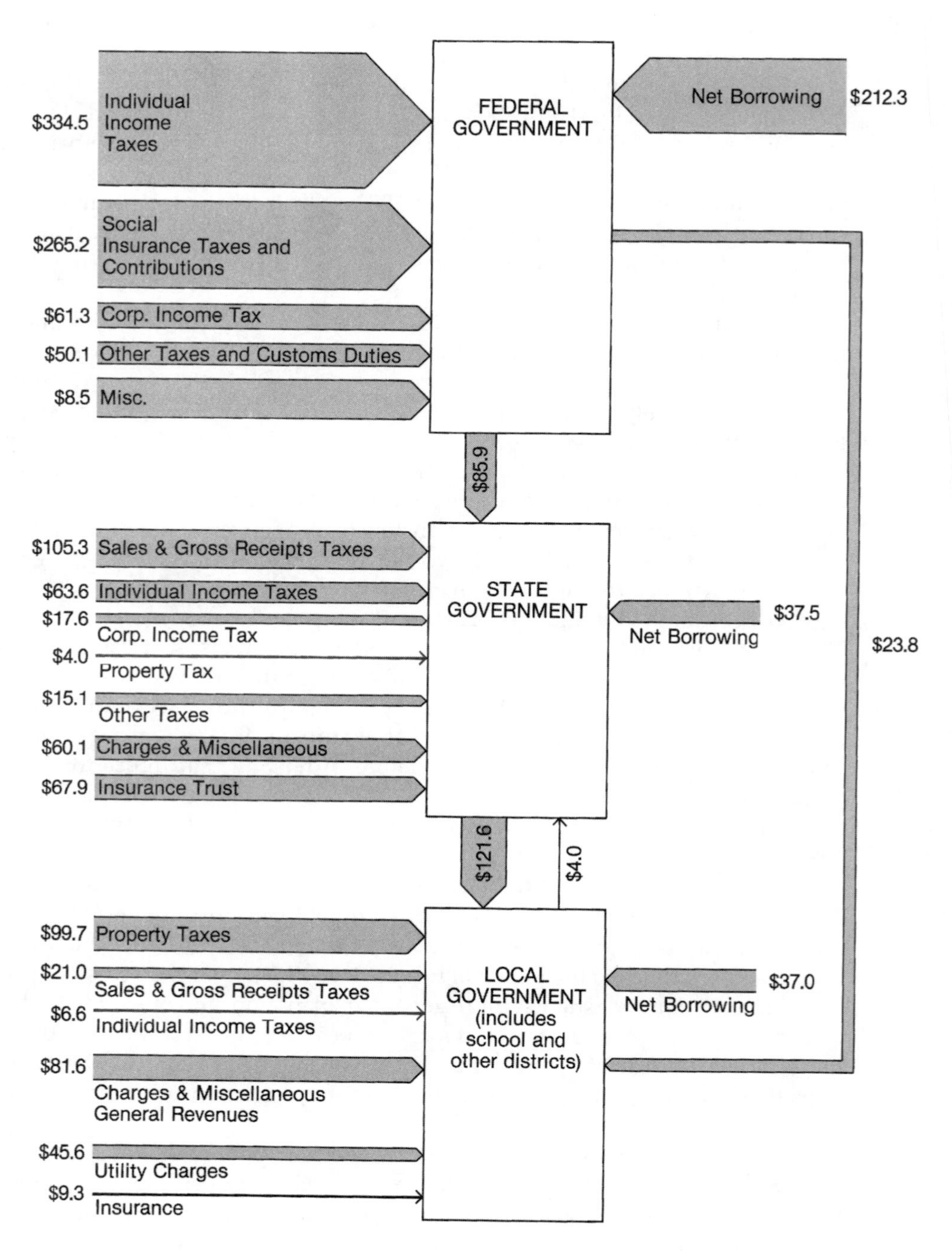

Sources of Revenues and Intergovernmental Funds, 1990 (in Billions)
Source: *Statistical Abstract of the United States*, 1992, 112th edition, Department of Commerce, Bureau of the Census, Government Printing Office, Washington, DC, Tables 450, 460, 461, 468
*Precise figure not available.

partly with federal funds, the federal government can achieve the effect of requirement simply by making citizen participation a requirement for the receipt of federal funds. And in fact, planning at the city, town, and county level is very heavily conditioned by such federal requirements.

Very often the federal government does not even need to monitor the behavior of the recipient government to achieve compliance. The reason is simple. If the local government violates a federal funding requirement, it is likely to face a lawsuit from some individual or group seeking to block its use of federal funds on the grounds that it has violated a condition of receiving such funds. For example, failure to take low- and moderate-income citizens into the decision-making process for community development planning is likely to bring such a suit from a low-income or minority advocacy group. Failure to heed guidelines attached to a federal grant for construction of a waste-water treatment plant might bring a suit from an environmental organization. Thus, from the federal perspective, many of the guidelines attached to grants are self-enforcing.

Another way to influence local behavior is simply by providing funds for the purpose. When Congress wanted to encourage states and localities to do water-quality planning, it provided grants for doing so. Many localities that did water-quality planning in the late 1970s and early 1980s did not want to do it enough to use their own funds. However, they were quite happy to do it with federal funds from section 208 of the Clean Water Act of 1977.

Political Ideology and Federal Grants

As a generalization, national administrations of a liberal political orientation have been quite comfortable with strong federal influence over local and state governments. This was true in the Kennedy-Johnson era from 1960 to 1968 and in the Carter period, 1976 to 1980. Administrations of a more conservative political temper have been less happy with the growth of federal power and have sought to reduce federal influence over local actions. For example, President Nixon was able to replace a large number of separate, or "categorical," grant programs with a small number of combined, or "block,"grants within which states and localities would have relatively more discretion about how they spent federal monies. General revenue sharing, initiated during the Nixon administration, delivered federal funds to state and local governments on a formula basis with little federal control.

The Reagan administration also moved to reduce federal influence over local expenditures through block grants and by readjusting grant programs to funnel relatively more of the funds to the states rather than localities.[12] The final distribution would then be in the hands of the states, moving the federal government further away from a position of direct control. The Reagan administration also sought to reduce the total flow of federal funds to state and local governments. For example, during its second term the administration succeeded in getting Congress to phase out general revenue sharing.

The Reagan administration argued in favor of shrinking the federal role on several grounds. One was that the process by which funds are obtained by taxation, sent to Washington, and then sent back to the jurisdictions where the taxpayers live is unnecessarily wasteful. They also argued for a reduced federal role on the grounds that the federal government cannot know local conditions as well as local governments and, therefore, that local decision making should not be subject to federal oversight. Finally, a reduction in federal transfers to local governments has been advocated as a means of reducing the federal deficit.

Perhaps a broader motivation behind Reagan's "new federalism" was simply to shrink the total role of government in the U.S. economy. If federal payments to state and local governments are cut, these governments may increase taxation somewhat to make up the shortfall but are unlikely to increase taxation to the full extent of the cuts. Presumably, local governments will be more parsimonious in the spending of monies they raise by taxing their citizens than in spending monies they receive from Washington. The overall effect, then, would be to reduce total public expenditures, regardless of the level of government, a change that is part of the conservative political agenda.

The Bush administration generally followed the same general direction as the Reagan administration. One reason for this was a similar view of the proper role of the federal government. Beyond that, the administration was boxed in by a reluctance to ask for new taxes—recall President Bush's "no new taxes" pledge—and by rising expenditures for entitlement programs, particularly Medicare and Medicaid. Thus the money for a more activist role was not available even had the administration been so inclined.

President Clinton, who assumed office in January, 1993 and who is clearly to the political left of either Presidents Reagan or Bush, showed a more activist disposition, particularly in regard to medical care and social services. The administration also showed signs of favoring a more active role in regard to industrial policy. President Clinton's Secretary of Labor and long-term economic advisor, Robert Reich, has long been an advocate of some form of industrial policy. The new administration's views regarding land use and resource use issues were, as of late 1993, somewhat less clear. Though the appointment of Bruce Babbit as Secretary of the Interior did suggest some impetus toward environmental activism.

Mandated Responsibilities

The federal government also influences local and state planning activities by direct requirements, or "mandates." For example, the Clean Air Act amendments of 1970 require the EPA to establish certain air quality standards. To meet these standards states are required to produce state implementation plans (SIP). Although the states have great latitude in the precise manner in which these air quality standards are to be met, the federal legislation does force them to plan and also establishes minimum targets (levels of air quality) for which to plan. The legislation also specifies in general ways the items that state plans must contain. For example, the state plan must contain provisions for reviewing plans for construction of facilities that might produce sufficient emissions to prevent achievement of federally mandated air quality standards. Thus plans for a solid waste incinerator that might push levels of air pollutants above federally mandated standards would have to be reviewed. Should a state government fail to make such a review or make the review in an inadequate manner, it might open itself up to legal action by an environmental group or other concerned parties.

The situation just described represents a particular style of regulation that is very commonly used by federal and state governments. That is, the regulating body does not tell the regulated party what to do in detail. Rather, the regulated party is told what must be achieved but is left with wide discretion concerning how to do so. Perhaps the best-known example of this regulatory style is seen in regard to rules pertaining to automobile fuel economy. Average mileage standards, Corporate Average Fuel Economy (CAFE), for the total fleet produced by a manufacturer were established and fines for exceeding this standard were set. But car makers were told nothing about what technologies to use in achieving these goals.

One advantage of this approach is that overall goals are formulated at a high level, where decision makers have an overview of "the big picture." But technical decisions are made by those who are closer to the problem and thus better informed about details. As a practical matter this style is also likely to be much more acceptable in a political system like that of the United States—one in which power is widely distributed and in which there are strong local governments and a tradition of resistance to excessive central authority.

SUMMARY

Planning occurs within a framework of state legislation, for the municipality as a "creature of the state" has only those powers granted it by the state. It also bears those responsibilities imposed on it by the state. The capacity of a municipality to implement plans is also circumscribed by constitutionally guaranteed individual rights.

Zoning, the best known of land-use control devices, is an exercise of the "police power." The contradictions, real or apparent, between the zoning process and constitutional guarantees relative to property and to due process go far to explain why the process of establishing the rights of municipalities to zone took several decades. Even today, the zoning power is still evolving through a process of legislation, litigation, and judicial decision.

Planning enabling legislation defines the powers of municipalities with regard to planning and, in many cases, also defines the obligations of the community with regard to planning. For example, it may require that the community have a comprehensive plan and that the plan include certain elements.

The federal government exerts a large influence over the local planning process. In some cases it does so by laws and regulation. More often, it does so through requirements attached to funding or simply through the pattern of federal grants. The predominant flow of funds is downward: from the federal government to state and local governments and from state governments to local governments.

NOTES

1. John F. Dillon, *Commentaries on the Law of Municipal Corporations*, 5th ed., Little Brown & Co., Boston, 1911, vol. 1, sec. 237. It can be argued that the "creature of the state" concept is not quite so literally true as it once was. Since World War II there has been a trend for the powers and obligations of local governments to be

defined in state constitutions rather than in laws or charters. If one takes the view that the state constitution comes from the people and creates both the state government and local governments, one could argue that the state and local governments exist in parallel and are thus coequal.

2. As an example of the antizoning position, both for legal and other reasons, see Jack C. Harris and William Douglas Moore, "Debunking the Mythology of Zoning," *Real Estate Review*, vol. 13, no. 4, Winter 1984, pp. 94–97.
3. For an account of the legal issues involved in "taking," see Daniel R. Mandelker, *Land Use Law*, The Michie Co., Charlotesville, VA, 1982.
4. For a history of the evolution of zoning, see Mel Scott, *American City Planning Since 1890*, University of California Press, Berkeley, 1971, chaps. 2 and 3.
5. See Charles F. Flory, "Shaping the Skyscrapers of Manhattan," *Real Estate Review*, vol. 13, no. 2, Summer 1983, pp. 48–53.
6. 272 U.S., 365 (1926).
7. Code of Virginia, 1950 (as amended), Title 15.1, chap.11.
8. A plat is a map or diagram showing a parcel of land divided into building lots.
9. By "local governments" are meant all municipal and county governments and also school districts.
10. *Statistical Abstract of the United States*, 1981 (102 ed.), Table 476.
11. The term *elastic* in this usage means that percentage increases in tax revenues exceeded percentage increases in income.
12. For a discussion of the present state and recent history of intergovernmental fiscal relations see John Gist, chaps. 10 and 11 of John M.Levy, *Urban and Metropolitan Economics*, McGraw-Hill Book Co., New York, 1985.

SELECTED BIBLIOGRAPHY

Buck, Peter L., ED., *Modern Land Use Control*, The Practicing Law Institute, New York, 1978.

Burns, James M., Peltason, J. W., and Cronin, Thomas E., *Government by the People*, Prentice Hall, Englewood Cliffs, NJ, 1987.

Mandelker, Daniel R., *Land Use Law*, The Michie Co., Charlottesville, VA, 1982.

CHAPTER 6

PLANNING AND POLITICS

WHY IS PLANNING POLITICAL?

For several reasons, planning generally takes place in a highly politicized environment.

1. Planning often involves matters in which people have large emotional stakes—for example, the character of a neighborhood or the quality of a school district. A planning decision that you do not like may intrude itself into your life every day because its fruits are located where you live or work. The often very emotional suburban resistance to subsidized housing is largely a matter of residents' fears about the effect it will have on the local school system. The residents may be right or wrong, but either way it is easy to understand why they become passionate about what they think will affect the happiness and safety of their children. (See the box on pages 90–92 about the City of Yonkers.) Vociferous citizens' opposition was the major force that ended Urban Renewal (see Chapter 12). Few actions of government can arouse more emotion than a program that might force the citizen to give up an apartment or relocate his or her business to make way for what one writer called "the federal bulldozer."
2. Planning decisions are visible. They involve buildings, roads, parkland, properties—entities that citizens see and know about. Planning mistakes, like architectural mistakes, are hard to hide.

3. Like all functions of local government, the planning process is close at hand. It is easier for the citizen to affect the actions of a town board or a city council than the actions of a state legislature or of Congress. That feeling of potential effectiveness encourages participation.
4. Citizens correctly assume that they know something about planning without having studied the subject formally. After all, planning involves land use, traffic, the character of the community, and other items with which residents are familiar. Therefore, citizens tend not to defer to planners.
5. Planning involves decisions with large financial consequences. Consider Mr. X, who owns 100 acres of farmland on the urban fringe. Land values in the area are rising and it is clear that the land will soon pass from agricultural to a more intensive use. If municipal sewer and water lines are extended along the road fronting the property, the land will be suitable for garden apartment development at 12 units per acre, making it worth, say, $100,000 per acre. On the other hand, if the land is not served with utilities, residential development there will be limited to single-family houses on 1-acre lots, and land will be worth $10,000 per acre. Mr. X now has a $9 million interest in whether the municipal master plan shows sewer and water lines down a particular road. Variations on this theme could easily be posed in terms of zoning, street widening, community development, construction of public buildings, flood control measures, and the like.

   Even those who own no property other than the house they live in may feel, quite correctly, that they have a substantial financial stake in planning decisions. For many people, their biggest single source of net worth is not in bank accounts or stock certificates but in home equity (what the home would bring when sold minus what is owed on it). Planning decisions that affect house values may thus assume major importance to home owners.
6. There can be a strong link between planning questions and property taxes. The property tax is one of the financial mainstays of local government as well as of public education. To the extent that planning decisions affect what is built within a community, they affect the community's tax base. That, in turn, affects the property taxes community residents must pay. And these taxes are hardly a trivial sum. In 1990 total property tax collections in the United States were approximately $156 billion or over $600 per capita. For practical purposes the tax is levied and used only by local governments and school districts. Concern over property tax levels has been very great in recent years. Witness the passage of Proposition 13 in California and comparable property tax limits in a number of other states.

PLANNERS AND POWER

Planners are basically advisors and in a literal sense are often virtually powerless. Alone, the planner has no capacity to do the things that cause change within the community: to commit public funds, to enact laws, to enter into contracts, or to exercise the power of eminent domain. Where the planner does have some legal powers, perhaps in connection with land-use controls, as discussed in Chapter 9, they are powers granted by the legislative body and removable by that same body. The planner's influence on events, then, stems from the capacity to articulate viewpoints and develop consensus and coalitions among those who do wield some power.

A plan is a vision of the future. A planner moves events to the extent that he or she can cause that vision to be shared. In the early years of planning—as noted in connection with the Plan of Chicago—the view was that the plan came solely, or almost solely, from the head of the planner. It was then his or her task to sell that vision to the public and to the political establishment of the community. This is exactly what was done with great success in the Chicago case by Burnham and his associates. But in this age, when citizens are much better informed and in which it has been demonstrated many times that one can "fight city hall" and win, such a top-down approach is no longer possible.

A more modern view is that good plans spring from the community itself. In this view the planner's proper role is to facilitate the planning process and to aid it with his or her own expertise, rather than to deliver the plan full blown. Several points can be made in favor of the modern approach. First, it avoids elitism. The planner has particular skills the average citizen does not have, but that does not make the planner wiser in general. Second, there is no way that the planner, or any other single individual or group, can have a complete and accurate view of the interests of the citizenry as a whole. Only the individual can really know his or her own needs and preferences. If that is true, only by taking the citizenry into the planning process at an early stage can their interests be fully represented. Last, it can be argued that a plan formed with substantial community input is more likely to be carried out than a plan of equal quality that has simply been drawn up directly by professionals. The very act of participating in the planning process informs the citizen about the details of the plan. Giving time and energy to the process of planning builds the citizens' commitment to the plan. What was "their plan" now becomes "our plan."

Planners now view involvement with politics very differently than they did a few decades ago. In the 1920s and 1930s it was common to try to isolate the planning process from politics—to keep planning "above" politics. A common political arrangement was to have the planner report solely to a "nonpolitical" planning board. In time it was realized that since the political sphere was where decisions were made, isolating the planner from politics rendered him or her much less effective. Then, too, it came to be realized that the term *nonpolitical* is misleading. If one appoints a group of prominent citizens as a lay board one has, in fact, made a political decision. A group of nonprominent citizens might give the planners a very different set of instructions. No one is really nonpolitical, for everyone has interests and values and that is the substance of which politics is made.

The notion of the planning function as one that should be nonpolitical is related to the urban political reform movement of the late nineteenth and early twentieth century.[1] Political power was wrested from the old machines like New York's Tammany Hall and vested in civil servants; so-called reform administrations; and in some cities, in professional, nonpartisan managers. The city manager form of government, in which the elected mayor has a largely ceremonial role and the real administrative responsibility and authority are vested in a city manager hired by the legislative body, comes from the reform movement.

In the reform view politics was a seamy and often corrupt process, and the more that planning could be kept out of it the better. A more modern view would be that the reform movement was a victory of the upper-middle class over machines, which often represented, albeit with some of the gravy skimmed off the top, the working class and newly arrived immigrants. In short, reform was not the elimination of politics so much as a transfer of political power.

THE FRAGMENTATION OF POWER

The environment in which the planner operates is characterized by a diffusion of political, economic, and legal power. This is probably true for any planner anywhere, but it is particularly true in the United States. Political power in the United States is fragmented in several ways. First, it is distributed among different levels of government. State and local governments are much stronger in relation to the national government than is the case in other democratic states of the Western world such as France or England. In general, also, state and local governments raise much more of their own revenues than do their counterparts in other democracies. Financial and political autonomy are related. The relatively greater autonomy of state and local governments in the United States is largely traceable to a point made in the previous chapter, namely, that the U.S. Constitution was essentially a compact among the states. Resistance to central authority is an old American political tradition.

Political power is also fragmented through the so-called "separation of powers" among executive, legislative, and judicial branches. That separation goes back to the founding of the country and the intent of the drafters of the Constitution to restrain government by structuring it so that the power of each branch would counterbalance the powers of the other branches. Planning as a government activity is clearly a function of the executive branch. However, implementing virtually any plan requires funding. Both the levying of taxes and the appropriation of funds are legislative functions. The powers of both the executive and legislative branches are, of course, constrained by the judicial branch.

In addition to being fragmented along the executive-judicial-legislative line, local government may also be fragmented in an administrative sense. A metropolitan area that constitutes a single economic and social entity may be divided into dozens or even hundreds of political jurisdictions. In addition to governments, there may be a variety of districts that have some governmental powers and responsibilities. School districts have some of the powers of government such as the power to tax and the power of eminent domain. In many states the school board members are elected directly by the residents of the district, and those members, in turn , choose the district's superintendent. The administrative structure that runs the schools thus exists in parallel to the structure of local government but is not a part of that government. Yet both structures tax the same population; both may make land-use decisions, and both may make capital investments. Similar comments might be made with regard to water, sewer, transportation, and other authorities.

As noted earlier, the United States has a strong tradition of respect for property rights. Conflict over the exact location of the boundary between the rights of the public and the rights of property owners is thus virtually inevitable. The determination of the boundary is ultimately made in the courts, that is, by the judicial branch. We also note that the courts are often the guardians of individual rights and in this role may require certain actions of the other branches of government. Court-mandated school integration is perhaps the best-known example, but there are many others. In years gone by court decisions about the rights of the handicapped determined what steps municipalities had to take in order to meet the needs of their handicapped residents. Now, how the courts interpret the language of the Americans with Disabilities Act (ADA) of 1992 will determine exactly what steps municipalities must take and what expenditures they must make for the handicapped.

Power in the nongovernment sphere is also widely distributed. The citizens in their role as voters are the ultimate power. But groups of individuals also constitute power blocs. The citizen as home owner is part of a very powerful bloc, as any planner working in a community with a large percentage of owner-occupied housing units quickly learns. In many communities the citizen as a member of a labor union is part of a powerful bloc. The citizen as a member of an environmental group such as the Sierra Club or a local conservation group is a member of another bloc. Those who own substantial amounts of property, whether vacant land or structures, constitute still another source of power. So, too, are the community's employers. There is a very strong relationship among land-use planning, capital investment, and construction activity. Thus the construction industry—both management and labor—is often a major participant in planning decisions and in planning controversies.

The planner usually finds little within the community on which there is unanimous agreement. Majority positions can often be found and compromises can be reached. But it is rare when all parties can agree on precisely what constitutes the public interest. When propositions are stated as generalities they often elicit more agreement than when stated as specific proposals. We all favor enhanced environmental quality. But raise the issue of shutting down a particular facility and you quickly find that one person's environmental protection is another person's unemployment. Planning, like politics, is in large measure the art of compromise.

STYLES OF PLANNING

We have suggested that the planner works in an environment of widely distributed power, conflicting interests, and less than total agreement. How, then, are planners to conduct themselves? Styles of planning vary with individuals and also with places. Few planners will fit exactly into any one of the types that follow, but rather will display different amounts of the several pure types in their professional role.

1. *The planner as neutral public servant*. In this role planners take a politically neutral stance and fall back on their professional expertise, which will be used to tell the community how best to do what it wishes to do. They will not, in general, try to tell the community what it ought to do. The advice and technical work they present to the community will largely be confined to "how to" and "what if" and not to "should" or "should not." When choices are to be made, planners will estimate how the various alternatives will play out. If the community decides it needs some low-rent subsidized housing, they may advise the community on where to locate it, how to design the site, how to finance it, what effect it may have on the tax base, how many additional children it will send to the schools, and what additional public services its residents might require. If the community is drawing up a comprehensive plan and zoning ordinance, they will help structure these to reflect the community's intent.

   If the community does not want such housing, planners will not urge a change of position, though perhaps they might point out legal or other consequences. Subject to the constraints of personal and professional ethics the planners might even advise the community on what sort of comprehensive plan and zoning law provisions will withstand court challenge brought by a group seeking to force the community to accept such housing.

2. *The planner as builder of community consensus*. This is essentially a political view of the planner. It became more popular in the postwar period as it became very clear to most planners that the older view of the planner as nonpolitical public servant was at great variance from the way that planning questions actually were resolved.[2]

   In this view planning cannot be separated from politics. Politics is the art of taking divergent views and divergent interests and bringing them into sufficient harmony to permit action to be taken. The role of the politician, then, is that of broker between various interests.[3] Since no plans can be implemented without political will and political action, the planner, too, must be very close to, or perhaps a part of, the political process. The advocate of this view, for example, would hold that the older notion of having the planner report solely to a supposedly nonpartisan lay planning board is a prescription for impotence: It is better to make the planner an integral part of the bureaucracy or the political structure where the decisions are made. This view is consistent with planners expressing their own values and trying to move the community in directions that they see fit. How much planners can move the community in their own direction varies. The planner who is visibly at great odds with the main values and desires of the community often becomes an unemployed planner.

3. *The planner as entrepreneur*. This is not a role that planners originally envisaged for themselves but one in which some find themselves. When the planners run an agency that is particularly task-oriented, they very often become entrepreneurs. For example, in Urban Renewal programs, public funds were used to clear and prepare sites, which were then sold or leased for development by private capital. The planner who ran an Urban

Renewal agency had to market sites, find developers, and negotiate contracts. Local economic development programs have as their primary goal increasing private investment in the community. Thus the economic development planner is necessarily drawn into an entrepreneurial role involving marketing, negotiation, and financing. In recent years many cities used Urban Development Action Grants (UDAGs) from the Department of Housing and Urban Development to revitalize declining areas. Here, too, the planner had to behave more as an entrepreneur than as a traditional planner.

4. *The planner as advocate.* In this role the planner acts as a representative for certain groups or certain positions and chooses to advance particular interests. The concept of advocacy planning, which developed in the early 1960s, sprang from the view that there are groups in society that lack the political and economic strength to advance their own interests adequately. Thus they need to be specially represented in the planning process. Specifically, advocacy planning cut its teeth on the issue of exclusionary zoning (see Chapter 9). Advocacy planners, the best known of whom was the late Paul Davidoff, took the position that suburban zoning laws locked out the poor and minority group members and then set about to change such laws by means of persuasion and, more important, litigation.[4] The advocacy planner, like the attorney, does not generally claim to represent the majority but rather the interests of a particular client. Those interests may or may not coincide with interests of the majority of the community or, for that matter, the nation.

   In general, advocacy planners who represent less prosperous subgroups of the population will have at least some element of a radical political perspective. It is the view that society exploits, mistreats, or otherwise abuses some of its citizens that is likely to propel one into an advocacy role. If, on the other hand, one sees society as generally fair and just, one is not likely to see much need for advocacy planning.

   The notion of advocacy may also be used in a slightly different sense. Rather than serve as the advocate of a particular group in society, the planner may advocate a particular cause or program, such as parks, mass transit, highways, or environmental preservation. The planner who represents a cause may have a somewhat easier time of making a claim to serving the public interest as a whole than does the planner who represents a particular group. But even here, if one picks almost any goal it will generally turn out that accomplishing it creates some gainers and some losers.

5. *The planner as agent of radical change.* This is a view held by few practicing planners. Planners who hold a full-blown radical perspective are likely to find the day-to-day work of planning in most organizations frustrating and painful because they will have to cooperate on a daily basis with a system for which they have little respect. Among planning academicians there are a fair number, though definitely a minority, who take a neo-Marxian or Critical Theory position and see the promotion of radical political and economic change as a proper long-term goal for planning. This subject is discussed further in Chapter 19.

HOW PLANNING AGENCIES ARE ORGANIZED

Planning agencies vary greatly in size and purpose. What follows is typical but far from universal. As noted, the old idea of a planning agency being outside of and "above" politics has been almost universally abandoned. The modern planning agency is a part of the executive branch of the municipal government. Its head, like the commissioners of other departments, reports to the chief elected official or, if there is a manager form of government, to the city or town manager. Very commonly, the planning director or commissioner is a political appointee nominated by the chief elected official and confirmed by the legislative body, just as the head of a federal department is nominated by the president subject to confirmation by the Senate. The commissioner is often required to have specific qualifications such as a master's degree in planning or membership in the American Institute of Certified Planners (a certification based on education, experience, and passing an examination). As any appointed official, the commissioner or director can be dismissed at the will of the chief elected official. In that sense, as in many other ways, the ultimate power to plan is vested in elected officials and, therefore, at one remove, in the body politic of the community.

Beneath the commissioner is a staff who, generally, have civil service status. A position such as assistant planner, associate planner, planner, and so forth has defined requirements such as degrees and education. The newly hired individual typically goes through a provisional period of six months or a year and then receives a permanent appointment. In some cases staff must be hired from a list of people who have passed the civil service examination for the position. In other cases, the agency may be able to hire people who have not taken the examination, but the applicants cannot receive permanent appointments until they have passed the exam. Because of the difference between a political and civil service appointment, the staff often has a good deal more permanency than the commissioner.

In addition to reporting to the chief elected official, the head of the planning agency also may report to a lay planning board, typically made up of citizens who have been nominated by the chief executive officer and confirmed by the legislative body. Its members serve with no or, at most, token pay. The purpose of the board is to provide some citizen input to and oversight for the planning agency. Such boards vary greatly: Some are merely rubber stamps; others may be very active and forceful. Some boards see their role as essentially supervisory, whereas others may use their own status within the municipality to advance the program of the planning agency. A board whose members are articulate and energetic can make a major contribution to building public interest in and support for the cause of planning.

The planning agency may also report directly to the community's legislative body. Often, the municipality's charter or bylaws will specify subjects on which the agency will report. For example, the charter might specify that the agency will deliver an annual report evaluating the various items proposed in the municipality's capital budget.

If the agency is of moderate or larger size, there are likely to be several sections that handle different aspects of the planning task. For example, there may be a group that handles comprehensive or long-range planning. There may be another group that handles land-use control issues and performs such functions as zoning and subdivision reviews (see Chapter 8). Still another group may review matters related to the capital budget such as investment in water and sewer facilities, roads, municipal facilities, and the like. In some agencies there will be a research section, which makes population forecasts and revenue estimates and, generally, tries to provide a solid quantitative and factual basis for the actions of the rest of the agency. In the 1970s, when community development funds began to flow from the Department of Housing and Urban Development, many planning agencies set up sections to handle the disbursement of these funds. For example, a county agency might have had a community development section that reviewed the plans of and funded the community development activities of subcounty units of government or private groups. From time to time, other planning-related functions of government may be lodged in planning agencies. In many communities, economic development agencies have been located within or attached to planning agencies; agencies that are heavily involved in environmental issues may have an environmental section, and so on.

Reaching Out to the Public

Because planning is a collective activity, and because no agency will be very successful without a broad political base, planning agencies generally have a number of links to the community through various advisory or lay groups. These links may be formal or entirely casual. One approach is the advisory panel: A group of citizens interested in a particular issue, say environmental preservation, will maintain liaison with the planning agency. The agency will solicit information and advice from the group on planning decisions that have significant environmental impact. Citizens interested in housing might constitute another group with which the agency has frequent contact. In the college town in which I live there are citizens' groups concerned with sidewalks, bicycle paths, and urban design, and the planning agency has frequent contact with all of them. Such groups often furnish support for planning department initiatives, as well as useful data and ideas. But even when the citizens and the planners disagree, it is generally better to communicate on a continuing basis than simply to meet occasionally in an adversarial situation. Differences that often can be negotiated through informal contacts may solidify beyond compromise if they first surface in a public environment and people take stands from which it is later awkward or embarrassing to retreat. As discussed in Chapter 8, planning agencies also make extensive use of public meetings and presentations when developing plans. Meetings are useful in building support, in helping the agency to understand and be responsive to citizens' preferences and concerns, and in meeting legal requirements for citizens' participation.

Beyond all these approaches, most planning agencies reach out to the community through a variety of informal means. The planning director or staff members will speak before the Rotary Club, the League of Women Voters, the

Chamber of Commerce, and other groups. Many agencies will send out press releases and otherwise seek media coverage so that people know what the agency is doing and why. The agency that does not build a base of popular support within the community is not likely to accomplish very much.

SUMMARY

Planning takes place in a highly political environment because (1) planning often involves issues in which citizens have a large emotional stake; (2) the results of planning decisions are often highly visible; (3) planning questions are more accessible to citizens than those handled at the state or national level; (4) citizens feel they have insight into planning questions and are not overly deferential to planners' expertise; (5) planning decisions often have large financial effects on property owners; and (6) planning decisions may have significant effects on property tax rates.

Planners exercise little or no power directly but rather affect events to the extent that they affect the political processes of the community. In the last several decades the idea of planning as a nonpolitical process has given way to a more realistic view of the planner as one of a number of participants in the political process. The older view of the planner as presenting a finished plan to the community has now been supplanted by the view that planning is a community process, which the planner facilitates and supports with technical expertise.

Depending on the community and the personality and ideology of the planner(s), a variety of planning styles can be identified: (1) the planner as neutral civil servant, (2) the planner as builder of community consensus, (3) the planner as entrepreneur, (4) the planner as advocate, and (5) the planner as agent of radical change.

NOTES

1. For a discussion of the reform tradition in urban politics, see Blake McKelvey, *The Urbanization of America*, Rutgers University Press, New Brunswick, NJ, 1963, particularly chaps. 6 and 7. See also, Edward C. Banfield, *City Politics*, Harvard University Press, Cambridge, MA, 1963.
2. One early work that examined the disparity between a purely rational and technical approach with the way decisions are actually reached is Martin Meyerson and Edward C. Banfield, *Politics, Planning and the Public Interest*, The Free Press, Glencoe, IL, 1955. A shorter presentation of some of the same arguments can be found in Edward C. Banfield, "Ends and Means in Planning" *International Social Science Journal*, vol. XI, no. 3, 1959. The article is reprinted in Andreas Faludi, *A Reader in Planning Theory*, Pergamon Press, New York, 1973. Another article in this connection is Norman Beckman, "The Planner as Bureaucrat," *Journal of The American Institute of Planners*, vol. 30, November 1964; also reprinted in Faludi, op. cit. See also Alan Altshuler, *The City Planning Process: A Political Analysis*, Cornell University Press, Ithaca, NY, 1965; Herbert J. Gans, *People and Plans*, Basic Books, New York, 1968; and Anthony J. Catanese, *Planners and Local Politics*. Sage Publications, Beverly Hills, CA, 1974.
3. A number of planners have become quite interested in mediation techniques in this regard. See, for example, Lawrence Susskind, "Mediating Public Disputes," *Negotiation Journal*, January 1985, pp. 19–22.
4. Paul Davidoff, "Advocacy and Pluralism in Planning," *Journal of the American Institute of Planners* (now the *APA Journal*), vol. 31, 1965. See also Paul Davidoff and Thomas A. Reiner, "A Choice Theory of Planning," *Journal of the American Institute of Planners* , vol. 28, May, 1962. Both are reprinted in Faludi, op. cit.

SELECTED BIBLIOGRAPHY

MEYERSON, MARTIN and EDWARD C. BANFIELD, *Politics, Planning and the Public Interest*, The Free Press, Glencoe, IL, 1955.

BANFIELD, EDWARD C., *City Politics*, Harvard University Press, Cambridge, MA, 1963.

CATANESE, ANTHONY JAMES, *Planners and Local Politics*, Sage Publications, Beverly Hills, CA, 1974.

CATANESE, ANTHONY JAMES, *The Politics of Planning and Development*. Sage Publications, Beverly Hills, CA, 1984.

FALUDI, ANDREAS, ED., *A Reader in Planning Theory*, Pergamon Press, New York, 1973.

FRIEDMANN, JOHN, *Planning in the Public Domain: From Knowledge to Action*, Princeton University Press, Princeton, NJ, 1987.

HARRIGAN, JOHN J., *Political Change and the Metropolis*, Little Brown & Co., Boston, 1985.

HEFLAND, GARY, ED., *Metropolitan Areas: Metropolitan Governments*, Kendall Hall Publishing Co., Dubuque, IA, 1976.

JACOBS, ALLAN, *Making City Planning Work*, American Society of Planning Officials, Chicago, 1978.

CHAPTER 7

THE SOCIAL ISSUES

The two professions from which modern urban planning sprang are architecture and landscape architecture, both of which are concerned largely with physical design. In earlier years planners often tended to emphasize design and physical issues over social issues, as the discussion of the Plan for Chicago indicated. But planners have long recognized that what at first glance appear to be simply matters of design can have powerful social implications.

In the 1960s and 1970s dissatisfaction within the profession over what many saw as an underemphasis on social issues reached major proportions. Many planners concluded that they should be focusing on social issues, and some began to define themselves as "social planners" and to speak of a subfield of "social planning." This change within the profession had a number of roots.

The Civil Rights movement of the late 1950s and 1960s focused attention on issues of justice and fairness. Many planners felt that they could not simply be neutral civil servants doing the bidding of "the establishment" if they did not approve of its goals and policies.[1] The wave of riots and arson that hit U.S. cities from Newark to Watts in the mid-1960s revealed a deep well of dissatisfaction and distress among minority populations and added to the perception that we as a society must be doing something wrong. Shortly thereafter, the Vietnam War split a generation of Americans. Those who felt that the war was wrong tended to carry that perception over into a more radical position on many domestic issues. If the establishment was wrong in Vietnam, they felt it was also wrong at home.

Another reason for the change in focus was that many projects that appeared to be well planned in physical terms did not work out well when considered in a broader view. Urban Renewal, discussed in Chapter 12, was one such case, as was public housing. The Pruitt-Igoe public housing project in St. Louis was a large project built according to what were considered good design practices of the time. In fact, it won a design award from the American Institute of Architects (AIA). Socially, however, the project was a failure, with high rates of crime, vandalism, illegitimacy, and so on. Ultimately, the city, unable to deal with the multiple social problems of Pruitt-Igoe, demolished the buildings and cleared the site, AIA award notwithstanding. Clearly, physical design does not solve people's psychological, family, economic, legal, drug, alcohol, and other problems. Building a project, however well done from an architectural and site design perspective, that isolated large numbers of people with serious problems in a small area simply set the stage for disaster.

WHAT ARE THE ISSUES

Housing is probably the area in which physical planning decisions have their greatest social effects. Land-use controls and decisions about capital facilities like water and sewer lines affect how much housing and what type of housing will be built. That decision affects rents and house prices, and thus who will live in the community. Through the mechanism of cost, one pattern of housing may favor racial integration whereas another will favor racial segregation. Because where children live determines where they go to school, housing policy can turn out to be educational policy as well (see the box on pages 90–92). Where one lives can determine one's access to recreation, to social services, and perhaps most important, to employment. Policies and economic forces that separate the housing that low-income workers can afford from the jobs for which they are qualified can produce unemployment. Prolonged unemployment can lead to family breakup, which may have links to welfare dependency, alcoholism, crime, and other social pathologies. It has been persuasively argued that the formation of the "urban underclass" is, in part, due to just such a separation.[2]

Even if we forget matters of race and class entirely, decisions about housing can have powerful effects on how people live. Suppose the land-use controls in a suburban town permit the building of only single-family houses on half-acre or larger lots. By limiting what can be built to a single, expensive type of structure, the town has made some very personal decisions for its residents. Many of the children who were raised in the town will not be able to afford to live there as young adults. When a couple is divorced, the partner who does not get the house may have to leave town because there is no housing that he or she can afford. That might not be the case if some rental apartments were available. A couple with a grown retarded child who cannot live alone but could function well in a group home may be very affected by whether or not the town permits large, old, single-family houses to be converted into group homes. This is, incidentally, not an idle example. Many communities have experienced bitter fights over whether or not to permit group homes. A middle-aged couple who would like an elderly parent to live with them will be concerned about whether or not the town's zoning law permits accessory, or so-called "mother-in-law," apartments to be attached to or constructed adjacent to single-family houses.

There are vastly more single-parent families in the United States today than there were a few decades ago. Among two-parent households, there is now a much higher percentage in which both parents work outside the home. Good planning might accommodate itself to these changes in a variety of ways. A pattern of land-use controls that permitted homes, workplaces, and child-care facilities to be close together would make the lives of many families simpler and happier. In some communities, as noted, expanding the variety of housing types to accommodate the increasing number of smaller households would be useful.

Economic development is another area in which issues of physical

THE YONKERS HOUSING CASE

Yonkers is an old city of about 190,000 located in Westchester County, New York. On the west, the city is bounded by the Hudson River and on the south by the Bronx, one of the five boroughs of New York City. To its north and east the city borders prosperous suburban areas of Westchester County.[3] The city contains 27 public housing projects, 26 of which are built in one area of the city, its southwest corner. In some ways this location makes sense. As the oldest and most densely developed part of the city, the southwest corner contained the largest share of old, substandard multifamily housing. Building the public housing there thus cleared many of these obsolete units.[4] The southwest corner of the city is also the part of the city with the best access to public transportation (bus, commuter rail, and New York City subway system). Thus a family that could not afford a car could live there and still have reasonably good mobility for such purposes as getting to work. The southwest corner was also the part of the city in which the poorer part of the city's population was living at the time the public housing was built.

But these respectable planning considerations were not the only reason public housing was concentrated there. An overriding consideration was *political feasibility*. This bland term meant that the predominantly white population of the rest of the city was adamantly opposed to public housing in their neighborhoods because they disliked and feared the poor black population that would occupy it. The city's politicians, administrators, and planners, as well as the officials of the federal government's Department of Housing and Urban Development (HUD), which funded the housing, bowed to that opposition by ruling out sites that failed the political feasibility test.

In 1980 the Justice Department, subsequently joined by the National Association for the Advancement of Colored People (NAACP), brought suit against the city and against HUD, alleging that the siting of the housing had created a condition of de facto school segregation. This violated the principles of school integration established in *Brown* v *Board of Education*, a landmark case decided by the Supreme Court in 1954.[5] In 1985 Judge Leonard B. Sand of the Southern District

Court in New York found both the city and HUD guilty. That decision was sustained on appeal by the U.S. Supreme Court of Appeals for the Second Circuit in 1987. In June 1988 the U.S. Supreme Court refused to hear an appeal by the City of Yonkers. At the end of its legal road, and under threats by Judge Sand of massive fines, the city in a consent decree agreed to a plan for the building of public housing in other neighborhoods. But the City Council subsequently refused to carry out the plan.

In spite of the disapproval of the city by Judge Sand and much of the press, many Yonkers residents did not feel guilty about their defiance of the court. Many felt that they knew all they had to know about street crime and school problems simply from living next to New York City. In fact, many Yonkers residents are ex-New Yorkers who moved to the suburbs to get away from crime and other urban problems and, particularly, to be able to send their children to suburban rather than city schools. Rightly or wrongly they were not about to be educated on the subject by judges, sociologists, planners, or editorial writers.

Defiant city residents were sustained in their view that they were morally right, even if legally wrong, because Yonkers had substantially more than its proportionate share of Westchester County's public housing. Many other municipalities in the county contained no public housing or subsidized housing of any type. By an unfortunate coincidence, Judge Sand had a weekend home in Pound Ridge, an upper-income Westchester town whose population was almost entirely white. Pound Ridge could never be accused of mislocating its public housing because it did not have any at all. To dramatize what they felt was the judge's hypocritical position, Yonkers residents took to driving up to Pound Ridge and picketing the judge's house.

Frustrated by the City Council's refusal to implement the plan to which the city had consented, Judge Sand invoked fines of $500 per day against the council members who voted against it. The council members still refused to comply. In November 1989 the city's mayoralty election turned on the issue of compliance or noncompliance. In what the *The New York Times* described as a "stunning upset," a hard-line proponent of noncompliance, a retired New York City detective named Henry Spallone, defeated the incumbent Nicholas C. Wasicsko, who had urged compliance and compromise. Then, in January 1990 the U.S. Supreme Court handed Spallone and the three dissenting council members a small and ambiguous victory. By five to four it ruled that Judge Sand should not have fined the council members until he was certain that fines against the city alone would not produce compliance. The decision did not, however, resolve the larger issue of whether a court could order a legislator to vote in a particular way.

Heartened by this small victory, Spallone and the three council members appeared determined to continue to resist Judge Sand. By the end of 1991 it was reported that a total of only 28 units of court-ordered housing had been built. At this time a newly elected mayor, Terence M. Zeleski, took office. He showed more willingness to compromise than had his predecessor and the city soon submitted a new plan to Judge Sand. The new plan would

> . . . involve 709 units of owner occupied housing, primarily in existing condominium and cooperative apartments. Under the plan, the city would provide mortgage assistance to buyers; people who now live in subsidized housing, most of whom are Black or Hispanic, would get priority.

Judge Sand then gave the city four months to prove that its plan would work. The plan represents a considerable scaling back from the original demands of the court for the plan would

> . . . replace another blueprint for desegregation, languishing since the judge ordered it in 1988, that called for 800 units of subsidized housing and the eventual construction of 3,200 units that would be rented at market rates.

The end result may be some hundreds of units of existing housing made available to low and moderate income tenants. That would clearly be a victory for the plaintiffs if it happens. On the other hand the years of resistance have apparently blocked the construction of court-ordered new housing that the citizens did not want.[6]

Yonkers residents protesting the proposed construction of public housing. The figure hanging in effigy is Judge Sand. (Mark Vergari, Gannett Suburban Newspapers)

planning quickly reveal a social side. Assume a community needs jobs and new tax revenues, but it is handicapped by a shortage of sites suitable for commercial development. It could use its power of eminent domain to take some land, carry out the necessary site preparation, and then market the land for commercial use. But the land now contains housing, whose residents will be forced to move. Should this be done? Will a functioning neighborhood be destroyed, and if so, are the new jobs and new tax revenues worth it? If it is to be done, what arrangements will be made to rehouse the displaced population? Or will the population that now lives there simply be given notice and then left to its own devices?

For another illustration, assume that a town's economic development director is excited because he thinks that with a little effort the town can obtain a new Wal Mart shopping center, which will provide hundreds of jobs and some much-needed tax revenue. But it is also clear that if this new facility is built, the competition from it will kill off much of the remaining activity in the downtown. That will change the look and feel of the community because the downtown will cease to be a focal point. From a pure balance sheet perspective, the new shopping center looks good. But how heavily should the intangibles connected with the downtown be weighted? When all is said and done, should the shopping center be encouraged or resisted?

Very often the promotion of the local economy involves giving subsidies or tax breaks to firms to encourage them to locate in the community instead of elsewhere. In that case public funds are being given, through the firm, to entrepreneurs, investors, and stockholders who may be a good deal wealthier than the average taxpayer in the community. Should we be troubled by this?

Some planners are very comfortable with this approach: That is the way the game is played in this capitalistic society, and by and large, the system works better than other alternatives. Others, such as Norman Krumholz, a former planning director of the City of Cleveland, are outraged by it.[7] Regardless of what position one takes on the point, it clearly contains serious questions of social philosophy.

Environmental decisions can have major social consequences. If an environmentally fragile area is the last site in town that might accommodate some low- and moderate-income housing, there is a serious question of values to be addressed. As noted elsewhere, one person's environmental protection may be another person's unemployment. Again, what looks like a physical question rapidly reveals a social side.

A recurrent theme of this book is that planning decisions impose gains and losses. This point is made in subsequent chapters in connection with growth control, environmental planning, and economic development planning, among other issues. Planners who define themselves as social planners often feel that they should attempt to tip society's scales toward the less fortunate (or tip them so they favor the fortunate a bit less). But many other planners take the position that their task is to serve the majority of the community or to serve a general public interest so far as they can identify it. These planners might also argue that a single community cannot do much about broad equity issues such as the distribution of income. Therefore such matters are best left to higher levels of government, whose means are more commensurate with the dimensions of the problem.

WHO DOES SOCIAL PLANNING?

If one asks practicing planners or planning educators whether there is a separate field of "social planning" within the planning profession, one will get answers ranging from "Of course" to "What is it?" If a planner is doing something that is directly devoted to a social end, say administering community development funds for day care or an adult literacy program, clearly that planner is engaged in "social planning." The great majority of planners, however, do not spend most of their time on explicit social planning. But almost any decision that involves how sizable blocks of land will be used or how sizable sums of public money will be spent has social implications. In that sense, any planner who is conscientious and competent is engaged in social planning.

SUMMARY

All planning decisions of significant size have social implications, for example, in connection with housing, economic development, and the environment. Whether or not one recognizes a separate field of social planning, it is clear that the social side of what at first might appear to be purely physical or design questions should not be ignored.

NOTES

1. *Establishment* is a commonly used but not precise term referring to that collection of individuals and institutions who constitute the main decision-making power within a society.
2. See William J. Wilson, *The Truly Disadvantaged,* University of Chicago Press, 1987.
3. The county, population of about 870,000, contains a total of 43 municipalities, of which Yonkers is the largest.
4. Whether clearing substandard units is always desirable is an arguable matter because it may have the effect of tightening the market and thus driving up rents. However, the removal of substandard units was standard Urban Renewal doctrine when Yonkers public housing was built.
5. In this decision the Supreme Court rejected the previous "separate but equal" doctrine and ruled that segregation itself, regardless of whether or not the facilities were otherwise equal, was unacceptable.
6. For the reader interested in the Yonkers case, the best source is *The New York Times Index,* for *The Times* has covered the case regularly since Judge Sand's 1985 decision. The two longer quotes come from Lynda Richardson, "U.S. Judge Lets Yonkers Try its Housing Approach," *The New York Times,* July 16, 1992, Sec. B, p. 6. *The Journal of Planning Education and Research,* vol. 8, no. 3, Summer 1989, pp. 177-196, contains a symposium on the case. The 1985 court decision is *United States* v *City of Yonkers et al.,* Civil Action #80 CIV 6761 LBS (S.D.N.Y. November 20, 1985). For a brief account, see *Journal of American Planning Association,* vol. 25, no. 4, Fall 1986, p. 387.
7. Pierre Clavel, *The Progressive City: Planning and Participation, 1969-1984,* Rutgers University Press, New Brunswick, NJ, 1987, chap. 3.

SELECTED BIBLIOGRAPHY

ANDERSON, WAYNE, F., FRIEDEN, BERNARD J., and MURPHY, MICHAEL J., EDS., *Managing Human Services*, International City Managers Association, Washington, DC, 1977.

BOLAN, RICHARD S., "Social Planning and Policy Development, " in *The Practice of Local Government Planning*, International City Management Association, Washington, D.C. 1979.

CLAVEL, PIERRE, *The Progressive City: Planning and Participation, 1969-1984*, Rutgers University Press, New Brunswick, NJ, 1987.

HOWE, ELIZABETH, "Social Aspects of Physical Planning," in *The Practice of Local Government Planning*, 2nd ed., International City Management Association, Washington, D.C. 1988.

CHAPTER 8

THE COMPREHENSIVE PLAN

In the planning literature one sees the terms *comprehensive plan, general plan,* and *master plan* used synonymously. At present, the term *comprehensive plan* is in most common use and will be used here for all three. It refers to the most basic plan prepared to guide the development of the community. One characteristic of the comprehensive plan is that physically it covers the entire community. Another defining characteristic is that it is long-term. Comprehensive plans typically have time horizons in the range of 20 years. Recall from Chapter 4 that having a plan may be optional or required by the state.

THE GOALS OF COMPREHENSIVE PLANNING

Since municipalities differ, the following list of goals will not be complete nor will every item necessarily apply to every community. Because the goals overlap, another writer might list them differently yet cover the same ground. Note that all of the following goals, with the possible exception of the last, readily fit within the rubric of the phrase, *health, safety, and public welfare,* cited earlier in connection with the police power.

1. *Health.* Achieving a pattern of land use that protects the public health is a well-established planning goal. One aspect might be prohibiting densities of development that threaten to overload water or sewer facilities. In

areas that do not have public water and sewer facilities, it may mean spacing houses far enough apart to prevent leakage from septic tanks from contaminating well water. It may involve separating industrial or commercial activities that produce health hazards from residential areas. It may mean banning certain types of industrial operations from the community entirely.

2. *Public safety*. This goal may manifest itself in numerous ways. It might mean requiring sufficient road width in new subdivisions to ensure that ambulances and fire equipment have adequate access in emergencies. In Sanibel, Florida, it means limiting the total number of housing units so that in the event of a hurricane the entire population can be evacuated within the minimum warning time over the one causeway that connects Sanibel to the mainland. Many communities have flood plain zoning to keep people from building in flood-prone areas. At the neighborhood level it might mean planning for a street geometry that permits children to walk from home to school without crossing a major thoroughfare. In a high-crime area it might mean laying out patterns of buildings and spaces that provide fewer sites where muggings and robberies can be committed unobserved.[1]
3. *Circulation*. Providing the community with adequate circulation is an almost universal goal of comprehensive planning. This means a system of streets, and perhaps also parking facilities, that make possible an orderly, efficient, and rapid flow of vehicular and pedestrian traffic. In many communities it also means providing for adequate public transportation. Planning for transportation and planning for land use are intimately connected, as is discussed in detail in Chapter 13.
4. *Provision of services and facilities*. An important part of most comprehensive planning efforts is determining the location of facilities such as parks, recreation areas, schools, social services, hospitals, and the like. In addition to planning for facilities, it is also important to plan for a pattern of land use that facilitates the provision of public services like police and fire protection, water, and sewers. For example, the pattern of land use will affect the feasibility and cost of providing public water and sewer facilities. The location of housing relative to the location of schools will determine whether children can walk or must be bused to school.
5. *Fiscal health*. There is a relationship between the pattern of development and the fiscal situation of the community. Any development will impose some costs on the community (fire protection, police protection, traffic, education, etc.). Similarly, virtually any development will generate some revenues for the municipality (property taxes, sales taxes, user charges, and other fees of one sort or another.) Some uses will yield surpluses and others deficits. Generally speaking it is not very difficult to predict in advance which uses will do which. In fact, a fairly substantial literature exists on this very point.[2] Many communities will plan for a pattern of land use that will hold down property taxes. But there are limits here. Does the community have the right to practice "fiscal zoning"—the use of its land-use controls to keep out types of housing or economic activity that are likely to cost the community more for additional services than they yield in additional revenue? In one form or another that question has been the

subject of much litigation, and the courts have not spoken with total unanimity on the matter. How much can a community limit the building of multifamily and small-lot single-family housing to control costs? The answer is far from clear, and many an attorney has earned a comfortable living litigating such points.

6. *Economic goals*. In thousands of communities economic growth or maintenance of the existing level of economic activity is an important goal. There is a link here with the fiscal goal, but there may be other motivations as well, most notably providing employment for community residents. Thus a community may seek to develop a pattern of land use that provides for commercial and industrial sites, provides good access to such sites, and facilitates supplying utilities to such sites. Other steps that a municipality may take to stimulate its own economic development are discussed in Chapter 14.
7. *Environmental protection*. This goal is an old one but, as noted in Chapter 16, has become much more common since the 1960s. It might involve restrictions on building in wetlands, steep slopes, or other ecologically valuable or fragile lands. It might involve preservation of open space, ordinances to control discharges into water bodies, prohibition or limitations on commercial or industrial activities that would degrade air quality, and so on. In a broader sense it may be connected to planning for the entire pattern of land use.
8. *Redistributive goals*. Some planners of the political left would argue that a goal of planning should be to distribute downward both wealth and influence in the political process.[3] In a limited number of communities, planners have been able to bend the planning process in that direction. For an account of a few such instances see the book by Pierre Clavel cited in Chapter 7.

THE COMPREHENSIVE PLANNING PROCESS

We noted that in the last several decades the comprehensive planning process has changed from one in which a small group handed down a plan to one in which the making of the plan is a participatory process open to the citizens of the community. This section describes a participatory plan-making process. The process will vary from one community to the next, but we can identify some common elements.

1. *A research phase*. One cannot plan very much if one does not have a sense of the present state of events and their probable future direction. Thus many comprehensive planning efforts begin with a data-gathering and forecasting phase.
2. *Clarification of community goals and objectives*. At some point, preferably early in the process, there has to be some agreement about what the plan is intended to achieve. This is not to say that agreement will ever be total.
3. *A period of plan formulation*.
4. *A period of plan implementation*.
5. *A period of review and revision*.

Though presented as a sequence, these items necessarily overlap. Insights gained in the research phase will reveal problems that affect the goals the community will formulate. But selecting goals will affect what things a community should know about itself. Thus the research and the goal-formation processes tend to proceed simultaneously. Research regarding population trends might lead to formulating the goal of acquiring an additional 500 acres of parkland. That, however, suggests another research question. Is a purchase of that magnitude realistic in terms of the community's revenues and other fiscal obligations? Thus steps 1 and 2 inevitably become intertwined.

Plan formulation tends to go on simultaneously with the first two processes. As one formulates a plan, one needs facts and estimates. The results of research modify the plan, and the needs of plan formulation tend to set the research agenda. Then, too, plan formulation tends to modify goals. That is, detailed planning tends to make plain the real implications of generalized goals, at that point goals may become modified. A community might set forth as a goal "an adequate supply of housing at affordable prices." It is hard to be against such a goal: Few will come out publically in favor of an inadequate supply of housing at exorbitant prices. But when the community looks at the matter in detail, it may not like what the goal implies. Getting prices down to affordable levels may mean building smaller housing units at higher densities than present residents want. Perhaps getting prices down will also necessitate a major increase in housing supply, with attendant increases in traffic congestion and overcrowding in the schools. In short, when the community begins to look at the consequences that flow from its goal statements, it may decide to modify the goals. Implementing the plan may also cause modification as it becomes apparent what can and cannot actually be accomplished.

In the following sections we discuss the five steps in detail.

Planning Research

Most planning agencies, particularly those large enough to have a research staff, make considerable use of planning-related research. One common type of study is the "population forecast." One cannot plan without knowing for whom one is planning, which means having some notion of how many people there will be in the community. It also means knowing something about the likely age structure of the population. One hundred people over the age of 65 make very different demands on the community than do 100 elementary school students.

There are various approaches to forecasting population. A very common technique is the "cohort survival" method. In this, the present population is mathematically "aged" into the future. In other words, each age and sex group, or "cohort," of the population is advanced through time and its numbers adjusted for expected mortality.[4] Adjustments are made for net migration (moves in minus moves out) and births. The advantage of the technique is that it presents a detailed picture of the structure of the population rather than just an estimate of the total number of people. The mathematics are relatively simple, but getting good results is another matter. At the city, county, or town level the big differences in growth rates between places are largely due to differences in net migration. Predicting net migration accurately is difficult. At the present it is much more an art than a science.

Then, too, there is an interaction between plans and forecasts that can muddy the waters.[5] For example, in many suburban areas housing stock is the factor that limits population growth. One might estimate net migration on the basis of past performance, but how does one factor into these estimates the effect on population of land-use control ordinances that will be enacted next year and that may be affected by this year's forecasts? In the ideal planning situation the making of plans and the making of forecasts should be related. However, such coordination between planning and forecasting is not easy to achieve.

Another basic study is the "land-use inventory."[6] Such a study generally begins with a mapping of existing land uses (residential, industrial, commercial, educational, recreational, etc.). The study also characterizes the undeveloped land in the community in terms of suitability for different uses. The common practice is to prepare a series of maps that show various land characteristics such as slope, whether or not the land lies within flood plains, whether the soil is well or poorly drained, and so on. In many cases the land-use study will also contain some information on land ownership, generally distinguishing between public, private, and institutional holdings at a minimum. The study might make further distinctions such as identifying major private or major institutional holders. The study may also identify some infrastructure characteristics, particularly water and sewer service. It may also identify some legal characteristics such as zoning categories, though these are less permanent characteristics than most of the other items mentioned.

In recent years the traditional paper map for the recording of the results of land use studies has been supplemented by electronic mapping systems generally referred to as Geographic Information Systems (GIS). In a GIS data is stored in digital form. For example, to store a contour line in the system a technician moves a digitizer along the contour line of a topographic map and the path of the digitizer is converted to digital form and stored in the computer's memory. Information such as assessed values, zoning category, census data and the like can also be entered as numbers or letters. The electronic data base can then be used to quickly produce a variety of maps, calculations, tabulations, etc. The map that might take a draftsman days to draw can often be produced by a GIS system in a few minutes.

At the regional scale GIS systems now make use of data from satellite cameras. Images, both from within and outside of the visible light spectrum, come from the satellite camera in digital form and are then "imported" into the GIS data base. Among the material that can be mapped from such digital information are vegetation, topography, hydrology, land use, temperature, and some geologic features. The level of precision is not usually sufficient for small parcels but may be quite adequate work at a large scale and costs only a small fraction of what it would cost if obtained by conventional methods.

Beyond these two most common studies are a host of others that may or may not be done, depending on needs and resources. If economic development is an issue, an economic base study may be undertaken. The degree of sophistication may vary from a simple listing of present employers to a highly sophisticated econometric model built by a consultant specializing in such work.[7]

Almost all comprehensive plans contain a circulation element. Thus studies of traffic flow characteristics along the existing transportation network are likely to be done early in the master planning process. Some general estimates of future traffic flows based on projections of future population and employment are also likely to be made at an early stage. There is a strong interaction between transportation planning and land-use planning in general. The amount of development in an area is a major determinant of the number of trips that will be made to and from the area. On the other hand, the accessibility of the area will in large measure determine how much development takes place there. Thus land use and transportation planning should go hand in hand.

Studies related to infrastructure are common. Water supply and the provision of sewer service are key elements in shaping the pattern of development in growing areas. Studies may be done to determine potential area for sewers and areas that are amenable to the development of public water supply systems. In areas where public water and sewer supply are not feasible, studies may be devoted to ground water supply and quality.

Soil characteristics may come in for serious study at this point. If an area is not to have sewers, for whatever reason, the amount of development that can occur may be limited by the capacity of the soil to absorb safely household wastes from septic tanks. This capacity will vary greatly with soil types. A sandy, well-drained soil may safely permit building several houses per acre. On the other hand, soil with a great deal of clay or bedrock lying close to the surface may require an acre or two of land per house for safe disposal of household waste. Soil characteristics such as shrinkage and swelling as the water content of the soil changes will affect the types of buildings that can be constructed. The capacity of the soil to absorb water will affect flooding potential, an important consideration in considering the type and intensity of development appropriate for the area.

Many communities will do recreation studies as part of a master plan, looking at population, recreational preferences, existing facilities, and so forth. In general, such studies will inventory the present supply of facilities and services. Future needs will be estimated by applying standards (so many acres of parkland per 1000 of population, for example) to the municipality's projected population. The gap between the existing situation and the estimated need is used to establish preliminary planning goals. Unmet recreational needs may also be estimated by survey techniques, simply asking residents what facilities they use and what additional facilities they would like to have.

In recent years planning at the comprehensive stage has taken on an increasingly fiscal cast. Many municipalities have found themselves under strong fiscal pressures, the sources of which are various. In many central cities and some small communities, expenses have risen while the tax base has stagnated. In other cases tax bases have grown substantially but municipalities have still faced very strong resistance to tax increases, as in California's Proposition 13 and comparable successful initiatives in other states. In the early and mid-1980s the Reagan administration's New Federalism, mentioned in Chapter 5, further increased fiscal pressures on local governments by reducing the flow of funds from the federal government. Those pressures continued under the Bush administration and will probably continue under President Clinton, for the need to deal with the federal deficit will probably preclude major new grants to localities for other than a few specialized purposes.

Fiscal studies generally involve analyzing trends and making forecasts of expenditures, revenues, and tax rates. Studies may also be done to estimate capital needs and capital costs. The basic purpose of a fiscal study is to permit the community to match the other elements of the plan to the resources it is likely to have to carry out the plan. In fact, it is very difficult to say whether a community's planning is realistic if one does not have some knowledge of its financial underpinning.

Formulating Community Goals

Ideally, goals should be formulated with a knowledge of the essential facts of the situation, a knowledge of the limitations under which the municipality operates and a realistic view of the options open to the community. In fact, developing a realistic view of financial, legal, political, physical, and other limits and possibilities is the ultimate purpose of the research component described previously.

The purpose of the process should be to formulate a limited number of goals that have a definite meaning, do not contradict one another excessively, and represent an implementable consensus of the community's populace.

The planning agency's role in this process might be to provide a forum for discussion (organizing meetings, obtaining media coverage, setting up advisory committees), providing facts and laying out options, and synthesizing and articulating the results of the discussions and deliberations. The process of setting goals should be an open one in that citizens and groups who have a stake in the outcome of the planning process are not excluded. This consideration is not just a matter of fairness or legal requirement but also of practicality. Those who have had a hand in shaping a plan are more likely to support it than those who have not.

Formulating the Plan

When the baseline studies have been done and agreement has been reached on goals, the work of formulating the plan can begin. In larger communities the plan is generally drawn up by the municipality's planning agency. In smaller communities, it is very common for the plan to be drawn up by a planning consultant and submitted to the community for approval. In the best of such situations, there is continuous interaction between consultant and community so that the plan suits the community and the citizens have a commitment to it because of their involvement in its formulation. In the worst of situations, there is little interaction, the consultant delivers the plan, takes his or her money, and is heard from no more. Often the citizens will have little commitment to the plan, and it will achieve little, other than, perhaps, fulfilling federal or state funding requirements.

The first step in plan formulating is generally to lay out a variety of options. For example, assume one goal is to reduce traffic congestion in the central business district. One option might be widening or straightening the main street; another, constructing a bypass; a third, building a parking structure and eliminating on-street parking on the main street; a fourth, converting from a two-way to a one-way street system; a fifth option, some combination of these.

When all of the reasonable options have been listed, it is time to begin considering their respective costs and merits. This is sometimes referred to as "impact analysis." One item to be considered is cost and what the costs would imply for the municipal tax rate and debt structure. That study might look not only at direct costs of the options but also indirect considerations such as estimated effects on sales tax receipts and property values. Another item would be the number of households and businesses affected by the taking of property and the disturbance of traffic flow during the construction phase. The planners would also examine the relative degree of improvement in traffic flow that might be expected from each option. Aesthetic and urban design issues would also be examined. When the impact assessments have been made, the preferred option can be selected. Note that it is often a good idea to bring affected parties such as the property owners, residents, and businesspersons into the impact assessment and option-choosing process. First, they are likely to make useful contributions. Equally important, no plan can be implemented without political consent, and politics is "the art of compromise." It is better to resolve differences early around a conference table than later in the courts or the press.

This impact analysis can be done for each main element of the plan. At some point, however, their combined effects must also be examined to know whether the total cost is manageable. If it is not, choices among goals must be made.

Implementing the Plan

As noted earlier the two most powerful tools for carrying out the physical side of the plan are capital investments as called for in the capital budget and land-use controls. Capital investments in roads, public facilities, and utilities create the basic conditions that permit development, which land-use controls then shape and channel. Ideally, capital investments and land-use controls should be consistent with one another and with the comprehensive plan. If coordination is lacking, the results are likely to be disappointing. For example, if capital investments create powerful pressures for development in areas that the comprehensive plan shows as developing at low density, the stage has been set for litigation and controversy. The end results are likely to be very different from what the community envisioned.

Review and Updating

Almost inevitably, community development will not unfold quite as envisioned in the master plan. Planning is anything but an exact science. Rather it is an art still in the early stages of development. Then, too, the pattern of development is shaped by all sorts of forces that are beyond community control and in many cases beyond prediction. Thus after a short time the community will not be quite where the plan would have it, and so some replanning is necessary. Just as a navigator takes frequent bearings and replots of the course accordingly, the community checks its situation periodically and adjusts its plans. But the analogy is not entirely accurate. In the case of the navigator, the destination remains the same. In the case of the municipality, the goals themselves may change as realities both inside and outside the municipality change.

For the plan to be effective over a long term, periodic review is essential. Ideally, the review applies to all of the major plan elements. First, it applies to the data base. Population, revenues, expenditures, housing stock, employment, and so on inevitably will not evolve exactly as predicted. Large disparities may show up fairly quickly. Consider, for example, cost projections for capital expenditures. A major component of debt service for capital expenditures is the cost of borrowing money, that is, interest rates. In 1981 the interest rate on long-term bonds was about twice what it was in early 1993. No one doing capital budgeting for a municipality in 1981 could have predicted that drop nor could anyone doing capital budgeting now predict what interest rates will prevail a few years hence.

Beyond updating the data base on which the plan rests, it is also necessary to update goals and strategies. Ideally, the municipal government should have a commitment to updating the plan at regular intervals. If this cannot be done the plan loses its relationship to reality. If government personnel and citizens perceive the plan as a static and increasingly irrelevant document, it soon loses its political force. The act of updating it keeps it relevant and keeps the body politic committed to it. It also institutionalizes planning as an activity within the community.

Maintaining community interest in the planning process is one of the most important tasks of any planning agency. Thus public relations is a major aspect of successful planning. The planning director's speech to the Rotary Club, the appearance in a high school civics class, and the periodic newspaper article on what the city or town or county is planning for solid waste disposal or parklands or economic development or housing or downtown business district revitalization are all part of that effort. In one southern town, planning agency staff have appeared in first- and second-grade classrooms and run six- and seven-year-old children through a simple experience in laying out a neighborhood. That may not pay off for a quarter of a century, but then planning is a long-term process.

SUMMARY

The comprehensive plan covers the entire municipality and has a long time horizon, typically 20 years or so. The goals of a municipality's comprehensive planning process might include issues of health, public safety, public welfare, circulation, provision of services and facilities, fiscal health, economic development, and environmental protection.

Since the 1920s when comprehensive plans (also called master plans and general plans) became common, the process has changed considerably. Early plans usually were prepared by a small "nonpolitical" group, and the role of the body politic was to support the plan with appropriate legislation and funding. In the years since World War II the process has become much more participatory. The modern planner is likely to facilitate and provide technical expertise for a community-wide planning process rather than simply prepare the plan for community acceptance.

The comprehensive planning process can be divided into five major stages.

1. Research
2. Clarification of goals and objectives
3. Plan formulation
4. Plan implementation
5. Review and revision

Though shown as separate steps, there is much overlap between them because what is learned in one step may cause the community to modify what was established in a preceding step. For example, the detailed work of plan formulation, by revealing the true costs of pursuing a particular goal, may cause the community to reconsider its goals. We also noted that periodic review of problems and progress and subsequent updating of the plan are essential if the plan is to continue to affect the development of the community.

NOTES

1. For a discussion of the relationship between design and safety from crime, see Oscar Newman, *Defensible Space*, The MacMillan Company, New York, 1972.
2. See, for example, George Sternlieb et al., *Housing Development and Municipal Costs*, Rutgers University Center for Urban Policy Research, New Brunswick, NJ, 1973; or Robert W. Burchell and David Listokin, *The New Practitioners Fiscal Impact Handbook*, Rutgers University Center for Urban Policy Research, New Brunswick, NJ, 1985.
3. Norman Krumholz, "A Retrospective on Equity Planning: Cleveland, 1969–79," with comments, *APA Journal*, vol. 48, no. 2, Spring 1982, pp. 163–84.
4. For an introductory account of this technique and comparison with other techniques, see F. Stuart Chapin and Edward J. Kaiser, *Urban Land Use Planning*, 3rd ed., University of Illinois Press, Urbana, 1979, chap.6.
5. The terms *forecast* and *projection* are often used interchangeably, but to demographers there is a distinction. The former implies the analyst's best estimate of what will happen. The latter is simply a mathematical exercise showing what the population will be if certain rates of birth, death, in-migration, and out-migration obtain. A forecast can be proven right or wrong by future events. But a projection, if the mathematics is done correctly, cannot be said to be wrong.
6. See Chapin and Kaiser, *op. cit.*, or either the 1968 or 1979 edition of *Principles and Practice of Urban Planning* for a further discussion on the land-use inventory.
7. For an account of different types of community economic studies see John M. Levy, *Urban and Metropolitan Economics*, McGraw-Hill Book Co., New York, 1985, chap. 4.

SELECTED BIBLIOGRAPHY

Branch, Melville C., *Continuous City Planning*, John Wiley, New York, 1981.

Chapin, F. Stuart, and Kaiser, Edward, J., *Urban Land Use Planning*, 3rd ed., University of Illinois Press, Urbana, 1979.

Kent, T.J., *The Urban General Plan*, Chandler, San Francisco, 1964.

So, Frank S., and Getzels, Judith, *The Practice of Local Government Planning*, 2nd ed., International City Management Association, Washington, D.C., 1988.

So, Frank, S., Irving Hand, and Bruce W. McDowell, *The Practice of State and Regional Planning*, The American Planning Association, Chicago, 1986.

CHAPTER 9

THE TOOLS OF LAND-USE PLANNING

The comprehensive plan, as described in the preceding chapter, largely pertains to the pattern of land use. In this chapter we discuss the tools available to the municipality to effectuate its land-use plans. Essentially there are two broad categories of direct actions by which a community can shape its land-use pattern.

1. *Public capital investment*. Public investment in facilities such as schools, municipal buildings, hospitals, and parks determines the use of publicly owned land. Public capital investment also exerts a powerful influence on the development of privately owned land. The construction of roads, water lines, sewer lines, schools, public buildings, and the like changes the pattern of that which is economically feasible and thus changes private decisions. In most communities the major share of land is privately owned and the major share of investment in land development and structures comes from private sources. Thus it is this second effect, the shaping of the market in which private investment decisions are made, that produces the most important and most visible effects on the land-use pattern. Unlike regulations, which are subject to legislative change and legal challenge, public capital investments exert their effects over very long time periods. A road or bridge or sewer main, once constructed, will exert its effect on the pattern of development for decades to come.
2. *Public control over the use of privately owned land*. Since government cannot directly compel anyone to invest or build, the control takes the form of

permitting some things and forbidding others. If one says that in the absence of controls all things would be permitted, then public control of land use essentially amounts to a set of prohibitions, even if some of the regulations are couched in terms of uses permitted. The controls may apply to the type of activity or the amount of activity. Or certain actions may be prohibited unless certain other actions are taken. For example, the community's land-use controls might stipulate that a certain size of commercial building may not be erected unless a certain amount of parking space is provided.

PUBLIC CAPITAL INVESTMENT

In general, accessibility is the main determinant of the development potential and, hence, of the value of land. Very high accessibility can produce spectacular land values. For example, in late 1985 a building site several blocks from the White House in Washington, D.C. sold for somewhat over $1,000 per square foot, or well in excess of $40 million per acre. Nor was this the first such sale recorded in the city. What gives the site its extraordinary value is its accessibility—its close proximity to commercial, residential, and government activity and the ease with which it can be reached from the region's highway and mass transit networks. Where land values have been studied for municipalities, the peak figure occurs in the most central (most accessible) point and then tails off peripherally. Smaller peaks occur at points of increased accessibility, for example, where two major roads intersect or at a mass transit stop.

Land values largely determine the intensity of development. It costs much more per square foot of usable floor space to build a high-rise than a low-rise building. The primary reason for building high is to economize on an expensive resource, namely, land. And the reason the builder wants to build there at all is because the high accessibility will be capitalized in a higher selling price or rental rate. For example, rental rates for new office space in midtown Manhattan in the mid-1980s were in the range of $50 per square foot per year. Thus floor space equivalent to that of a typical suburban single-family house rented for the better part of $100,000 per year. It is the accessibility of the site that makes it possible to obtain such rentals. In an economic sense, the height of a city's skyscrapers is largely due to the existence of a regional transportation system that makes those buildings accessible to the population of the region. To a considerable extent land values also determine the type of use for the site. For example, with these sorts of land values, the city does not need to zone out manufacturing activity, for virtually no manufacturer would want to locate there. Accessibility is simply not that important in most manufacturing operations.[1]

The point is that accessibility is shaped by public investment in roads, mass transit, parking facilities, and the like. The pattern and the timing of public capital investment can thus be an extremely powerful shaper of the land values and hence of the manner in which land is used. In the Washington, D.C. region mentioned before, the building of the subway system, the Washington Metro, has created hundreds of millions of dollars in land values. Simply the announcement that a metro stop is planned for a certain location has been sufficient to set off waves of real estate speculation for a radius of several blocks around the site.

One can see the relationship among accessibility, land value, and land development in the suburbs. The results may be even more striking than in an urban area because a single capital investment can produce much larger changes in accessibility than can investment in an already-developed area. The construction of a stretch of road in, let us say, a developing suburban area may quite literally create hundreds of millions of dollars in land values. In fact, the land values created may be a large multiple of the value of the public investment. For example, in a typical major metropolitan area, land that is suitable only for single-family housing might be worth $20,000 an acre. Land suitable for office or shopping center development might be worth $200,000 an acre. The difference in suitability may simply be road access. If access is by a low-capacity two-lane road, only low-density residential development is feasible. If access is by a high-capacity four-lane road, commercial development is feasible. Suppose replacing a mile of two-lane secondary road with a mile of four-lane highway costs $5 million. Its construction creates a strip of land a mile long and 500 feet deep on either side, which is now suitable for commercial development. Taking these numbers at face value, 121 acres have now increased in value by $180,000 apiece, for a total increase in land values of roughly $22 million—four and one-half times the cost of the public investment.[2]

The placement of road intersections is a major determinant of land values. A favorite location for a shopping center, for example, is at the intersection of two major roads. Convenient access means more customers and more customers mean a higher volume of business. That means higher rentals for the shopping center developer. The importance of intersections as a determinant of commercial location can be seen easily by driving along the beltway surrounding a major metropolitan area. Simply note the clumps of commercial development that occur where the beltway intersects radial routes from the core of the region.

In urbanized areas where parking is difficult, parking structures can produce drastic increases in accessibility. Such structures are often a centerpiece of downtown revitalization projects. The city of White Plains in New York State boasts a large mall, known as the Galleria, in its urban renewal area. The mall, completed in the early 1980s, has annual sales of over $200 million. To make the site attractive for a mall location, the city built a 2,800-car parking structure at a cost of $29 million. The city's 3 percent sales tax applied to annual sales in excess of $200 million should quickly recoup the outlay on the parking structure. Without the increase in accessibility provided by the structure, the mall would not have been possible. Instead, most of the retailing development that went into the mall would have gone into surrounding suburban areas, where large amounts of at-grade parking space are available.

Public capital expenditures for water and sewer facilities are major shapers of residential and commercial growth. Without such facilities development is limited to the relatively low densities permitted by dependence on wells and septic tanks. Just as investment in transportation facilities can produce drastic increases in land values, so, too, can investments in water and sewer lines.

One could go on in the same vein. Public capital investments in airports, shipping facilities, parklands, and educational facilities all shape land values and through that mechanism shape the pattern of development.

LAND-USE CONTROLS

Although land-use controls are not quite so powerful a shaper of land use as is public capital investment, they are still extremely important. Their development and implementation often constitute a major share of the work effort of many planning agencies. In the minds of many citizens, land-use controls are almost synonymous with planning.

In this section, we discuss subdivision controls, zoning, and several miscellaneous types of land-use controls.

Subdivision Regulations

Subdivision regulations are an old form of land-use control going back to the early nineteenth century and before.[3] Their enforcement is an exercise by the municipality of the police power within the framework of the powers granted it by the state.[4] Subdivision regulations control the manner in which blocks of land over a certain size may be converted into building lots. Before building lots can be sold or the owner can make improvements, the municipality must approve a plat (map) of the property. The ordinance will require at a minimum that the map show streets, lot lines, and easements (rights of way) for utilities. It also will stipulate what improvements must be made before building lots can be sold or before building permits may be granted. Thus the community is able to compel the property owner to construct internal streets that link up in a satisfactory manner to the municipality's street system and meet its standards for width, safety, and quality of construction. Similarly, it can compel the developer of the property to provide sewer, water, and drainage facilities that meet the community's standards. Subdivision requirements frequently also stipulate that certain land dedications (or payments in lieu of such dedications) be made to the community by the developer for schools, recreation, or community facilities. Many subdivision regulations require that the design of the subdivision be compatible with the municipal master plan and zoning ordinance, thus reinforcing the implementation of these documents. In general, subdivision regulations apply to residential development, but in some communities they also govern some commercial and industrial subdivisions.

Though less well known than zoning laws, subdivision regulations give communities substantial power to ensure that new residential development meets community standards and fits in with community development plans. Like zoning laws, subdivision regulations are subject to litigation and various forms of political pressure. Like the power to zone, the power to regulate subdivision can be abused. For example, some communities seeking to screen out less affluent people have enacted subdivision regulations that impose unnecessarily high costs on builders, thus blocking the construction of moderately priced housing.

Zoning Ordinances

The best known form of land-use control is the zoning ordinance,[5] which is generally prepared by the community's planners or planning consultant. The document acquires its legal force when the community's legislative body passes a measure adopting it. Generally speaking, there are two parts to the zoning ordinance. The first part is a map that divides the community into a number of zones. The map is sufficiently detailed so that it is possible to tell in which zone(s) any given parcel of land lies. Most commonly, all of the community is zoned. However, there are some cases, particularly nonurban counties, in which part of a community is zoned and part is not. The second part is the text, which specifies in considerable detail what may be constructed in each zone and to what uses structures may be put. The box on pp. 112–13 shows some of the details for one zoning classification in Fairfax County, Virginia.

Among the items generally specified by the ordinance are the following:

1. *Site layout requirements.* These may include, among other things, minimum lot area, frontage and depth, minimum setbacks (minimum distance from structure to front, side, or rear lot line) maximum percentage of site that may be covered by structure, placement of driveways or curb cuts, parking requirements, screening requirements, and limits on the size or placement of signs.
2. *Requirements for structure characteristics.* These may include maximum height of structure, maximum number of stories, and maximum floor area of structure. The last is often cast in terms of floor area ratio (FAR), which indicates a maximum permissible ratio of floor area to site area.
3. *Uses to which structures may be put.* In a residential zone the ordinance might specify that dwellings may be occupied only by single families and then proceed to define what constitutes a family. The ordinance might also enumerate certain nonresidential uses permitted in the zone such as churches, funeral homes, and professional offices. In commercial zones the ordinance will generally specify which uses are permitted and which are not. For example, in a manufacturing zone the ordinance might specify that sheet metal fabrication operations are permitted but that rendering operations are forbidden.
4. *Procedural matters.* The ordinance will specify how it is to be determined whether building plans are in conformity to the zoning ordinance. (A common arrangement is that the building inspector shall make such determination and must deny a building permit application if they are not.) The ordinance will generally also specify an appeals procedure by which an applicant can apply for relief. In many communities the initial appeal authority is vested in a special body generally referred to as the Zoning Board of Appeals. When this is not the case the review process is often assigned to the planning board or to the municipal legislative body.

The Popularity of Zoning Zoning has been, since shortly after its inception, by far the most common means by which communities have sought to control land use. What accounts for its popularity? The answer is quite simple. It has considerable power to achieve goals that the community favors, and it is almost free. No compensation need be paid to property owners for reductions in property values caused by limitations imposed by the zoning ordinance on the type or intensity of use permitted. The only costs to the municipality are administrative and legal expenses.

In principle, the same effects could be achieved by exercise of the power

THE INGREDIENTS OF A ZONING ORDINANCE

This material is reproduced from a Fairfax County, Virginia, zoning ordinance. Note that it specifies permitted uses, site geometry, ground coverage, and building height and bulk.

Commercial District Regulations
Part 5 4-500 C-5 Neighborhood Retail Commercial District

4-501 Purpose and Intent The C-5 District is established to provide locations for convenience shopping facilities in which those retail commercial uses shall predominate that have a neighborhood-oriented market of approximately 5000 persons, and which supply necessities that usually require frequent purchasing and with a minimum of consumer travel. Typical uses to be found in the Neighborhood Retail Commercial District include a food supermarket, drugstore, personal service establishments, small specialty shops, and a limited number of small professional offices.

Areas zoned for the C-5 District should be located so that their distributional pattern throughout the County reflects their neighborhood orientation. They should be designed to be an integral, homogeneous component of the neighborhoods they serve, oriented to pedestrian traffic as well as vehicular. The district should not be located in close proximity to other retail commercial uses.

Because of the nature and location of the Neighborhood Retail Commercial District, they should be encouraged to develop in compact centers under a unified design that is architecturally compatible with the neighborhood in which they are located. Further, such districts should not be so large or broad in scope of services as to attract substantial trade from outside the neighborhood. Generally, the ultimate size of a C-5 District in a given location in the County should not exceed an aggregate gross floor area of 100,000 square feet or an aggregate site size of (10) acres.

4-502 Permitted Uses

1. Accessory uses as permitted by Article 10.
2. Business service and supply service establishments.
3. Churches, chapels, temples, synagogues and other such places of worship.
4. Drive-in banks, limited by the provisions of Sect. 505 below.
5. Eating establishments.
6. Fast food restaurants, limited by the provisions of Sect. 505 below.

7. Financial institutions.
8. Offices.
9. Personal service establishments.
10. Private schools of general education, private schools of special education.
11. Public uses.
12. Quick-service food stores, limited by the provisions of Sect. 505 below.
13. Repair service establishments.
14. Retail sales establishments.
15. Telecommunication exchanges.

4-506 Lot Size Requirements

1. Minimum lot area: 40,000 sq. ft.
2. Minimum lot width: 200 feet
3. The minimum lot size requirements may be waived by the Board in accordance with provisions of Sect. 9-610.

4-507 Bulk Regulations

1. Maximum building height: 40 feet
2. Minimum yard requirements
   - A. Front yard: Controlled by a 45° angle of bulk plane, but not less than 40 feet
   - B. Side yard: No Requirement
   - C. Rear yard: 20 feet
3. Maximum floor area ratio: 0.50
4. Refer to Sect. 13-108 for provisions that may qualify the minimum yard requirements set forth above.

4-508 Open Space 20% of the gross area shall be landscaped open space

4-509 Additional Regulations

1. Refer to Article 2, General Regulations, for provisions which may qualify or supplement the regulations presented above.
2. Refer to Article 11 for off-street parking, loading and private street requirements.
3. Refer to Article 12 for regulations on signs.
4. Refer to Article 13 for landscaping and screening requirements.

of eminent domain or by contract between municipality and property owner. But either of those courses would necessitate major expenditures by the municipality.

In fact, contracts between governments and property owners have been used to affect land use. Generally, the contract is referred to as an easement. This is an agreement by the property owner to forego some right(s), for example that of subdividing the property or developing it in some way, in return for a payment. For example, Suffolk County, New York, has made widespread use of easement purchases to maintain land on eastern Long Island in agricultural use. Such a device can be highly effective, for the purchase of an easement provides an ironclad guarantee to the community in the form of an enforceable contract that property will not be used in a manner proscribed by the easement. In other places a similar effect has been obtained through special tax treatment. In many jurisdictions where farmland preservation is a goal, land that is kept in agricultural use is taxed very lightly compared to the tax that must be paid on it when it is placed in some other use.

Easements and special tax treatment are used in most states, but their application is quite spotty compared to the near universality of zoning. The explanation is cost.

The Effectiveness of Zoning How effective is zoning in shaping land use? There is tremendous variation among communities, ranging from almost totally ineffectual to highly effective. Zoning may be quite effective in a growing area where the land-use pattern is not yet fully determined. Here zoning can shape the urban pattern by blocking or limiting growth in some areas and thus, in effect, diverting it to other areas. Often in prosperous developed areas in which there is substantial pressure for change in land use, zoning may be effective in preventing or moderating that change. For example, a prosperous inner suburb might successfully resist the transformation of single-family neighborhoods to multifamily neighborhoods even though the economics of the local housing market favor such a change.

On the other hand zoning may be relatively ineffective in older urban areas where the land-use pattern is essentially established and where growth forces are not very powerful. Zoning, by itself, cannot address the redevelopment problem, for controls cannot compel anyone to invest in an area. Zoning may also be relatively weak if the community is so eager for investment that it readily adjusts its zoning to suit developers' preferences. At the other end of the scale, zoning may be weak, or even absent altogether, in semirural or rural areas where the residents do not see much need for public control of land use.

One key to effective zoning is synchronization between land-use controls and public capital investment. It is possible for a community's land-use and capital investment policies to be at odds with one another and for each to undermine and frustrate the intent of the other. For example, a capital investment program might generate forces for a type or intensity of development that is proscribed by the zoning. In this case either the capital investment has been partly wasted or economic pressures will force changes in the zoning. Conversely, if the zoning permits levels of development that are not supported by necessary road and utility investment, nothing is likely to happen. The community will have the pleasure of watching its industrial or office zone grow weeds year after year.

The Limitations of Zoning Zoning is limited by both economic and legal forces. If the value of land in a use permitted by zoning is very much lower than the value of that land in a use that is forbidden, but for which a market exists, property owners have strong motivation to try to change the zoning. They may expend substantial funds on litigation, or they may devote substantial effort to building a coalition of forces to lobby for zoning change. If the community is hungry for jobs and additions to its tax base, property owners may indicate to the community that if it does not show flexibility their capital will be invested in some other community, which can recognize a good thing when it sees it.

To illustrate, consider a prototypical suburban scenario. Mr. X owns 100 acres of vacant land, which has been in his family for generations. He rents the land to a local farmer for enough money to cover his property taxes. The land in its present low-density residential zoning category has a market value of $10,000 per acre. A major real estate developer perceives that were development of condominiums at medium density possible, the land would be worth $50,000 an acre. She approaches Mr. X and offers to buy an option. Specifically, for $10,000 Mr. X gives the developer the right to buy the property for $12,000 an acre at any time during the next two years. If the developer chooses not to exercise her option, Mr. X still keeps the $10,000.

Having purchased the option, the developer now tries to change the zoning. If her attorney tells her that the municipality's zoning of the property is on weak legal ground, she may approach the municipality, indicate to them why their position is weak and suggest that compromise is in everyone's best interest. The municipality's legal position may be weak for any number of reasons. Comparable parcels in other areas of the municipality may be zoned for more intensive development. Hence a charge of inconsistency (of treating equals unequally) may be leveled against the municipality in court. Perhaps the zoning of the property is not in keeping with the municipality's master plan. If so, the developer can argue that the zoning is capricious and inconsistent. Perhaps the developer can show that on the basis of utilities, access, and other considerations, the property could sustain far more development than the zoning permits. In this case she can argue that the present zoning cannot be justified on the grounds of the police power.

Hearing all this and after due consultation with its planning consultant and attorney, the municipal officials might well decide that compromise is indeed in order. In that case they may recommend to the municipality's legislative body that it amend the zoning ordinance. If the community is adamant and the developer is sure the legal situation favors her, she might bring suit and begin to fight it out in court. The issue might be settled in court or, seeing the tide of legal battle flowing against, it, the municipality might decide to compromise.

Alternatively, the developer can take a less confrontational tack. She can engage a local planning consultant to design a condominium development for the site. The consultant comes up with a proposal nicely presented with attractive drawings and a model. The consultant performs a set of calculations referred to as a "fiscal impact analysis," which shows that for every additional dollar the project will cost the community for services its property taxes and other contributions to the municipal treasury will amount to two dollars. (See box on property taxes on page 117.) The developer's proposal does not fail to note how many dollars of retail sales within the community will be made to condominium residents, a point that will not be lost on the municipality's business community. The report will also note how many years of on-site construction labor the project will require, a point that should bring in a few more allies, particularly if construction employment has been soft recently.

At this point the report is presented to the town government with appropriate newspaper and other publicity. When public hearings are held, the developer or her spokespeople adopt a posture of reasonableness and conciliation. If there are aspects of the plan to which the citizens object, they will listen attentively and endeavour to find mutually satisfactory compromises. For example, if residents worry that the development will send too many children to the local schools, she may offer to build more studio and one-bedroom units and fewer two- and three-bedroom units, thus bringing in more childless couples and fewer large families. The relationship between unit size, household size, and number of school-age children has been studied often and can be predicted fairly well. Thus this sort of "architectural birth control" can often be practiced quite effectively[6]

The developer will also structure the proposal to give herself room to be reasonable. If she would have been satisfied with building six units to the acre, the initial plan may call for eight units to the acre. This leaves her something that can be given up after suitable protest but without causing real pain.

The developer may or may not obtain a zoning change in this manner. Any planner who has spent some time working in the suburbs has seen such situations go both ways. The point, however, is that the party desiring the zoning change has numerous avenues open.

The playing of zoning games is hardly limited to those on the private side of the fence. Municipalities often zone substantial amounts of land in economically unrealistic categories. This suits the municipal interest quite well, for it gives the municipality a bargaining position that it would not have were the land zoned realistically in the first instance.

In the late 1970s the town of Harrison, New York, became the home of Texaco's corporate headquarters. The headquarters imposes few costs on the town yet provides a very substantial property tax payment, clearly a very desirable situation from the town's perspective. How did it happen? The site was 100 acres or so of land zoned for single-family houses on two-acre lots. As it happened the site was in a developing commercial area and was close to the intersection of two interstate highways. It clearly had potential for much more valuable use than low-density single-family housing. The fact that a zoning change was needed before economically realistic development could occur put the town in a strong negotiating position. First, the town was able to turn away any development proposal it did not like. In addition, the need for a rezoning gave the town the power to insist on a variety of site features, like below-ground parking and deep setbacks, on which the corporation might not otherwise have chosen to spend money.

Similar comments might be made with regard to residential development. If a rezoning is necessary to permit the building of multifamily housing, the municipality might say no to a low-income housing proposal but yes to a structurally similar development intended for affluent singles—a form of discrimination that few if any courts would sustain were it written into the zoning ordinance.

Zoning and the Courts As noted in earlier chapters, zoning and other land-use controls all involve some abridgement of the rights of ownership. Specifically, they may limit the intensity or the manner in which real property may be used. Over the years the courts have expanded the amount of abridgement that they will tolerate. But the boundary between what is and is not permissible is

PROPERTY TAXES AND ZONING

Zoning cannot be fully understood without some understanding of property taxes. Property tax collection by local governments and school districts in the 1990s totalled $149.8 billion and accounted for approximately three-fourths of all local tax collections.[7] Given the size of that number, few significant zoning decisions are made without considering the property tax implications. Here, very briefly, is how property taxes are levied. The municipality maintains a ledger (either on paper or electronically), referred to as the property tax roll. Each property in the municipality appears on this roll. Generally speaking, the roll will have one column for "land" and another column for "improvements," the latter essentially meaning structures. In each column is recorded the assessed value of the land or structure. The value, determined by the municipality's assessor, presents his or her estimate of the value of the property were it to be sold at market in an "arm's length" transaction.[8] Some municipalities have "full value assessment." Other use fractional assessment. Where fractional assessment is used, all properties should be assessed at the same fraction of market value.[9] The municipality and other taxing jurisdictions each have a property tax rate that is applied to the assessed value of the property to determine how much tax is owed. For example, if the tax rate is $2.50 per 100 of assessed value and the property is assessed at $50,000, the tax owed is $50,000 × 2.50/100 = $1,250.

For the municipality as a whole the equation is tax base × tax rate = tax yield. Tax base in this equation is the sum of all of the assessed values on land and improvements subject to tax.[10]

The tax rate is set to produce the amount of revenue needed. If a given development will bring in more in taxes than it will cost in additional municipal expenses, either (1) the same level of municipal services can be maintained for a lower tax rate or (2) a higher level of services can be maintained at the same tax rate. If the costs of servicing the new development exceed the tax revenues it will yield at the current tax rate, those relationships are reversed.

Though this discussion is cast in terms of a municipal tax rate, there may actually be several property taxes within a given community. For example, properties in a town located within a county and having an independent school district may be subject to a town tax, a county tax, and a school tax. In some suburban areas, where the structure and responsibilities of government are not so large as in a city, and where a large percentage of all households have school-age children, the school tax constitutes the majority share of the total tax burden.

The property tax has been subject to a barrage of criticisms over the years. However, it remains in universal use. For one thing it is easy to administer and enforce. The assessor assesses and the Receiver of Taxes sends the bill. If the property owner fails to pay the bill, the municipality can foreclose the property and sell it at auction to recover the back taxes. It is probably the hardest tax to evade. The individual or business may be able to conceal some income, but no one has yet figured out how to hide a house or a factory.

somewhat ambiguous and may vary from place to place and court to court, leaving much room for controversy and litigation.

At one time it could have been said that the question was one of adjudicating the rights of the property owner versus the rights of nearby property owners and of the community. That is still a major part of the matter, but in the last two decades or so another major element has been introduced.

The new element is consideration of the rights and interests of those who are neither members of the community nor own property in it. In a very general sense the inclusion of these formerly outside parties can be considered a part of the national concern with civil rights, which has characterized the last few decades. Admitting that outsiders have a valid interest in the community's land-use controls gives them standing to bring suit, a standing that formerly they did not have.

Numerous suits have been brought against suburban communities for zoning land in an overly restrictive way, many, for example, by restricting development to single-family houses on large lots. Such controls may make it almost impossible for low-income people to live in the community. Opponents of suburban zoning often claim that policies that kept out lower-income persons also constituted racial discrimination. The argument was that since blacks have, on average, significantly lower family income than whites, keeping out low and moderate income families had the de facto effect of excluding blacks. A number of suits against suburban communities have been brought by minority group organizations for this reason.

The courts have also recognized as a legitimate concern the question of regional housing needs. The argument, very generally, is that if the municipality is part of a metropolitan region it is part of the regional housing market. If it limits the amount of housing that may be built within its borders, it tightens housing markets and drives up housing costs within the entire region. The courts have thus overturned some suburban zoning ordinances on the grounds of regional housing needs.

For example, in 1965 the Supreme Court of Pennsylvania stated in overturning an ordinance that established a 4-acre minimum lot size requirement,

> It is not difficult to envision the tremendous hardship, as well as chaotic conditions, which could result if all the townships in this area decided to deny to a growing population sites for residential development within the means of at leasta significant segment of the population.11

In 1975 in what is perhaps the best known of the exclusionary cases, *Southern Burlington County NAACP* v *Township of Mount Laurel* (generally referred to simply as *Mt. Laurel*), the Supreme Court of the State of New Jersey found that the entirety of the township zoning ordinance acted to exclude whole classes of individuals (including the poor and minorities) and was invalid under the New Jersey state constitution. The township was instructed to prepare a new ordinance that remedied these defects.

In 1983 a group of cases, collectively referred to as *Mount Laurel II*, pushed the judicial interpretation of a community's areawide obligations even further.[12] Among the points made in the decision were that all municipalities have an obligation to provide housing opportunities for their low- and moderate-income residents, that any municipality that permits economic growth must create opportunities for provision for some portion of the region's low- and moderate-income housing needs, and that municipalities must take steps to make certain that said housing opportunities are realistic.

The court noted certain concrete steps municipalities could take to bring themselves into conformance with the court's findings. One of these was the removal of all present legal barriers to the building of low- and moderate-income housing. This could be interpreted to mean that any land-use control regulation that increases costs but cannot be shown to be essential to maintenance of the public health, safety, and welfare would not be sustainable. Thus regulations involving matters of minimum street width subdivisions, buffering from adjacent land uses, and like the might be struck down. So might exactions, discussed later in this chapter. Tax abatement for low- and moderate-income housing, inclusionary zoning devices, and set asides might also be required to bring a community into conformance with *Mt. Laurel II*. The term *set aside* means that the law would require that in housing developments over some specified size, a given percentage of units be set aside for low- and moderate-income renters or purchasers. Conservatives might argue that this provision translates into saying that such purchasers would be subsidized by either the developer or the buy-ers of the units not set aside. They might argue that such subsidization should be done explicitly by the taxpayers as a whole rather than implicitly by the developer or by other buyers. Nonetheless, that was the position the court took.

Finally, the decision discussed the possibility that large blocks of land might have to be zoned for low-cost housing types such as mobile homes. (Mobile homes are anathema to many affluent communities both because they are considered to represent a lower standard of housing than conventional units and because, due to their lower cost, they carry low assessments and thus pay less property tax.)

After the Mt. Laurel decisions it appeared that the exclusionary walls would be breached in many New Jersey suburbs. One hundred and thirty-five suits, most of them by developers, were brought against suburban communities. Many of these suits were close to settlement when a series of events leading to what has been termed *Mt. Laurel III* occurred.

In 1985, responding to pressures from suburban towns that were facing legal challenges based on *Mt. Laurel II* the New Jersey Legislature passed the Fair Housing Act. The act established a Council on Affordable Housing. Towns could submit to the council plans for supplying their fair share of low-cost housing. When the plan was accepted by the council, the town would then be protected from Mt. Laurel-type lawsuits. Rather than have the courts acting as a sort of statewide zoning authority, an administrative function that does not typically fall within the scope of the judiciary, a statewide administrative agency was set up to deal with the process.

The new procedure seems entirely sensible. The decision-making authority is placed by legislative act in an administrative agency and the issue of housing can be addressed on a coordinated, statewide basis. However, the actual effect, and apparently the intent as well, was to shield communities from the impact of *Mt. Laurel II.* The deadlines for meeting the agreed-upon goals were very long. In addition, a community could buy its way out of up to half of its low-cost housing obligation by contracting with another community that agreed to provide the units. For example, a wealthy suburban town that did not want low-cost housing could make payments to a less-affluent urban area that would agree to provide low-cost units, and in fact, at least one such contract has been made. One might ask what is wrong with allowing such contracts. The city gets housing funds, which it needs, and the town, for a price, is allowed to continue a housing policy that the majority of its residents want. The answer depends on one's viewpoint. If one simply wants to see low-cost housing built somewhere within the state, nothing is wrong with it. If, on the other hand, one feels that restrictive zoning perpetuates a pattern of segregation, which is inherently wrong, then one must object to the contract. In fact, one could argue that the contract voids the basis of *Mt. Laurel I.*

For the moment it appears that the Mt. Laurel story is at an end. In 1986 a builder challenged the constitutionality of the Fair Housing Act, for as noted, the act prevented builders and others from suing a community once the community's plans had been accepted by the council. In *Hills Development Co.* v *Township of Bernards* (*Mt. Laurel III*) the Supreme Court of New Jersey rejected the developer's claim and held the law to be constitutional.

The Mt. Laurel story illustrates how difficult it is for a court to make a community or a group of communities do what their citizens are adamantly opposed to doing. In the Yonkers case, the community resisted by all sorts of foot-dragging. In this case the communities resisted by making an ingenious and successful end run around the courts through the legislature.

The exact limits of the zoning power fluctuate from time to time and from place to place, for in the final analysis the zoning power is what the courts say it is. A conservative judiciary will, in general, limit the zoning power more than will a liberal judiciary. In 1987 planners were alarmed by a Supreme Court decision in a California case. In *First English Evangelical Church of Glendale* v *County of Los Angeles,* the Court ruled that if landowners had been unduly burdened by land-use control regulations they were entitled to compensation by the regulating agency or body of government. Previously, it was understood that a property owner might sue to have a regulation overturned, but it was not required that compensation be paid for losses incurred while the regulation was in force. The Court based its decision on the last line of the Fifth Amendment, "nor shall private property be taken for public use, without just compensation." Undue restriction of use in the Court's view meets the meaning of the word *taken* and thus requires compensation.

Subsequently, when the case was remanded (sent back) to a lower court, it was found that a "taking" had, in fact, not taken place. Thus the church was not entitled to compensation. However, given the Supreme Court's decision, there exists the possibility that a body of government or regulatory agency might be forced to pay a large judgment in the event that its actions were found to constitute a taking. The thought that local governments might have to pay large judgements to litigants who could show that the zoning power had been overused was intimidating. Many planners feared that this possibility would make local governments far more timid in their efforts to control land use. But so far there have been no such judgements.

A more recent judgement authored by the very conservative Supreme Court Justice, Antonin Scalia, in *Lucas* v *South Carolina Coastal Council* also created some alarm among planners regarding the matter of compensation. The litigant, Lucas, had purchased two beachfront lots on a South Carolina barrier island with the intention of constructing single-family houses on these lots. Two years later the South Carolina legislature passed the Beachfront Management Act. Enforcement of the act prevented Lucas from building and thus rendered his $975,000 investment essentially worthless. In the decision which sent the case back to the state court for a finding of facts the Supreme Court instructed the South Carolina courts to award damages to Lucas unless they were able to find that construction of the houses would have been prohibited by previous legislation unrelated to the Beachfront Management Act. Again, the specter of the payment of compensation was raised. In one comment the decision suggested that the one circumstance in which there might not need be compensation even though the owner was deprived of all use of his or her property was if use might violate established nuisance law. This suggested the legal basis of zoning might be pushed back to depending upon nuisance law. Land-use controls as in *Hadacheck* v *Sebastian* (see Chapter 5) originally sprang from nuisance law but had long since gone past these simple origins to a much more extensive conception of the public good. Whether or not the Lucas case will have a measurable effect on land-use control remains to be seen. Inquiries by the author among practicing planners suggest that they are interested but not overly concerned. The point is that land-use law is continually evolving and at its edges there will always be some uncertainty.

Recent Developments in Zoning

Zoning, as we have described it, is a rather crude instrument. It essentially tells one what cannot be done but it cannot make anything happen. Its very rigidity may lead to less than optimal results. For example, a zoning district permits a certain amount of development on a given sized lot within a given zone. If some lots are developed to the full amount permitted but other lots remain vacant or are developed to only part of the permitted intensity of use, the entire district may function quite well. On the other hand, if every lot is developed to full intensity, the congestion, traffic, and noise may be overwhelming. Yet one can hardly tell a property owner that he or she cannot develop as much as the owner of an adjacent plot simply because the other property owner was first. Such a position would carry little weight in court.

"Zoning saturation" studies have frequently shown that if a municipality were developed to the full extent that the zoning allowed, its population would be several times the present level and often far beyond what most people would regard as tolerable. New York City, the most densely developed city in the United States, has had populations in the 7 to 8 million range in recent decades. Some time ago a saturation study showed that if built up to the full extent the law allowed, the city could have a population of some 30 million. A saturation study of Yonkers, New York, with a population of about 200,000 on 20 square miles, showed that the city could, if fully developed as the law permitted, have a population of about 600,000. This would make it the most densely populated city in the United States. In neither case is there any chance of such development occurring.

The disparity between actual and theoretical development does raise questions about the precision of zoning. Clearly, zoning is not determining the structure of the city in fine detail if there is that much space between the overcoat of zoning and the body of development.

Zoning is vulnerable to the criticism that it severely limits the freedom of the architect and site designer and may thus lower the quality of urban design. Rules promulgated to cover the substantial blocks of land are likely to be suboptimal with regard to particular sites or parcels.

Zoning has also been criticized for producing a sterile environment through an excessive separation of uses. The most influential criticism of this sort was delivered in the 1960s by Jane Jacobs.[13] She argued that by excessive separation of uses—residents here, stores there, and so on—planners produced urban environments that were sterile and sometimes dangerous as well. They were sterile because of lack of diversity, she argued, and dangerous because the single-use street was deserted for some part of the day and thus an inducement to crime.

One area of which Jacobs spoke very highly is the West Village, part of Manhattan's Greenwich Village. The West Village is a very old area, characterized by small and frequently irregularly shaped blocks and a great mix of uses. Most buildings are not very high, typically four to six stories. The same block will often contain a fine-grained mix of residential and nonresidential uses. In fact, many buildings have stores, restaurants, coffee houses, and the like on the ground level with apartments above. The area has a very lively street life, which lasts into the late hours of the night, and it is generally considered a desirable neighborhood in which to live. Jacobs argued that the sort of diversity, charm, and activity that characterize the West Village is often blocked by the rigidities of zoning and the planners' excessive concern with separation of uses. She argued that the area owed much of its charm to the fact that it had developed before the advent of zoning (zoning is not retroactive). Though she is not a planner herself, Jacobs' criticism made many planners rethink the intent and effects of zoning on neighborhoods.

Making Zoning Flexible In an effort to make zoning a finer instrument, a variety of techniques have evolved in recent years. These, in general, are designed to make land-use controls more flexible and more negotiable. The basic idea is that increasing flexibility allows the parties of land-use negotiations to bargain and thus realize what economists sometimes refer to as "the gains of trade."

Let us say that the land developer would like to do something that is prohibited under the letter of the zoning law. On the other hand the municipality might like the developer to do something that he or she is not legally required to do. Why not have an ordinance so structured that some bargaining is possible? Presumably we need not fear that the municipality will lose out. If, on balance, the trade is not in the municipal interest, the municipality will not consent. A number of newer techniques follow.

"BONUS" OR "INCENTIVE" ZONING Many communities will allow increased residential densities if developers will include some units earmarked for low- and moderate-income tenants. For example, the law might stipulate eight units to the acre in a particular zone but permit an increase to ten units if 15 percent of the units are reserved for low- and moderate-income tenants. The developer gets the scale economies of denser development and the community moves a bit closer to meeting its low- and moderate-income housing goals.

Many cities have made comparable arrangements with regard to office

Glass-roofed arcade connects two parallel streets at AT&T headquarters building in Manhattan. Some willingness to deviate from the rigidities of traditional Euclidean zoning is usually necessary to achieve an interesting and unusual result like this.

development. The zoning ordinance might stipulate a certain height limitation but permit additional height or stories above that if the developer will provide certain amenities at ground level—for example, a plaza in front of the entrance to the building, a direct entrance to a subway station, or a "vest pocket" park or sitting area.

TRANSFER OF DEVELOPMENT RIGHTS The intent of transfer of development rights (TDR) is to concentrate development in areas where it is wanted and to restrict it in areas where it is not. To do so, a sending and a receiving area are designated. Property owners in the sending areas who do not develop their properties to the full extent permitted by the law may sell their unused rights to property owners in receiving areas. The technique might be used to preserve open space, to limit development in an ecologically fragile area, or to achieve historic preservation goals, among others.[14]

One might ask, "Can this not be done with conventional zoning simply by permitting high densities in some areas and low densities in other areas?" In a literal sense the answer is yes. However, in a practical sense the answer may be no. Assume that the intent of the community master plan is to keep development very sparse in a particular area. If one simply zones that way, say a minimum lot size of 10 acres for a single-family house, one may have imposed large losses on property owners. Perhaps when the property owners bring suit the municipality will be sustained and perhaps it will not. Even if it can win in court, the municipality has created a constituency opposed to the plan. On the other hand if it gives the property owners salable development rights, both their motivation and grounds for suit are eliminated or, at least, much diminished. If the municipality wishes to preserve old buildings in a historic zone, one way to do it is to let the property owners there have salable development rights. When they sell their development rights to property owners in an area where the municipality wants growth (the receiving area), they are no longer motivated to tear down their old buildings, for having sold their rights, they no longer can redevelop at higher densities.

Won't the property owners in receiving areas object to, in effect, having to buy off owners in sending areas? Not necessarily, for if purchasing development rights is not profitable, receiving area property owners will not purchase them. Presumably a market in development rights will develop, the price moving to a position high enough to motivate owners in the sending area to sell yet low enough to make purchase profitable for property owners in the receiving area.

For the municipality, the technique, like zoning itself, is essentially costless. The payments to some property owners come not from the municipality's taxpayers but from other property owners. Whether the municipality's taxpayers may ultimately pick up some of those costs in the form of higher rents and higher prices is another issue.

The technique is relatively new and a matter of some controversy. One way in which it could be misused would be if development rights were to be assigned to areas where the actual possibility of development is small. If one gives the owner of a property in "bottomless swamp" or "rocky promontory" a development right, it is just a windfall since he or she could not realistically expect to develop anyway. But a developer in an area of high land values may still be willing to buy that right. The possibilities for abuse seem to be considerable.

INCLUSIONARY ZONING In inclusionary zoning, developers who build more than a specified number of units must include a certain percentage for low- and moderate-income households or some other designated group of households.[15] It differs from the incentive or bonus approach in that the inclusion of low-and moderate-income units is not discretionary. It is the same, however, in that it shifts some of the costs of housing such households to the developer. He or she, in turn, is likely to shift at least some of that cost to the other buyers or renters.

PLANNED UNIT DEVELOPMENT Planned unit development (PUD) has been widely used in the last decade or two and its popularity is still growing. PUD techniques vary from one ordinance to another but a prototypical ordinance might work like this: The entire community is zoned in a conventional (Euclidean) manner. However, the law provides that a property owner with a minimum number of acres, say 20, has the option of applying to develop his or her holdings as a PUD. In this case the property is subject to a different set of controls. The density permitted may or may not be the same as that stipulated by the conventional ordinance and the uses permitted may or may not be the same. The entire site plan will be reviewed as a single entity under a review process specified by the PUD ordinance.

Some PUDs are entirely residential and some are entirely commercial. In many cases, however, PUDs contain a greater mix of uses than would be permitted under conventional ordinance. Many PUDs that are predominantly residential contain some retailing. Numerous PUDs contain a mix of residential and commercial uses. Because the entire site plan is reviewed at one time, the benefits of mixing uses can often be had without risking some of the disadvantages. For the urban designer, PUDs can offer vastly more room for creative and innovative design than can be had working under a conventional ordinance.

An economic advantage of the mixed-use PUD is that the various uses tend to strengthen each other. For example, the Glenpointe development in Teaneck, New Jersey places 292 condominium units, a 350-room hotel and conference center, 461,000 square feet of office space, 72,000 square feet of retail space, several restaurants, and some miscellaneous uses on the site of about 50 acres. According to the development's planner,

> Much of the beauty of the planned mix . . . is that each on-site activity center creates support and demand for every other activity center. Office tenants, for example, help support the hotel, restaurants, health club, and shops. . . . In turn, these amenities help to create a demand for the office space. Thus mixed use feeds on itself and creates its own symbiotic universe.[16]

One problem with many business areas, both downtown and suburban, is that they become almost deserted in the evening. Mixing residential uses with commercial uses tends to make the area more active in the evenings and on weekends. The mixed-use concept can make both commercial and residential areas more interesting and less sterile. Essentially, the PUD technique places some power to control land use in the hands of a review board or other group, which looks at that particular site design. It allows a degree of innovation and flexibility that cannot be obtained under an ordinance and procedure that have to fit all cases within the municipality.

CLUSTER ZONING Cluster zoning is another technique intended to free the site designer from the rigidity of conventional Euclidean zoning while still letting the community retain control of the overall effects of the development. Cluster ordinances, which generally apply to residential development, permit the building of houses on smaller lots, provided the space thus saved is used for community purposes. For example, the zoning ordinance might specify a minimum lot size of $\frac{1}{2}$ acre but cluster provisions permit building houses on $\frac{1}{4}$ acre lots provided that the completed development shall have no more houses in it than it could contain if developed with $\frac{1}{2}$ acre lots. The space saved is to constitute an open area accessible to all residents of the clustered area, often maintained by a residents' association.

Cluster zoning is very popular with planners. It permits the preservation of substantial blocks of open space and reduces development costs in a number of ways. Placing houses closer together reduces the amount of road surface and utility line required per house. Smaller lots also mean less money spent per house on grading and other site preparation costs.

Although clusters have been built in many communities, the cluster plan is often greeted with some public suspicion. The community sees the combination of closely spaced houses and open space blocks and suspects that sooner or later the open blocks will fill in with housing. In point of fact, the permanency of the open blocks is easily protected with appropriate legal documents at the time the cluster development is approved by the community, but it can be difficult to convince a community that this is the case. With the passage of time and the accumulation of favorable experience, community resistance to clustering should diminish.

PERFORMANCE ZONING Performance zoning is relatively new and not yet in widespread use, but its use is growing and it holds much promise. Performance zoning codes stipulate what may or may not be done in terms of end results instead of giving detailed regulations on the exact form of development. It can be regarded as an attempt to achieve the same goals as conventional zoning but in a more flexible manner.

In Largo, Florida, a conventional or Euclidean system of 20 zoning districts has been replaced by a performance zoning system. Five residential categories differ only by the maximum density permitted. Intensity of use is controlled by limits on floor area ratio (FAR) and the percentage of site that can be under impervious cover. There are no limitations on the type of housing, side yard and rear yard setback, and building height.

Four separate commercial zones have been created. The zones are distinguished by their FAR and impervious cover requirements. For the downtown zone, a FAR of .90 and impervious cover of 100 percent are permitted. On the other hand, for the flood-prone zone, the FAR is limited to .12 and impervious cover to 40 percent. There are no height limitations and no side or rear yard setback limitations. Gail Easley, the community's assistant director of planning, explains the decision to go to performance zoning in this way.

> One particular problem [with conventional zoning] . . . is the proliferation of zoning districts. As the number of districts grows, it becomes harder to distinguish among them; as the distinctions become less clear, the purpose of any given district becomes blurred, and the formal distinctions become less defensible. An increase in the number of districts results in fewer uses being permitted in any single district. This decreases the likelihood that an available site will be properly zoned to meet a developer's needs. This, in turn, increases the probability that a zoning amendment will be sought.[17]

DEVELOPMENT AGREEMENTS The state of California passed enabling legislation that permits municipal governments to enter into "development agreements." These essentially bypass the existing zoning, though they must be in conformity with the comprehensive plan. The contract between the developer and the municipality specifies what the developer may do and also what he or she is required to do within the project area. The developer benefits by being permitted to do things not permitted under the existing zoning. The developer of a multistage project also gets the security of knowing that zoning and other controls will not change during the development process or "build out" period because the municipality is legally bound by the contract. The municipality benefits by being able to require things of the developer as a condition for signing the contract.

In the case of Colorado Place, an office development in Santa Monica, the developer benefitted by being allowed to build above the 45-foot height limit specified in the zoning ordinance and also by being able to include in the project some uses not permitted under the existing zoning. The city benefitted by requiring that the developer build some off-site low-income housing and provide and maintain a small on-site park and a child-care center. Both city and developer evidently saw themselves as being better off under this arrangement than under the traditional Euclidean approach, for both parties entered into the contract freely.

EXACTIONS In recent years a variety of charges, often referred to as exactions, have become part of the land development scene. Numerous communities have resorted to exactions, sometimes quite substantial, for permission to develop. In some cases they are required only if there is to be a rezoning or zoning variance. In other cases the exactions are charged for development within the existing zoning law. In general, the exaction is charged to pay the costs that the development is presumed to impose on the community.

In some cases the exaction may be for a very closely related cost, for example, nearby road construction needed to carry the additional traffic new commercial development will generate, or school or park construction that the population of a new residential development will require. In other cases, the connection may be more tenuous. For example, San Francisco decided that new office development increases the demand for housing in the city. Since 1981, builders of office structures of over 50,000 square feet of floor space must earn housing credits by either building new units themselves or contributing funds to housing rehabilitation or affordable housing projects. Typically, the exaction runs to about four dollars per square foot of office floor space. The number of credits is based on estimates of how many square feet of office floor space are required per worker, what percentage of the San Francisco office work force lives in the city, and how many workers live in the average housing unit. A somewhat comparable amendment was added to the Boston zoning ordinance in 1983.

The exaction technique may be used to achieve similar results as incentive zoning. For example, Hartford, Connecticut, instead of using exactions, offers density bonuses to office developers who build downtown housing. Clearly, both the exaction and the bonus or incentive technique will work best where growth pressures are strong and land availability limited. If the community is hungry for development it will not burden developers with the additional costs of exactions, nor will density bonuses be particularly attractive. Rather than demanding exactions, the municipality may be offering subsidies or tax abatements.

These examples do not by any means exhaust the variations on traditional land-use controls. Rather, they are a sample of how planners in recent years have added elements of bargaining, negotiation, and flexibility to the land-use control process.

Other Types of Local Land-Use Controls

In addition to subdivision and zoning regulations already described, there are a number of other controls that are not quite so widely used. Several are described here very briefly. In some cases these other types of controls are part of the zoning ordinance. In other cases they are separate.

SITE PLAN REVIEW Typically, site plan review applies to developments over a certain size. The community vests its planning or zoning agency with the responsibility of reviewing site plans for such considerations as internal circulation, adequacy of parking, and buffering from adjacent uses, and makes site plan approval necessary before building permits may be granted. Site plan review does not supersede zoning but rather is another layer of review. It is applied to commercial and multifamily development.

ARCHITECTURAL REVIEW In architectural review, building plans are reviewed for essentially aesthetic considerations. For example, a town with a predominantly colonial style of housing might review to ensure that new development would be in keeping with the established style. Architectural boards of review are often found in older, upper-income residential areas where preservation of the past and of property values weighs heavily on the minds of those who make up the body politic. They are also frequently found in new planned developments. Often they will become involved in what seem like small issues, for example, whether or not a satellite dish antenna can be placed in a yard or what colors are acceptable for the exterior of houses in the development. Feelings about review boards vary. Although some applaud them for maintaining the visual quality of the town or development, others may regard them as a dead hand of conformity, which achieves no major purpose and may actually make the community a less interesting and stodgier place. There is a tradeoff. If one wants variety and spontaneity, one must risk some instances of bad taste.

HISTORIC PRESERVATION Many communities designate historic districts and then exercise control over development within them. Controls may dictate that new structures must be in a style and at a scale consistent with the past. They may dictate that when repairs and remodeling are done, historic appearance must be maintained. For example, if adjacent buildings have old-fashioned leaded glass windows with small panes, a modern window would not be permitted. In some cases community development funds may be used to assist property owners in maintaining the historic character of their buildings. Often responsibility for historic preservation will be vested in the planning agency. In other cases some or all of the responsibility will lie with a separate agency, such as New York City's Landmarks Commission. Although there is historic preservation activity in all parts of the United States, it is probably most prominent in New England, where a great deal of colonial era development remains to be preserved. Historic preservation is unquestionably motivated by a love of the past, but in areas where tourism is a major part of the economy there is economic motivation as well.

State, Regional, and Federal Controls on Land Use

The assertion of some control over land-use decisions by higher levels of government, primarily state governments, has been termed "the quiet revolution." The phrase comes from the title of a book by Bosselman. In the introduction he states,

> The *ancien regime* being overthrown is the feudal system under which the entire pattern of land development has been controlled by thousands of individual local governments, each seeking to maximize its tax base and minimize its social problems, and caring less what happens to all others.
>
> The tools of the revolution are new laws taking a wide variety of forms but each sharing a common theme—the need to provide some degree of state or regional participation in the major decisions that affect the use of our increasingly limited supply of land.[18]

Much of the force for such laws comes from environmental concern, which as noted earlier, increased greatly during the 1960s. In general, land-use controls emanating from higher than local levels of government do not supersede local controls. Rather, they add another layer of control. The applicant must satisfy not only the local jurisdiction but also the higher-level jurisdiction. Higher-level controls are found most often where there is a clear public interest beyond the borders of the single community. Very often, also, higher-level controls are found in environmentally fragile areas, for example, coastal zones.

Why Is Higher-level Control Necessary? One might ask why higher-level control of things like wetland development is necessary. After all, do not individuals as residents of a locality have the same degree of concern with environmental quality that they have as citizens of the state?

Part of the answer comes down to the issue of "externalities." [19] If a community grants a rezoning that enables a shopping center development to obliterate a wetland, the fiscal gains of that development accrue to that community. So, too, may many of the employment gains. At least some of the increases in land values are also likely to be captured by community residents. On the other hand, the unfavorable effects may be largely felt outside the community. For example, increased stormwater runoff may have no significant effect on the community but may cause flooding downstream. Expanding the level of decision making to the state reduces the chance that gains for a few individuals will swing the decision and increases the chance that widespread effects will be given their due weight.

The other big reason for higher-level controls over environmental issues is technical complexity. Most local governments do not have the time and expertise necessary to do the data gathering and analysis required for good decision making. A variety of state level controls on development are mentioned in Chapters 15 and 16.

COMBINING CAPITAL INVESTMENT AND LAND-USE CONTROLS

Since capital expenditures and land-use controls are the two principal methods by which municipalities may affect land use, the enlightened community strives to coordinate them so that they reinforce each other. Capital investment in transportation, public facilities, and infrastructure can shape the land market. Land-use controls can permit what is desired and, within the sorts of limitations described, prohibit what is not desired.

For example, consider the case of Westchester County, New York's so-called "Platinum Mile." The name was chosen by local promoters with the usual lack of modesty that attends such christenings, but it is reasonably accurate. Along the border between two municipalities, the city of White Plains and the town of Harrison, is a massive collection of corporate headquarters and other office development. All told these facilities provide many thousands of jobs and constitute hundreds of millions of dollars of tax base. It is the sort of complex that most communities would be delighted to have. How did it come into being?

First, the basic preconditions were there. One fact was a good location within the New York metropolitan area. This made it possible to capture firms that were moving out of New York City but wished to remain within the metropolitan area. It also made the area attractive to firms that were moving into the metropolitan area but did not need a Manhattan location, with its very high costs. Second, the Westchester County–Fairfield County (Connecticut) area was attractive to corporations for "quality of life" reasons, such as parklands, good public schools, and an attractive pattern of development. Many corporate decision makers thus favored the location because they themselves wanted to live there. The same "quality of life" factors also made it easy to recruit managerial and technical personnel.

But given the existence of these preconditions it was still necessary to turn them into reality. At the end of the 1950s White Plains had been planning to build a bypass along its border with the town of Harrison. The road was to have been called the White Plains Arterial. At this time the interstate highway system was being laid out by the federal government in coordination with the states. City officials were quick to see the opportunity. They dropped the concept of the bypass and pushed to get the pathway of the arterial incorporated into the design for the interstate highway system.

The city was successful and interstate highway I-287 now runs between the two municipalities, increasing accessibility and greatly increasing land values and the potential for development. The crucial role of capital investment is clear. However, we note that 90 percent of the cost of building the interstate came from the federal government. Only the remaining 10 percent was paid by state and local governments. State and local funds were used to construct wide service roads on either side of the interstate and a series of overpasses across the interstate linking these roads. Thus a motorist leaving the interstate at one of the several interchanges would have quick access to any point in the entire strip.

Having used capital investment—whether local funds or "foreign aid" from the federal government—to create demand on the site, it now remained to control land uses to produce a desirable result. The strategy used was to permit that which was desired and to prevent other land uses from blocking desirable development. Clearly, zoning to permit office development was one part of the strategy. Requiring large minimum sites for development prevented land from being chopped up by small, scattered development. Where there is good highway access in a relatively populous area, retailing is clearly a possibility. But strip commercial development would foreclose the possibility of office park development, both by eating up road frontage and also by creating an environment that was not attractive to corporate headquarters and other "upscale" office development. That eventuality was blocked by simply prohibiting retail uses. Thus, as a gardener favors the plants he or she wants by weeding out others, land-use controls were used to favor particular types of development by blocking other types. The combined effect of coordinated capital investment and land-use control was highly successful.

SUMMARY

Two major ways in which a municipality may shape its pattern of land use are through (1) public capital investment and (2) legal controls over the use of privately owned property.

Public capital investment creates specific public facilities, which make up part of the total land-use pattern. Most important, however, public capital investment shapes the market in which the development of privately owned land occurs.

Subdivision regulations essentially control the manner in which raw land is subdivided and placed on the market for development. Though subdivision regulations have been the object of less discussion than zoning, they represent a powerful means of control over the development process. The rigid "Euclidean" zoning, which came into being in the early twentieth century, has now been supplemented with a variety of techniques to make it more flexible, more subject to negotiation, and more adaptable to the planning of large developments as single entities. These devices include "bonus" or "incentive" zoning, transfer of development rights (TDR), planned unit development (PUD), cluster zoning, and a number of others. Although the right to zone has been clearly established since the 1920s, the limits of the zoning power are still subject to some change as a result of the process of litigation and the establishment of legal precedent. In particular, since the 1960s the courts have redefined municipal obligations to nonresidents as a result of suits brought against suburban communities.

For the most effective shaping of the land-use pattern, public capital investment and land-use controls should be coordinated. Public capital investment affects the demand for land and structures, and land-use controls channel and shape the way demand forces play themselves out.

NOTES

1. "Accessibility" has more than one dimension. A central city site will typically be much more accessible to pedestrians, transit users, and in some cases, automobile drivers than a suburban site. On the other hand it is likely to be a good deal less accessible by truck or rail. It would be more precise to say that the type of accessibility offered by a central city site is not likely to be of great value to a manufacturer.
2. Calculated as follows: $(5280 \times 1{,}000)/43{,}560 \times (200{,}000 - 20{,}000)$, where 5,280 is the number of feet in a mile and 43,560 is the number of square feet in an acre.
3. For a history of subdivision regulations, see Richard M. Yearwood, *Land Subdivision Regulation: Policy and Legal Considerations for Urban Planning*. Praeger, New York, 1971.
4. For an account of the subdivision process, see *The Practice of Local Government Planning*, International City Management Association, Frank So and Judith Getzels, eds., Washington, D.C., Chap. 8.
5. For a general account of the zoning process, see Frank So, ibid, Chap. 9.
6. For an example of a work that relates housing type to household size and pupil load, see George Sternlieb, et al., *Housing Development and Municipal Costs*, Rutgers University Center for Urban Policy Research, New Brunswick, NJ, 1973.
7. For data on the sources of revenue for local governments, see "State and Local Government Finances," *Statistical Abstract of the United States*, published annually by the Bureau of the Census, Department of Commerce, Washington, D.C.
8. Other criteria may sometimes be used, particularly for commercial property. For example, assessors may use estimated cost of replacement or income generating potential.
9. When fractional assessment is used an "equalization rate" is generally computed so that the assessed value can be converted into "full value." This is particularly important when funding such as state aid for public education is conditioned by the property tax base of the receiving community. In recent years there has been a general trend toward full value assessment to avoid such complications.
10. Typically, properties owned by nonprofit institutions, as well as properties owned by government itself, are exempt from property taxation.
11. *National Land and Investment Company* v *Kohn*, 215, A. 2d 597 (Pa. 1965).
12. For a brief account of the collective effect of these decisions, see Wendy U. Larsen, "The Failure to Legislate: Mt. Laurel II," *Urban Land*, April 1983, pp. 34 35. For *Mt. Laurel III*, see Harold A. McDougal, "From Litiga-

tion to Legislation in Exclusionary Zoning Law," *Harvard Civil Rights Civil Liberties Law Review*, vol. 22, 1987, pp. 623–63.

13. This point is forcefully argued in Jane Jacobs, *The Death and Life of Great American Cities*, Vintage Books, Random House, New York, 1961. See, in particular, the section entitled "The Conditions for City Diversity."
14. For an example of the use in regard to historic preservation, see "Large Tower Would Use Depot's Rights," *The New York Times*, September 17, 1986, section B, p. 1. See also George M. Raymond, "Structuring the Implementation of Transferable Development Rights," *Urban Land*, July-August 1981, pp. 19–25.
15. See Seymour I. Schwartz and Robert A. Johnston, "Inclusionary Housing Programs," *Journal of the American Planning Association* , vol. 49, no. 1, Winter, 1983, pp. 3–21. See also Barbara Taylor, "Inclusionary Zoning: A Workable Option for Affordable Housing," *Urban Land*, March 1981, pp. 6–12; and Gus Bauman, Anna Reines Kahn, and Serena Williams, "Inclusionary Housing Programs in Practice," *Urban Land*, November 1983, pp. 14–19.
16. James D. Moore, "Glenpointe: The Birth of a Second Generation MXD," *Urban Land*, June 1983, pp. 14–19.
17. Gail Easley, "Performance Controls in an Urban Setting," *Urban Land*, October 1984, pp. 24–27. See also Tam Phalen,"How has Performance Zoning Performed," *Urban Land*, October 1983, pp. 16–21.
18. Fred Bosselman and David Callies, *The Quiet Revolution in Land Use Controls*, Council for Environmental Quality, Superintendent of Documents, U.S. Government Printing Office, Washington, D.C., 1973, p. 1.
19. An economist's term that refers to effects that are visited on "third parties," that is, parties who are not participants in the transactions and whose interest, therefore, may not be taken into account by the participants in the transaction.

SELECTED BIBLIOGRAPHY

CHAPIN, F. STUART, and KAISER, EDWARD J., *Urban Land Use Planning*, University of Illinois Press, Urbana, 1979.

J. BARRY CULLINGWORTH, *The Political Culture of Planning*, Routledge, Inc., New York, 1993.

HAAR, CHARLES, *Land Use Planning: A Casebook on the Use, Mis-Use and Re-Use of Urban Land*, 3rd ed., Little, Brown & Co., Boston, 1980.

SO, FRANK, and GETZELS, JUDITH, *The Practice of Local Government Planning*, International City Management Association, Washington, D.C., 1988.

NOTE: For the reader interested in keeping up with trends in land development and land-use control techniques, the magazines *Urban Land, Planning,* and *Real Estate Review* are a good and highly readable sources. For a more technical and formal current source on land-use regulation see the journal *Zoning Digest*.

CHAPTER 10

URBAN DESIGN

Charles W. Steger

> Mind *takes form* in the city; and in turn, urban forms condition mind. For space, no less than time, is artfully reorganized in cities: in boundary lines and silhouettes, in the fixing of horizontal planes and vertical peaks, in utilizing or denying the natural site, the city records the attitude of a culture and an epoch to the fundamental facts of its existence. The dome and the spire, the open avenue and the closed court, tell the story, not merely of different physical accommodations, but of essentially different conceptions of man's destiny. . . . With language itself, it remains man's greatest work of art.[1]

The design of cities has been the conscious task of many throughout history. However, only in the 1950s with the advent of university degree programs did the term *urban designer* and the profession of urban design emerge with a distinct label.

Cities develop over time because of the conscious and unconscious acts of man. Urban design assumes that in spite of the vast scale and complexity, cities can be designed and their growth shaped and directed. A major example of human ability to shape the urban environment is the work of Baron Haussmann from 1855 to 1868 in Paris during the time of Napoleon III.

During this period, Haussmann was responsible for creating a new pattern of boulevards that reshaped the character of Paris. The façades of buildings along the grand boulevards were required to be uniform, giving a sense of rhythm and order to the streets. The grand tree-lined boulevards he created became and

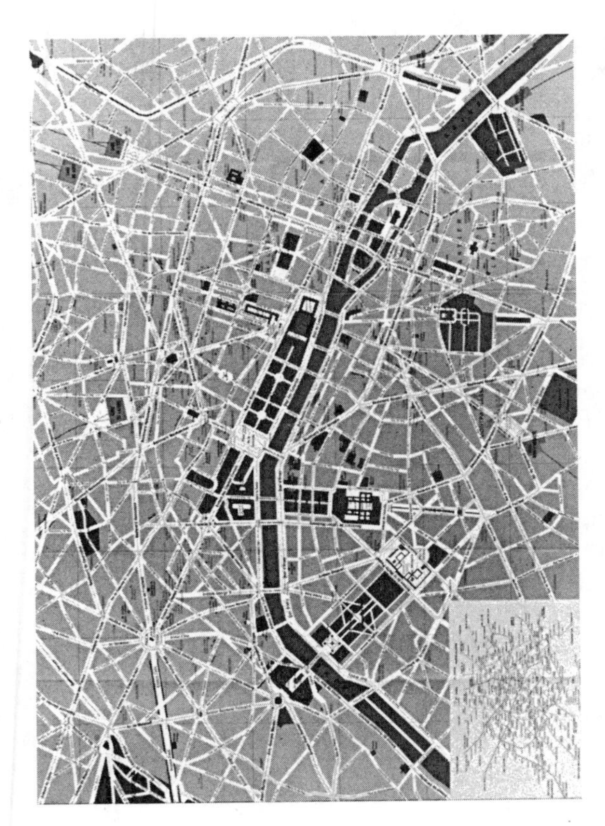

Street map of Paris (left) shows Haussmann's grand design. Photo of the Place de la République (below) shows the reality a century later.

remain some of the major public spaces of Paris. He addressed the problem of the flow of traffic and what the appropriate land uses should be. He shaped the skyline and the proportion of space by limits on height and rules governing the space between buildings. The vistas shaped by the boulevards focused on major public buildings and on gardens, giving new character to the nineteenth-century city. This plan for Paris, using grand boulevards as a major orienting force, was copied throughout the world.

WHAT IS URBAN DESIGN?

Urban design falls between the professions of planning and architecture. It deals with the large-scale organization and design of the city, with the massing and organization of buildings and the space between them, but not with the design of the individual building.

Several factors distinguish urban design from architectural design. Urban design deals with a large scale, such as entire neighborhoods or cities, and with long time frames, frequently 15 to 20 years. For example, Haussmann's work in Paris required 17 years. This is a sharp contrast to the 1, 2, or 3 years usually required for the construction of a single building. Urban design also deals with a large number of variables such as transportation, neighborhood identity, pedestrian orientation, and climate. This complexity, combined with the long periods of time involved, results in an environment characterized by high uncertainty. The control over specific development is less direct than with a single building. As a result, many of the techniques employed by urban designers differ from those of the architect.

Although the urban designer and planner have complementary roles, they do have separate and distinct functions. Most commonly, the modern urban designer deals with a part of the city. Very often, the site on which the urban designer works has been allocated as part of a larger planning process. It is after that allocation is made that the urban designer examines the site in terms of massing and spatial organization. The planner, by contrast, must typically consider the entire city. In fact, very often he or she must look beyond the bounds of the city and understand how the city functions as part of a larger region, for example, how the transportation system of the city relates to surrounding suburbs and communities. Thus the planner plays a central role in allocating the uses of land among the competing functions. Planners are more likely than urban designers to be involved in the political process whereby public policy is formulated. In other words, planners and urban designers are each involved with a spectrum of social, cultural, and physical design issues. The difference is a matter of degree.

Urban designers operate in both the public and private sectors. For example, an urban designer might be involved in laying out a planned unit development (PUD) or a mixed-use development such as the Teaneck, New Jersey, project described in Chapter 9. In such a situation the urban designer will be employed by the developer. But urban designers are also employed by public bodies. For example, during the period of Urban Renewal (see Chapter 12) sites were acquired, cleared, and planned by Urban Renewal agencies. Parcels were then sold or

Market Street in San Francisco remodeled, as visualized by the urban designer. Widened sidewalks and open-air arcades make it an attractive pedestrian area. There is a strong design influence from Haussmann's grand avenues in Paris.

leased to developers, who put up buildings or groups of buildings in accordance with the agency's overall plan. In this case the urban design was done by designers on the public payroll, and the architectural design was done by individuals or firms on the developer's payroll.

The Battery Park City development illustrated in this chapter represents a large and highly successful urban design effort done under public auspices. The developing organization, Battery Park City Authority (BPCA), was set up as a public benefit corporation by the New York State Legislature in 1968. Its purpose

Commercial development at Battery Park City (right) and residential section and riverfront promenade (below).

was to develop 92 acres to be created by landfill on the Hudson shore of Manhattan adjacent to the World Trade Center and the city's financial district.

Streets, blocks, open spaces, utilities, a 1.2 mile long esplanade along the Hudson River, and the allocation of land uses were all laid out by the project's designers. The buildings, designed by independent architectural firms, conformed to height, bulk, and other guidelines provided by BPCA.

Note the long time horizon characteristic of major urban design efforts. BPCA came into being in 1968. Funds were obtained through a bond issue in 1972, and the landfill was completed in 1976. Work was suspended for several years because of New York City's financial difficulties, and BPCA was reorganized in 1979. In 1980 construction of the first building began. By 1990 the development contained about 4,000 apartments and roughly 10 million square feet of commercial floor space. Another 8,000 apartments and several million square feet of commercial space still remained to be built. From concept to completion the project will have taken a quarter of a century.

In years to come the role of the urban designer is likely to grow because of an important trend in land development in the United States: A growing percentage of all development is taking place within PUDs or other large-scale, unified developments, rather than as lot-by-lot filling in under traditional Euclidean zoning. One reason for this shift is that often better results are obtained with a unified design approach. Another reason is the emergence of large development organizations that can put together the huge blocks of capital—often in the hundreds of millions and, occasionally, in the billions of dollars—that such projects require.

But even more important have been changes in the market for residences and commercial space. The emergence of a large and prosperous older population created a market for retirement communities that contain not only houses and apartments but community and outdoor recreation facilities as well as—all to be put together in an attractive and unified design. Comparable comments can be made for the residential demand of affluent "yuppies," who want their squash courts and jogging paths close at hand. Many businesses prefer a business park location because it permits the sharing of common facilities like parking and telecommunications, and because a well designed development gives an "upscale" image that impresses clients and customers. It must also be admitted that a large-scale project may sell partly because its size and physical separation provide a degree of social isolation. Personal safety, security for personal or business property, and even protection from urban unpleasantness like panhandling can be powerful selling points.

THE URBAN DESIGN PROCESS

Although each city and its problems are unique, there are some general sets of activities in most urban design studies. Following are four basic phases and some subphases.

1. Analysis
   a. Gathering of basic information

b. Visual survey
c. Identification of hard and soft areas
d. Functional analysis
2. Synthesis
3. Evaluation
4. Implementation

Analysis

Gathering of Basic Information Basic information is gathered on such items as land use, population, transportation, natural systems, and topography. In addition, the designers make a careful examination of the varied character of areas and the structure of neighborhoods and business areas. Problems and design goals are identified. If, for example, the project were to provide 250 housing units for a section of the city, the designer would have to determine the following, among other items:

1. Suitability of the topography, that is, slope or floodplains
2. Land area required for the new units
3. Amount of traffic generated and necessary roadways to accommodate it
4. Adequacy of public utilities
5. Parking space requirements
6. Additional requirements for schools, parks, and playgrounds
7. Relevant zoning and subdivision ordinances

For a commercial development, many other basic items would also be included, such as the buying income of surrounding residential areas, facts about the recent demand for various commercial space, estimates of likely "absorption rates" for commercial space, the competitive strength of nearby commercial areas, and the like.

Within the analysis phase, several activities are particularly important in understanding the structure, organization, and pattern of urban areas.

Visual Survey In *The Image of the City,* Kevin Lynch describes the concept and key elements of the visual survey.[2] The idea is based on the assumption that as each of us walks around a city, we create in our minds a map that orients us to the urban environment. This mental map makes us feel less anxious about finding our way about. Lynch developed a vocabulary of symbols that enables the urban designer to characterize in graphic form the key elements of the urban fabric. The visual survey is now considered a standard part of any urban design study and is used as a tool by designers to communicate their perceptions of the structure and organization of a city or neighborhood to one another. The visual survey examines and identifies components of the city such as the location and views of landmarks and activity nodes. It reveals the boundaries between neighborhoods and whether they are clear and distinct or amorphous. The survey also explores the sequence of spaces a pedestrian might encounter in walking from one part of the city to another.

Identification of Hard and Soft Areas Cities, and the neighborhoods and districts that comprise them, are in a constant state of change. Although this dynamic condition may not be seen easily from one day to the next, over the time span of 5, 10, or 15 years it becomes quite apparent.

The delineation of hard and soft areas helps the designer to know what parts of a city can accommodate growth and change and what parts are essentially fixed because they may be occupied, for example, by a historic landmark or cemetery. A good example of a hard area is a public park near the central business district of a large city. Given the shortage of open space, it is extremely unlikely that any development will be allowed to take place in that area. A soft area may be a neighborhood or business district with an increasing number of vacant buildings. Intervention and development there might be quite desirable from the point of view of the residents and the city. New development may improve the quality of the physical environment as well as increase the diversity of the economic base of the community. Such information is of considerable value in the latter stages of the urban design process when proposed plans must be evaluated for feasibility of implementation.

Functional Analysis The functional analysis examines the relationship of activities among the various land uses and how they relate to circulation systems. This builds very heavily on the work of the land-use planners. However, the urban designer carries the study into three dimensions.

For example, in virtually every major urban area, there is the constant problem of excessive congestion and traffic on the streets. Traffic has grown so enormously that the pedestrian has very little space in which to walk. Why are the streets too small to accommodate our needs? If we look back into history, there is an explanation: When the cities were first laid out either in the colonial period in the United States or in response to the massive growth of urban populations during the industrial revolution, the technology of building was such that most structures were no more than three or four stories high. Advances in construction, particularly the invention of steel frames and the elevator, made it economically and structurally possible to build much higher. Structures such as the World Trade Center are over 100 stories high. Consequently, the number of users and the demand for services have increased dramatically, but the streets have remained the same size.

It is therefore very important to consider the real consequences of our plans in three dimensions and how they might change over time.

Synthesis

From the synthesis phase emerge design concepts that reflect an understanding of the constraints of the problem and propose optimum solutions, given the many tradeoffs that must be made. The designer is often confronted with the resolution

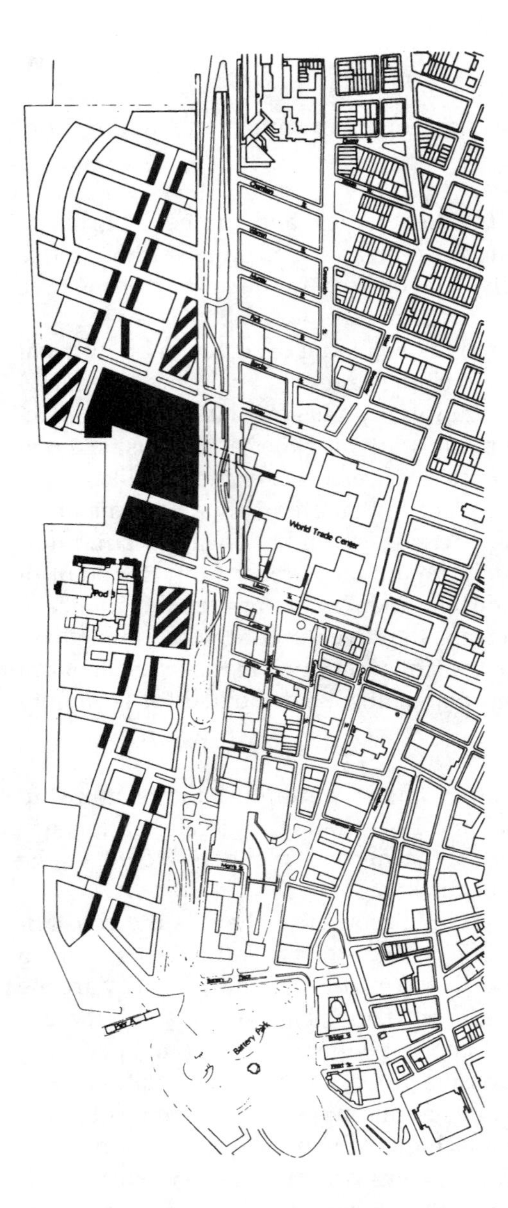

Residential
Permitted Retail Center
Commercial/Retail Center
Potential Commercial or Residential Sites

Land Use Allocation

0 200 400 600

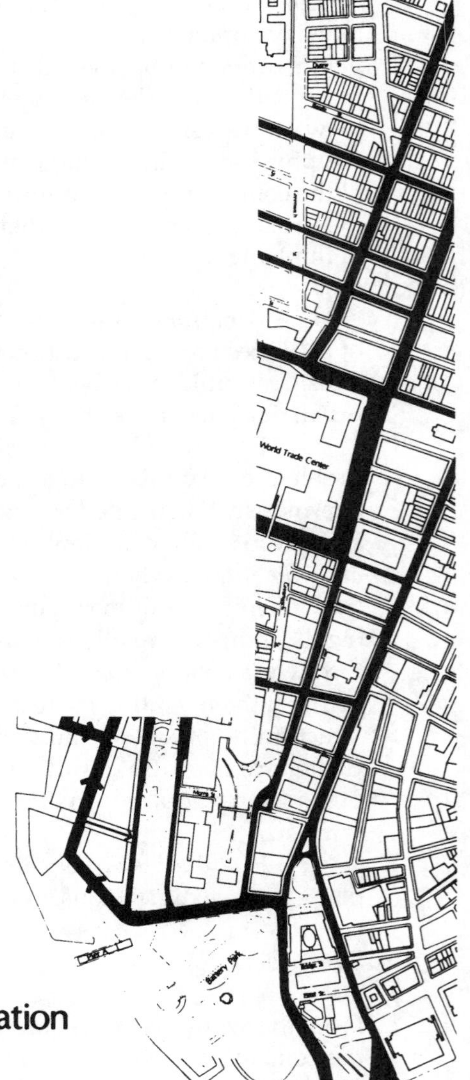

Primary Circulation
Secondary Circulation

Vehicular Circulation

Three schematic drawings for Battery Park City, a 92-acre mixed commercial and residential development built on landfill in the Hudson River. Though built on new land, the development's street pattern is closely linked to the city's existing pattern. Immediate proximity to Manhattan's financial district and World Trade Center makes the new land some of the most valuable property in the United States. Below, the designer's vision of the streetscape as seen looking east from the Hudson River.

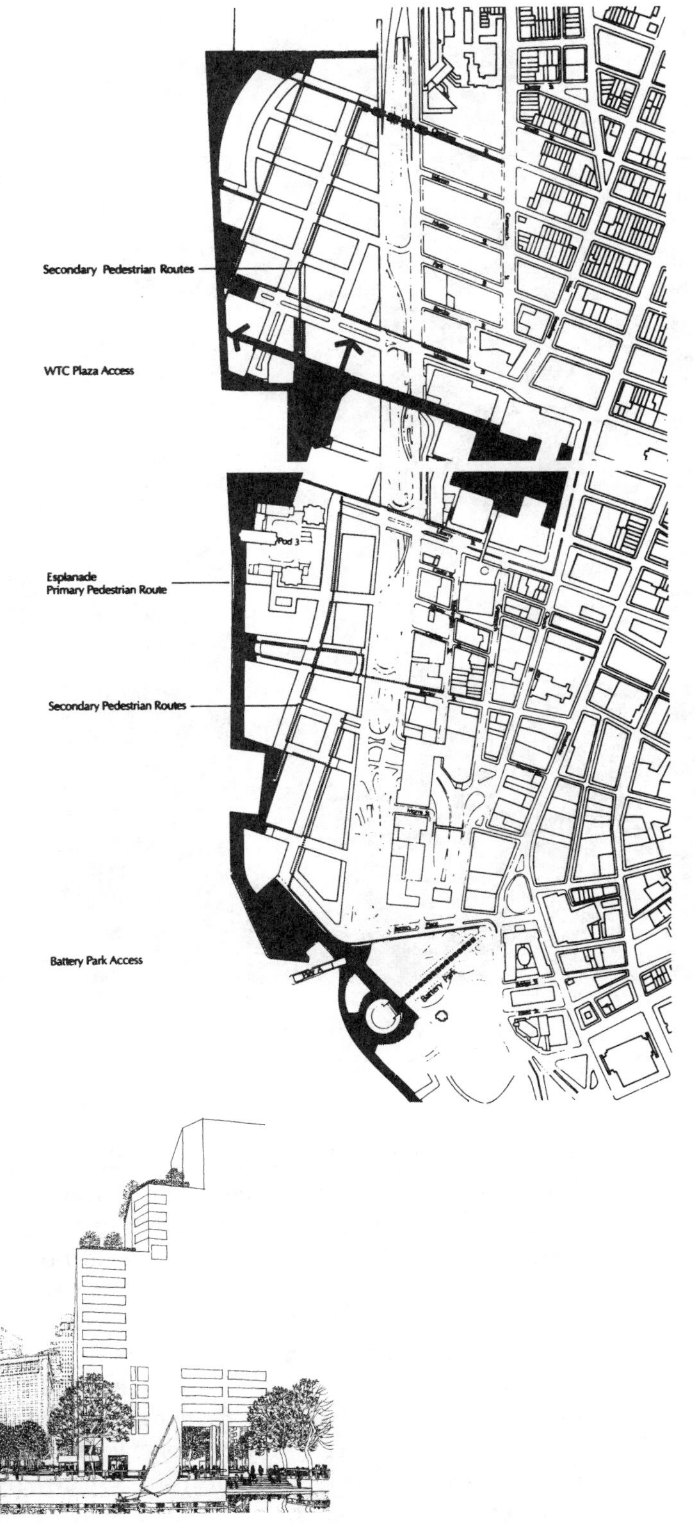

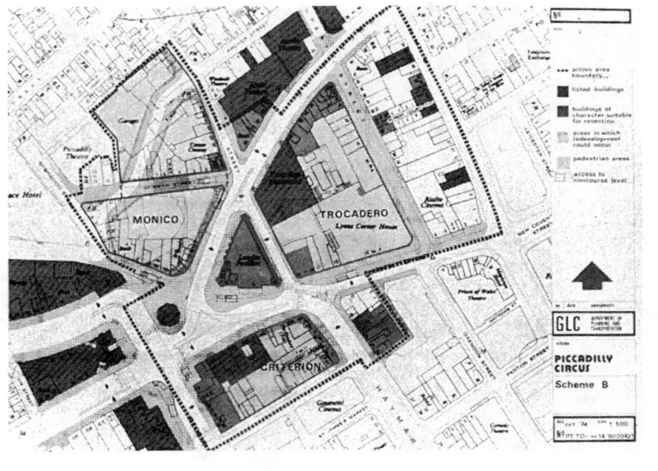

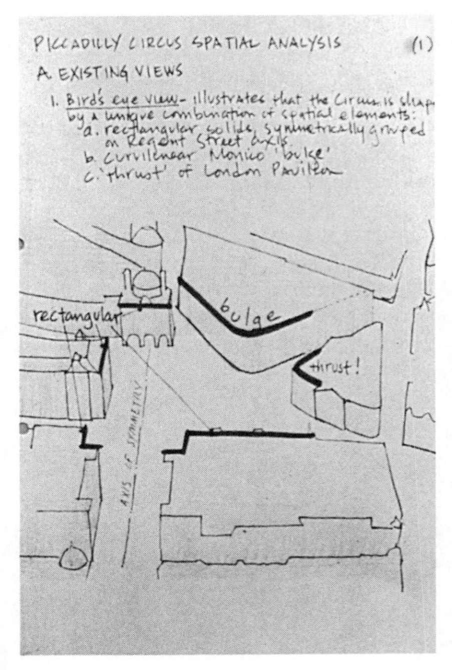

Spatial analysis, plan, and reality,
Picadilly Circus in London.

of many conflicting demands. For housing units, there is an inherent conflict between pedestrian and vehicular traffic. If traffic flow is too fast or too heavy, it will hamper pedestrian crossing unless either traffic lights or pedestrian bridges are installed. Each of these solutions takes additional resources.

It is in the synthesis phase that the data gathered and the analysis of the problem must be translated into proposals for action. Prior to the complete development of the urban design plan, there are several preceding activities. The first component of the synthesis phase is the evolution of concepts that address the problem. In the initial phases, there may be a number of concepts proposed. There is usually more than one way to solve a particular set of problems. Concepts are followed by the development of schematic design proposals. These are more specific in nature. Schematics are followed by preliminary plans.

Evaluation

Evaluation occurs at many levels, ranging from meeting technical demands to the ability to gain public acceptance. It is the time at which the preliminary plans generated in the synthesis phase are compared to the original goals and problem definitions.

After the design proposals are complete, it is essential that they be evaluated in light of the original problem or issue they were intended to address. One of the more complicated tasks associated with evaluation is determining what criteria should be employed. There are two basic categories: (1) how well the solutions fit the problem and (2) how readily the proposals can be implemented.

The task is further complicated by the fact that cities are dynamic, and their problems are constantly changing. Developing solutions for problems that are in a state of flux is like shooting at a moving target. Our understanding of how problems change over time has grown as citizen participation has gained importance. Citizen participation was greatly increased by the Environmental Protection Act of 1969, which mandated citizen review and comment on projects that received federal funding (see Chapter 16).

Implementation

During implementation, the strategy for actual financing and construction is devised. Detailed phasing studies and tools such as zoning ordinances are called into play to realize the project.

Once an urban design plan is developed, the principal tools through which it is implemented are land-use controls and capital expenditures. The land-use controls available to the urban designer include not only the traditional or Euclidean zoning ordinance but also a variety of modern techniques including PUD, incentive or bonus zoning, and transfer of development rights, as described in Chapter 9.

Capital expenditures shape the pattern of land development as noted earlier by altering land values through the provision of access and utilities. When there is public participation in a project, capital expenditures combined with the power of eminent domain may be used to assemble the land on which the project is to be built.

WHAT IS GOOD URBAN DESIGN?

To this point, we have described the process of urban design. Of equal importance is how to evaluate it. What is good urban design?

In its most general sense, urban designers intend to improve the quality of people's lives through design. They accomplish this through the elimination of barriers as well as the creation of opportunities for people to move about the city in a free, safe, and pleasant way. For example, one should be able to walk through a reasonable portion of an urban area in inclement weather without major difficulty, so the urban designer may find ways to link buildings or portions of entire

The planned community of Reston, VA. Clockwise from upper left: The town center viewed from across Lake Ann (an artificial lake), a pedestrian bridge connecting the town center with adjacent residential areas, a mixed housing area with parking and road access behind the buildings, and closeup of the town center on Lake Ann. Note how the curved layout of the buildings is used to create a public area fronting on the lake.

blocks with covered walks. Minneapolis has accomplished this goal through its skyway system, in which the upper floors of its downtown core are linked by enclosed walkways. This feature is very desirable from the point of view of the pedestrian. It has also enhanced the value of second-story retail space.

People like to see other people and to be seen. Many cities provide incentives for developers who will create public plazas in conjunction with new developments. Such spaces provide an opportunity for people to sit in the sun at lunch and observe the general activity of the street. William Whyte in his work on the *Social Life of Small Urban Spaces* has done a systematic study of the factors contributing to successful urban spaces.[3] He concludes that some form of movable seating and the opportunity to purchase food and drink are key elements.

Another way to evaluate the success of urban space is the way in which it assists in orienting the user. For example, can users find their way from one place to the other without confusion or fear? Are the signs easily understood? Are major pedestrian areas well lighted in the evening so that users can make their may easily and safely? Jane Jacobs made this point forcefully in the early 1960s in *The Death and Life of Great American Cities*.[4]

Other functional criteria such as safety are also important. For example, separation of pedestrian and vehicular traffic reduces accidents. Yet the spaces and circulation areas must be organized so that they can be readily accessible to emergency vehicles and can accommodate delivery vehicles to the shops we find so desirable along pedestrian streets.

Good design achieves its intentions and often more. For example, the developer's intention in constructing a mixed-use project may simply be to achieve a profitable combination of commercial and residential structures. Yet if the project is well-situated and aesthetically attractive, its benefits will spill over onto adjacent areas. The project might increase pedestrian traffic and hence enhance property values in adjacent retailing areas. Its presence might also enhance the value of adjacent neighborhoods by making the area more interesting and varied.

A myriad of factors can affect the success of an urban design project. A list of a number of the more important criteria for judging urban design follows:

1. Unity and coherence
2. Minimum conflict between pedestrians and vehicles
3. Protection from rain, noise, wind, and so on
4. Easy orientation for users
5. Compatibility of land uses
6. Availability of places to rest, observe, and meet
7. Creation of a sense of security and pleasantness

But it must be admitted that urban design is not an exact science, for there is always the element of personal taste. One person's peace and tranquility will be another person's boredom and sterility. One person's excitement will be another person's soul-destroying cacophany. And most of us will have very differing needs from our environment at different stages in our lives. The area that suits a single person in his or her twenties may seem very unsuitable ten years later when the same person has a spouse and two children.

The Neighborhood Concept

A very central concept in urban design, and a place where one can see many of the previously noted criteria applied, is in the concept of "neighborhood." Though we now take the idea of neighborhoods and of planning for neighborhoods for granted, it is actually not a very old idea. In fact one of the first clear articulations of the neighborhood concept in the United States was that by Clarence Perry in work done in the 1920s for RPAA (see Chapter 3). A neighborhood is a unit that

The neighborhood concept circa the 1920s. The separate boys' and girls' playgrounds seem archaic today, but the plan otherwise has many modern features—separation of commercial and residential areas, a curvilinear street pattern to discourage through-traffic, the preservation of community open space, concentration of high-density housing near public transportation. Note that the neighborhood is centered around a public school.

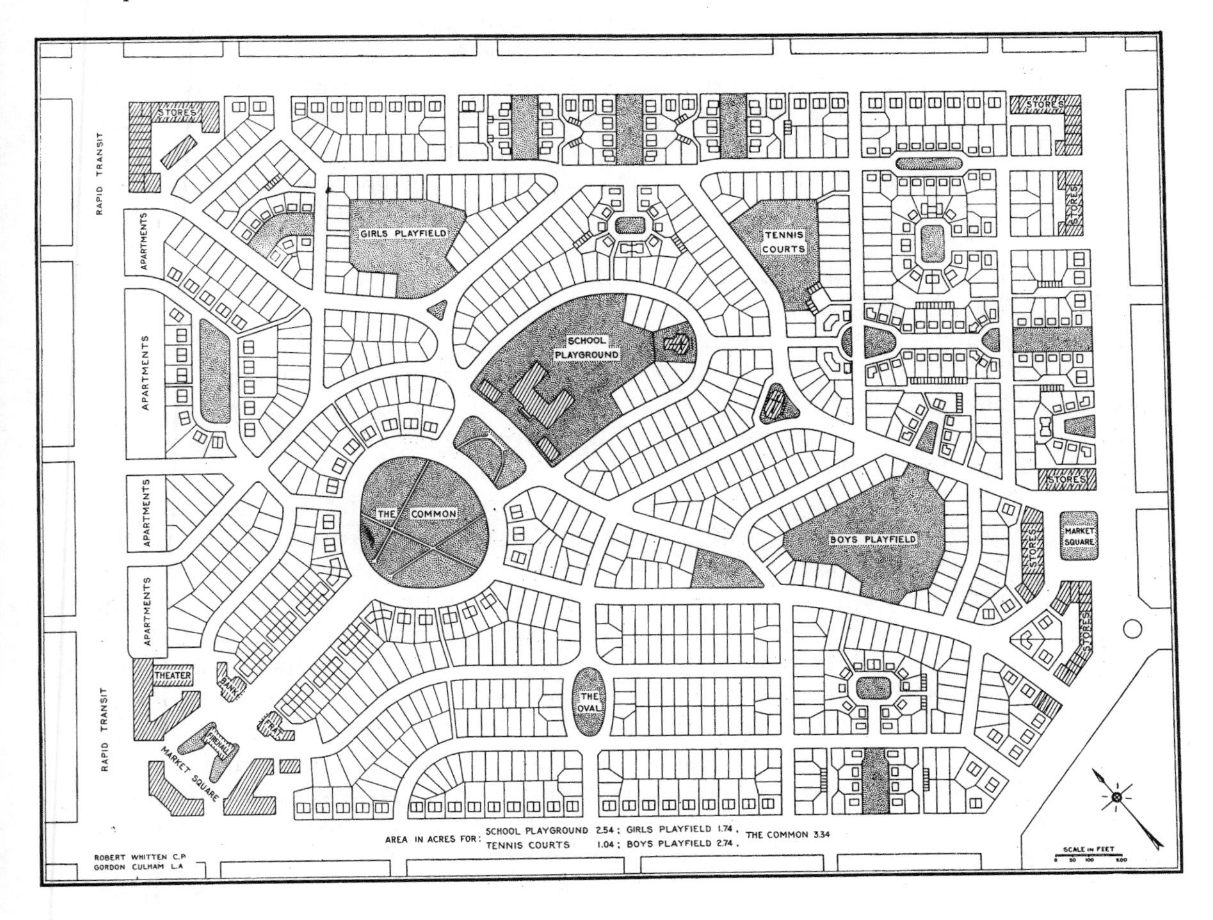

matches the daily scale of most people's lives. Traditionally, the neighborhood planning unit is the area that would contain a population sufficiently large enough to supply the pupils for one elementary school. Perry wrote in terms of 1,000 or 1,200 pupils, which in the 1920s implied a total neighborhood population of perhaps 5,000 or 6,000. Other writers have suggested other numbers, but the exact numbers are not the central point.

Typically, the neighborhood plan will provide for residences, a school, shopping facilities for goods one buys frequently (grocery, drug, and stationery stores but not department stores or automobile dealers), playgrounds, and perhaps small parks. The street pattern will serve the resident population but discourage through traffic. Major thoroughfares will often serve as neighborhood boundaries. In some communities, for example, Reston, Virginia, the residents will be further isolated from traffic by separate paths for pedestrians and cyclists. The well-designed neighborhood is likely to be laid out with common areas so that residents encounter each other in ways that promote social relationships. The neighborhood is thus structured to provide conveniently and safely much of what most people need and use in their daily lives.

One complaint about the planning of many suburban areas is that the separation of land uses and, particularly, the large expanses of tract housing eliminate much of what we to associate with neighborhoods. One does not meet one's neighbor walking to the corner store because there is no corner store and, given the spreadout nature of many suburbs, one is not likely to walk to many destinations. Similarly, children do not casually encounter each other walking home from the neighborhood school because there is no neighborhood school. Rather, they are bussed to and from a consolidated school several miles away.

REPLANNING SUBURBIA: ANDRES DUANY AND NEOTRADITONAL PLANNING

Ask a group of planners to name one urban designer and there is a good chance that the name that will come first to most lips is that of Andres Duany. Not everyone in the profession agrees with him. But agree or disagree, most planners take his design ideas seriously.

Most of America's population growth is going into the suburbs and Duany says that, by and large, the suburbs are being planned wrong.[5] He lays the biggest single portion of the blame on the highway engineers but still reserves a good bit for the planners. Suburban planning, according to Duany, suffers from several major sins. First, there is an overemphasis on planning for the automobile. As Duany says, highway engineers "want cars to be happy." In his view, meeting traffic flow and parking goals often takes precedence over designing for people in suburban areas. He also faults suburban designers and planners for excessive separation of uses and for laying out land use at too coarse a grain. If land uses are rigidly separated and each land use occupies a substantial area one result is inconvenience. Distances between uses become too great for walking and so one is forced into total dependence on the automobile.

He notes that the excessive automobile dependence has great effect on the texture of everyday life. Old people lose their independence in the suburbs not when they are too infirm to walk, but when their eyesight becomes too dim to drive. At that point an adult who may otherwise be entirely capable of independent living becomes dependent. At the other end of the scale young people who have not yet reached the legal age to drive are extremely dependent on adults to drive them to activities, an unusual circumstance in an urban area. The child's freedom and mobility are severely restricted and the parent finds herself or himself very tied down by the need to be a chauffeur for the children.

Duany notes that the emphasis on designing for the automobile produces pedestrian-unfriendly patterns that inhibit walking even when the point-to-point distances are short. In one illustration he shows an office park and a shopping center perhaps 200 feet apart and separated only by a road. But the road, with its turning lanes, is five lanes wide. The office park, for purposes of buffering as required in many zoning ordinances, is surrounded by a berm (a mound of earth) several feet high. At noon time almost no one who works in the office park will walk to the shopping center for lunch simply because the combination of berm and five-lane-wide roadway is too inhibiting. Instead, the worker at the office park will use his or her car, which is parked nearby in the lots surrounding the office buildings, and drive to lunch. Duany notes that in many suburban commercial areas the greatest congestion occurs at midday, caused largely by workers driving to lunch.

Duany's solution to the design faults of the suburbs is what has come to be called "neotraditional" planning. It is so named because much that he advocates harks back to traditional city and town planning practices that have been rejected in modern suburban planning. He advocates the mixing of uses at a fine grain. He notes that zoning originated to separate incompatible uses but that there is much less need for this today than at the turn of the century. For example, much manufacturing today is quiet and clean and there is no reason why it cannot be located relatively close to housing. It is important that buildings in an area be in scale with each other, but not that they all be for the same type of use or for the same type of inhabitant. Like Jane Jacobs, he argues that excessive homogeneity of use and building type leads to sterility and inconvenience. He suggests, for example, that apartments over stores and accessory apartments on single-family lots (for example, the garage that has been converted to a one bedroom apartment) would go a long way to solving the problems of low- and moderate-income housing. And he notes that, regretably, most suburban zoning codes prevent construction of these types of units.

He places great importance on pedestrian-friendly streets. The traditional city street with, say, two lanes for traffic, one lane on each side for parked cars, and sidewalks is pedestrian friendly. Because it has only two lanes of traffic that move at a moderate speed it is easy to cross. The lines of parked cars offer the pedestrian on the sidewalk a sense of security because there is a barrier between him or her and the moving vehicles in the street. Buildings, according to Duany, should be brought up close to the street and parking beyond what can be accommodated on the street should be located behind the building. The typical shopping center or office park design in which the building is set back and isolated from the street by a large parking lot is, in Duany's view, a design disaster. Even the most unattractive building "gives more to the street" than does a sea of parked cars or, when the cars are not there, a sea of asphalt. Duany is an advocate of alleys, for these permit parking to be placed behind buildings. The alley avoids the need for the typical suburban residential design in which half of the frontage of a house consists of a garage door. And a street scape that consists largely of garage doors is not a very interesting or inviting public space. Duany's vision of good design necessarily implies fairly small lots, for widely spaced houses discourage walking.

In arguing the case for his design views Duany rests much of his case on the market. He points out that people will pay very high prices for the fine grained, pedestrian-friendly pattern he advocates. Note, for example, the high price of residential real estate in Georgetown (Washington, D.C.) or Marblehead, Massachusetts.

This writer finds much that is attractive in Duany's vision. It must be said, though, that much of the rigid suburban zoning that Duany decries is not neces-

WHAT IS WRONG WITH THE POD AND COLLECTOR PLAN

The pod and collector system, with each pod connecting separately to the collector as in the top half of the figure is a common suburban design approach. It looks good on paper but, Duany argues, it works badly. First, every trip from a point in one pod to a point in another pod becomes an automobile trip on the collector. This is a prescription for traffic congestion. The problem is not that there is a shortage of total road surface, but that this design forces a large part of the traffic onto a small fraction of the total road surface.

Walking for purposes like shopping is discouraged because there is no direct path from the houses in the pod at the upper right to the mall or the stores fronting on the collector. Walking for purposes of visiting, say between the single-family houses and the apartments, is also discouraged for the same reasons. Even walking from one store to another is discouraged, for the customer at the mall cannot easily walk to the strip shopping because the only link between them is the collector. Thus in addition to concentrating automobile trips as noted above, the pod and collector system also increases the total number of automobile trips.

The half of the drawing below the collector shows a pattern that Duany regards as far superior. The same elements—single-family houses, apartments, stores, and a public school—are contained in each half of the drawing. But circulation is very different. In the bottom half most trips for shopping and social purposes can be made through secondary streets without having to go out onto the collector. In addition, many trips are easily made on foot. Residents of the single-family houses and apartments can walk to the mall by a reasonably direct path along secondary streets with sidewalks. Similarly, school children can walk to and from school on secondary streets. The student who stays after school for an activity and misses the school bus can walk home rather than wait to be picked up by a parent. The design promotes a greater degree of social integration because the two different types of housing, apartments and single-family houses, are not isolated from each other in separate pods.

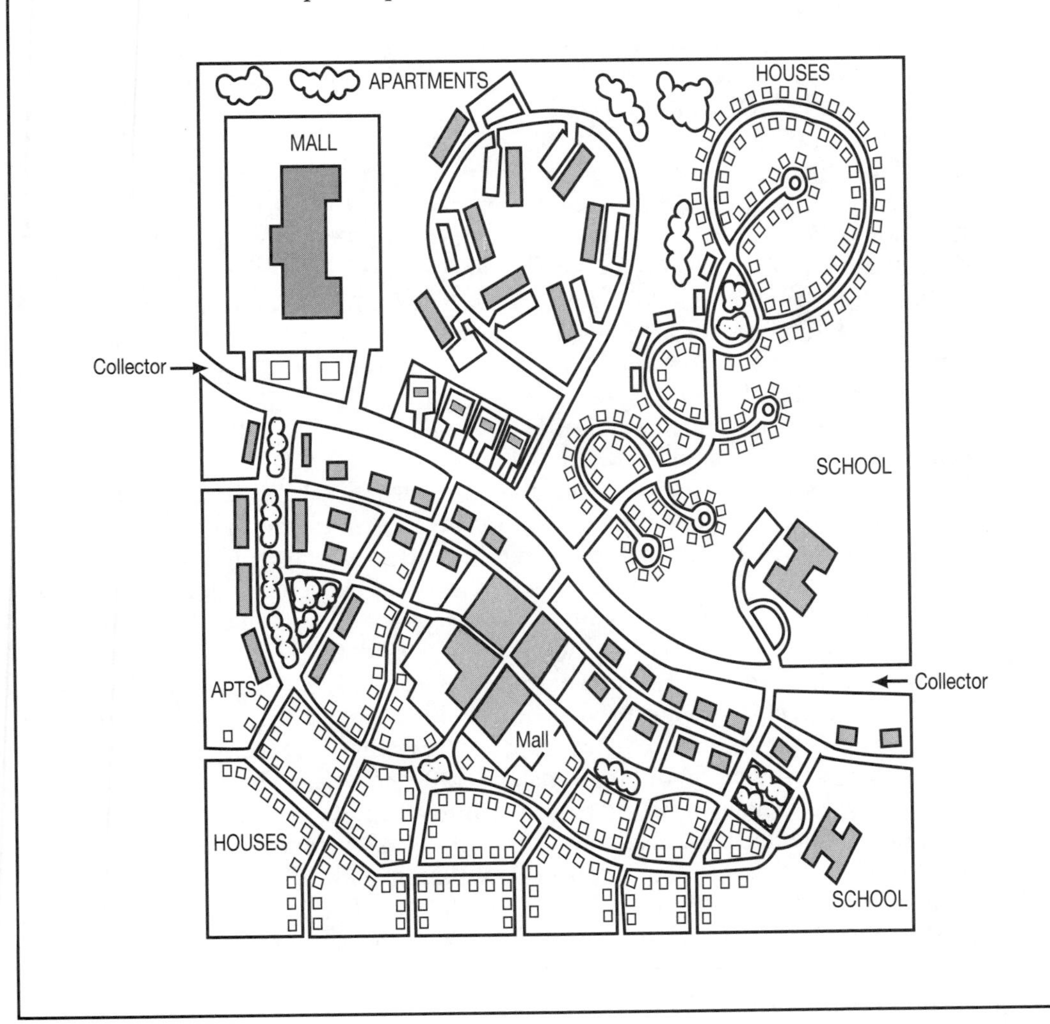

sarily the planners' first choice, but, rather, represents the will of the citizens. The suburban planner who urges more flexible zoning and greater mixing of uses on the citizen often gets quite a negative response from them. And, it is not only the highway engineers who, in Duany's words "want cars to be happy." The citizens also want their high speed mobility and ease of parking.

The large residential lot is the enemy of Duany's neotraditional vision, for one cannot have a pedestrian-oriented community if houses are spaced, say, 200 or more feet apart.[6] In fact, with the limited amount of pedestrian traffic that occurs at such spacing it is very hard to justify the cost of sidewalks. But one cannot be a planner in the suburbs for long without realizing how many people prize having a big piece of property and regard large lot zoning as an ideal form of development. Frank Lloyd Wright's vision of Broadacre City (see next section) spoke to the taste of a great many people. Thus though Duany's design philosophy appeals to many, there are also many to whom it does not appeal and who, in fact, embrace the automobile-served pattern against which he inveighs.

VISIONS OF THE CITY OF THE FUTURE

Given that the urban designer is concerned with the development of the city not only in the present but 15 to 20 or more years into the future, it is important to have some concept of what cities in the future might be like. The literature of architecture, planning, and urban design is fortunate to have many such references. Ideas range from Frank Lloyd Wright's Broad Acre City to R. Buckminster Fuller's mile-wide geodesic dome for Manhattan to Le Corbusier's Ville Radieuse. Behind each of these concepts was an idea about how city dwellers should respond to social and technological change.

For example, in the Ville Radieuse (Radiant City), Le Corbusier envisioned high-rise residential towers in a park-like setting. Major roadways would link together sectors of the city. Two of his key ideas are reflected in this urban design proposal. The first stemmed from his idea of returning the land for human use. It is for this reason that his buildings are raised off the ground on columns or pilote; in this way, buildings are not barriers to our movement along the ground. The second idea is how the organization of the city should change if we were to accept the automobile. Major roadways connected the high-rise housing with commercial and industrial sectors of the city. Le Corbusier sought to find ways for people to be in closer contact with nature and to use advances in technology to free themselves to reflect on their future and place in the world.

The organization of buildings and patterns of land ownership conceived for La Ville Radieuse are in sharp contrast to Wright's concepts for Broad Acre City. In La Ville Radieuse the land would be owned in common, whereas Wright would have each individual or family own a one-acre lot. Homes and industry would be connected by major roadways. Wright felt that individual ownership of land by broad segments of the population was important in preserving a democratic society. His political and social philosophy was translated into the design proposals contained in the plans for Broad Acre City.

By comparing the plans for La Ville Radieuse and Broad Acre City, one can gain insight into the political ideologies of the two men. Wright places great value on the independence and autonomy of the individual, as suggested by each person owning a plot of land. In contrast, Le Corbusier sees a role for collective ownership of property, suggesting that the overall welfare of society is enhanced if individuals see themselves as part of a larger group.

Other visionaries have suggested more radical approaches to structuring the future city. Drawings and models by Paulo Soleri depict megastructures with heights as great as the tallest skyscrapers but covering as much as several hundred acres of ground. The structures contain both housing and employment for a

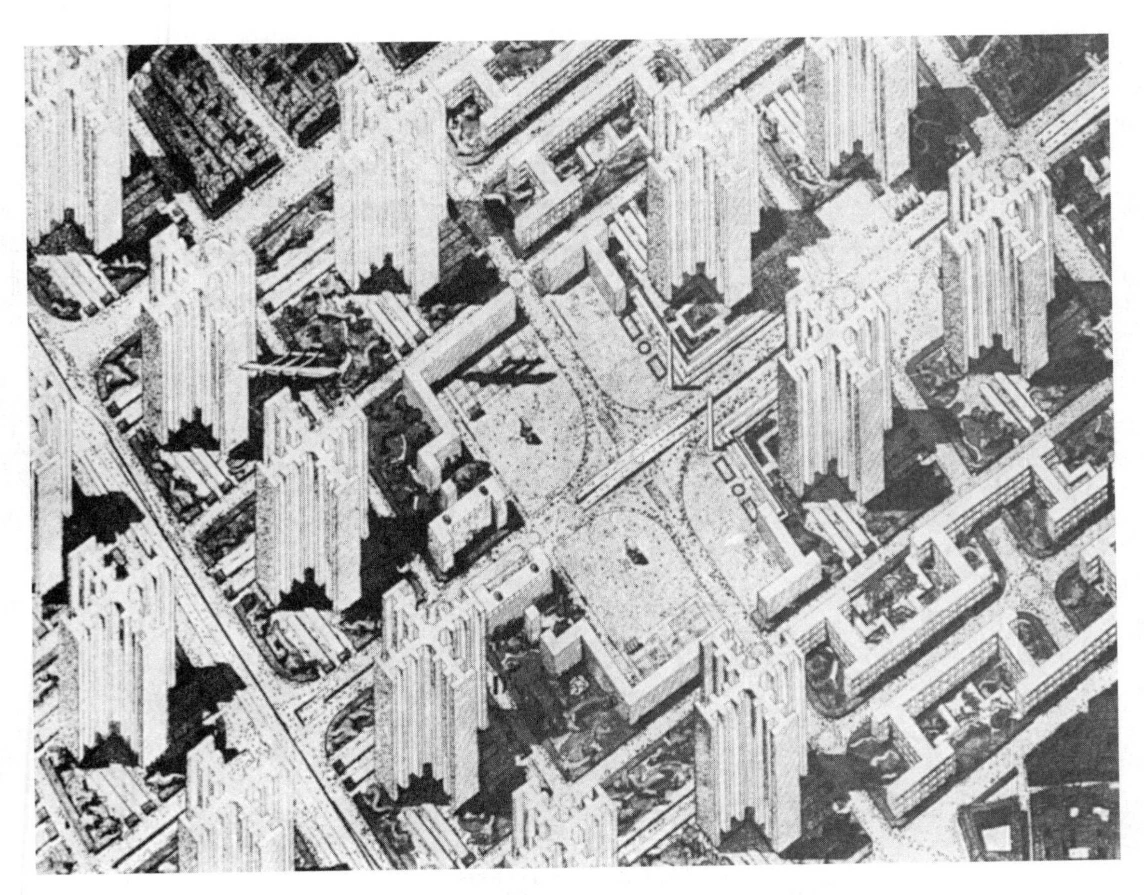

Corbusier's "Voisin" plan for Paris 1922–25 (top). Building very high permitted extreme population density while leaving 95 percent of the land vacant. Though never built, this plan exerted enormous influence on design, both for better and worse, in many countries. At left is the planned community of Roehampton in Great Britain. Note the large amounts of interior open space and the use of columns referred to as *pilote*.

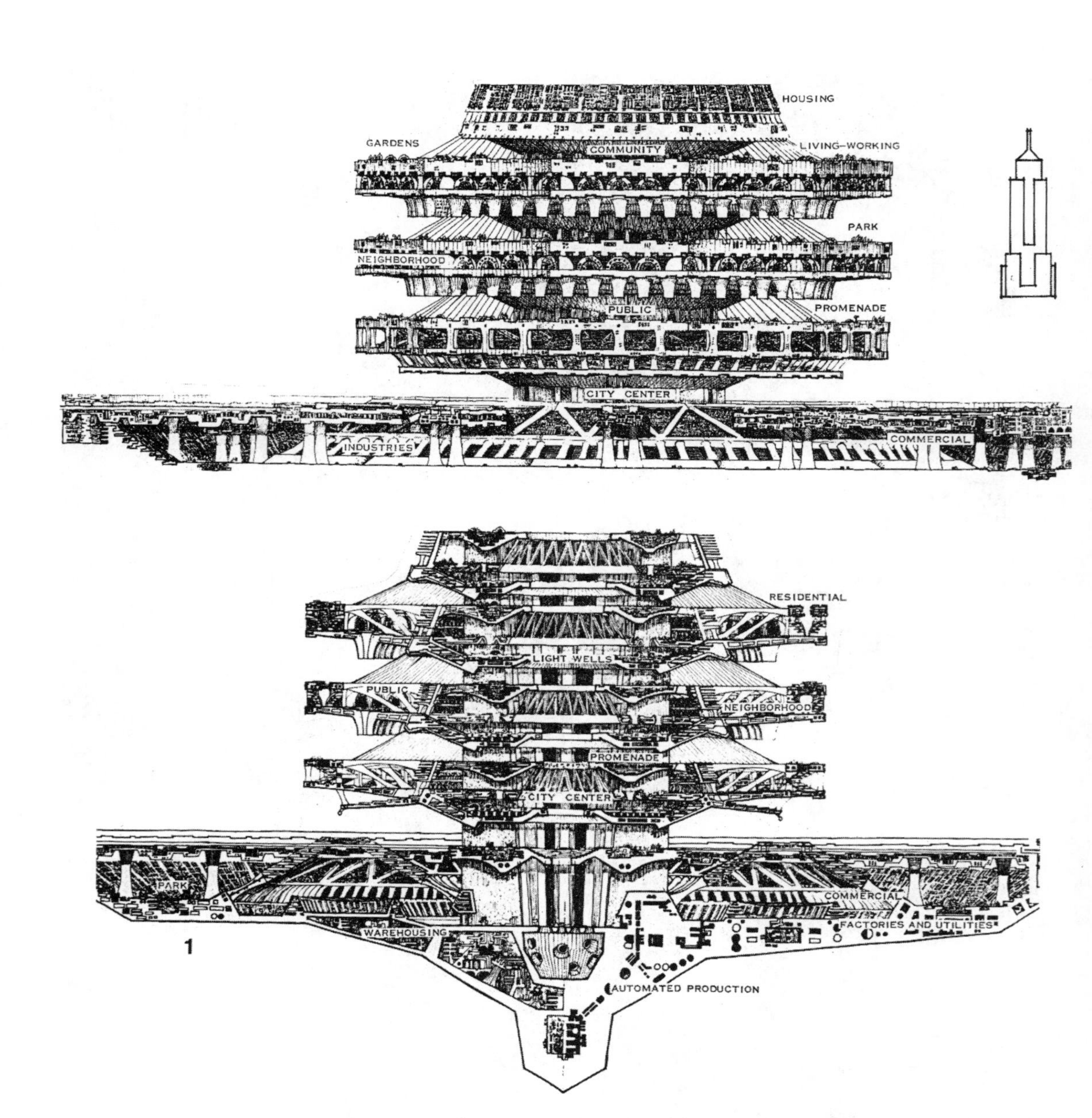

Paolo Soleri "hyperstructure" in ground level view (top) and cross section (bottom). Figure at upper right is Empire State building at same scale. Structure would be 3,444 feet (1050 m) high, 10,367 feet (3,160 m) across the base. Population would be 520,000 or about 171,000 per square mile of ground covered, roughly seven times the population density of New York. Soleri's work is informed by an extremely strong environmental consciousness. The hyperstructure would house and employ a very large number of people with a very small "footprint" on the earth and with a very low per capita energy consumption. Though hyperstructures are not likely to be built in the near future, Soleri's designs have influenced a generation of planners and architects. The influences of his thought can be found in the Houston Galleria and the Atlanta Hyatt-Regency.

population of 100,000 or more. Soleri has labeled this general set of studies "arcology." Like ecology, which is the study of animals in their natural homes, arcology is the study of how best to build urban structures to accommodate homes, manufacturing, and public facilities in a fashion compatible with nature. In addition to suggesting new ways of organizing living space, Soleri's proposals contain predictions of completely automated manufacturing facilities that might be placed underground. Soleri is constructing a small new community called Arcosanti in the desert north of Phoenix, Arizona. Arcosanti will test, on a very small scale, some of the concepts embodied in his megastructure designs.

Have such visions of the future city been a useful guide? None of these proposals offers a plan in its entirety. Instead they tend to focus on one or two factors that their authors consider to be of primary importance. However, there is an underlying assumption in each of the proposals that the design of the physical environment affects human behavior.

One task for the urban designer is to combine aesthetic considerations with what we have learned about the relationship of physical design and human behavior to obtain a result that actually improves the quality of people's lives. We have learned through experiences with programs such as Urban Renewal and federally assisted housing that although physical design does affect human behavior, it is not the single most powerful determinant. Rather, it is one aspect of a complex array of physical, social, and economic, cultural, and psychological factors that are present in our everyday lives.

For example, public housing experience has taught us that high-rise construction does not necessarily work out well for all populations. It is hard for a mother living on the twelfth floor to keep an eye on her children as they play outdoors. The relative anonymity of a high-rise seems to make high-rise public housing prone to crime and may also make it more difficult to build a feeling of community and mutual help. On the other hand high-rise development may work very well for a young, affluent population, as many a successful condominium developer could testify. The negative sociological effects that we now know to be associated with some high-rise, high-density housing were not anticipated by Le Corbusier. Rather than take his proposals literally as ideas to be applied to all urban areas and all urban populations, it is best to consider them as options to be explored and evaluated. The modern city needs a coherent vision of the future to guide its development, yet it must accommodate a wide diversity of values, hopes, and perspectives. Concepts of the future must address how urban people should live, how neighborhoods should be organized, and how we can preserve natural beauty and the quality of the environment as increasing numbers of people inhabit the globe.

SUMMARY

Urban design generally occupies a middle position between architecture and planning. Rather than focusing on the design of the individual structure, the urban designer concentrates on the massing and organization of buildings and on the spaces between them. The physical focus of the urban designer may be somewhat smaller than that of the planner, who often is concerned with the entire city or even the city as part of a larger metropolitan system.

The urban design process is broken into four main phases: (1) analysis, (2) synthesis, (3) evaluation, and (4) implementation. Judging a particular piece of urban design is always a somewhat subjective matter. However, there are some generally accepted criteria, including

1. Unity and coherence
2. Minimum conflict between vehicles and pedestrians
3. Protection from rain, noise, wind, and so on
4. Ease of orientation
5. Compatibility of land uses
6. Availability of places to rest, observe, and meet
7. Creation of a sense of security and pleasantness

The urban designer, in producing a design that not only looks good but also functions well, must consider many factors beyond the purely physical. These include financial, political, psychological, and sociological considerations.

NOTES

1. Lewis Mumford, *The Culture of Cities*, Harcourt Bruce Jovanovich, New York, 1970, p. 5, originally printed in 1938.
2. Kevin Lynch, *The Image of the City*, MIT Press, Cambridge, MA, 1960.
3. William H. Whyte, *The Social Life of Small Spaces*, The Conservation Foundation, Washington, D.C. 1980.
4. Jane Jacobs, *The Death and Life of Great American Cities*, Vintage Books, Random House, New York, 1961.
5. Ruth Eckdish Knack, "Repent, Ye Sinners, Repent," *Planning*, August 1989, pp. 4–13.
6. An acre is 43,560 square feet. This corresponds to a square approximately 209 feet on edge. Thus the 200 feet figure approximates the minimum possible spacing under zoning that specifies a minimum lot size of one acre. Given that there are likely to be some oversized lots and pieces of land that cannot be developed for topographic or other reasons, the actual spacing will be greater.

SELECTED BIBLIOGRAPHY

ALEXANDER, CHRISTOPHER, *A Pattern Language*, Oxford University Press, Oxford, 1977.

BARNETT, JONATHAN, *An Introduction to Urban Design*, Harper and Row, New York, 1982.

BENEVELO, LEONARDO, *History of Modern Architecture, Volume 2, The Modern Movement*, MIT Press, Cambridge, MA, 1982.

BRAMBILLA, R., and LONGO, G., *For Pedestrians Only*, Whitney Library of Design, New York, 1977.

CIUCCI, DAL CO, and MANIERI-ELIA, TAFURRI, *The American City: From the Civil War to the New Deal*, trans. Barbara La Penta, MIT Press, Cambridge, MA, 1979.

DUANAY, ANDRES, and PLATER-ZYBERK, ELIZABETH, *Towns and Town-Making Principles*, Rizzoli, New York, 1991.

MORRIS, A.E.J., *History of Urban Form*, John Wiley, New York, 1972.

PUSHKAREV, B., and ZUPAN, J., *Urban Space for Pedestrians*, Regional Plan Association of New York, MIT Press, Cambridge, MA, 1975.

Regional Plan Association, *Urban Design Manhattan*, New York Regional Plan Association, 1969.

TRANCIK, ROGER, *Finding Lost Space: Theories of Urban Design*, Van Nostrand Reinhold, New York, 1986.

CHAPTER 11

CAPITAL FACILITIES PLANNING

Alan Walter Steiss

THE NEED FOR CAPITAL FACILITIES PLANNING

As noted in Chapter 9, investment in capital facilities is often the single most powerful tool available to the community to shape its development and implement its comprehensive plan. Capital facilities such as roads, bridges, schools, parking structures, public buildings, water supply, and waste disposal facilities will shape the pattern of land use for decades to come. They generally represent very large investments of public resources and are not easy to modify once built. The acquisition of parkland, a capital investment, can shape the development of a community for decades thereafter even if it is not improved in any way and there is no subsequent investment made on it. In terms of the urban design it will constitute a hard area. Development will have to flow around it and thus will be shaped by it.

There are few, if any, areas of local government in which a systematic planning effort is more important than in making decisions about capital investment. The planning process can assist public officials in developing long-range capital investment strategies by

1. Making projections and forecasts of population needs and economic conditions.
2. Analyzing future revenue and expenditure requirements.

3. Evaluating costs and benefits associated with alternative investments.
4. Assessing various fiscal policies and methods of financing capital facilities.

COMPONENTS OF CAPITAL FACILITIES PLANNING

The planning activities described in this chapter are known by a variety of labels—public works planning, long-range capital improvements programming, capital outlay planning, public investment planning, or capital budgeting. Regardless of the label, the principles and objectives are the same: to guide, within the limits of available financial resources, the provision of major public facilities having a relatively long life. Thus effective *capital facilities planning*—the term we have chosen to use—must involve planning, financing, and programming.

The *planning* phase begins with the formulation of goals and objectives for the desired levels of public service. These goals and objectives must be related to population and economic trends and projections of future demands for public services and facilities. By comparing needs with the capacity of existing facilities, it is possible to determine the additional supply necessary to meet the anticipated demand.

The *financing* phase determines how payments are to be made and specifies the sources of funds. As discussed later in greater detail, capital facilities can be financed in several ways—on a pay-as-you-go basis, from reserve funds, and through long- or short-term borrowing.

Programming refers to a detailed plan for the raising and disbursement of funds and the construction or acquisition of facilities over a relatively short period of time. Programming is necessary because few if any local governments have the resources necessary to make all desirable capital improvements simultaneously. Programming should be based on a system of priorities that is tied to the goals and objectives set forth in the planning phase. A process for the continuous evaluation of public services and facilities also must be developed.

THE PLANNING PHASE

In the planning phase, the emphasis is on the identification of community preferences and the formulation of goals and objectives. This often requires the preparation of population estimates, economic forecasts, and other studies that will give some picture of what the community might be like in the future. The community's estimated or projected future needs can be compared with the present infrastructure (such as roads, water and sewer capacity, and recreational facilities) to suggest how that infrastructure might need to be augmented and modified. Note the close parallel here with the early phases of the comprehensive planning process described in Chapter 8. The following elements should be considered in this long-range planning framework:

1. *External factors that may influence public programs.* Such factors include shifts in land-use patterns and demographic characteristics, changes in economic activities, social trends, and scientific and technological change.

2. *Total public service needs and demand.* Assumptions, standards, and criteria used to quantify and project public facility and service needs should be clearly identified.
3. *An inventory of the present capital facilities of the community.* This should include the state of repair and estimated remaining service life of these facilities.
4. *An evaluation of the present and future roles of various levels of government, as well as private enterprise, in the provision of public facilities and services.* The evaluation may include recommendations for the elimination of overlaps through the coordination or realignment of agency responsibilities.

Forecasting Community Growth and Change

Population projections are usually the most fundamental component in forecasting capital facility requirements. A frequently applied projection technique is the cohort-survival method (see Chapter 8). It is more useful than some other techniques because it gives the picture of the composition of the population rather than just a total number. As noted, the mathematics of the technique are simple. The difficult part is making the right assumptions.

Mistakes in projecting population can be quite costly. For example the baby boom, which began in the late 1940s and lasted until the early 1960s, produced huge increases in public school enrollments. In the 1960s and early 1970s, many localities looked back on a succession of increases, assumed the trend would continue into the foreseeable future, and made substantial investments in new school buildings. In fact, however, enrollments peaked a few years into the 1970s and then declined. As a result, many school districts found themselves paying the debt service on school buildings for which they had no use and often trying to sell empty school buildings at a fraction of cost. In fact, there was considerable interest in the question of how to convert school buildings to residential and commercial use. In the middle 1980s births began increasing as the large numbers of children born in the baby boom reached childbearing age (the "echo" of the baby boom) and by the beginning of the 1990s many school districts were beginning to confront capacity shortages. The municipality or the district was then confronted with the question of whether this upturn was a temporary phenomenon or a long-term trend. Thus, multi-million dollar investment decisions must be made under conditions of considerable uncertainty.

Economic projections are also basic to capital facilities planning. Note that these are not independent of population forecasts since there is generally a relationship between population and employment. If a locality is having rapid industrial growth, for example, it will probably have a wave of worker in-migration. The needs of these new workers and their dependents must be forecast to ensure adequate provision of basic public facilities and related services. Employment projections will also assist in estimating future traffic flows, water and sewage disposal requirements, and so forth.

Land-use studies, also noted in Chapter 8, are a part of planning for capital facilities. These are important for determining what types of development are likely in what areas, which in turn has implications for what types of capital facilities must be provided. Land-use studies also are important for identifying land suitable for various types of capital facilities and for estimating the cost of such public improvements; the cost of sewers, roads, and other facilities can be greatly influenced by topography, subsoil conditions, and the like. The results of the land-use studies should be consistent with the economic and population forecasts. For example, if a land-use study does not indicate enough developable area to accommodate projected population and employment increases, the planner should think seriously about scaling down the projections.

The Computer in Capital Facilities Planning

The computer's capacity to "crunch" large amounts of data quickly makes it practical for types of calculations and estimates that otherwise would be too laborious and time-consuming to contemplate. The computer became available to planners in the late 1950s and early 1960s. It was first used in transportation planning, particularly at the regional level. As computer technology improved, computer modeling was applied to a wide range of planning problems, usually in large organizations such as regional transportation planning agencies. The age of large-scale land use and transportation modeling was thus begun. By *model*, we mean a set of equations that to some degree duplicate the behavior of the real "system" (e.g., a metropolitan area) under study. In a transportation model, for example, the equations might relate the number of vehicular trips to the size and distribution of the population, personal income, number of jobs, and density of development. In an economic model, equations might relate retail sales to population, earned income, transfer payments, and tax rates. Once a model is constructed, various assumptions about the future conditions can be tested.

Models are commonly used to explore various "scenarios," that is, a sequence of events and conditions. For example, suppose a model is being used to forecast the cost of a major construction project, say, a sewer system that will be built over the next decade. The user of the model might make a number of assumptions about future interest rates, other assumptions about future labor costs, and still others about future costs of construction materials. If six assumed levels are made for each of the three variables, 236 possibilities ($6 \times 6 \times 6$) can be calculated to get an idea of the range of possible costs for the project from the best to worst case. The speed with which the computer can process data permits all sorts of explorations that would not be practical if the analyses had to be done by hand. But whether the results of a computer model turn out to be a reliable guide to the future depends on the assumptions that went into the model. Thus, the ultimate responsibility is placed squarely in the hands of the model builder and model user.

THE FINANCING PHASE

Many local governments operate under a condition of considerable fiscal strain. Government officials feel themselves pinched between the need to provide funds for an expensive array of public services and the resistance of the citizens to further tax increases.

In the late 1970s citizen resistance to increases in local taxation rose to such levels that commentators began speaking of the "tax revolt." The most notable example was Proposition 13, passed in California in 1978.[1] In this referendum, California voters passed a proposition that rolled back local property tax assessments to an earlier period; capped the rate at which these assessments could be increased; placed limits on the maximum property tax rate; and barred all units of government, other than counties, from using the property tax. The effect was to cut property tax revenues in California from $12.5 billion to $5.4 billion. Comparable, although not as severe, tax limitations were subsequently passed in a number of other states.

During the Reagan and Bush administrations federal aid to state and local governments for most purposes shrank as a percentage of gross national product and as a percentage of state and local government expenditures. The states managed during the long Reagan era economic expansion. But the recession of 1990–91 pushed many into a near crisis condition. For example, in 1992 the state of California confronted a budget deficit in the $12 billion range with resulting cutbacks in services, layoffs of public employees and a long-running political standoff between Gov. Pete Wilson and the State legislature. Nor was federal help likely, for as of late 1993 the Clinton administration had evidenced no interest in across-the-board increases in aid to state and local governments. Given the nation's concern with the federal budget deficit that was hardly surprising. It appears that state and most local governments will operate under considerable fiscal pressure for some time to come.

Municipalities borrow extensively to fund capital expenditures. However, there are restraints on borrowing. In general, states impose borrowing limits on substate units of government. Typically, these limits are cast in terms of dollars of outstanding general obligation depth as a percentage of the full value of taxable real property within the municipality's borders.[2] Beyond any state-imposed limits on borrowing, municipalities are constrained by the fact that this year's borrowing must be paid back from revenues in subsequent years. Then, too, when the debt service burden of a municipality becomes overly large in comparison to its tax base, the municipality's bond rating may be lowered and the cost of borrowing increased. Companies that rate municipal bonds (and thereby influence the interest rate that must be offered to place such bonds) emphasize the importance of "good fiscal stewardship" in this regard.

Revenue Analysis

Revenue analysis disaggregates (separates) sources of revenue into appropriate categories, like property tax, sales tax, fees and licenses, and projects these over a number of years. Demographic and economic forecasts are very important in estimating the future size of the tax base from which these revenues will come. The future magnitude of intergovernment aid also must be estimated. Finally, some assumptions must be made about inflation or deflation, and particularly, about interest rates; the former is important because revenues from sources like sales and property taxes are greatly affected by inflation, and the latter is important because it affects the cost of borrowing. Considerable uncertainty is involved in such analyses, and the chance that a municipality will project its revenues correctly over, say, the next decade is quite small. Nevertheless, there is no good alternative. As noted previously, with a computer it is possible to run "best case" and "worst case" scenarios to provide an "envelope" within which to plan.

Expenditure Analysis

Expenditure analyses also require disaggregation of data on expenditures into major categories. Data from past fiscal years provide a basis on which to calculate rates of increase or decrease. Subsequently, these data assist in the computation of multipliers appropriate to each expenditure category. For example, past data might be examined to project the cost per pupil of primary school education. Population projections for the community provide enrollment estimates in future years. Multiplying these two quantities yields a first approximation of the real costs. The projected costs might then be adjusted for projected inflation to yield the actual dollar costs. Note that we are multiplying one uncertainty (projected cost per pupil) by a second uncertainty (number of pupils) by a third uncertainty (changes in the value of the dollar). Therefore, the result is necessarily only a very rough approximation.

An Expenditure Model An expenditure model that has particular application to long-range financial planning was developed by Claudia Scott.[3] The model produces separate estimates of future expenditures for nine major categories of public service. Each class of expenditure can be based on various explicit assumptions regarding the supply and demand associated with a particular service. The model permits the testing of different assumptions even where a high degree of confidence cannot be attached to particular projections.

The data shown in Table 11–1 are quite old, but they indicate how repeated runs on the computer can be used to establish upper and lower limits and indicate a range in which the actual values will probably lie. Multiple runs are also useful in showing how sensitive the outcome is to each of the variables in the model. In the run shown all possible outcomes are listed for low, medium, or high values for three different variables: population, level of service, and public employee salary levels. This produces a total of 27 (3 × 3 × 3) combinations. Note that there is about a 15 percent spread between the lowest and the highest figure in any given year. The highest projection was obtained when salary and service levels were high and population was medium. The medium population number yielded a higher cost figure than the high population cost because it assumed higher proportion of minority population with higher per capita service needs. Whether or not this assumption about minority population service needs is correct, it emphasizes the point made earlier that in forecasting population it is not only total numbers that are important.

This and other similar computer-assisted modeling techniques have been successfully applied in the financial planning efforts of various localities. These

TABLE 11–1 Projections of city expenditures under alternative assumptions concerning population, service, and salary levels for 1971 through 1975 (thousands of dollars)

Code[a]	Ranking of 1975 Projection[b]	PROJECTION 1971	1972	1973	1974	1975
1. LLL	1	$59,000	$65,004	$70,004	$ 75,810	$ 81,394
2. LLM	5	59,802	66,607	72,560	79,458	86,267
3. LLH	12	62,118	69,034	76,592	85,160	94,026
4. LML	4	59,973	66,949	72,754	79,093	85,905
5. LMM	10	60,801	68,605	75,426	82,925	91,014
6. LMH	18	63,436	71,110	79,527	88,900	99,326
7. LHL	13	61,574	70,151	77,272	85,451	94,342
8. LHM	19	62,452	71,906	80,153	89,268	100,178
9. LHH	25	65,518	74,559	84,572	95,817	109,432
10. MLL	3	59,489	65,980	71,244	77,355	83,266
11. MLM	3	60,304	67,611	73,853	81,091	88,275
12. MLH	16	62,888	70,079	77,864	86,929	96,247
13. MML	9	59,037	68,249	74,658	81,593	88,949
14. MMM	14	61,564	70,131	77,414	85,603	94,366
15. MMH	22	64,542	72,699	81,700	91,779	102,961
16. MHL	20	62,807	72,616	80,621	89,846	100,291
17. MHM	24	63,733	74,469	83,652	94,343	106,598
18. MHH	27	67,279	77,206	88,332	101,326	116,599
19. HLL	2	59,388	65,779	71,036	77,136	83,020
20. HLM	6	60,201	67,404	73,637	81,856	88,004
21. HLH	15	62,686	69,863	77,695	86,150	95,922
22. HML	7	60,709	68,420	74,055	80,813	88,032
23. HMM	11	61,282	69,567	76,784	84,743	93,368
24. HMH	21	64,078	72,110	82,438	90,858	101,906
25. HHL	17	61,911	70,824	79,433	87,871	98,666
26. HHM	23	62,997	73,151	80,919	92,240	101,825
27. HHH	26	66,287	75,855	86,413	99,076	114,577

[a]L = low, M = medium, H = high. The first letter describes population level; the second describes service level; the third describes salary level. Thus, for projection 12, code MLH means that this computer run was based on the medium population estimate, the low service estimate, and the high salary estimate.
[b]Rankings range from lowest (1) to highest (27) expenditures.

Adapted from Claudia DeVita Scott, *Forecasting Local Government Spending,* The Urban Institute, Washington, D.C., 1972, p. 98.

techniques offer a significant improvement over the "best guess" extrapolations traditionally used to estimate future expenditure levels and, therefore, future revenue requirements.

Methods of Financing

In financing public facilities, the options are similar to those available to any individual or family. A municipality may (1) pay cash, (2) save money for future acquisitions, or (3) borrow on anticipated earning power. A sound, long-range revenue program will seek to develop an appropriate mix among these three methods. Some fairly straightforward calculations can assist public officials in evaluating alternative mixes.

For example, assume that a municipality is considering a major addition to its community health center. Construction costs are estimated to be $500,000 (in current dollars), with an additional $50,000 for site preparation and $150,000 for equipment. Construction costs are increasing at 12 percent per year, and the cost of equipment is estimated to be increasing at 15 percent per year. The municipality might consider four different financing approaches:

1. Fund the project from general tax revenues over a period of four years, with site preparation in year 1, construction in years 2 and 3, and equipment acquisition in year 4.
2. Build a capital reserve fund over four years until the total project costs were accumulated, at which time the project could be constructed.
3. Fund site preparation out of current revenues and issue bonds for the $650,000 in equipment and construction costs.
4. Establish a capital reserve fund, annual payments from which to cover the project schedule outlined under the first alternative.

The calculations associated with each of these alternatives are shown in the box on pp. 168–169. As can be seen from the data, given the assumptions noted, the fourth approach is the least costly alternative. Note, however, that achieving the least cost is not necessarily the only consideration, for there are other pros and cons to any financing strategy.

Pay-as-you-go financing encourages government to "live within its income." It minimizes premature commitments of funds. The credit of government is conserved for times of emergency, when ample credit may be vital. Since the pay-as-you-go approach avoids the added cost of interest payments, it also is usually less costly than borrowing.[4]

On the other hand, the pay-as-you-go approach may result in an undue burden being placed on present taxpayers to finance some future need from which they may not fully benefit. Thus, it may be argued that public projects providing services over many years should be paid for by people according to their use or benefit—financed on a pay-as-you-use basis. Achieving *user-benefit equity*—if that is an important goal—may require financing a facility so that the burden is spread over the life of the improvement. That means repayment over a period of many years. Then, too, excessive commitment to pay-as-you-go may prevent a municipality from doing things that really need to be done because the projects are too costly to be carried out with only annual operating funds. In fact, few governments today have the capability to finance vital public facilities strictly on a pay-as-you-go basis. Therefore, the power to borrow is one of the most important assets of government.

Like all government powers, the capacity to borrow must be used with a clear understanding of its safe and reasonable limits. A sound borrowing policy is one that seeks to conserve rather than exhaust credit. The ability to borrow when necessary on the most favorable market terms is an objective that applies to governments just as it does to business and industry.

Localities often will borrow to finance major facilities on the assumption that future economic and population growth will make the payment of the debt service (principal and interest) more feasible. Future events may or may not prove this assumption correct.

Communities also may borrow on the assumption that inflation will make repayment easier. As inflation erodes the real value of the dollar, the actual burden of a given dollar of debt declines. A municipality that issued 30-year bonds in 1960 was paying off the last of that debt in 1990 with dollars that were worth no more than 30 cents in terms of 1960 prices. However, unless one's crystal ball is unfailingly accurate, relying on inflation to lift the burden of debt can be a high-risk strategy.

Financing capital facilities through the accumulation of a reserve fund (sometimes called a capital reserve) can be thought of as the opposite of borrowing in that the timetable is reversed. A portion of current revenue is invested each year to accumulate sufficient funds to initiate some particular project in the future. Thus, an investment of $100,000 each year for ten years at 6 percent interest will yield a reserve fund of $1,318,000.[5] Conversely, should the objective be to develop a reserve fund of $2 million at the end of ten years, a municipality must be willing to invest $151,736 per year at 6 percent. The reserve fund approach is clearly a conservative and prudent strategy. Whether it is the lowest cost approach depends on whether project costs inflate at a rate higher or lower than the rate of interest the municipality gets for the money deposited in the reserve fund.

Bonding Strategies When municipalities borrow, they generally do so by issuing bonds. A bond is a promissory note ensuring that the lender will receive periodic payments of interest and that at the due date the original sum invested will be repaid. Thus, a ten-year municipal bond for $10,000 with a 7 percent interest rate will pay the bondholder $700 each year (usually in semiannual installments). Then, at the end of ten years, the $10,000 principal itself is repaid.

In general, interest on municipal bonds is exempt from federal taxation (and from state taxes in the state in which it is issued). The buyer does not even have to report as income the interest received from such bonds. Thus, municipal bonds carry a lower interest rate than taxable bonds of even the most blue-chip corporations. In effect, this tax exemption is a very substantial federal subsidy to local governments because it effectively reduces their borrowing (debt service) costs. For 1993 the federal government's office of Management and the Budget (OMB) federal revenue loss (tax expenditure) on tax exempt bonds issued by local governments was approximately $15.6 billion.[6]

Municipal bonds backed by the "full faith, credit, and taxing power" of the issuing locality are referred to as *general obligation bonds*. Some bonds, however, are backed instead by a pledge of the revenues generated by the facility that is being financed. Such *revenue bonds* often are used to build parking structures, sewage treatment plants, toll roads and bridges, and other facilities that have fairly predictable revenue-generating capacities.

Municipal bonds fall into two general types according to the method of redemption: (1) term or sinking funds bonds and (2) serial bonds. *Term bonds* become due in a lump sum at the end of the term of the loan (all bonds in the issue reach maturity and must be paid off at the same time). The lump sum principal

FOUR ALTERNATIVES FOR FUNDING A CAPITAL INVESTMENT

Alternative 1.
Pay-As-You-Go Funding from General Revenue

Year	*Project Phase*	*Cost Calculations*	
1	Site preparation		= $ 50,000
2	Construction: First phase	$250,000 (1.12)	= $ 280,000
3	Construction: Second phase	$250,000 $(1.12)^2$	= $ 313,600
4	Equipment Acquisition	$150,000 $(1.15)^3$	= $ 228,130
	Total cost		$ 871,730

Alternative 2.
Capital Reserve Fund over Four Years
(8% Annual Interest)

Project Phase	*Cost Calculations*	
Site preparation	$50,000 / $(1.12)^3$	= $ 70,246
Construction costs	$500,000 / $(1.12)^3$	= $ 702,464
Equipment acquisition	$150,000 / $(1.15)^3$	= $ 228,130
Total reserve required		$1,000,840
Annual payments (adjusted for interest that unused balances in reserve fund will earn)		= $ 222,107
	Total cost $222,107 × 4	= $ 888,428

Alternative 3.
Bond Issue—Five-Year Annuity Serial
(6% Annual Interest)

Annual debt service on $650,000		= $ 154,300
		× 5
		$ 771,500
Site preparation		50,000
	Total Cost	$ 821,500

Alternative 4.
Capital Reserve Fund
With Annual Funding of Project

Year	*Carry Forward*	*Payment to Reserve*	*Cost*	*Reserve Balance*
1		$196,500		
		× 1.08		
		$212,220	$ 50,000	$162,220
2	$162,220	$196,500		
	× 1.08	× 1.08		
	$175,198	$212,220	$280,000	$107,418
3	$107,418	$196,500		
	× 1.08	× 1.08		
	$116,011	$212,220	$313,600	$ 14,631
	$ 14,631	$196,500		
	× 1.08	× 1.08		
	$ 15,801	$212,220	$228,130	$ 0
		Total cost $196,500 × 4		= $786,000

The four alternatives in the box are compared in terms of the actual total cash outlay required for each one.

In alternative 1 the construction work is divided equally between year 2 and year 3 but year 3's cash figure is 12 percent larger because of the effect of another year's inflation. Equipment is acquired in year 4 so that its cost increases by three year's inflation.

In alternative 2 we assume that the municipality puts away money in four equal installments. Site preparation is done in the first year, but construction and equipment acquisition are put off for three years. During those three years the monies deposited in the reserve fund earn interest, but at the same time, construction and equipment acquisition costs rise because of inflation.

In alternative 3 the $50,000 in site preparation cost is paid out of current revenues and the remaining $650,000 is funded by a bond issue. Both construction and equipment acquisition are done in the first year.

In alternative 4 equal payments are made into a reserve fund. Construction is done in the second and third year and equipment is acquired in the fourth year. This alternative differs from alternative 2, in which construction does not begin until all the funding has been accumulated. Because the rate at which costs inflate is greater than the interest rate, alternative 4 is less costly than alternative 2.

The reader may note that alternatives 2 and 4 involve 8 percent interest rates, whereas alternatives 3 involves a 6 percent interest rate. The assumption here is that the municipality can invest its unspent funds at prevailing market interest rates, and it can borrow at lower rates because the interest that its bonds pay is exempt from taxation.

payment is met by making annual payments to a *sinking fund*. When invested at compound interest, these annual payments should produce the amount of principal required at maturity. An issue of *serial bonds*, on the other hand, is retired by annual installments directly from tax revenues or, in the case of revenue bonds, from earned income.

Term bonds require some expertise in fund investments. Frequent actuarial computations are required to determine the adequacy of sinking funds to meet principal payments at maturity. Bonds for which the principal is funded solely through a sinking fund are not legal in some states. With proper investment safeguards, however, term bonds do offer some advantages. They may serve to finance public utilities and other enterprises that do not have established earning records. The accumulations in the sinking fund may afford a means of disposing of new bond issues when the general market is unsatisfactory. That is, a municipality may "buy" a portion of its own bonds in a new issue. Providing prompt repayment is made, sinking funds also afford an opportunity for short-term borrowing when the cost of bank loans is prohibitive.

Serial bonds are preferable for most purposes and for most cities, particularly for smaller communities. Serial bonds have simpler retirement requirements and offer greater flexibility in marketing and in arranging the debt structure of the community. There are two types of serial bonds: annuity serials and straight serials. With *annuity serials*, the debt service payment is approximately the same each year (like a home mortgage). The portion of the annual payment that covers interest is higher in the early years of the issue but declines as payments toward principal are made (i.e., as the outstanding principal is retired). *Straight serial bonds* require annual payments of principal of approximately equal amounts. Interest payments are large in early years and decline gradually as the number of bonds outstanding declines.

Evaluation Criteria

Most municipal governments will be asked to consider many more projects than can actually be funded. Thus, it is necessary to have some way of assigning priorities. Hatry, Millar, and Evans have suggested 11 criteria for the evaluation of capital projects.[7] These criteria, summarized in Table 11–2, are based on a recent survey of capital facilities planning procedures in 25 cities. Typically, capital project requests originate in the various municipal departments such as public works, parks and recreation, education, and social services. Most cities require a description or justification for each project as part of the departmental submissions. Often these statements are so general, however, that the process of comparing and selecting among competing projects may become very subjective. For the planning agency to review a capital project effectively, a systematic set of evaluation criteria is extremely useful. Each of the criteria listed in Table 11–2 is briefly examined in the following sections.

1. Fiscal Impacts All local governments require data on the expected costs of each capital project. In many cities, information is also requested on the operating and maintenance (O & M) costs of the proposed project. Often capital

TABLE 11–2 Suggested evaluation criteria

1. Fiscal impacts
2. Health and safety effects
3. Community economic effects
4. Environmental, aesthetic, and social effects—impact on the quality of life
5. Amount of disruption and inconvenience caused by the project—impact on the quality of service
6. Distributional effects—who is affected and how
7. Feasibility, including public support and project readiness
8. Implications of deferring the project
9. Amount of uncertainty and risk
10. Effects on interjurisdictional relationships
11. Advantages accruing from relationships with other capital proposals

Adapted from Harry P. Hatry, Annie P. Millar, and James H. Evans, "Guide to Setting Priorities for Capital Investments," *Guides to Managing Urban Capital*, vol. 5, The Urban Institute Press, Washington, D.C., 1984, p. 9.

projects, particularly those involving rehabilitation of existing facilities, are intended to reduce future O & M costs. Therefore, estimates of such reductions may be an important factor in justifying such projects. Explicit consideration of initial costs for development (site acquisition and preparation, construction, and capital equipment acquisition) and subsequent costs for operations, maintenance, and repairs of the capital facility is sometimes referred to as *life-cycle costing*. Other fiscal impact considerations include

1. Changes in revenue: Capital projects may generate new revenues for the locality (e.g., when charges are levied for public services) or may result in a reduction in government revenues (e.g., when private land is taken off the tax roll for a capital project site).
2. Impact on energy requirements: Estimated changes in energy requirements (increases or decreases) should be included as part of a project's O & M cost impacts.
3. Legal liability: Estimates should be made of any potential cost liabilities of undertaking (or not undertaking) a capital project, such as for flood damages resulting from the diversion of a natural stream course.

2. HEALTH AND SAFETY EFFECTS Project justifications should include an assessment of such health- and safety-related effects as anticipated reductions in traffic accidents, elimination of health hazards arising from sewer problems or poor water quality, and long-term health hazards like asbestos in public buildings. Data on the estimated number of persons affected and the severity of the effect should be provided. The data should indicate the anticipated improvements in such conditions if the proposed project is implemented.

3. COMMUNITY ECONOMIC EFFECTS Economic effects should include the likely impact of the project on (a) property values, (b) the tax base, (c) employment opportunities, (d) personal income, (e) business income, and (f) the stabilization or revitalization of declining neighborhoods. These impacts may be more evident in capital projects that are proposed in response to community growth and ex-

pansion. However, projects aimed at maintaining or upgrading the existing infrastructure also may have significant economic effects.

4. QUALITY OF LIFE AND QUALITY OF SERVICE Both beneficial and adverse effects on the quality of life—environmental, aesthetic, and social—in the community should be considered. Although perhaps not resulting in major health problems, the potential for noise, air, or water pollution should be taken into account. Increased travel times and other inconveniences to the public should also be evaluated.

5. DISRUPTION AND INCONVENIENCE Some projects can involve lengthy disruptions of service and inconvenience to users. Repairs or construction of bridges, streets, and water and sewer lines can involve rerouting of traffic, temporary interruptions of service, or even relocations of households.

6. DISTRIBUTIONAL EFFECTS Capital projects can deliver financial gains or losses to individuals or firms (e.g., loss of trade because of street blockage during construction). Where appropriate, these benefits and costs should be broken down by (a) age groups, (b) economic status, (c) neighborhoods or districts, (d) residential or commercial areas, (e) handicapped persons, and so forth.

7. PROJECT FEASIBILITY Projects should be evaluated in terms of any special implementation problems (e.g., requirements to obtain state or federal permits or other authorization) and legal issues. The compatibility and compliance of the project with the comprehensive plan should be assessed. If the project is a continuation of previous improvements, the impact on prior investments should be identified. And finally, the degree of public support for or opposition to the project should be evaluated, and any special interest groups involved should be identified. Jurisdictions should explore the availability of needed staff; the time required to obtain federal or state approvals; the time required to ensure the necessary citizen support; and the lead times for architectural and engineering plans, construction bidding, material acquisition, and the like.

8. IMPLICATIONS OF PROJECT DEFERRAL The impact of deferring the project should be explored. What will be the added costs? Who will be harmed and how? Is intergovernment assistance more or less likely to be available in the future? What are the trends in the municipal bond market? Deferring projects is especially tempting for public officials when the locality is financially hard-pressed in the current fiscal year. Before the decision to defer is made, however, local officials should estimate possible effects.

9. RISK AND UNCERTAINTY All capital projects involve some risk and uncertainty. The uncertainty, for example, can arise from cost estimates (especially in projects involving new technologies or procedures) and in terms of the effects on the quality of service (because of uncertainties about the durability and reliability of new materials). As noted, there are always risks in the bond market.

10. INTERJURISDICTIONAL RELATIONS Special coordination may be required if a proposed project has significant adverse or beneficial effects on other jurisdictions or agencies that serve the same area. Examples include water supply projects where the source (reservoir or aquifer) is outside the municipality or a landfill project where one jurisdiction handles the waste produced in other jurisdictions.

11. ADVANTAGES ACCRUING FROM OTHER PROPOSALS The relationship between capital projects should be identified, particularly if the initiation of one project will affect the costs or benefits of another. For example, improvements to water mains could be undertaken at less cost if coordinated with street improvements in the same area. If two or more projects could be undertaken together at a lower cost than if done separately, the combined effort might rate a higher priority.

Some of the criteria described above are more objective than others. Even though fiscal impacts cannot be estimated precisely, the terms in which they are measured, namely, dollars, are unambiguous. On the other hand, such items as "aesthetic and social effects" are necessarily less precise, although not necessarily less important. There is thus much room for differences of opinion about how to weight the various items in Table 11–2. In that sense, evaluation is always somewhat subjective. Nonetheless, systematic approaches such as that described here are useful in organizing and clarifying thinking about capital expenditures.

When projects have been evaluated by these criteria, they can be *ranked* or sorted into various categories. One set of categories to which proposed projects might be assigned is shown in Table 11–3.

TABLE 11–3 General criteria for capital facilities priority system

Category	*General Criteria*
1. Urgent	Projects that cannot reasonably be postponed; projects that would remedy conditions dangerous to public health, welfare, or safety; projects required to maintain a critically needed program; projects needed to meet an emergency situation
2. Essential	Projects required to complete or make fully usable a major public improvement; projects required to maintain minimum standards as part of an ongoing program; desirable self-liquidating projects; projects for which external funds for over 65% of costs are available for a limited period
3. Necessary	Projects that should be carried out within a few years to meet clearly demonstrated anticipated needs; projects to replace unsatisfactory or obsolete facilities; remodeling projects for continued use of facilities
4. Desirable	Adequately planned projects needed for the expansion of the current programs; projects designed to initiate new programs considered appropriate for a progressive community; projects for the conversion of existing facilities to other uses
5. Acceptable	Adequately planned projects that can be postponed without detriment to present operations if budget reductions are necessary
6. Deferrable	Projects recommended for postponement or elimination from immediate consideration in the current capital facilities plan; projects that are questionable in terms of overall needs, adequate planning, or proper timing

Adapted from Alan Walter Steiss, *Local Government Finance: Capital Facilities Planning and Debt Administration*, Lexington Books, Lexington, MA, 1978, p. 38.

THE PROGRAMMING PHASE

When all proposed projects have been examined and analyzed, a composite *capital improvements program* should be prepared for presentation to the chief executive. A capital improvements program (CIP) represents the more immediate and more detailed portions of the long-range capital facilities plan, usually spanning a five-to-six-year period. Governments have found with experience that six years is a convenient period for the detailed programming of capital expenditures, permitting sufficient lead time for the design and other preliminary work required by such projects. Projects included in the CIP should be ranked according to priority.

The capital improvements program is then reviewed and adopted, with appropriate modifications, by the chief executive and the governing body. When adopted, the CIP should be made available in report form to civic groups and interested citizens in addition to being distributed to the operating departments. The detailed description of each project should include a brief statement of its general purpose and reason for its inclusion in the CIP. Capital costs, operating costs, source of funds, method of financing, and financing schedule should be set forth in the report for each project.

Even after legislative action has been taken in adopting the CIP, funds must still be made available. The final step in the capital facilities planning process is the preparation and adoption of a *capital budget*. This sets forth, in dollar terms, the policy decisions from the preceding steps. Of course, even after appropriations are made, changes and adjustments are still possible before construction or acquisition. However, if the original project requests are based on a sound planning foundation, the need for such changes should be minimal.

SUMMARY

Capital expenditures are often the most powerful tool available to the municipality for shaping the patterns of development. Capital-expenditures involve decisions that exert their effects over long time periods and can be altered only with considerable difficulty. In most cases, needs for capital facilities as the municipality sees them will exceed the funds available. For all of these reasons it is important for the municipality to have an effective capital facilities planning process. This process should be synchronized with the comprehensive planning process as described in Chapter 8. Its time horizon should be similar to that of the comprehensive plan, typically 20 or 25 years.

Generally, the capital facilities planning process can be divided into three main phases.

1. *Planning*. In this phase demographic, economic, and other studies are done to form an estimate of the municipality's future capital needs. The present facilities are inventoried to determine how many future needs can be met from existing facilities. The difference provides an estimate of the need for future capital investment.
2. *Financing*. Sources of revenue and methods of paying for proposed facili-

ties are examined in detail. A variety of financing techniques are available to municipalities: pay-as-you-go; the establishment of reserve funds, which are essentially a form of prepayment; and borrowing through the issuance of bonds.

3. *Programming*. In this phase a detailed schedule for the execution and financing of the projects decided on in the first two phases is developed. The time horizon for programming is considerably shorter than for the capital facilities planning process as a whole. Many municipalities use a period of about six years for programming purposes.

NOTES

1. For details of Proposition 13 as well as a general account of the tax limitation movement, see Alvin Rabushka and Pauline Ryan, *The Tax Revolt*. The Hoover Institute, Stanford University Press, Stanford, CA, 1982.
2. The term *full value* refers to the market value of the property in question. The reason for using this term is that many communities use fractional assessment, wherein properties are assessed at some fraction of market value. This figure is then multiplied by a correction factor (sometimes referred to as an "assessment ratio" or "equalization rate") to obtain the full value.
3. Claudia Devita Scott, *Forecasting Local Government Spending*, Urban Institute Press, Washington, D.C., 1972.
4. An exception to this generalization is the case in which a municipality borrows at low interest rates and then a period of strong inflation ensues. In this case the municipality is paying back with dollars whose real value shrinks each year. If the inflation rate is greater than the interest rate, the reduction in the real value of the debt service payments more than cancels out the burden imposed by the interest charges.
5. Computed by $S = N\left(\frac{(1 + r)^{n-1}}{r}\right)$, where N is the amount of payment, n is the number of payments, and r is the interest rate.
6. *Statistical Abstract of the United States,* 112th edition, Department of Commerce, Washington D.C., 1992, Table 497.
7. Harry P. Hatry, Annie Millar, and James H. Evans, *Guide to Setting Priorities for Capital Investment,* Urban Institute Press, Washington, D.C., 1984.

SELECTED BIBLIOGRAPHY

HATRY, HARRY P., MILLAR, ANNIE P., and EVANS, JAMES H., *Guide to Setting Priorities for Capital Investment,* Urban Institute Press, Washington, D.C., 1984.

STEISS, ALAN W., *Local Government Finance: Capital Facilities Planning and Debt Administration,* Lexington Books, Lexington, MA, 1975.

CHAPTER 12

URBAN RENEWAL AND COMMUNITY DEVELOPMENT

For several decades community development has been a major preoccupation of planners. It covers a wide range of goals and activities.

1. *Facilitation of economic growth or, in more desperate cases, measures to retard the loss of economic activity.*
2. *Attempts to increase the quality—and sometimes the quantity—of the municipality's housing stock.*
3. *Attempts to sustain or improve some particular commercial function of the city, most commonly retailing.* (Note the link here with item 1.)
4. *Improvement of some physical aspect of the community such as its parks, recreational facilities, parking facilities, or street pattern.*
5. *Furtherance of urban design goals.* This is often tied to some of the previously listed goals. For example, attempts to beautify—or de-uglify—a downtown street might be tied to attempts to increase downtown retailing activity, which might be part of a larger effort aimed at employment expansion.
6. *Provision of a variety of services.* Examples might be provision of social services such as day care, job training, or drug rehabilitation. Service provision is likely to be directed primarily to less affluent segments of the community's population.

Although the term *community development* is of post-World War II origin it is not a totally new departure for planning. Planners' concerns with housing go back to the nineteenth century. Then, too, the facilitation of economic growth had been a major motivation behind city planning for decades.

This chapter begins with an account of Urban Renewal, a program that is now history. The reader may wonder why this look backward is necessary. Although the Urban Renewal program is now over, many of its main elements are still central to the urban development process. It is instructive in that it illustrates how hard it can be to formulate policy that is free of major side effects and actually does what it is intended to do. For its critics, who grew to be very numerous indeed, Urban Renewal was a classic illustration of the old expression "The road to hell is paved with good intentions."

URBAN RENEWAL

Urban Renewal began with the Housing Act of 1949 and was officially ended in 1973 (though some funding of projects started before 1973 continued far into the 1980s). The goals of the program, as expressed in legislation and congressional debate, included

Eliminating substandard housing
Revitalizing city economies
Constructing good housing
Reducing de facto segregation

The method used was clearance and rebuilding directed by local agencies and supported by large federal subsidies. It was and still stands as the largest federal urban program in U.S. history, and it reshaped parts of hundreds of communities.[1] Statistics published in 1973 when the program was terminated showed that more than 2,000 projects had been undertaken on 1,000 square miles of urban land. Some 600,000 housing units, the dwelling places of perhaps 2 million people, had been demolished and those people forced to move. Roughly 250,000 new housing units had been built on the same sites. Approximately 120 million square feet of public floor space and 224 million square feet of commercial floor space had been built on renewal land.[2] As a measure of economic impact, the floor space figures translate into workplaces for almost one-half million employees. The assessed value of land and structures in renewal areas increased by a factor of 3.6 from what it had been before the program started. Today all of these figures would be even larger because the 1973 figures, which actually represented the facts as of about 1971, caught many renewal areas after the demolition phase but well before the construction phase was complete.

By 1973 the Urban Renewal program had spent approximately $13 billion in federal funds, a figure that would be at least three times as large if converted into 1990s dollars. To this figure should be added several billion dollars in local funds. Beyond that were the private investments on Urban Renewal Sites. These substantially exceeded the total public investments.

The Origins of Urban Renewal

The rationale for Urban Renewal stems from two very simple economic circumstances. To build on virgin land the builder need only pay the cost of the land plus the cost of construction. But to build on land containing structures that must be demolished, the builder must also pay the residual value of those structures. A building may be obsolete. Its owner or any objective observer might agree that under present circumstances it would never make sense to build a building like it on the present site. Nonetheless, if the building yields some stream of income to its owner, he or she will not give up the building without compensation.

Consider the following example. Mr. X owns a 90-year-old tenement near the core of the city. The building contains 12 apartments, which rent for an average of $200 per month—a low figure, which represents the fact that these apartments are close to the bottom of the city's housing market. Mr. X is approached by a developer who is interested in the land under the building but must acquire that building to get at the land. A rule of thumb for rental properties is that buildings are valued at 100 times the monthly rent roll, so Mr. X responds with an offer to sell for $240,000 (12 × 200 × 100). If the building occupies a 50-by-100-foot lot, that works out to about $48 per square foot, or roughly $2 million per acre. Even if the developer thinks Mr. X may come down considerably, that number makes vacant land on a suburban highway at, say, $5 per square foot, or roughly $200,000 per acre, look very attractive.

The second factor that impedes development in built-up areas is the land assemblage problem. Typically, urban land ownership is highly fragmented. A single city block is likely to be owned by many separate individuals or business organizations. In fact, in many cities the basic unit into which land was originally subdivided is the 25-by-100-foot lot (25-foot frontage and 100-foot depth). For the developer setting up a major project it may be necessary to deal with dozens of different owners. In some instances their titles may have legal problems that cannot be resolved without substantial delays. In other cases the owner of a small parcel may exploit his or her capacity to block a large project by holding out for a price that far exceeds the fair market value of the land. Compared to the urban fringe, where land is generally owned in much larger blocks, the situation can be very discouraging.

These impediments to urban redevelopment were recognized during the latter part of the Great Depression and there was interest by the federal government in taking steps to improve the competitive position of the central cities. In December 1941, hardly good timing for proposing a new civilian program, Greer and Hansen published an article suggesting the creation of City Realty Corporations.[3] These organizations would be able to use eminent domain to assemble land and would have funds from higher levels of government for the acquisition and clearance of sites. The proposed corporations would thus be able to deal effectively with both the residual value and land assemblage problems.

The idea lay dormant through World War II but was revived shortly thereafter. The Housing Act of 1949 brought the program into being very much as

Hansen and Greer envisioned it. The act provided for the creation of Local Public Agencies (LPAs) analogous to the City Realty Corporation. The LPA would have the power of eminent domain to acquire sites. Two-thirds of the LPA's funding was to come from the federal government and the remaining third from the municipality. However, some of the local share could be services in kind (services of city personnel, donation of city-owned land, etc.) so that in cash terms the federal government paid more than the nominal two-thirds. The LPA would use its legal powers and financial resources to acquire, clear, and otherwise prepare sites (grading, provision of utilities, widening and straightening of streets, etc.). These would then be sold or leased to private developers at substantially below cost.

By absorbing the residual value as well as many other development costs, the program would greatly accelerate the redevelopment process within the designated renewal areas of cities. By using public powers to acquire and clear large sites, the program would permit far more coordinated and imaginative development than would otherwise be the case.

In order to work as described Urban Renewal introduced a new practice into law. It previously had been understood that eminent domain could be used to take private property and convey it to a public body for public use, for example the building of a public school. But under Urban Renewal government took property from one private party, say, the owner of a dilapidated tenement and ultimately conveyed it to another private party, the developer building on the Urban Renewal site. This seemed questionable on constitutional grounds and a property owner took an Urban Renewal Agency to court. But in 1954 in *Berman* v *Parker* the Supreme Court sustained the agency. Had the case gone the other way the Urban Renewal process as it was then structured would have come to a virtual halt, another indication of the decisive role that the courts often play in planning.

Intention and Reality

Congress intended Urban Renewal as a housing program, as the goals listed earlier indicate. The initial legislation confined renewal activity to sites that either were or would be largely residential. In fact, the initial legislation stipulated that for each new unit of housing built at least one old unit of housing must be torn down. The intent to eliminate slums by replacing bad, old housing with good, new housing was very clear.

The goals, though praiseworthy, contain some internal contradictions and some not-so-pleasant side effects, which become apparent on reflection. For instance, rebuilding the city's economy is likely to be furthered by a program that demolishes substandard housing and replaces it with a purely commercial development. But where does that leave the goal of adding good, new units to the city's housing stock? Who could be against eliminating substandard housing? Rephrase that as reducing the supply of low-cost housing, driving down vacancy rates, and thereby tightening the housing market in which the poor must find shelter and it does not sound so good. Achieving a higher degree of racial integration is a praiseworthy goal. One way to achieve racial integration in a poor, black neighborhood is to knock down dilapidated older housing occupied by low-income blacks and replace it with high-quality—and more expensive—housing to be occupied by middle- or upper-income households, most of whom are not black. Of course, that is a rather stiff price to pay for integration.

These points are not made to ridicule the program. Rather, it is to say that Urban Renewal was major urban surgery and as such it had many side effects, not all of which were desirable or foreseen. Any major program will have all sorts of secondary effects, some of which are good and some of which are bad. Some will be foreseen and others will not. Doing good is not simply amatter of good intentions.

One fact that soon became apparent as the federal funds began to flow was that local intentions and federal intentions were not always the same. With the passage of time, local desires began to change both federal law and federal practice. From the federal point of view housing was central. But many localities did not care about housing. If rundown housing occupied by lower-income households was demolished and replaced with commercial development, the municipality solved both a housing and a tax base problem. The population that lived in the housing to be demolished would not vanish from the face of the earth. But if it settled in adjacent communities after being dehoused by "the federal bulldozer," it became someone else's problem. From the local perspective, that solved the problem. Of course, from the federal perspective that was no solution at all. At best, it was a "zero sum game" played with federal funds. Clearly, what constitutes a problem and what constitutes a solution vary, depending on whom one considers to be one's constituency.

What happens when federal and local goals differ? The "locals" wanting the federal money do some compromising and accept some conditions that they do not like. On the other hand, the federal official whose job it is to spend the allocated funds wants to see agreements with LPAs signed and projects underway. So he or she does some compromising too. In time the program gets bent from its initial shape into something that both the "locals" and the "feds" can "live with." Gradually both the legislation and the regulations adapt to this reality. In the case of Urban Renewal that meant relaxing the residential requirements and permitting many projects that had a predominantly commercial emphasis.

But that was hardly the end of the story. With the passage of time some of the program's side effects became apparent, and both those who suffered from them and their allies began to exert pressure for change.

The most easily identified and numerous victims were those people who lost their housing because of Urban Renewal. In the typical project all the land was acquired at the beginning. Before clearance could begin all those who resided on the site had to relocate. There then followed a clearance phase during which all the demolition was accomplished. The construction phase might then spread out over a number of years. It might not even begin for several years after clearance was completed. When the construction phase was completed, the number of new units might or might not approximate the number of units demolished. In either case the new units were not likely to do the original residents much good. First, there was the question of where they were to live in the intervening years. Equally important was the cost issue. Good, new housing costs a lot more to rent than bad, old housing. Urban Renewal typically took place in the urban core, where housing was old, relatively inexpensive, and largely occupied by poor people. Most of them could not afford the new housing even if they could wait for it. As Martin Anderson, probably Urban Renewal's most effective critic, noted,

> The people are poor. A great many of them are Negroes and Puerto Ricans. Good quality, conveniently located housing is scarce; good quality, conveniently located housing for $50 or $60 a month is almost impossible to find. It is difficult to picture hundreds of thousands of low-income people, many of them subject to racial discrimination, moving from low quality into higher quality housing at rents they can afford. And then, one might ask, why if all this good housing at low rents is available, didn't they move before urban renewal nudged them along?[4]

When studies were done of people dispossessed by Urban Renewal, it was often found that the relocatees were worse off than before. The process of forced moving tore up individuals' connections to friends, relatives, neighborhood organizations, and the like and generally left people less happy with their life situation than previously. The only way people seemed better off was that their standard of housing was somewhat better. That effect was almost inevitable since renewal often tore down the most deteriorated units in the municipal housing stock. Of course, with the tightening of the housing stock, they often paid more for their new housing than they had for their old housing.

The effect of Urban Renewal on the city's economy also came under some criticism. There was no question that Urban Renewal did stimulate economic development as described earlier. The question that critics raised was how much damage the process did to the existing economic structure. The first argument was that simply the announcement of impending renewal froze investment both within the designated area and also nearby. Within the area no investor would commit funds, for obvious reasons. But even outside the area investors would be inhibited because they did not know how much competition—subsidized with federal monies—would soon be coming to the renewal site. Whether it be old housing, old retailing space, or old commercial space, spending money on its renovation or modernization would be made more risky if new, competing structures were soon to rise on the nearby site. Another argument was that when businesses were forced to close because their buildings were condemned, they often never reopened. The loss of customers to competitors or the expenses of reopening simply overwhelmed them. It was also said that renewal generally demolished relatively cheap commercial space. This is the space often occupied by struggling new enterprises, which cannot afford newer space. Thus it attacks the "incubator" role of the city and may do long-term damage, which does not show up in short-term statistics.[5]

Ultimately, Urban Renewal accumulated so many enemies that in 1973 Congress terminated the program, although, as noted, funding pursuant to contracts signed previously continued into the 1980s.

Urban Renewal in Retrospect

On the negative side, there seems little argument about the human costs of Urban Renewal. The paralyzing effect of impending renewal action seems less important in retrospect, for once the project has been completed the effect disappears. Somehow, the argument regarding the incubator role of the city also seems less powerful in retrospect. Many cities still retained large amounts of cheap space after Urban Renewal. If there is a substantial vacancy rate on low-cost commercial space, as is the case in many cities, it is hard to argue that very much long-term damage has been done by the loss of some low-cost space.

On the positive side what can be said? Probably the biggest gain has been that Urban Renewal projects have given many cities the ability to compete with their suburbs. For example, White Plains, New York (as noted in Chapter 9) has grown as a retailing center in an age when most cities have been losing retail sales and jobs to the suburbs. Clearly, it was the new and efficient street pattern and the availability of large cleared parcels of land with marketable titles at below cost that made it possible for White Plains to swim against the tide. Without Urban Renewal most of the retailing activity now in downtown White Plains would be out on the highway.

One of Manhattan's big selling points as a commercial and residential location is its preeminence as a cultural center. A part of that preeminence resides in Lincoln Center, a cultural complex built as an Urban Renewal project on several blocks of deteriorated residential structures.

The Boston waterfront pulls in millions of tourists dollars and also makes the city more attractive as a residence for a young and affluent population, which might otherwise settle in the suburbs. In that sense it acts as a promoter of "gentrification," a trend that most cities, rightly or wrongly, seem to welcome.[6]

Writing in the 1960s Charles Abrams stated of Urban Renewal,

> It [Urban Renewal] allows room for more squares and parking spaces and is a useful tool for the long overdue rebuilding of cities enslaved to the 20- to 25-foot lot, and the gridiron pattern. It provides the opportunity for enlarging the street system surrounding the new projects, the closing of streets where necessary, the diversion of traffic, the addition of streets or widening of intersections. It facilitates running the new highways into the city's shopping centers and the creation of off-street parking and enclosed parking space. In short, the renewal project supplies a multipurpose opportunity in place of the piecemeal efforts to correct traffic problems, provide playgrounds and open spaces, provide neighborhood amenities, and new housing public and private.[7]

In referring to the failure of firms that were unable to compete successfully, the economist Joseph Schumpeter applauded the "creative destruction" of capitalism. At its best, Urban Renewal was "creative destruction." It tore away an old and obsolescent urban fabric and replaced it with something newer and brighter and, presumably, more economically viable. But such destruction is not without pain to individuals and enterprises. Reasonable people may differ over whether the gains justified the pain.

Baltimore's Inner Harbor redevelopment done jointly by the city and the Rouse Corporation. The development includes tourist attractions such as the restored USS Constellation at lower right, restaurants and retailing, large amounts of office space, and hundreds of hotel rooms to accommodate tourists and business travelers. The project works because the mix of uses is mutually reinforcing. Thus such redevelopment can only be done as a unified effort involving many adjacent parcels of land.

The Stamford, Connecticut Urban Renewal area as it appeared in the 1960s before redevelopment began and as it will appear in the early 1990s when redevelopment is complete. Note the ready access to interstate 95 and the revised street pattern.

COMMUNITY DEVELOPMENT

A year after the termination of Urban Renewal, Congress passed the Housing and Community Development Act of 1974. This omnibus act replaced Urban Renewal as well as a variety of urban "categorical" programs, that is, programs that provide funds for specific categories of activity, such as sewage treatment, recreation, or housing. The act provided Community Development Block Grants (CDBG) to permit localities to pursue a very wide range of activities including, but not limited to, activities that had been pursued under the Urban Renewal program. The intent of the block grant approach, as opposed to the categorical approach it superseded, was to reduce the federal role in local affairs by allowing municipalities more discretion. In that sense it was in keeping with the more conservative political philosophy of the Nixon administration in contrast to preceding Democratic administrations. Community Development (CD) funds were distributed on a formula basis, which counted population, age of housing stock, and poverty. Thus virtually every municipality in the nation received some funds. Municipalities were free to expend funds on a wide range of projects, including many types of service provisions as well as capital expenditures. Among the purposes for which CDBG funds could be used were acquisition of real property, public facilities and improvements, parks and playgrounds, centers for the handicapped, neighborhood facilities, solid waste disposal facilities, parking facilities, public utilities, street improvements, water and sewer facilities, pedestrian malls and walkways, flood and drainage facilities, clearance activities, public services, rehabilitation of public residential structures, rehabilitation financing, temporary relocation assistance, and a variety of economic development purposes.[8]

The act emphasized services for the poorer segment of the population, but in many communities there was a tendency to spend most of the funds on bricks and mortar. There were several reasons for this. Bricks and mortar last longer and are more visible. Then, too, services are hard to discontinue, so if the source of funding is cut off, the municipality that spent most of its CD funds on services could find itself out on a financial limb.

According to the legislation, municipalities were not to use CD funds for expenditures they would make in the absence of such grants, nor were they simply to use CD funds for tax relief. In the terminology of public finance, CD funds were to be "stimulative," not "substitutive."[9]

The legislation also required the predominant share of CD funds to be used in a manner that primarily benefited low- and moderate-income persons. Essentially, this means either spending CD funds in areas that have substantial proportions of low- and moderate-income residents or spending the funds on facilities or services that will be used by or will benefit these persons. Presumably day care or land clearance for a factory or warehouse would so qualify; repairing the seawall at the municipal yacht basin would not.

The act required each community to include as part of its grant application a Housing Assistance Plan (HAP), which spelled out community housing needs and laid out plans for dealing with them. The act also imposed significant "citizen participation" requirements on communities. The regulations state, among other things,

> There shall be involvement of low and moderate income persons, members of minority groups, residents of areas where a significant amount of activity is proposed or ongoing, the elderly, the handicapped, the business community, and civic groups. . . . The applicant shall make reasonable efforts to insure continuity of involvements. Citizens shall be provided adequate and timely information. . . . Citizens, particularly low and moderate income persons and residents of blighted neighborhoods, shall be encouraged to submit their views and proposals.[10]

Clearly, these requirements were motivated in part by criticisms of Urban Renewal, which accused these programs of riding roughshod over the residents of renewal areas. Even if the federal government were to make no effort to enforce these rules directly, they would have considerable force. Any citizen or any group that felt slighted in the community planning process could bring suit against the municipality on the grounds that it had failed to provide an adequate citizen participation process. A successful suit might well enjoin the municipality from spending further federal or perhaps even local funds until this fault was remedied.

In 1977 Congress expanded the scope of community development efforts somewhat by providing additional funds intended specifically for local economic development. These funds were provided under the Urban Development Action Grant (UDAG) program.[11] Communities that met certain criteria for poverty, age of housing stock, unemployment, and slowness of employment growth were eligible to apply for grants. UDAG grants were typically used for site acquisition and clearance to facilitate local economic development. Unlike the CD grants there was no entitlement. Obtaining a UDAG grant was a completely competitive process. In effect, UDAG monies enabled municipalities to do, on a small scale, a commercial renewal project—site acquisition, site clearance and improvement, and then sale or lease at below cost. In that sense, UDAG was a direct descendant of Urban Renewal. It differed in scale and in the absence of a housing element.

UDAG funds were used in hundreds of cities, and the competition for grants was intense. Although the program was popular with the cities, it was phased out at the end of the Reagan administration, whose hostility stemmed at least in part from ideology. Such grants constitute a public allocation of capital to which the free market conservative is likely to be opposed. But two other factors also contributed to the program's demise: the fact that some instances of corruption and excessive profits were turned up and the general budgetary pressures generated by the federal deficit and the Gramm-Rudman bill.[12]

Community Development versus the Urban Renewal Approach

In general, Community Development has differed from Urban Renewal primarily in its gentler approach and in its emphasis on rehabilitation and preservation, as opposed to Urban Renewal's clear-and-start-from-scratch approach. For example, in the realm of housing, CD programs have expended substantial funds on grants or low-interest loans to home owners and to the owners of rental properties for rehabilitation and modernization.

One program that has been highly successful in some cities is urban homesteading. In declining residential areas, cities often come into ownership of residential properties, primarily through foreclosure for unpaid property taxes. (This is not likely to happen in thriving areas since the higher market values will cause the owner who cannot pay taxes to sell out rather than simply walk away.) In the homesteading program the house is essentially given to a new owner, who promises to "bring it up to code" within a given time period. If the new owner succeeds in doing so, the title then passes to him or her without charge. In effect, the cost of acquiring the property is the expenditure required to bring the building up to the standards set forth in the municipality's building code. That expenditure may be primarily financial, that is, money spent on contractors, or it may largely be labor by the new owner, so-called "sweat equity."

In the city of Baltimore the program has worked quite successfully on old row houses. The lure of home ownership has been strong enough to attract an adequate number of urban homesteaders, but according to city officials, the potential profitability has not been so great as to bring in many speculators. Not only does the program improve housing quality, but also it fills neighborhoods with individuals and families who have a strong commitment to those neighborhoods. It thus contributes greatly to neighborhood stability, a goal that in the long run is probably more important than simply the maintenance of building quality.

In commercial areas many CD programs have taken a less radical approach than Urban Renewal. Low-interest loans have been made to local businesses, sometimes for operating purposes and sometimes for renovation and expansion. Pedestrian malls designed to attract shoppers have been constructed. Of course, some expenditures quite reminiscent of Urban Renewal have been made, for example, the construction of parking structures and street widening and realignment. But in general, the emphasis has been on preservation, rehabilitation, improvement, and gradual change. The intent has been to achieve the same goals as Urban Renewal but with less damage to the existing urban fabric.

In many cases municipal governments have given up the idea of competing head-to-head with suburban retailers on the grounds that it was impossible to match the automobile access and parking advantages of the suburban shopping center (the case of White Plains, noted earlier, is an exception in this regard). Instead, there has been more of an emphasis on strengthening those assets of the city that are not so readily matched by suburban areas. Such assets might include cultural facilities and areas designed largely for pedestrian traffic, where the denser and more varied pattern of land uses gives the city an advantage over the suburbs. For example, the revitalized downtown in Roanoke, Virginia, includes a museum, a theater, a number of specialty shops, and a small farmers market, all laid out for pedestrian access. There has been no serious attempt to compete with outlying shopping centers.

In a number of cities waterfronts that have long since lost their shipping functions have been converted to areas where one strolls, has lunch or dinner, shops, or uses some cultural or entertainment facility. The Boston Waterfront, Manhattan's South Street Seaport, and Baltimore's Inner Harbor are examples. Very often there is an element of historic preservation in such efforts. For example, South Street Seaport includes a number of restored buildings as well as several old, restored sailing vessels tied up at city-owned piers. Again, one might view this as an attempt to capitalize on an asset that the city has and the suburbs generally do not have, namely, the charm of the old.

THE HOUSING QUESTION

Housing, defining the term broadly, is probably the most important issue in urban planning. Housing constitutes the biggest single land use in most cities and towns; in many places it occupies more land than all other uses combined. There are few if any planning issues that touch most people more deeply than the condition of their immediate neighborhoods, because that is where they spend most of their time. Moreover, housing is often the single largest item in a family's budget, and the house is the most expensive possession that most people acquire. Equity in a house often constitutes the major share of the estate a person passes on to his or her descendants.

We may all agree that housing problems should be solved, but when we are asked to define the housing problem we are likely to give very different answers. In the 1970s and 1980s the prices of both new and used houses increased considerably more rapidly than did personal income. Thus for many young adults the housing problem was that the price and down payment requirements for a house put home ownership out of their reach. That is a young, middle-income perspective. Home ownership is not a problem for the rich and, generally, it is not an option for the poor. For the poor the housing problem might be finding decent housing at a rent that does not take an inordinate share of their total income. A social worker who works with the mentally handicapped or with deinstitutionalized mental patients might say that the biggest housing problem is the shortage of group homes for people who do not need to be in institutions but who cannot quite function on their own. For the resident of an exurban town experiencing rapid growth, the housing problem may be that too much housing is being built nearby, turning exurban tranquility into urban hustle and bustle. For a 60-year-old couple living in an almost paid off $200,000 house that they bought in 1970 for $35,000, there is no housing problem at all. They are well housed now and they are sitting on top of a big capital gain.

National policies that deal with housing reflect this jumble of interests. The biggest housing "program" is not a program at all but rather the favorable tax treatment of home ownership. (See chapter 18 for details.) Interest paid on home mortgages is tax deductible, whereas interest paid on most other things, for example, the purchase of an automobile, is not. Property taxes paid by home owners are tax deductible, whereas the property taxes a renter implicitly pays through his or her rent are not. The favorable tax treatment is largely a subsidy for middle- and upper-income people, but there are also subsidies at the other end of the income scale. There are over 1 million units of public housing in the United States, all very heavily subsidized.[13] There are also several million units of housing that although privately owned, have varying amounts of public subsidy behind them. In some cases the subsidy was delivered to the builder to reduce construction costs. In other cases the subsidy was delivered to the tenant in the form of a rent allowance.

Neither the Reagan nor the Bush administration put housing very high on its list of priorities. Housing subsidy funds declined during the latter part of the Reagan administration, and the Bush administration did not move to restore them to earlier levels. The main Bush housing proposal was for revisions of the tax code that would permit potential first-time home buyers to save for their downpayments out of pretax rather than posttax income, somewhat in the manner of an Individual Retirement Account (IRA). This proposal was clearly aimed at younger, middle-income people and not at the poorest members of the population.

The Department of Housing and Urban Development (HUD) was, shortly after President Reagan left office, shaken by major revelations of financial mismanagement and corruption. Its Reagan-era secretary, Samuel J. Pierce, was under investigation and facing possible indictment. Bush's secretary, the former New York State Congressman Jack Kemp, was necessarily preoccupied with restoring the agency's integrity and credibility. As of mid-1993 a distinctive Clinton approach to housing had not emerged.

Just as federal housing policy goes in several directions at once, so, too, may local policy; and as is true in the federal case, the effects of the various policies pursued by the community may at times be in conflict. For example, land-use controls designed to preserve environmental and neighborhood quality may push up the cost of new housing at the same time that the community pursues policies designed to help low- and moderate-income families afford housing.

PLANNING FOR HOUSING

For housing that is to be built purely by the private market, meaning without direct subsidy of any kind, the main step a community can take is to provide the opportunity for the market to work. At the physical level this means providing infrastructure, namely, roads, public water, and sewers. Land cannot be developed for housing without road access, and it cannot be developed at more than very low density without public water and sewers. Beyond these absolutely essential items, other public investment will affect the rate of new housing construction. For example, recreational facilities or an elementary school may make a developing area more desirable.

Land-use controls will control the quantity of the housing stock by setting an upper limit on the number of units per acre; they will also affect price by the types of units they permit. For example, garden apartments cost less per unit than do row houses. Row houses, in turn, cost less per unit than do free-standing single-family houses on small lots. These cost less than houses on large lots. Land-use controls that require particular amenities, for example, recreational facilities, for new developments will affect the price that the builder must ask. Subdivision requirements affect the site preparation costs, which in turn will be reflected in the price of the finished units.

What can the community do to provide low- and moderate-income housing? As stated, it can provide the infrastructure to support, and the land-use controls to permit the building of less expensive housing types. It can encourage builders to seek out and use federal and state subsidies for low- and moderate-income housing. It can make it community policy not to use its land-use control and other legal powers to obstruct the building of subsidized housing. Similarly, it can take an accommodating rather than a resisting stance toward group homes. This last item is not an idle point: In many communities citizens' resistance to group homes can be ferocious. Also, the municipality can use CD funds, or even funds raised through its own tax efforts, to subsidize low- and moderate-income housing. For example, CD funds have been used to make low-interest rehabilitation loans to low- and moderate-income home owners and to the owners of low-rent apartment houses. This may be done through a revolving loan fund or through the banks, with the municipality picking up a portion of the interest cost and perhaps also guaranteeing the loan. The municipality's zoning laws can provide density bonuses to developers who will include a certain number of units reserved for low- and moderate-income buyers or renters (see Chapter 9).

A number of municipalities ranging from New York City to Santa Monica have attempted to render housing more affordable through rent controls. Economists, by and large, are against the practice. They argue that it encourages disinvestment in those units subject to controls and that fear that controls will be extended to new units reduces the rate of new construction. Thus, they conclude that controls reduce housing quality and exacerbate housing shortages. However, regardless of one's view on the wisdom of controls, no list of steps that a community can take to address the question of affordability would be complete without mentioning them.

What a single community can do regarding low- and moderate-income housing is not great. Federal monies for housing are in relatively short supply. Even if the community makes every effort to see that its land-use controls do not preclude lower-cost housing types, the fact is that any new housing is expensive. The ability of the community to subsidize housing through either CD funds or its own revenues is limited by other demands on the budget and the willingness of the majority of the citizens to be taxed for that purpose. Still, there is a certain amount that can be done if that is what the community wants, but as noted elsewhere, not every community wants to do it.

Federal Requirements

The particular federal program that has propelled literally thousands of communities into preparing formal housing plans has been the CDBG program. One requirement for the receipt of funds, whether to be used for housing or other purposes, is the Housing Action Plan (HAP). At present, the rules require the community to certify in its application for CD funds that it is following a HAP approved by HUD. Briefly, HUD requires the plan to contain an inventory of the community housing stock and numerical goals for its improvement. It also requires the plan specifically to provide an analysis of the housing needs of lower-income renters. Finally, the plan must contain a statement of how the goals are to be met.

Exactly what aspects of the housing stock and the housing market the study covers may vary substantially from one community to another. If the study is oriented primarily toward matters that are eligible for federal funding, it is likely to focus on the quality and cost of units available for less affluent households.

Good objective measures of housing stock quality are hard to come by. Several decades ago the Bureau of the Census had its census takers enumerate "deteriorated" and "dilapidated" units but subsequently decided that such judgments were too subjective to provide good data. However, the bureau does provide data on the number of units that do not contain complete kitchen and bathroom facilities. Imperfect as this measure is, it has been used as a "proxy" for housing quality. Another measure of housing quality, though it has little to do with the physical quality of the unit, is overcrowding. The Bureau of the Census defines overcrowding as a situation in which there is more than 1.0 resident per room.

Finally, much attention has been paid to the question of whether low- and moderate-income households can afford housing. For this judgment planners tend to rely on rent/income ratios, a data item that is also supplied by the Bureau of the Census. At one time it was thought that a household should not have to spend more than 25 percent of its income on rent. More recently, housing economists have used 35 percent as a rule of thumb. Obviously, either figure is somewhat arbitrary.

Thus, the community can make some estimates of the number of units that may be substandard and the number of households in need of rental assistance.Vacancy rates may give some indication of whether the community should be seriously concerned with increasing the total number of units.

A More Comprehensive Approach to Planning for Housing

The community, in studying its housing situation, need not be bound by the necessities of federal approval and federal subsidies. One long-term issue to be considered is simply the numerical adequacy of the municipal housing stock. Projections of population and employment can be used to approximate future housing needs. A general understanding of market dynamics is also important. Units are added by new construction, sometimes by the subdivision of existing units and sometimes by the conversion of nonresidential to residential units. Units are lost-through fire, demolition, abandonment, and the conversion of residential to nonresidential units (e.g., the conversion of a single-family house into an office). Market forces such as personal income, rents and prices in adjacent communities, land costs, the competition between residential and commercial uses for space, and so on shape the long-term change in the municipal housing stock.

For a long-term analysis, attention should be paid to supply factors, including land, utilities, street capacity, and the like. Thus a really comprehensive study would go well beyond the low- and moderate-income housing questions and attempt to understand the dynamics of the entire housing market. We might also note that housing for low- and moderate-income residents and housing for more prosperous residents are not totally separate entities. If neighborhood conditions deteriorate, we may witness a flight of the prosperous and their replacement by low- and moderate-income households. Conversely, if demand for housing is strong and the supply of housing limited, we may see prosperous households displacing poor households, the "gentrification" process now visible in parts of many U.S. cities.

How Effective Are Housing Plans?

Most plans do not have major effects on the character of the community's housing stock, for several reasons. First, there will necessarily be some plans to which the community has little or no commitment. If having a housing plan is a precondition of getting CD funds and the community wants the funds, it will prepare a plan even though its real interest in low- and moderate-income housing may be negligible. But beyond that there is the issue of magnitude.

Consider the situation as of 1990. Americans spent approximately $547 billion to obtain housing and another $434 billion on household operation such as heating, waste disposal, and the like. The federal tax expenditure on mortgage interest and property taxes for owner occupied housing was about $51 billion. Federal expenditures on housing assistance, the main federal effort on behalf of low- and moderate-income people, was about $16 billion.[14] These figures are hardly the complete story. They exclude state and local expenditures for housing and some minor categories of federal housing expenditure. But they do make the point that direct public expenditures on housing are a relatively small part of the total expenditure on housing.

The tax expenditure on interest and property taxes has the effect of shifting the nation's housing market toward ownership and away from renting, of probably exerting some upward pressure on the prices of owner occupied housing, and of delivering a very substantial benefit to middle- and upper-income households. It does not make much direct contribution to meeting the housing needs of low- and moderate-income people.

Thus because of both the limited amount of public funds and the frequent fact of municipal ambivalence about housing goals, most housing plans do not make major changes in the composition of the municipal housing stock. Housing is often one of the most frustrating items on the planner's agenda.

SUMMARY

The Urban Renewal program began with the Housing Act of 1949 and was terminated by Congress in 1973. Local public agencies used a mixture of local and federal funds plus the power of eminent domain to acquire and clear redevelopment sites. Sites or portions of sites were then made available to developers at a fraction of their cost. The combination of heavy subsidy and eminent domain was intended to solve two major obstacles to urban redevelopment: problems of residual value and site assembly.

As Urban Renewal progressed it acquired many enemies, primarily because of its displacement effects. By the time Congress ended the program it had demolished approximately 600,000 housing units, forcing perhaps 2 million people, most of them having low or moderate income, to relocate. It also forced the closure of thousands of small businesses, many of which never reopened. The destruction of the social and economic fabric of neighborhoods was ultimately considered to be an unacceptably high cost.

The year after Urban Renewal was ended, Congress passed the Housing and Community Development Act of 1974. In place of Urban Renewal's clear-and-rebuild approach, Community Development programs have tended to emphasize preservation and improvement. The urban homesteading program noted in connection with the city of Baltimore typifies the emphasis on preserving the existing urban fabric that characterizes many CD programs. As a reaction to what were regarded to be the excesses of Urban Renewal, CD legislation contains numerous requirements for citizen participation, particularly that of low- and moderate-income citizens.

Housing plans may be narrowly keyed to federal funding programs, or they may take a broader approach. In the latter case, estimates of housing demand based on employment and demographic studies are compared with projections of future supply in order to estimate future needs. In general, housing is one of the more frustrating items with which the planner deals. The sums of money on the public side are very small compared to total expenditures. Thus the capacity of government programs to affect the basic housing picture is limited. In addition, housing issues are often major sources of social and political controversy within the community.

NOTES

1. It can be argued that two other federal programs or policies have actually had more effect on cities than did Urban Renewal. These are (1) the construction of the interstate highway system and (2) the structure of the IRS code and the tax benefits it provides for home ownership. However, powerfully as these may affect cities, they are not specifically urban programs nor were their urban effects foremost in the minds of the legislators who enacted them. In fact, it seems likely that their urban consequences, though now well recognized, were largely unanticipated.
2. Congressional Research Service, Library of Congress, "The Central City Problem and Urban Renewal Policy," prepared for the Subcommittee on Housing and Urban Affairs, Committee Banking, Housing and Urban Affairs, United States Senate, Washington, D.C. 1973. Note: Subsequent figures on Urban Renewal expenditures or any other federal housing or urban development programs can be found in the *Annual Yearbook*, Department of Housing and Urban Development (HUD), Washington, D.C.
3. Guy Greer and Alvin W. Hansen, "Urban Redevelopment and Housing," National Planning Association, 1941.
4. Martin Anderson, *The Federal Bulldozer*, MIT Press, Cambridge, MA, 1964, p. 64.
5. The hypothesis, an old one in urban economics, is that the city incubates small, growing industries. When they reach a certain degree of maturity, they then move out to more peripheral areas, which provide lower costs, albeit in a somewhat less rich and varied business environment. The city survives even though it loses one mature industry after another because it is constantly generating new industries. For an account of this idea see Wilbur Thompson, *A Preface to Urban Economics*, Johns Hopkins Press, Baltimore, 1965.
6. The term *gentrification* comes from gentry and refers to the movement back into older neighborhoods of people of higher economic or social status than the present occupants.
7. Charles Abrams, "Some Blessings of Urban Renewal," in *Urban Renewal: The Record and the Controversy*, James Q. Wilson, ed., MIT Press, Cambridge, MA, 1966, p. 560.
8. This partial listing is drawn from regulations published in the *Federal Register*, March 1, 1978, p. 8441. The *Federal Register* is a daily publication of the federal government, which provides detailed regulations for the implementation of legislation passed by the Congress. It runs to many thousands of pages per year.

9. Enforcing such a distinction is not always easy. If the community intended to build a playground in any case but allocates part of its CDBG to that purpose, how can we ever say with certainty how the general purpose funds thus freed have been used? Can we say with certainty that the funds freed by the CD grant have not been used for a purpose that is not an approved CD activity? In fact, can we say with certainty that the knowledge that it was to receive a CDBG did not cause a municipality to tax its property owners at a somewhat lower rate than it would otherwise have done?
10. See *Federal Register* op. cit., p. 8,462.
11. The basic ground rules for the UDAG program were spelled out in the *Federal Register*, October 25, 1977, part III, and January 10, 1978, part IV.
12. The bill set annual deficit ceilings. If the ceilings were not met by specific program cuts, they were to be met by across-the-board percentage reductions. The effect of the bill, as intended, was to put strong pressures on the administration to cut programs wherever it could.
13. Public housing means that the units are owned and operated by a unit of government. This is distinct from publicly assisted housing, which is privately owned and operated but subsidized in some manner by government.
14. *Statistical Abstract of the United States*, 112th ed., U.S. Department of Commerce, Bureau of the Census, 1992, Tables 495, 547, and 681.

SELECTED BIBLIOGRAPHY

CHRISTENSON, JAMES A., and ROBINSON, JERRY W., EDS., *Community Development in America*, Iowa State University Press, Ames, 1980.

SO, FRANK S., and GETZELS, JUDITH, *The Practice of Local Government Planning*, International City Management Association, Washington, D.C. 1988, chap. 12.

WILSON, JAMES Q., ED., *Urban Renewal: The Record and the Controversy*, MIT Press, Cambridge, MA, 1966.

CHAPTER 13

TRANSPORTATION PLANNING

In this chapter we consider transportation planning as practiced at the municipal and metropolitan level. There is an emphasis on planning for automotive transportation, for it is the predominant mode in the United States. The chapter does, however, include some material on transit as well.[1] Before turning to the transportation planning process, some general background on transportation trends since World War II would be useful.

RECENT TRENDS IN URBAN TRANSPORTATION

In 1945, the year World War II ended, the population of the United States was approximately 133 million and there were about 25 million passenger cars registered, approximately 1 car for every 5.3 people. By 1990 the population had grown to 249 million and there were approximately 143 million cars registered, 1 for every 1.7 people. Whereas the human population of the United States had grown by 87 percent, the automobile population had grown by about 472 percent.[2]

One powerful force behind the increase in automobile ownership was the large increase in average real personal income in the years following World War II. Not only did the general prosperity enable more people to own automobiles, but that same prosperity also facilitated a great wave of suburbanization. The postwar suburbanization and the increase in automobile ownership were complementary phenomena. Widespread automobile ownership facilitates suburbanization. On the other hand, moving from central city to the suburbs increases one's need for an automobile.

The public transportation situation in the postwar period was very different. Ridership reached an all-time high in 1945, when wartime employment peaked, gasoline was rationed, and civilian production of automobiles had been suspended for several years. From 19 billion trips by fare-paying passengers in 1945, the total declined to a postwar low of 5.6 billion in 1975. By the 1980s the figure had risen slightly but was still barely one-third the 1945 figure.

To a large extent the decline in public transportation is the opposite side of the coin from the forces already discussed. Increased automobile ownership eliminated millions of potential transit customers. Suburbanization meant the movement of millions of households into areas where, because of reduced congestion, the automobile works better than in central cities. Conversely, the dispersed suburban land-use pattern makes the provision of public transportation, which depends on high volumes on fixed routes, more difficult.

PAYING FOR TRANSPORTATION

To understand public policy in regard to transportation it is important to understand how private and public transportation are financed. In terms of direct costs, private transportation is essentially self-financed. Vehicle purchase, fuel, maintenance, insurance, parking, and other costs are paid directly by vehicle owners and operators. Roads and highways are, by and large, paid for by a variety of taxes and charges levied on automobile users. Such charges include license fees, registration fees, and state and federal gasoline taxes. For example, federal contributions to road construction come from the Highway Trust Fund, which is supplied by federal excise taxes on the sale of motor fuel.

It has been argued, however, that the automobile exacts a variety of hidden costs that are not so covered—air pollution; death and injury from accidents; and a more scattered pattern of land use, which results in increased costs of public services. If one dislikes the suburbs, one might argue that suburbanization is a cost the automobile has imposed on America. Conversely, if one prefers the suburbs to the city, as millions of Americans evidently do, one can say that suburbia is a blessing the automobile has conferred on America. But regardless of these arguable matters, the fact is that in a direct sense automobile transportation is paid for by those who use it.

In contrast, the economics of public transportation in the United States are such that very little of it would survive had it to be financially self-sustaining. At present, most public transportation capital costs are paid for with public (mostly federal) funds. The city buses operated by a typical transit system were bought primarily with federal money and stored and maintained in a facility funded in the same way. Several cities have recently built or expanded subway systems. The funds for such construction are largely federal, as are the funds by which the systems acquire their rolling stock. Moreover, almost all transit systems in the United States receive substantial operating assistance, again largely from the federal government, either on a vehicle mile or passenger mile basis. On balance, receipts at the farebox cover somewhat less than half of all transit operating expenses in the United States and effectively none of the capital costs.[3]

We subsidize public transportation for several reasons. There are people who cannot use private transportation, and society must provide them with some means of personal mobility. Such people include those too young to drive, those too old to drive, those who have some handicap that prevents them from driving, and those who cannot afford automobile ownership. We also subsidize public transportation because we think it improves circulation in urban areas by reducing the number of private vehicles in use. Shifting people from cars to buses or trains may also improve environmental quality by reducing the total amount of vehicle emissions. Heavier reliance on public transportation also permits a more compact urban design, which many planners favor. These last several points suggest that subsidizing public transportation confers benefits on nonusers as well as users.

Finally, it has been argued that we ought to subsidize public transportation as a matter of income redistribution. The argument here is that by providing at below cost a product used by low-income people we are, in effect, transferring income to them. This is probably the weakest of the arguments because subsidizing transit is, at best, a very inefficient means of transferring income. Not all poor people use public transportation, nor are all users of public transportation poor. In fact, the patrons of at least one type of transit, commuter rail lines, generally have above-average incomes.

TRANSPORTATION PLANNING AND USE

Land use and transportation planning are very much a chicken and egg situation. In the short term, land use shapes the demand for transportation. Many a highway has been built because population or commercial growth produced congestion and delays, which generated political pressures to deal with the situation. On the other hand, the provision of roads changes land values and thus alters the intensity with which land is used. The interstate highway system, to take the largest example, was designed to facilitate movement of vehicles from one existing urban center to another, something it does very successfully. However, it has also done a great deal to reshape urban areas, as discussed earlier, an effect that was not one of the motivations behind its construction. Beyond that, it has reshaped the balance between metropolitan and nonmetropolitan areas in the United States by making formerly isolated rural areas far more accessible than they were a generation ago. In fact, it is believed that much of the movement of manufacturing activity out of metropolitan areas and into rural areas has occurred for just this reason. Thus it can be argued that the system has had a major impact on the economies of both metropolitan and nonmetropolitan areas.

In the ideal case, transportation planning and land-use planning would go hand in hand. At the national level, this has clearly not been the case. At the state level, it sometimes is and sometimes is not. In the best case, state highway departments will take into account the fact that their decisions not only affect how the population now in place is served but also shape land use for decades to come. Highway planning and more general land-use planning are coordinated. In the less satisfactory case, the highway engineers tend to think in terms of meeting demand rather than a combination of meeting demand and shaping the future of land use.

It is often at the municipal level that transportation and land-use planning are most closely coordinated. The issues are simpler and the numbers of people involved are smaller. Thus coordination is easier. Then, too, the fact that both the planners and the highway department report to the same mayor and the same city council can prevent them from going off in different directions.

THE TRANSPORTATION PLANNING PROCESS

Transportation planning is a basic function of many planning agencies, for adequate circulation is and traditionally has been a major planning goal. As practiced in the last several decades, particularly at the multijurisdictional level, it is perhaps the most elaborate and mathematically well-developed area of planning. The modern multijurisdictional transportation planning process represents a fusion of engineering, economics, and urban planning, all facilitated by modern computing equipment. The field in its present form was brought into being by a coincidence of forces shortly after the end of World War II. The rapid increase in automobile ownership and the suburban housing stock created a massive demand for increased highway capacity. The Highway Act of 1954 provided 50 percent matching subsidies for urban highways and funds for transportation planning. It also required planning as a condition of eligibility for the matching subsidies—still another example of the conditioning of the local planning scene by federal funding requirements. In 1956 Congress passed the National Defense Highway Act, which initiated the building of the interstate highway system. Federal legislation and funding thus set off a wave of highway building in the decades after the war. The digital computer, which was invented at the end of the war and became a practical planning tool a decade to a decade and a half later, made it possible to "crunch" huge amounts of data and thus make possible the modern style of highway planning.

The following pages focus on highway planning at the metropolitan level. At smaller geographical levels the process is necessarily somewhat simpler and generally less mathematical. More than most planning processes, transportation planning necessitates a multijurisdictional effort, for the flow of travelers is no respecter of municipal boundaries. Thus the same communities that may do their land-use planning in relative isolation will often be part of an areawide metropolitan transportation planning process.

Modeling Metropolitan Area Transportation

The goal of the transportation planning process is to assist governments in providing an adequate transportation system at an acceptable cost. This involves modeling the behavior of the present system, estimating future travel demand, and estimating how changes in the system will affect travel behavior and the operation of the transportation system in the future.

The interstate highway system with its ring-road, or "beltway," design creates masses of highly accessible land outside the city, particularly where radial routes coming out of the city intersect the beltway. Though not intended in that way, this feature of the system has been a powerful force for moving people and jobs out of the central city.

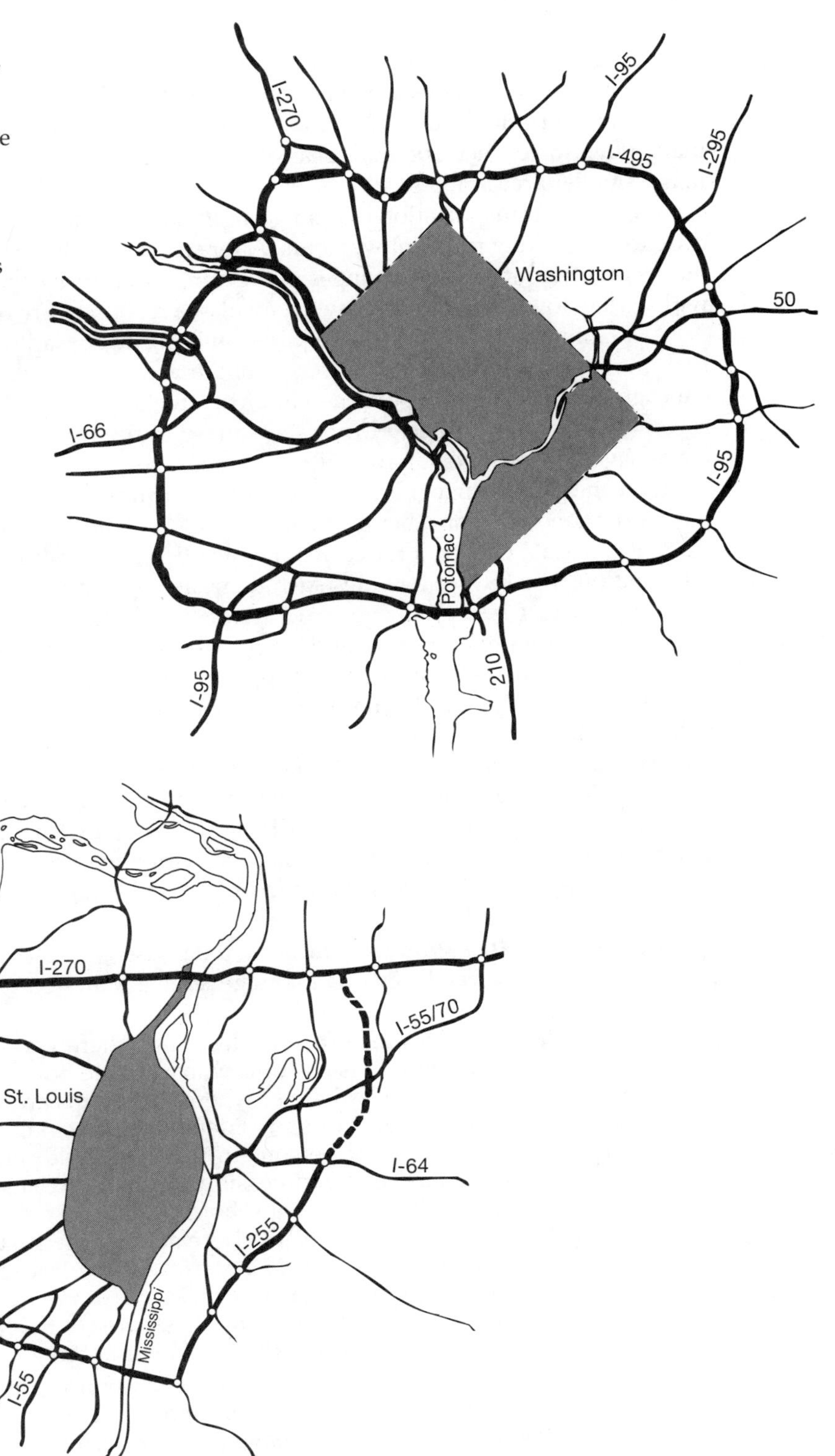

The approach described below was first used in the 1950s in the Chicago Area Transportation Study (CATS).[4] Variations of it were subsequently done in many other major metropolitan areas. The general approach has also been used in many smaller area studies.

Major transportation planning projects usually involve a four-step procedure for estimating travel movements. After such estimates are made, the relative merits of different possible changes in the transportation system can be evaluated with a view toward deciding how the available resources are best allocated.

Going through the steps requires building a geographic data base. In general, the area in question, say a metropolitan area, is divided into zones. In the Chicago study and many patterned after it, a rectangular grid is imposed on the region and data are collected for each square in the grid. A typical grid might cover several thousand square miles. In other cases, particularly in smaller studies, the zones may be irregular, with shapes determined by terrain features, neighborhood boundaries, or other characteristics of the land-use pattern.

The data gathered for each zone includes both population and economic information. The former includes such items as the number and type of housing units, number of residents, age structure of the population, household income, number of automobiles owned, and similar items. The economic information will include such items as the number of people employed in the area in various occupations and the number of square feet of floor space and land area devoted to retailing, wholesaling, manufacturing, office operations, and other activities. Each of these broad categories may be broken up into a number of subcategories. Floor space, a widely used measure because it can be determined with a fair degree of accuracy, has proven to be a good predictor of how many trips will be attracted to a zone. The purpose of the data base is to provide the information from which a model of travel behavior (trips from each zone to each zone) can be built.

The Four-Step Process Once the data base is in place any given transportation alternative can be evaluated. In general, a four-step process is used.

1. *Estimating trip generation.* Before deciding where people will go from a given point of origin, it is customary to estimate how many trips a given place will generate regardless of where those trips are destined. For estimating trip generation from a residential area, variables such as household income, number of persons in the household, number of vehicles owned by the household, and possibly population density might be used to estimate average trips per household per day. In general the number of vehicular trips would be positively related to the first three items and negatively related to the last. The reason for the last relationship is that trips that may be made on foot or by mass transit in a dense area are likely to be made by auto in a sparsely populated area, where trip distances are longer and parking and congestion problems absent.
2. *Estimating trip distribution.* After trip generation has been resolved, the next issue is to distribute the trips. Suppose a given zone in a region contains 1,000 households, whose average size, vehicle ownership, and in-

come are known. The total number of trips can thus be estimated, but the question is how the trips will be distributed among possible destinations. A variety of estimating methods has been developed over the years. The most commonly used is the gravity model, originally developed in the 1920s to analyze shopping patterns. (The original formulation was known as Reilly's Law of Retail Gravitation, and in the past gravity models were sometimes known as Reilly models.) The force of gravitation between two objects is proportional to the product of their masses and inversely proportional to the square of their distance. By analogy, the force of trip attraction between, say, a housing complex and an office complex would be proportional to the product of the number of households and the number of square feet of office floor space and inversely proportional to some function (perhaps the square or some value near the square) of the distance between them. In principle, then, one might estimate the relative number of trips made from origin A to destinations B and C by computing the relative force of attraction between A and B and between A and C. Again, the force of attraction is proportional to the product of the "masses" divided by some function of the distance. By extension, the model apportions the trips from zone A to all the other zones by a similar process. The model then does the same for zone B, zone C, and so on. At the end of the process one has a complete picture of trip distribution; that is, the number of trips from each zone to every other zone. For a region with a large number of zones, the data base and the number of calculations are very large. Thus, as a practical matter such a planning exercise would not have been possible before the computer.

Such an exercise could be done for an actual distribution of housing and floor space or for a hypothesized one. Distance might be taken as straight-line distance from the center of one zone to the center of another. Or it might be taken as actual road mileage, travel time, or some composite of both.

3. *Estimating modal split*. Where there is more than one mode of transportation available, say, automobile and bus, it is important to apportion by mode the trips distributed in the previous stage. Over the years considerable experience has been accumulated and a the number of mathematical estimating techniques worked out. In general, the two main criteria that determine which mode an individual takes are quality of service and cost. Quality of service is largely a matter of travel time. Quite frequently there is a clear tradeoff between speed and cost. For example, in public transportation, commuter rail service is generally much faster than bus transport and also substantially more expensive. Knowing something about the income distribution of the population using public transportation would thus enable the planner to make some estimates of how that population would divide between the two modes.

4. *Trip assignment*. Once the choice of mode has been settled the last issue is predicting how trips will be distributed between alternate routes from the same origin to the same destination. Again, the question is resolved by mathematical modeling. Consider that there are two routes, A and B, from Zone X to zone Y. Imagine, also, that we begin with all traffic on

route A. As travelers shift from A to B, travel times on route A fall while those on route B lengthen. Transportation planners have available a number of mathematical models to predict when equilibrium will be reached.

In general these modeling steps are used in the following way. First, the existing state of the transportation system is modeled mathematically, using the steps described above. Then the model is calibrated to produce results that correspond to the actual flow of traffic. The data used for calibration will come from actual measurements of traffic flow, for example, those made by counters that are tripped by the weight of a vehicle passing over a rubber hose. Once the model duplicates the observed travel behavior, alternative situations can be modeled. For example, a planner might assume an increase in the number of households in a given zone. The model can be run again, and the region will show a slightly different pattern of trips. The transportation planners might then postulate changes in the road pattern to see how these will affect the pattern of trips. Since the speed of travel on a road depends on its volume of traffic, such simulations will give planners insight into how potential changes in the road system will affect travel times. Travel in metropolitan areas has morning and evening peaks, corresponding to commuting hours. Traffic flow is very different in peak and nonpeak hours. The model can be run to simulate different times of the day.

The real strength of the computer model is that the speed with which it does calculations makes it possible to experiment with numerous different possibilities. In principle, there is no calculation done by the computer that could not be done by hand, but as a practical matter the computer opens up a range of exploratory possibilities that would otherwise be prohibitively time-consuming and expensive.

The Policy Decision

Computer modeling can and does help to examine possible improvements and additions to the transportation system but by itself cannot make any decision. How is the actual decision about policy reached?

One technical aid to decision making is benefit/cost analysis. This is a process of systematically enumerating the benefits and costs of a particular option, say, a new link in the road network or an extension of a transit line, and assigning to them monetary values. The ratio of benefits to costs can then be calculated. Where many projects are competing for limited funds, the benefit/cost ratios may be used as a means of deciding which ones to fund.

On the benefit side of a proposed improvement might be listed time saved by travelers. This means that a monetary value must be assigned to time, and in fact, a large number of studies have been done by transportation analysts to find out how travelers value their time. Other benefits might include lives saved and injuries avoided if the new route is safer than the old one. Savings in vehicle operating costs would be considered if the new route were shorter or reduced stop-and-go-traffic. Costs would include land acquisition costs, construction costs, and repair costs, among others. Typically, the three biggest items in highway benefit/cost studies are construction and land costs, time savings, and vehicle operating costs.[5]

Benefit/cost analysis has its subjective side. For example, how does one assign precise values to human life and health? Measures like estimated lifetime earnings or awards of courts in negligence cases have been used, but presumably even the most ardent advocate of benefit/cost analyses would admit that these measures are hardly ideal. There are also many other items that cannot readily be converted into dollar terms. For example, urban design and aesthetic issues do not lend themselves well to being "monetized." Nonetheless, benefit/cost analysis is far superior to reliance on pure intuition.

Transportation questions often generate tremendous citizen involvement and can become highly emotional and political. New construction takes people's property and can have great impact on neighborhoods. A freeway through a neighborhood can constitute a formidable barrier between the remaining halves, greatly raise the noise level, lower the air quality, and generally make life there a good deal less attractive. Changes in the flow of traffic may bring windfalls to some businesses and large losses to others.

Some citizens' disillusionment with highway building has come from what planners and engineers refer to as the "induced demand" phenomenon. When the capacity of the road network is increased, for example, by the opening of a new expressway, it is often observed that traffic congestion does not fall very much on the other roads and that in the peak hours the new road may be operating at close to maximum capacity in a very short period of time. The building of new capacity has induced additional traffic; also, some people who previously traveled during off-peak hours because of congestion now travel in the peak hours. The highway planner may be satisfied with the result in that more people are now getting what they want, namely, the ability to travel where they want when they want. But to the citizen who used to drive to work in the morning rush in one hour and now drives in 59 minutes, it may appear that there has been much disruption and much expenditure for very little gain.[6] The next time a highway bond issue comes up for referendum, he or she is likely to vote no.

In recent years citizens' opposition to highway building has become formidable. In San Francisco in the early 1970s the Embarcadero Freeway was halted in midconstruction by opposition, based largely on concerns that this elevated road would block views of San Francisco Bay. When the portion that had been built and was in use was damaged in the October, 1989 earthquake the city did not move to rebuild it. Rather, the city-council voted to replace it with a less obtrusive below-grade roadway, providing that outside funding could be found for this purpose. Whether the freeway will be rebuilt if such funding is not found remains to be seen. In 1985 New York City abandoned Westway after more than a decade of determined opposition. The term *freeway revolt* has been used to describe rising resistance to highway building. Not only does resistance come from affected residents, business people, and property owners, but a certain amount also comes from environmentalists, who in general do not favor anything that will increase automobile use.

Thus political considerations weigh very heavily in decisions about transportation policy. In some cases rights-of-way may be determined partly on the basis of which neighborhood or municipality is least able to resist them. However scientific and rational transportation planning may be, the total decision will rest only partially on technical considerations.

Planning for Public Transportation

The approach to planning public transportation infrastructure is similar in principle to that of highway planning. The same sorts of computer studies done for automotive travel can be done for transit. Then, too, benefit/cost analysis is as applicable to transit as it is to highways and streets.

In recent years the public in large cities and metropolitan areas has generally been more favorably disposed to transit improvements than to the building of new highways. Improving transit tends to decongest the streets by reducing automobile travel. It appeals to environmentalists for reasons of air quality and fuel consumption. Those concerned with urban design often favor transit because it leads to a more compact land-use pattern that is much friendlier to pedestrians than is a city designed for automobile transportation. Distances between destinations are shorter and less land area is given over to streets. Taking a walk in a transit-oriented city like Chicago or Boston and then taking a walk in an automobile-oriented city like Albuquerque or Los Angeles is likely to convince one that there is some truth in this argument.

A major problem with transit, as noted before, is that financially it is far from self-sustaining. It must be heavily subsidized, and, most of that subsidy must come from higher levels of government.

In the mid 1970s the long-term decline in transit ridership halted and a slight increase in ridership was noted. This reversal was due in large measure to increased federal funding. The Urban Mass Transit Acts (UMTA) of 1964 and 1966 provided modest funding for planning studies and operating subsidies. UMTA 1970 provided over the next decade approximately $10 billion in operating subsidies and construction funds. Several new transit systems came on line during the 1970s. But the 1980s saw federal funding for transit, along with many other forms of federal aid to state and local government, scaled back. Behind the less than overwhelming political support for subsidizing transit is a basic geographical fact. To function adequately transit requires population densities of at least several thousand persons per square mile. Therefore, a substantial part of the U.S. population, including much of its metropolitan area population, lives in areas that cannot adequately be served with transit at any conceivable level of public expenditure. Thus many members of Congress do not have constituencies that care much about transit.

The continuing suburbanization of the U.S. and, particularly the development of major employment centers in the suburban ring around the central city may cause some change in the pattern of transit development. Traditionally, commuter rail lines were built on a radial plan to bring suburban workers to downtown jobs. However, at present there are plans afoot in a number of metropolitan areas for suburban rail lines that run circumferentially to carry commuters to suburban subcenters rather than downtown. Suburban rail design is thus beginning to follow the pattern of suburban highway design, in part because of the economic realities fostered by several decades of suburban highway building.[7]

Transportation Management Systems

In the 1980s it appeared that for many years to come the transportation infrastructure of the United States would not be greatly enlarged. Population growth was slightly less than 1 percent per year and automobile ownership was so high that large future increases seemed unlikely. The interstate highway system, approximately 40,000 miles in all, was virtually completed.

Thus attention turned to transportation management systems (TMS), essentially practices and technologies that make an existing infrastructure operate more efficiently. For example, an old subway system such as New York City's charges the same fare at all times of day or night and for a trip of any length. The Washington Metro uses a computerized fare card system, which adjusts the charge both for time and trip length. Thus the price of the service is adjusted for changing demand conditions. As another example of a TMS technique, many areas during the morning and evening rush hours set aside special lanes for vehicles carrying more than one occupant. The idea is to encourage carpooling and thus reduce peak-hour congestion. A list of TMS techniques is provided in Table 13–1.

A Look Ahead

For planners concerned with transportation the most important event of recent years was the passage of the Intermodal Surface Transportation Efficiency Act (ISTEA) of 1991. Often pronounced as "ice tea," the act retains the basic structure of very substantial federal transportation aid to the states and localities financed largely by the Highway Trust Fund. But the act also contains some new features that hold out the prospect of integrating transportation planning with land-use and environmental planning into one sensible whole.

For several decades it has been widely understood that the building of transportation facilities, especially highways, has had a huge effect on how and where people lived. But, in too many cases, highway planning has been based almost solely on pure transportation issues with little respect for its effect on the overall pattern of settlement and on the natural environment. ISTEA requires

> states and cities to incorporate nontransportation into their transportation planning. In effect, ISTEA moves the side effects closer to the center of the planning process by forcing states and localities to look ahead and if possible, eliminate the negative consequences of road building.[8]

In areas where current air quality is not up to federal standards, so called "non-attainment" areas, the metropolitan planning organization will not be able to receive federal funding unless it produces a plan that deals with automotive

TABLE 13–1 Transportation System Maintenance (TSM) Techniques

1. Improved vehicular flow:
   Improvements in signalized intersections
   Freeway ramp metering
   One-way streets
   Removal of on-street parking
   Reversible lanes
   Traffic channelization
   Off-street loading
   Transit-stop relocation
2. Preferential treatment of high-occupancy vehicles:
   Freeway bus and carpool lanes and access ramps
   Bus and carpool lanes on city streets and urban arterials
   Bus preemption of traffic signals
   Toll policies
3. Reduced peak-period travel:
   Work rescheduling
   Congestion pricing
   Peak-period truck restrictions
4. Parking management:
   Parking regulations
   Park-and-ride facilities
5. Promotion of nonauto or high-occupancy auto use:
   Ridesharing
   Human-powered travel modes
   Auto-restricted zones
6. Transit and paratransit service improvements:
   Transit marketing
   Security measures
   Transit shelters
   Transit terminals
   Transit-fare policies and fare-collection techniques
   Extension of transit with paratransit services
   Integration of transportation services
7. Transit management efficiency measures:
   Route evaluation
   Vehicle communication and monitoring techniques
   Maintenance policies
   Evaluation of system performance

Source: U.S. Department of Transportation, Urban Mass Transportation Administration, *Transportation System Management: State of the Art,* Washington, D.C., 1977.

emissions. These plans might involve car and van pooling, increased investment in transit, elements of land-use planning designed to place jobs and housing closer to each other, and the like. Foot and bicycle paths might also be part of such a plan.

A total of $24 billion over the life of the act are earmarked for "flexible" funds that can be allocated to a wide range of transportation projects ranging from highways to bike paths. Ten percent of each grant must be earmarked to safety and another 10 percent to "enhancement." The latter might include scenic, recreational, or other improvements along or near the transportation route in question.

The planning processes that are specified in the regulations associated with the act should broaden the transportation planning process so as to bring a wider range of participants into it and thus reduce the relative power of highway engineers, construction companies, and construction unions. To the extent that the process is done by a broader group, a wider range of concerns will be represented and the transportation facility building will have to take greater account of planning concerns.

SUMMARY

Since World War II, per capita ownership of automobiles in the United States has more than doubled, partly because of the increase in real income. Increases in automobile ownership have gone hand in hand with the process of suburbanization, each reinforcing the other. In terms of direct costs, private transportation more or less pays for itself, whereas public transportation requires heavy suburbanization. The decline in public transportation since World War II was attributed partly to increased automobile ownership and partly to a more spread-out pattern of land use.

The present pattern of land use shapes the present demand for transportation, and transportation investment decisions shape the future pattern of land use. In the best of circumstances, land-use and transportation planning proceed as coordinated rather than isolated processes.

Large-scale transportation planning is a four-step process:

1. *Estimating trip generation.* Without considering destinations the planners, using such variables as household size, household income, and number of vehicles per household, estimate the total number of trips which will originate from each zone.
2. *Estimating trip distribution.* Using a gravity model or other mathematical model, the planners will then estimate the number of trips from each zone to each zone.
3. *Modal split.* If more than one mode of transportation is available, say automobile and bus, the planners will use mathematical models to estimate the number of travelers using each mode from each origin to each destination. The main variables in such models are cost and travel time.
4. *Trip assignment.* Where there is more than one route from one zone to another zone, the final item to be modeled is the number of trips which will be made via each route.

After the model is built, it is calibrated, that is, adjusted so that its output duplicates the actual travel behavior of the region. Then the model can be used to examine different transportation alternatives. Benefit/cost analysis is frequently used to evaluate and rank different investment possibilities. Ultimately, though, deciding on major investments is a political matter because transportation system investments can have large consequences for land values, for neighborhood quality, and for the entire pattern of development.

For a variety of reasons it is not likely that there will be a repetition in the foreseeable future of the massive highway construction that occurred in the 1960s and 1970s. Thus, much interest has focused on transportation system management (TSM) as a means of extracting more performance from a relatively stable infrastructure. The Intermodal Surface Transportation Efficiency Act (ISTEA) of 1991 offers promise of integrating future transportation planning into overall land-use planning than has previously been the case.

NOTES

1. The term *transit* generally includes public (not chartered) buses, subways, commuter rail, and trolleys.
2. Figures are from the chapter "Transportation-Land," *Statistical Abstract of the United States*, 1992 and earlier years.
3. For overall statistics on transit costs and revenues, see ibid. For more detailed information, see American Public Transit Association, *Transit Fact Book*, Washington, D.C. annual.
4. *Chicago Area Transportation Study: Final Report* (3 vols.), published jointly by the State of Illinois, County of Cook, City of Chicago, and the U.S. Department of Commerce, Bureau of Public Roads, 1959–62.
5. See John W. Dickey, *Metropolitan Transportation Planning*, McGraw-Hill Book Co., New York, 1983, chap. 6.
6. Anthony Downs, "The Law of Peak-Hour Congestion," *Urban Problems and Prospects*, Rand-McNally, Chicago, 1976.
7. "Suburban Choo Choo," *Planning*, June 1991, pp. 24–30.
8. F. K. Plous, Jr., "Refreshing ISTEA," *Planning*, February, 1993, pp. 9–12.

SELECTED BIBLIOGRAPHY

DICKEY, JOHN W., *Metropolitan Transportation Planning*, 2nd ed., McGraw-Hill Book Co., New York, 1983.

CHAPTER 14

ECONOMIC DEVELOPMENT PLANNING

HISTORIC ROOTS

Planning for economic development is an old American tradition. In many ways it antedates the sort of city planning we have discussed in this book. In the nineteenth century a great many cities took steps to strengthen their competitive position vis à vis competing cities. Quite naturally, much of the push came from the city's merchants, for they were the individuals who would profit most from municipal economic success. Most often, such planning efforts were directed toward the transportation infrastructure—to increasing the accessibility of the city. In a day when overland transportation costs per ton/mile were a large multiple of what they are today, a significant reduction in those costs could give the merchants in one city or town an overwhelming advantage over competitors in other cities.[1]

Probably the best-known example in the nineteenth century was the building of the Erie Canal. A group of New York City merchants perceived that obtaining good access to the Midwest would confer a tremendous economic advantage on the city. The way to do this in the pre-railroad era was to build a canal connecting the Hudson River to Lake Erie. By the 1830s, a decade or so after its completion, the canal was carrying something close to 1 million tons of freight per year and giving New York an enormous commercial advantage over its two main rivals of the time, Boston and Philadelphia. In fact, the great age of canal building in the United States, roughly 1800 to 1830, was largely a matter of municipal initiative, each city trying to steal a march on its competitors.

The age of canal building ended abruptly with the coming of railroad technology, but the same story of municipal competition was repeated. Many of the early railroads were built with municipally raised funds, and the competition between cities and towns to be on a rail line was intense. In many cases municipalities purchased railroad bonds to provide the capital to build a line that would put them on the map commercially. In other cases municipalities guaranteed bonds to make them marketable. One writer described this period as an age of "urban mercantilism," so intense was the competition.[2]

When the U.S. rail system was fairly well developed, competition switched to other areas. For example, in the period after the Civil War a number of southern communities actively promoted the development of the textile industry by offering various forms of financial assistance to firms in New England, then the textile manufacturing center of the United States. Again, the impetus came largely from local merchants, whose primary motivation was to promote commerce and development that would boost profits and property values. These motives for local economic development efforts are not unknown today, but some additional and in some cases more altruistic motives have been added.

PERSPECTIVES ON LOCAL ECONOMIC DEVELOPMENT

To discuss the present situation in local economic development it is necessary to make clear two different perspectives. For several decades local economic development efforts have been heavily shaped by federal funding and federal legislation. Thus there is a national perspective to be considered. There are also strong local motivations, and what is good for a particular municipality or state may or may not be good for the nation as a whole.

The Federal Presence in Local Economic Development

In the years after World War II a new term was added to the economic vocabulary of the nation: *structural unemployment*. It refers to a mismatch between the supply of labor and the demand for labor. The mismatch may apply to skills. For example, in the 1960s numerous former farmers and farm workers were unemployed because the postwar mechanization of agriculture had forced them off the land, and they lacked skills for doing other kinds of work. At the same time the burgeoning computer industry was experiencing shortages of programmers, systems analysts, and technicians. In the mid-1980s there was high unemployment among many manufacturing workers and labor shortages in many service occupations as the nation's job mix shifted rapidly. Thus labor shortages may coexist with labor surpluses because of a mismatch between the skills of the labor force and the needs of employers. To a great extent this type of structural unemployment is the result of technological change. The faster the change occurs, the more serious the problem is likely to be.

The other aspect of structural unemployment is geographical. An area may lose jobs because firms have moved out or because changes in technology have reduced their labor needs or because they have gone out of business. If the loss of employment is not matched by corresponding out-migration of population, a sustained condition of high unemployment may result. In general, it appears that capital is more mobile than population, so that structural unemployment does in fact occur in just this way. A company's board of directors can in a single, rational, "bottom line"–based decision decide to close a plant here and transfer their production operations to a site elsewhere in the nation or, for that matter, elsewhere in the world. It is not so easy for a comparable part of the population to decide to pull out of a labor-surplus area and move to a labor-short area.

The structural unemployment problem did not become apparent immediately after World War II. In welcome contrast to the Great Depression, the postwar period was one of great prosperity. Thus for a time it appeared to many that the only important economic function of government was to maintain this desirable state of affairs by competent management of national (macroeconomic) economic policy.

After a few years, however, it became apparent that even though the nation was generally prosperous, not all regions or all subgroups of the population were doing well economically. The first region for which serious concern developed was Appalachia. Lying between the prosperous eastern seaboard and the then-thriving industrial Midwest, the Appalachian region seemed to be in a permanent depression of its own.

Beginning in 1961 Congress began legislation designed to address both the skills and the geographical mismatch of the structural unemployment problem. The measures designed to alleviate structural unemployment because of a mismatch in skills do not bear directly on urban and regional planning as the term has been used in this book. They are thus not discussed here. Place-related programs are of direct interest and are summarized below.

In 1961 Congress created the Area Redevelopment Administration (ARA).[3] This agency was empowered to make grants to localities to support local economic development. Eligibility for ARA funding was based on county-level data on unemployment and poverty. Similar criteria have characterized the federal presence in local economic development ever since. There is obvious logic to this approach. If structural unemployment is the reason for local economic development programs, how better to decide whether an area needs federal aid than by looking for the consequences of structural economic difficulties, namely, poverty and unemployment? The ARA was replaced in 1965 by the Economic Development Administration (EDA), which essentially did the same thing as ARA. Poverty and unemployment statistics developed by the federal government were examined to draw up a list of counties that were to be eligible for EDA assistance. Eligible counties were then encouraged to set up economic planning organizations, which would submit funding applications to EDA.

A typical EDA-funded project was the community industrial park. A combination of EDA and local funds would be used for purposes like site acquisition, grading, and provision of utilities. When the site was ready, it, or parts of it,

DOES PUBLIC INTERVENTION MAKE SENSE?

Whether such federal subsidies to local development make sense has been the subject of considerable argument. From an economist's viewpoint, subsidies were being used to move economic activity into an area that was not its most efficient location in order to achieve some gains in equity. This so-called equity-efficiency tradeoff deserves a short explanation since it underlies much argument about what is the proper role of government in influencing the location of economic activity.

In brief, the argument is as follows: If the location in question were the most efficient location for the firm, ordinary market forces would cause it to locate there without any government action. If a subsidy (say, in the form of an industrial park site delivered at a fraction of actual cost) is necessary to cause the firm to locate there, by definition, the site is not the most efficient location. Thus, following this logic, there is a loss of efficiency for the whole economy stemming from the use of subsidies to influence economic locations. This occurs simply because encouraging a firm to locate at other than its most efficient location means that the cost of producing a given bundle of goods or services will be higher. In return for this efficiency loss, there is an equity gain in the sense that economic activity is directed to areas of more than ordinary need. This, then, is the efficiency-equity tradeoff. Those who support powerful public intervention in locating economic activity generally, either explicitly or implicitly, place heavy weight on equity. Those who generally oppose such public intervention are apt to place heavy weight, again explicitly or implicitly, on efficiency.

In general liberals have tended to favor place-related programs. Conservatives, such as Presidents Reagan and Bush, have generally opposed such programs, taking the view that it is the proper role of the national government to provide conditions under which private economic activity can flourish but that the marketplace itself should decide how and where capital is invested.

would be sold or leased at below cost to firms, which would then build and operate plants there. From the municipal viewpoint the expenditure of local funds would be justified by two things: the provision of jobs for local residents and the increase in property and other tax revenues from the new facility. The federal contribution was presumably justified by the decrease in structural unemployment.

Substantial federal support for local economic development has also been available from the federal government through Community Development Block Grants (CDBG), mentioned in Chapter 12. Community development funds can be used for a wide variety of economic development purposes. The Urban Development Action Grant (UDAG) program, described in Chapter 12, was another federal initiative that supported local economic development efforts, as were Industrial Revenue Bonds (IRB). No funds passed from the federal government to localities, but the tax breaks (more formally, tax expenditures) that these bonds made possible constituted a revenue loss to the federal government of about 2 billion dollars a year by the late 1980s.

The federal role in local economic development efforts peaked during the

Carter administration and then was gradually scaled back under Reagan and Bush. As the box above suggests, there is an ideological issue involved. Attempting to reshape the geographical pattern of business investment by means of government programs is a decision to replace the judgement of the market with the judgement of government and that is a decision with which conservatives are uncomfortable. Thus, it is not surprising that under Reagan and Bush funding for EDA was cut back and UDAG was ended. Industrial revenue bond funding was slated to be phased out but it had so much support from municipalities that Congress continued it, albiet in somewhat scaled back form.[4]

The new Clinton administration does not have the same reservations about the wisdom of government relative to the wisdom of the market as had the Reagan and Bush administrations and so a more activist federal role seems a strong possibility. A Clinton policy would probably not have the geographic focus previously described, but would focus on using federal funds to aid those sectors that appear either to have the most growth potential or to be most threatened by foreign competition. President Clinton's Secretary of Labor and longtime economic advisor, Robert Reich, is an ardent supporter such of "an industrial policy." Very early in his administration President Clinton spoke of forming a U.S. aerospace consortium. The precipitating event was substantial layoffs by Boeing Aircraft. Boeing was still the largest commercial aircraft producer in the world, selling about three times as many aircraft as each of its two nearest rivals, McDonnell Douglas and Airbus Industrie. However, the latter, a European consortium, has received some billions of dollars in government subsidies and thus drew President Clinton's ire as a form of unfair trade competition. Exactly what the U.S. aerospace consortium would do and whether it would receive federal grants or special tax treatment is not clear at this writing. The incident does suggest, however, that the Clinton administration may seek to implement some sort of U.S. industrial policy. Though an industrial policy might have no spatial intent it will inevitably have spatial consequences and one can predict intense political activity by states and localities in favor of their particular industries.

STATE ECONOMIC DEVELOPMENT EFFORTS

For many years the states have supported local economic development efforts. State departments of commerce provide information on the state and try to guide firms to municipalities within the state. States have for many years offered a variety of financial incentives, such as investment tax credits, to encourage firms to locate or expand within the state's borders. In recent years state governments have become increasingly active in economic development and deeply involved in major business expansions and relocations. States have shown an increasing willingness to use their funds to provide sites and site improvements and to use their powers to borrow money in tax-exempt markets to provide low-cost capital. States have also shown a substantial willingness to offer a variety of tax forgiveness for new industry. The state of Pennsylvania used all of its powers to provide Volkswagen with a subsidy package of many millions of dollars. For several years thousands of Volkswagens, and the only ones produced in the United States, were made in Pennsylvania. However, demand for the car declined and the company suspended all production in the United States, leaving the state sadder and perhaps wiser.

When General Motors indicated that it was seeking a site to manufacture its Saturn car, numerous governors and state representatives made pilgrimages to Detroit, and a keen bidding war developed, with states offering sites, promises of major investments in roads, and substantial tax abatements. As events worked out, GM chose a location near Columbia, Tennessee, which seemed to offer advantages in terms of labor force, transportation, and utility rates, and which did not offer as large a subsidy package as did many other places. But the willingness of states and localities to, in effect, make multimillion dollar bids for GM's presence does indicate the eagerness of states for economic development. Illinois was reported to have offered $200 million in infrastructure, tax concessions, and other expenditures for the Saturn facility.[5]

In 1981 a group of U.S. computer firms formed a consortium called Microelectronics and Computer Technology Corporation (MCC) to pool their research and development activities and thus enable themselves to compete with the Japanese challenge. "Fifty-seven cities in 27 states vied fiercely to become the host city for MCC. Austin ultimately was chosen primarily because of the quality of the engineering and science programs at the University of Texas at Austin, local 'quality of life' factors, and the state's considerable private and public incentives."[6] The incentive package included a $15 million endowment for the university's Electrical Engineering and Computer Science Departments, creation of 30 new faculty positions in those departments, additional research and graduate student support, and the construction of a new building leased to MCC for a nominal sum. From both the city and state point of view, bringing in MCC not only represents a significant amount of employment and economic activity in its own right but also holds the potential for attracting numerous other firms. In some cases firms may be attracted to the area because they have or hope to have business relationships with MCC. In other cases they may feel that they will benefit simply by being where the most advanced work is being done, so that, for example, their scientists and engineers can do graduate work in departments that are at the leading edge of technology. In this age of high technology, the university-industry linkage is well understood.

In some cases states have offered major packages to firms not to move in but simply not to move out. Perhaps this is inevitable. Bids to move will be matched by bids to stay.

> Illinois officialdom breathed a collective sigh of relief last June [1989] when word came that Sears, Roebuck and Company had chosen the Chicago suburb of Hoffman Estates as the new location of its 6,000-worker merchandise group. Sears had announced earlier in the year that it would leave its landmark building, the Sears Tower, in downtown Chicago.
>
> Although keeping Sears cost the state some $178 million and didn't create a single new job, Gov. James R. Thompson hailed the decision as "a great victory" for his state.[7]

Whether all this interstate bidding serves a useful purpose when viewed at the national level is arguable. But from the viewpoint of the state it may make good sense. Bringing in a big firm means thousands of jobs and millions in tax revenues. And it looks good to the voters. Losing a big firm means just the reverse.

The process, of course, contains the seeds of escalation. A big offer is likely to bring forth an even bigger counteroffer. Then, too, firms become very skilled at using the threat to move out or the possibility of moving in to motivate state officials. In some cases the threat to move out may be a bluff, but it may take a very nervy and politically secure governor to call it.

LOCAL ECONOMIC DEVELOPMENT EFFORTS

At the local level there is intense interest in economic development. It is estimated that there are more than 15,000 organizations in the United States devoted to economic development. The vast majority of these are organizations that operate at the local level—city, county, town, or neighborhood.

Communities have several motives for pursuing economic development. One is employment, as noted earlier. Increasing the size of the local economy seems like an obvious way to reduce unemployment. Recall that it is unemployment and its concomitant, poverty, that are the usual bases for eligibility for federal assistance.

Another major motivation at the local level is property tax relief. As noted in Chapter 9 the property tax is by far the largest source of locally raised revenue for substate levels of government. It is also by far the largest locally raised source of revenues for school districts. Most local governments and school districts find themselves under pressure on the subject of property taxes because they are caught between citizens' resistance to tax increases and demands for services. One obvious way out of the dilemma is to expand the tax base so that a given tax rate produces more revenue. In many localities the property the tax motivation is actually more important than the employment motivation. For one thing, essentially all citizens pay property taxes, whereas at any given time only a minority of citizens are unemployed. Then, too, there is no ambiguity about who captures the tax benefits. If a facility is built within the city or county or town lines, that body receives the tax payments. On the other hand, the labor market and business stimulation effects are likely to spread far beyond the municipal boundaries. Small communities within metropolitan areas generally are more motivated by tax than labor market considerations. This because they sense that they are part of the metropolitan labor market and are too small to affect it very much. On the other hand it is possible for them to calculate quite clearly how much a new project will add to their tax rolls.

There are other motivations as well. Economic growth is likely to be good for various sectors of the business community. Real estate brokers will benefit from an increased number of transactions. Property owners will benefit from increased demand for land and structures. Retailers will benefit from increased sales resulting from increased personal income. Construction firms—and their workers—will benefit from increased construction activity. In short, there is a good deal of general support from business and labor for local economic development efforts.

A Crucial Difference

Most of the planning discussed in this book does not involve intermunicipal competition. If town A improves its park system, that will not make the park system in town B worse. In fact, it may stimulate town B to improve its park system. But if town A through infrastructure improvements, tax abatements, or other inducements causes Universal Valve and Faucet to locate there instead of in town B, its gain is town B's loss. In that sense of intense head-to-head competition between municipalities, local economic development efforts represent a unique area of public policy and planning.

What a Community Can Do to Promote Economic Growth

In a very general way there are three major things a community can do to facilitate its own economic growth. As will become apparent, there is a certain amount of overlap.

SALES AND PROMOTION The community can engage in a variety of public relations, advertising, selling, and marketing efforts. In effect, it can view itself as a product and then make a concerted effort to sell that "product." For a firm seeking a location, there is no feasible way to gather objective information about all the possibilities. The community that makes itself highly visible thus gives itself an advantage.

SUBSIDIZATION The community can subsidize development in a variety of ways. One form is tax abatement. Since the main tax used by local government is the property tax, abatement most commonly takes the form of reduced property taxes for new commercial or industrial development. Some communities will set up revolving loan funds or other credit-granting arrangements to facilitate business growth. If the municipality levies sales, inventory, commercial occupancy, or business taxes, it may offer reductions in these.

The Enterprise Zone is a variation on this theme.[8] The city, town, county, or state designates an area as an enterprise zone. Within this zone a variety of tax breaks are offered for new investment. These may include property tax reductions, sales tax reductions, reduced corporate income tax and so on. In addition, direct grants may be offered. Another inducement may be the waiving of some land use regulations to permit higher densities. The technique has most commonly been used in the attempt to restore deteriorated central city areas but has also been used in some rural areas.

MAKING SITES AND BUILDINGS AVAILABLE Availability of sites or buildings is a key factor in determining whether a community can attract new commercial activity and retain existing activity. Let us begin by asking what constitutes a usable site. Consider a planning agency in a suburban or metropolitan fringe area setting up preliminary criteria for identifying potential industrial or commercial land. A first cut might be to rule out any land with a slope of more than 10 percent, for steep slopes push up site preparation and construction costs. Subsoil conditions such as drainage problems, rock outcroppings, and other characteristics that add to construction costs might be a second cut. If the municipality is traversed by a river or stream, land in the flood plain might also be eliminated from consideration. Availability of utilities such as water, sewers, and electric power is also a criterion. For light manufacturing, retailing, wholesaling, and office activities, adequate road access would also be a requirement. For heavy manufacturing, rail access as well is likely to be needed. In addition to having an adequate number of acres available, there is also the matter of site geometry. For heavy industry, a minimum site depth of 800 feet might be a good rule of thumb. For light manufacturing, minimum depths of 400 to 600 feet are desirable.

To ensure that adequate sites will be available in the foreseeable future, there are various steps a municipality can take. The most direct step is the public provision of sites. Numerous cities, towns, and counties have municipal industrial parks. The community uses public funds (and sometimes the power of eminent domain as well) to acquire and develop sites. The prepared sites are then sold or leased long term to firms, which erect and operate manufacturing or other commercial buildings on them. Very often, there is a significant public subsidy in such operations in that the rent or sales price only covers a fraction of the costs incurred in site acquisition, grading, drainage, building of access roads, running water and sewer lines, and so on.

Some communities will go even further in providing a place for economic activity by erecting a building and then seeking a firm(s) to occupy it. Very often the structure put up is a "shell building." The community puts up the outer shell of the building and then waits until it has found a firm to use the building before it completes the interior. Again, there may or may not be an element of subsidy in the process.

Another community might take a somewhat more tentative approach and engage in land banking, that is, acquiring land or perhaps options on land with a view simply to hold it as a potential commercial site. Of course, such a method is expensive. The financial cost to the community is the loss of interest on whatever funds are tied up in the land. If the community sinks $1 million into land banking and the current rate at which the community borrows is 10 percent, the carrying cost is $100,000 for this year, a burden that must be borne by the municipality's taxpayers.

Beyond the direct provision of land, the community can use its land-use control powers to attempt to ensure that adequate privately owned land will be available for commercial development. One obvious step is simply zoning an adequate amount of land in the appropriate categories. The zoning should be applied to land that actually has real development potential; land that meets the sorts of topographic and geometric standards previously described. It also means land that either already has been or has the potential for being provided with adequate access and utilities. As noted in Chapter 8 the zoning should be coordinated with the land uses shown on the comprehensive plan.

The infrastructure question is addressed through the community's capital budget. For sites with near-term development potential, capital funds can be spent to provide utilities and access. For sites with longer-term potential, it is hard to justify immediate expenditure. However, providing infrastructure to these sites can be an item on the community's capital improvements program scheduled for some years hence.

None of these measures will guarantee that a given parcel of land will be used for commercial or industrial use or that it will not be put to some other use. However, by declaring its intent through master planning, zoning, and capital budgeting, the community decreases the odds that lands with economic potential will be preempted by other uses. Assume that a block of 100 acres has good potential for economic development in the long term, but its chances for such development in the next few years are small. The owner has the chance to sell 5 acres out of its center for residential use now. However, dividing the site in that manner will greatly reduce its ultimate commercial or industrial potential. By telegraphing its long-term intentions as described, the community encourages the property owner to take a long-term rather than a short-term view of his or her situation.

A Systematic Approach to Economic Development Planning

What follows is a brief systematic account of how a community might approach economic development planning.[9]

1. Needs Assessment In this stage the community in effect asks itself what needs the program will try to meet. The two most common reasons for economic development programs are improvement of the labor market and expansion of the property tax base. In the first case the community might see the need simply as more jobs to soak up some local unemployment.[10] Or it might see the need as tightening the labor market to put upward pressure on wages generally. It might see a generalized need for more jobs or a need for more jobs for particular types of workers. As an example of the latter case, consider, say, a suburban county that has been gaining corporate headquarters activity and losing manufacturing jobs. It may be experiencing shortages of secretarial and clerical labor while running a 20 percent unemployment rate among factory operatives. The community might thus define its labor market goal as providing additional blue-collar jobs rather than simply increasing total employment.

A community that did not see itself as having serious labor market problems but had high rates of property taxation might still have a strong interest in economic development. Here, the goal would be expansion of the tax base, and projects would be judged primarily in fiscal rather than labor market terms.

By clarifying its goals, the community will have a better idea how to use its limited resources. It also will have some basis on which to make choices. For example, assume that the community has enough funds to subsidize site development for one of two projects and that neither project is feasible in the absence of subsidization. One project is a data-processing center for a major corporation. It will provide relatively little employment for presently unemployed city residents but will produce a large property tax yield. The other project is a warehouse. It promises to create a number of jobs that might be held by city residents who are now unemployed. However, warehouses are a very inexpensive form of construction compared to computer centers, so that the property tax yield will be only a fraction of that of the data-processing center. Which project should the community back? If the community has sorted out its goals in advance, the choice should be easy to make. In the absence of clearly articulated goals, making the choice will be difficult and the decision will be hard to justify. City officials may find themselves answering charges of favoritism or arbitrariness from disappointed applicants or political opponents.

2. A MARKET EVALUATION After the community has decided what economic development it would like to foster, the next step is a realistic assessment of the types of economic activity it might reasonably be expected to attract and retain. This means taking an objective look at the community's strengths and weaknesses as they would appear to a firm thinking about locating in the community or to a firm already in the community and thinking about whether to remain or relocate.

Among the items to consider would be wage rates, labor force, land costs, land availability, utility costs, transportation system, cost of living, price and availability of housing, tax rates, accessibility to major markets, and an elusive but important factor that generally goes by the name "quality of life." This last item includes such diverse factors as the quality of public education, recreational and cultural facilities, climate and environmental quality, and crime and public safety. Quality of life is becoming an increasingly important factor in the ability to attract economic activity. It affects the ability of a firm to recruit workers, which in turn affects the firm's ability to compete. It is particularly important in the so-called "high tech" industries, where technological change is rapid and the ability to recruit highly qualified engineers, scientists, mathematicians, and other specialized personnel is crucial.

3. AN ASSESSMENT OF THE CONSEQUENCES OF DEVELOPMENT POLICY Understanding how economic development will affect the community is important. Part of this assessment might be financial, particularly if the program is being mounted for property tax relief. This sort of study, generally referred to as "fiscal impact" or "revenue/cost" study, estimates both the new revenues from a given development and also the new costs that such a development is likely to impose on the community. From these estimates a revenue/cost ratio or net benefit (loss) figure is calculated. This figure may give the community guidance about whether to pursue economic development or, given that initial determination, what types

of development to pursue. If the community plans to offer subsidies to encourage economic development, it may yield some guidance about what level of subsidization makes fiscal sense. In Chapter 13 we mentioned benefit/cost analysis. A fiscal impact analysis is really part of a benefit/cost analysis. It happens to be the part most commonly done, primarily because it is relatively easy to do and because there is no ambiguity about what its results mean.

Economic development will also have a variety of effects on the community beyond those that show up in the fiscal impact study. It is well to anticipate these. For example, economic development will increase traffic within the community. Does the community have the capacity to handle this traffic? Will there be opposition from affected citizens? Almost inevitably economic development will have some environmental effects. How serious are these and how might the community deal with them? Creating new jobs within a community will increase the demand for housing. How will that affect housing prices and rents? If the housing stock is fairly elastic (can grow easily), increases in demand will manifest themselves largely in increases in supply. If the housing stock is fairly inelastic, increases in demand will manifest themselves in increased prices and rents.[11]

4. PLAN FORMULATION Once the issues of community needs, community abilities, and the effects of development on the community have been considered, an economic development plan can be formulated. The plan might include some or all of the following elements.

Advertising and marketing. In effect, the community is a product that the community's economic development agency attempts to "sell" to firms. This part of the plan may include items like brochures, advertising, press coverage, and visits to firms. The plan should include not only efforts to bring in new firms but also efforts to retain existing economic activity and encourage the expansion of firms now in the community.

A plan for the subsidization of economic development. This might involve tax abatements, grants, loans, or loan guarantees.

A program of capital investments. This element is likely to include plans for road construction or improvement and for the provision of public water and sewer facilities to make land suitable for commercial and industrial development. In particular communities, it might also include other elements. For example, in a community seeking to facilitate commercial development in the downtown area, it might include widening sidewalks and providing public parking. In a riverfront community, it might include dredging and channel widening. For many types of commercial activity, good air transportation is an economic asset. Thus lengthening the runway at the municipal airport might be part of an economic development-oriented capital budget.

Plans for dealing with the land-use aspects of economic development. These might involve channeling economic growth into some areas and attempting to keep economic development out of other areas. It might simultaneously involve seeking to protect residential and recreational areas from the impact of economic activity while trying to protect large blocks of land in industrial and commercial areas from being chopped up by piecemeal residential and commercial development. Should the community decide to play a direct entrepreneurial role, for example, the community-owned industrial park, the plan would also include elements pertaining to site acquisition and development.

Nonphysical elements. Most of the items mentioned so far are physical. However, there may be other steps the community can take. For example, if the municipality has a community college, its curriculum might be tuned to the economic development program by offering courses synchronized with the labor needs of the sort of firms the municipality hopes to attract. At the state level, particularly in the South, labor-training programs have been used quite effectively as devices for recruiting firms.

5. Plan Review and Updating Inevitably, events will not work out exactly as planned. Seeking new firms for a community is a bit like fishing. One can never be entirely sure what one will catch or just when one will catch it. Then, too, opportunities may come along that bend the plan into a somewhat different shape than its makers anticipated. For example, a community strongly desires a particular type of industry and has certain ideas about just where it should be located. An entrepreneur appears who is interested in building just what the community wants but is adamant about locating it in an area the community does not consider a good location. Does the community turn the project away or does it bend its land-use plan into a slightly different shape? With the passage of time the plan and reality will almost inevitably diverge, and some readjusting of the plan becomes advisable.

A LOOK AHEAD

In recent years the competitive situation of many U.S. industries has changed. In the first years after World War II the main competitor usually faced by a U.S. manufacturer was another U.S. manufacturer. In the last two decades or so the combination of cheap transportation, reduction of tariffs, and the diffusion of manufacturing technology to parts of the world with lower labor costs has produced a drastic change. The strongest competitor that many a U.S. producer faces today is located overseas. Very different economic development planning strategies will be called for when the chief competitor is across the ocean rather than across the state line. The formation of MCC noted earlier and, more recently, a consortium of computer component makers called Sematech are examples of groups of competitors banding together to face a common external threat. Exactly how the economic development efforts of governments will respond to the changed competitive situation is not clear at this point. Perhaps we will see an increased role for the states relative to local government to correspond to the increased geographic scale of competition.

It is widely believed that in relatively simple industrial operations that require substantial amounts of labor, the United States simply cannot compete with producers in low labor-cost areas. The corollary is that the competitive hope for the United States is in high technology, where a technical lead may make up for higher labor costs. Thus we may see considerable emphasis on the subsidizing and fostering of high-technology industry. As noted, the Clinton administration appears to be inclined in this direction. The strength of international competition is likely to focus federal efforts on strengthening the hand of U.S. industry as a whole rather than on "leveling the playing field" between communities or regions within the United States.

In recent years the relocation of firms, often manufacturers, has hit some communities very hard. As a result, there has been discussion of legislation that would either limit the rights of companies to move or impose some fairly heavy burdens on them if they did move. Those who favor such legislation base their arguments on what are sometimes termed "equity" considerations. Those who oppose such legislation generally base their arguments on questions of efficiency and personal freedom.[12] Which way the nation will move on this issue remains to be seen. To some extent it is an ideological issue, with the left favoring legislation and the right opposing it. There are also some constitutional issues involved, particularly the Interstate Commerce Clause, which prohibits states from interfering with the flow of interstate commerce.

SUMMARY

Planning for economic development dates back many decades. Early efforts tended to focus on transportation and generally were initiated by the commercial elite of the city.

Beginning in the 1960s the federal government began to subsidize local economic planning and development efforts with a view to combating structural unemployment. This policy continues to the present time though it was weakened somewhat during the Reagan and Bush presidencies.

Virtually all states strive to foster their own economic growth through a variety of programs involving marketing, subsidization, and the use of capital expenditures. Many thousands of municipalities also promote their own economic development using marketing and subsidization. Very often, the community will use its capital budget and its land-use policies to assure the availability of an adequate number of suitable sites.

Steps in a simple systematic approach to planning for economic development are

Needs assessment
Market evaluation
Assessment of development consequences
Plan formulation
Plan review and updating

The growing strength of international competition may shift the focus in local economic development from intermunicipal competition to collective efforts to compete with distant rivals.

NOTES

1. For a picture of the economics of transportation in the United States at the beginning of the nineteenth century, see Alan Pred, *City Systems in Advanced Economies*, John Wiley, New York, 1977.
2. Alfred Eichner, *State Development Agencies and Employment Expansion*, University of Michigan Press, Ann Arbor, 1970.
3. A brief review of programs through the end of the 1970s can be found in John M. Levy, *Economic Development Programs for Cities, Counties and Towns*. Praeger, New York, 1981, chap. 11.
4. For information on tax expenditures see the table on revenue losses in the chapter on federal government finances in the *Statistical Abstract of the United States*, various editions.
5. Robert Guskind, "The Giveaway Game Continues," *Planning*, February, 1990, pp. 4–8.
6. Josh Farley and Norman J. Glickman, "R&D as an Economic Development Strategy: Microelectronics and Computer Technology Corporation Comes to Austin, Texas," *Journal of the American Planning Association* vol. 52, No. 4, Autumn 1986, p. 408.
7. Guskind, op. cit.
8. For a summary of experience with enterprise zones see Rodney A. Erickson, "Enterprise Zones Lessons from the State Experience," in *Sources of Metropolitan Growth*, Center for Urban and Regional Studies, Rutgers, N.J., 1992, pp. 161-182.
9. The reader should not assume that all communities approach economic development in this systematic manner. In many cases, for a variety of political reasons, communities jump into economic development programs without much planning and the program largely amounts to a matter of shooting at targets of opportunity. See John M. Levy, "What Local Economic Developers Actually Do: Location Quotients vs Press Releases," *Journal of the American Planning Association*, Spring 1990, pp. 153–60.
10. It should be noted that 100 jobs added to the local economy will not generally reduce unemployment by anything close to that amount. Some of the jobs will be taken by people outside the labor force who have been drawn into it by the new employment opportunities. Additional jobs are likely to be taken by people who migrate into the area because of the availability of jobs. For a summary of experience on this point, see Gene Summers, *The Invasion of Nonmetropolitan America by Industry: A Quarter Century of Experience*, Praeger, New York, 1976.
11. This effect is commonly seen in the suburban areas of large metropolitan areas. For example, the Fairfield County area of Connecticut and the Fairfax County area of Virginia have experienced major growth in corporate activity, and many communities in the area have fairly restrictive residential land-use policies. The situation of increasing demand pressing on a relatively inelastic supply has produced extraordinarily high housing prices.
12. For a view that favors public regulation, see Barry Bluestone and Bennet Harrison, *The Deindustrialization of America*, Basic Books, New York, 1982. For an opposing view, see Richard B. McKenzie, *Fugitive Industry*, Ballinger Publishing Co., Cambridge, MA, 1984; or *Plant Closings: Public or Private Choice*, Cato Institute, Washington, D.C., 1982.

SELECTED BIBLIOGRAPHY

BEYARD, MICHAEL D., *Business and Industrial Park Development Handbook.*, Urban Land Institute, Washington, D.C., 1988.

BLAKELY, EDWARD J., *Planning Local Economic Development: Theory & Practice.*, Sage, Newburg Park, CA., 1989.

INTERNATIONAL CITY MANAGEMENT ASSOCIATION, *Shaping the Local Economy: Current Perspectives on Economic Development*, Washington, D.C., 1984.

LEVY, JOHN M., *Economic Development Programs for Cities, Counties & Towns*, 2nd ed., Praeger, New York, 1990.

LYONS, THOMAS S., and HAMLIN, ROGER E., *Creating an Economic Development Action Plan: A Guide for Development Professionals*, Praeger, New York, 1991.

MORIARTY, BRIAN J., and COWAN, DAVID M., EDS., *Industrial Location and Commercial Development*, University of North Carolina Press, Chapel Hill, 1980.

CHAPTER 15

GROWTH MANAGEMENT PLANNING

Growth management is generally defined as the regulation of the *amount, timing, location,* and *character* of development. Since the late 1960s hundreds of cities, counties, and towns in the United States have instituted growth management programs.

The goals of these programs vary. Growth management programs often are heavily motivated by environmental considerations. A related consideration may be ensuring a desirable pattern of land development in future years. Preserving an existing lifestyle and community ambiance is a common motivation, as is ensuring that community facilities such as schools, road utilities, and recreation will be adequate to future needs. In some cases a major goal of growth management will be fiscal, ensuring that the community will not be swamped by development-imposed costs. Finally, like the exclusionary zoning discussed earlier, growth management may have an exclusionary, or "keeping the good things to ourselves," motivation. Rarely will a program be instituted for a single reason. Untangling the various motivations and saying exactly why a community has entered into growth management may be extremely difficult.

In general, growth management plans or systems are made up of elements that have been well known to planners for years. In that sense, there is nothing unique about them. Growth management systems differ from traditional comprehensive planning not in the elements that compose them but in the synthesis of those elements. Specifically, growth management systems are generally characterized by very close and long-term coordination between land-use controls on the one hand and capital investment on the other. They are often also characterized by the use of more modern approaches to land-use control and often by a great sensitivity to environmental issues. In that all of these points are to be found in planning efforts that are not specifically labeled as growth management, it must be admitted that no absolutely hard line separates growth management from more traditional planning.

When growth management appeared in the late 1960s and early 1970s, several different terms with overlapping meanings came into being. A multivolume anthology of articles on the field, published in 1975, carried the title *Management and Control of Growth.*[1] Hence, we had the terms *growth management* and *growth control*. At the same time the term *no growth* also came into use. The same anthology carried articles with titles like "Problems Which Sprout in the Shadow of No-Growth" and "Should the Poor Buy No-Growth?"[2]

Growth management might be taken to mean management without any implication of limiting growth. *Growth control* carries the implication that growth is not only to be managed or guided but also limited. The term *no growth* carries the obvious implication of an intent to stop growth entirely.

With the passage of time growth management became more or less universal in the field. In fact, however, some growth management programs may really be growth control or no-growth programs under a somewhat more acceptable name. Growth management has had, among many, a bad name precisely because many programs were believed to be no more than disguised attempts to stop or unduly limit community growth.

In general, growth management policies are not common in older central cities, for there the problem is more likely to be shrinkage or stagnation rather than rampant growth. Growth control policies are common in suburban areas and in those cities where there is still substantial growth potential. They are also common in counties and towns outside of metropolitan areas. The potential for rapid growth and a high degree of environmental consciousness appear to predispose communities toward the establishment of growth management policies. So, too, does a high degree of general prosperity. If people or communities are poor they are more likely to be pro-growth because that implies jobs and revenues. In that case, environmental and quality-of-life issues are likely to seem less important.

THE ORIGINS OF GROWTH MANAGEMENT

Several strands came together to bring about the growth management movement. First was the rush to suburbanize after World War II. People moved outward in metropolitan areas partly to obtain relief from central-city conditions: to breathe cleaner air, to be less crowded, to be safer, and to be closer to nature. The person who has made such a move would in many cases want to be the last person who does the "I'm on board, now pull up the ladder" syndrome. No one who is active in suburban planning can long remain unaware of such motivations.

These motivations were joined by growing environmental consciousness beginning, roughly, in the early 1960s. Growth control proponents could gather strength and respectability from a general climate of environmental concern. Proposals to limit growth could now be supported on environmental grounds. At a local level of analysis it is hard to refute such arguments, for it is undeniably true that any development, whether residential or commercial, will have some adverse environmental impact.

Whether environmentally based opposition to growth can be justified when the physical scale of analysis is expanded is another matter. If a town takes some action that keeps a particular area in, let us say, low-density residential use when it might otherwise have gone into high-density residential use, it has unquestionably reduced the environmental impact on that area. Fewer trees will be cut down, less ground will be covered with impervious cover, fewer sources of air and water pollution will be present in the area, and so on.[3] However, it is obvious that much of the growth that was prevented will be displaced elsewhere. In that case one cannot say, *a priori*, whether the total effect of the growth limitation has been to decrease or increase environmental impact. The environmental impact argument is commonly used by proponents of growth limitations, but the issue of displacement effects is rarely discussed.

Regardless of the displacement effects issue, there is no doubt that the growing environmental consciousness of the 1960s and 1970s lent much strength to the growth management movement. Even global concern with overpopulation lent some strength to the growth control movement simply because of the superficial resemblance between planetary population control and local population control.

> Undoubtedly this [local efforts to stop populations growth] has much to do with the new Malthusian concern with the consequences of unlimited population growth at national and world levels. Some seem to think that the place to start controlling the nation's population growth is at the level of their city, metropolis or state. Others hope that, as the nation moves to zero population growth (ZPG), so will their communities. Both these views are misleading half-truths.[4]

Schumacher's book, *Small is Beautiful*, and similar works that railed against the increasing scale and complexity of modern life also lent strength to growth control movements.[5]

THE MECHANICS OF GROWTH MANAGEMENT

To consider growth management in detail let us examine one of the earliest and best-known growth management systems, that adopted by the town of Ramapo, New York, in 1969. The plan is well known in planning circles not because it had major effects on shaping the pattern of land use—for it did not—but because it raised key legal issues and then survived court challenge.[6] Among advocates of growth management it was the cause of much enthusiasm and was hailed as the wave of the future. Among those who saw in growth management simply the old exclusionary zoning in new garb, the system was roundly condemned. Even the appellate court that sustained the Ramapo plan on appeal did so with a split decision.

The town of Ramapo is located about 40 miles north of New York City in Rockland County, New York, on the west side of the Hudson River. It is at the outer fringe of commuting distance to Manhattan but within easy commuting distance of much employment in the inner suburbs of the New York region. In the 1960s the town feared that it would be overwhelmed by suburban growth and determined to gain some control over its fate. The town had a zoning ordinance that essentially limited new construction to single-family houses. That, critics have argued, might have been considered sufficient protection against growth pressures. In fact, some argued that such an ordinance was not only sufficient but also exclusionary. Nevertheless the town board enacted an ordinance that stated that a permit to build a house could not be granted unless the developer could show 15 development points.[7] These were to be calculated as follows:

1. Sewers
   Public sewers .... 5 points
   Package sewer plants .... 3 points
   County-approved septic system(in a large-lot zone) .... 3 points
   All others .... 0 points
2. Percentage of required drainage capacity
   100 percent or more .... 5 points
   90 to 99.9 .... 4 points
   80 to 89.9 .... 3 points
   65 to 79.9 .... 2 points
   50 to 64.9 .... 1 point
   less than 50 .... 0 points
3. Improved park or recreation facility including public school site
   Within ¼ mile .... 5 points
   Within ½ mile .... 3 points
   Within 1 mile .... 1 point
   Further than 1 mile .... 0 points
4. State, county, or town major, secondary, or collector road(s) improved with curbs and sidewalks
   Direct access .... 5 points
   Within ½ mile .... 3 points
   Within 1 mile .... 1 point
   Further than 1 mile .... 0 points
5. Fire house
   Within 1 mile .... 3 points
   Within 2 miles .... 1 point
   Further than 2 miles .... 0 points

The term *developer* meant any party seeking to build one or more houses. The ordinance meant that even if the applicant for a building permit(s) wished to build in conformity with the existing zoning, his or her application could be turned down if the site in question did not have the requisite 15 points. An appeals procedure was provided, and the ordinance was drafted so that the developer might be able to proceed in the absence of the necessary points if he or she would provide the infrastructure necessary to reach 15 points. The point system was keyed to an 18-year capital improvements plan. In effect, then, the ordinance reversed the usual sequence of land development. Typically, development tends to lead to the provision of an infrastructure. Frequently infrastructure is provided when the demands of a population in place for better public services (water, sewer, traffic, school, recreation, and the like) become sufficiently strong to motivate government to provide them. The Ramapo plan turned this around by blocking development until those services were in place.

As might be expected a court challenge was mounted. A lower court overturned the ordinance. However, the town appealed to the state's appellate court and by a split decision the town's appeal was sustained. The town took the position that its concern with providing infrastructure prior to residential development was a reasonable response to strong growth pressures and a legitimate exercise of the police power. It argued that denying permission to build did not constitute a total destruction of the value of property because the infrastructure would ultimately be provided and thus permission ultimately granted. Essentially, the court accepted this position.The court's decision could be regarded as a substantial expansion of the scope of the police power. In an article written after the town's successful appeal, an attorney for the plaintiff stated,

> . . . New York has opted for the police power. The breaking up of a community's lands into different use categories and reasonable changes in zoning designation have been consistently upheld as a proper exercise of the police power. Ramapo now adds to this traditional exercise of police power (solely with respect to its residentially zoned land), a novel time factor mandating when such use can be employed. The building of new residences on property now residentially zoned is phased for the next eighteen years.[8]

Leaving the purely legal issues behind, strong arguments can be made both for and against the Ramapo plan. Basically, they are similar to arguments that might be made for and against most growth management plans of the period. On the positive side it can be argued that the plan places the horse before the cart, where it should be. Planning for and provision of infrastructure now precede rather than trail development. Communities are not burdened with obligations they cannot meet and populations whose needs they cannot serve. The natural environment is protected against being overloaded. For example, if the capacity to treat the sewage of a housing development is not available, the development is blocked until that capacity is created. Hence streams and ground water supplies are protected against being overloaded with untreated human waste.

On the negative side several points can be made. Most generally, it can be argued that all this concern with property planning is simply a hypocritical stratagem for the defense of privilege. The plaintiff's attorney noted that the plan placed development point requirements on residential development but not on commercial development. The reason for this omission, he argues, is not because commercial development is less environmentally damaging or less needful of infrastructure, but rather that it is believed to yield a property tax surplus. In other words, a plan that blocks only residential growth looks suspiciously like a plan to skim off the fiscal cream and divert the costs of serving a residential population to other communities.

It can also be argued that applying controls only on the housing side constitutes a policy of social exclusion. The moderate-income person may work at a new plant in the community but the chances are that he or she will not be able to find housing there. Nor will his or her children be able to attend school in that community.

Another argument against the plan is that it ignores regional needs—specifically, regional housing needs. Even the majority opinion (the opinion that sustained the town's position) conceded this point. Referring to the regional need question Judge Scileppi, writing for the majority, stated,

> Of course these problems [regional housing needs and other regional planning considerations] cannot be solved by Ramapo or any single municipality. . . . To that end, State-wide or regional control of planning would ensure that interests broader than that of the municipality underlie various land use policies.

In effect, then, the judge was saying that—viewed in a larger framework—the Ramapo plan might deserve rejection or modification. But he was also saying that it was not the role of the judiciary to make that decision. Should his position be characterized as admirable judicial restraint or as an abdication of responsibility? That is a judgment for the reader.

The Ramapo plan could be faulted as being exclusionary in that it contained no provision for multifamily housing, row housing, or even single-family housing on small lots. In other words, it contained no provisions for the less expensive housing types. However, it must be noted that this is not strictly a criticism of the growth management aspects of the plan, for there are numerous communities with no explicit growth management plan but whose zoning permits only a limited range of housing types. Perhaps this caveat also emphasizes that the line between growth management and other types of land-use control is blurred.

The town took (and still takes) the position that the fact that it does not allow certain housing types, and therefore possibly keeps out certain types of people, is not so terrible. Is it not true that the region is made up of many communities? If so, why must any one community offer housing for all types of households? If Ramapo does not permit building of, say, garden apartments, will not the builder who wishes to construct such units simply take his or her capital elsewhere? One could go further and say that if Ramapo severely curtails the building of single-family houses, does that not simply mean that more units will be built elsewhere. After all, no action Ramapo takes will diminish the regionwide demand for housing nor will it diminish the regionwide supply of capital and labor for building housing.

There is some truth to these arguments. There are also some counterarguments. Although Ramapo cannot diminish regionwide supplies of capital and labor, it can diminish the regionwide supply of land available for development. That may elevate housing costs not only locally but also regionally.[9] If development that would have occurred in Ramapo is displaced to more peripheral communities, it may produce a kind of inefficiency at the regional level because it spreads out residential and commercial activity. That pushes up commuting times and costs, makes it more difficult to supply public transportation, and increases the cost of utility service. In other words makes for suboptimal regional planning.

WINNERS AND LOSERS IN GROWTH MANAGEMENT

In principle many municipalities could slow growth with equal effectiveness by limiting either residential or commercial development. Slowing residential growth would slow commercial growth by limiting the size of the labor force and the number of consumers. Similarly, limiting commercial growth would slow the growth of the housing stock because the presence of jobs is a major factor in the demand for housing.

In fact, however, most growth management systems emphasize limiting residential growth because such a policy tends to produce tight labor markets and high housing prices. That is much more attractive to the population already in place than a commercial limitation policy, which would produce higher unemployment and lower housing prices. And, of course, it is the population resident at the time who establishes the growth management policy.

Assume that a growth management program has the effect of slowing residential growth relative to employment growth. Who wins and who loses? The home owner wins simply through the workings of the law of supply and demand. Restrict the supply of any item, and all other things being equal, its price rises. The owner of rental property benefits in the same manner. A lesser supply of rental units in the long run means higher rents, which is capitalized as a higher value for the apartment building in question. Of course, by the same token, the renter loses. The nonresident of the municipality, if he or she has the desire to become a resident, is also a loser, for it is now more difficult to find housing in the community. In a general sense, those who own developed property in the community benefit and those who would like to own property lose. Those who would profit from community growth, for example, builders, construction workers, and real estate brokers, also tend to be losers. Owners of undeveloped land within the community are likely to be losers in the process for there is a general relationship between the value of land and the intensity with which it can be developed. Restrict that intensity and the value of land is necessarily diminished.

Financial effects will be felt outside the municipality as well. If town X and town Y are in the same metropolitan area, they are to some extent part of the same housing market. If town X reduces its rate of housing construction, it deflects some housing demand to town Y. Thus housing prices in town Y (as well as in X) will rise, benefiting those who already own housing there and penalizing those who seek to buy there. Comparable effects may be seen for rental property owners and renters as well.

Fiscal effects can also be demonstrated. If town X restricts residential development but accepts a new corporate headquarters, its tax rate may go down because the tax revenues from the headquarters exceed the new expenses the headquarters will impose on the town. In effect, town X is capturing the tax surplus from the headquarters while shifting the population-related costs to other towns. Town Y now has to pay the cost of educating the children of people who work in town X and whose place of work contributes handsomely to town X's tax base.

The "Defense of Privilege" Issue

Beyond the purely financial issue of winners and losers is a larger but less demonstrable issue. Much argument over environmental and planning issues is bedeviled with the question of "defense of privilege," with charges of hypocrisy by opponents of growth management and protestations of virtue by its proponents. Without trying to pass a blanket judgment over a complex situation let us simply present an argument.

There are some goods whose enjoyment by one party does not diminish the enjoyment of comparable goods by another party. If I enjoy a fine steak, that does not diminish your enjoyment of another steak. On the other hand, my enjoyment of a day on the ski slope may well diminish your enjoyment of your day on the slope because my presence makes the trails and the lift lines just a bit more crowded for you.

As the U.S. population becomes more prosperous, the possession of goods of the first type becomes less significant as a way of distinguishing between the affluent and the nonaffluent. Instead, the distinction increasingly becomes a matter of being able to enjoy goods and services of the second type—those whose value is lessened the more that others have access to the same or similar items. Increasingly, wealth becomes important not because it buys consumer goods but because it buys quiet, solitude, clean air, or access to relatively unspoiled nature. We can always produce more automobiles or more stereos, but the supply of mountain streams is fixed.

If one accepts this argument it is only a short step to seeing much environmental and planning conflict in terms of the defense of privilege. The population of a prosperous, attractive community that seeks to limit growth is simply defending its privileges. It is seeking, by means of political action, to protect or enhance the value of those goods of the second type that it now enjoys. One might say that it is using the political process to impose losses on outsiders, that is, denying them temporary or permanent access to the community.

An interesting aspect of this argument is the lineup of combatants in fights over environmental issues. Very often business and labor will be allied in favor of development, and the opposition will be largely upper-middle class, perhaps as represented by a coalition of environmental groups like the Sierra Club. The lineup of players is not hard to understand. The same project that means profit to the developer means jobs to the construction worker, and so they make common cause. The upper-middle-class opposition neither earns its living by investing capital nor by doing construction or industrial labor. If one accepts the defense of privilege argument, this class opposes the project for the reasons presented earlier.[10]

A SAMPLING OF GROWTH MANAGEMENT PROGRAMS

The city of Boulder, Colorado, limits the buildings permits it grants to a number that it estimates will hold population growth to 2 percent per year. At one time permits were awarded by a competitive scheme. At present, all the permits applied for are totaled and applicants receive a percentage share of their application. The city does not limit commercial growth in a comparable manner.

Boulder also uses requirements and exactions to reimburse the municipality for costs imposed by new development and to achieve, at the developer's cost, some public purposes. For example, the city requires that for developments of 10 or more units, 15 percent of the units must be for low- or moderate-income people. Initially, this is a cost the developer absorbs. In reality, economic theory would suggest that some of this cost is borne by the developer and some is shifted to buyers of the remaining 85 percent in the form of higher prices.[11] In any case, it is a cost not chargeable to the city government. Exactions are also made for park and community development funds. The exactions clearly are part of the fiscal aspect of growth management noted at the beginning of the chapter. However, placing additional costs (even if doing so is entirely justifiable) on the developer may have the effect of reducing somewhat the rate of development. That is not a matter of planning but of economics. Increasing the production cost of any item will, in general, raise its selling price and thus reduce the amount that can be sold.

The city of Davis, California, also limits residential permits. In the late 1970s community residents in a citizen-originated referendum voted to limit growth so that by the year 2000 the city's population would not exceed 50,000. Every two years the planning department calculates the number of new dwelling units that would be consistent with that target. Building permit applications are ranked and permits are granted only to that number. The city uses a scoring system, with points granted for energy efficiency, provision of low-cost units, past performance of the developer, environmental impact, design diversity, and compactness, among others. Like Boulder, Davis does not apply comparable limits to commercial development.

Bucks County, Pennsylvania, in the Philadelphia metropolitan area, reacted to growth pressures in a somewhat different manner. Here, the county has no direct control over local land use since, under Pennsylvania state law, zoning powers reside at the municipal level. Thus the county has only an advisory role. The county planning department designates development districts largely on the basis of projected population change. Within those districts it recommends infrastructure (such as sewer lines, water mains, and roads) to facilitate development consistent with the natural environment and expected or planned population change. It suggests that the county outside of those districts be considered a "holding zone," with land-use controls that hold population to very low density levels. This is achieved by large, lot zoning requirements and tax policies that encourage farmers to keep their lands in agricultural use.[12]

Within the development districts the county agency suggests the use of performance zoning, specifically, density and impervious cover requirements. Rather than specifying the nature of residential development in great detail, as does the conventional or Euclidean ordinance, the county will simply suggest zoning districts that specify the number of units per acre. Whether, for example, the units in question are to be single family or multifamily is a matter for community determination. The impervious cover requirements are cast in terms of percentage of the site covered. The intention is to control land use in terms of what is really important (in this case population housed in an area and volume of storm water runoff) rather than to specify a large number of details of secondary importance. From a design point of view, performance zoning achieves the overall goals of zoning but gives the designer far more freedom and should encourage much more interesting and varied design. It relies on the marketplace rather than the zoning ordinance to achieve functional, aesthetically sound development.

As is common, limitation is heavier on the residential than on the commercial side. Whereas commercial development is regulated by a variety of environmental controls as well as conventional zoning requirements, the performance approach is applied only to residential development.

In March 1989 Pasadena, California, enacted a growth moratorium through a citizen-initiated referendum (see box on page 234). Although many growth moratoria apply only on the residential side or, less commonly, only on the commercial side, the Pasadena moratorium takes a balanced approach. Commercial growth will be limited to 250,000 square feet per year (enough space for 600 to 800 office workers). Residential growth will be limited to 250 units per year (about one-half of 1 percent of the present housing stock). All new developments, whether residential or commercial, will have to meet a requirement of no significant "negative impact" with regard to environment, traffic, municipal expenditures, and affordable housing. The municipal expenditures criterion means that the proposed development must not add more to municipal costs than it will contribute in tax revenues; the details of how this result is to be determined have not been worked out as of this writing. The affordable housing requirement means that the building of the proposed units must not result in any net loss of "affordable" units; affordable units are defined in terms of household income. Median family income in the Los Angeles metropolitan area in 1989 for a family of four was $38,900. Affordable housing for a family of four is defined as that which could be afforded by a family earning up to 120 percent of the median, or roughly $46,700. A rule of thumb is that a family can afford a house whose price is up to 2 ½ times its annual income. If that figure were used, it would yield a maximum price in the range of $115,000 to $120,000. If a 25-percent-of-income rule were used for rents, it would yield a figure of slightly less than $1,000 a month. Thus, "affordable" housing does not mean low-cost housing.

In many California communities a combination of slow residential construction and strong economic growth (which increases the demand for housing) had produced extremely high house prices by the end of the 1980s. The balanced limitation approach and the affordable housing requirement were a limited attempt to deal with this problem. The motivations behind the initiative included traffic congestion, environmental quality, and a general feeling of being overwhelmed by growth. Tax considerations apparently did not play a major part in the decision.

INITIATIVE FOR CITIZEN CONTROL AND DEVELOPMENT IN THE CITY OF PASADENA

Pursuant to California Elections Code Section 4001 and the attached published Notice of Intent, we, the undersigned, registered qualified voters of this City, hereby present this Initiative Petition and request that the following ordinance be passed without alteration by the Board of Directors, or failing Board of Directors' adoption, be submitted to a vote of the people.

The people of the City of Pasadena do ordain as follows:

Section 1. Statement of Purposes and Intent.

The purposes and intent of this initiative are to:

A. Defend the quality of life in the City of Pasadena by controlling and limiting future growth in the City in a manner that maintains the special character of Pasadena.
B. Ensure through the exercise of the right to vote that the citizens of Pasadena rather than a small number of developers establish the growth policy for the City.
C. Set reasonable annual limits on the development of major commercial projects and the construction of multiple unit residential developments.
D. Require that Major Development Projects which are likely to have significant impact on the City's future be carefully and publicly reviewed by the City through a discretionary process that grants approval only to those projects which benefit the City.
E. Protect Pasadena's affordable housing by controlling demolition and conversion of Pasadena's older housing stock.
F. Ensure that all new development "pays its own way" for all public facilities, services, and infrastructure, such as streets, sewers, water, power, solid waste control, and police and fire protection, so that residents of Pasadena are not required to subsidize new growth with their tax dollars.
G. Improve the City's public notice of development and planning matters so Pasadena's citizens can have a better opportunity to participate in the planning and review process for new development.

Section 2 spelled out the "findings," that is, the basis in fact for the initiative. Subsequent sections specified the details of the growth management program and its implementation.

Many jurisdictions have seen the growth management problem as a largely financial issue—how to provide the infrastructure for growth before growth occurs and how to pay the infrastructure costs that growth imposes. As noted in Chapter 9, an exaction is a payment a jurisdiction demands in return for permitting development to take place. Fairfax County, Virginia, uses a system of "proffers," a variation on the exaction theme, which requires developers to offer to pay the infrastructure costs of major projects. The county is immediately west of Washington D.C. and is experiencing extremely rapid growth, particularly in office activity. It is very concerned with providing the infrastructure to keep up with this development. Because demand for commercial space is very strong, the county has considerable leverage in its dealings with developers.

The county uses the ability to grant or deny rezonings as a means of obtaining proffers. For example, in the Fairfax Center area, roughly speaking a 3,000-acre development node in the county, the master plan recognizes three levels of development. There is a base level, which is essentially single-family large-lot development; an intermediate level; and an overlay level, which permits intensive commercial and multifamily residential development. The developer who wishes a rezoning to either the intermediate or overlay level must offer to pay for the estimated infrastructure costs that development will impose on the county. In 1985 these costs were estimated at $2.83 per square foot of commercial floor space and $631 per residential unit. Outside of the Fairfax Center area, the proffer system is also in use but the numbers involved are not so precisely defined.

Under Virginia state law, government cannot literally demand a contribution from a private party. Thus if the developer builds "by right"—that is, under the existing zoning—he or she cannot be compelled to contribute to infrastructure costs. However, if a rezoning is required, the county can choose not to grant the request unless a "proffer" is made. The making of the proffer is thus, in a sense, voluntary. The developer makes it in the hopes of receiving something of value in return, namely, the higher profit obtainable from developing at a greater density. The county has also used the proffer system to obtain some nonstructural contributions from builders. For example, several developers have included the provision of van pooling in their proffers as a means of dealing with the increased vehicular traffic their developments can be expected to generate.

Fort Collins, Colorado, uses a technique designed to direct growth into specified areas and also to require new development to pay its own infrastructure costs first. The city is located within a county, and over the years it has grown by annexation. Under the terms of a joint city-county agreement, a 65-square-mile "urban growth area" has been defined. The understanding is that all land within the growth area is ultimately subject to annexation. Within this area urban services will be provided and urban development standards—paved roads, public water, public sewer facilities, and the like—will apply. As urban development takes place the city annexes the area. In addition to providing necessary infrastructure on site, developers are required to provide off-site infrastructure such as roads and sewer and water lines. How much they are required to provide is based on traffic and other studies, for which they themselves are required to pay.

In the Fort Collins case, rather than contribute to a development fund, the developer, is literally required to provide the specified infrastructure. A subsequent developer may be required to make payments to a prior developer if he or she makes use of the infrastructure the latter has provided. For example, if developer A builds a mile of road to serve his or her project and developer B subsequently builds in such a manner as to make direct use of that road, a compensating payment from B to A may be required.

The city also makes much use of planned unit development (PUD), which applies in all newly annexed areas. In older areas developers may use either the existing traditional zoning or apply for development under the PUD system. The city also requires that all property under single ownership be developed under a single "master plan." Note that the term *master plan* is used in a different sense than elsewhere in this book. The effect of these two approaches is to make land development much more a cooperative and negotiated process than it would be under traditional zoning. The planners and the developers together are able to look at the entirety of what is proposed and approve it or renegotiate it as a single entity.

The Fort Collins approach, as seen by the city's planning agency, is "growth management" as opposed to "growth control" in the sense that the effort is to shape growth rather than to limit it. In fact, in the late 1970s a growth limitation initiative analogous to Boulder's was soundly defeated by Fort Collins voters.

STATE-LEVEL GROWTH MANAGEMENT

Many states exercise considerable control over the process of growth, particularly in environmentally sensitive areas. These controls constitute much of Bosselman's "quiet revolution," noted in Chapter 9. The first statewide land-use controls were instituted in Hawaii in the early 1960s. The motivation behind them was that the land area of the islands is small, growth pressures were strong, and agriculture was important to the state economy. Specifically, according to Bosselman, the goal was to keep Honolulu, the main center of population in the state, from sprawling out, Los Angeles-like, into the adjacent Central Valley of Oahu. Under legislation passed in 1961 all land in the state falls into one of four major categories: urban, rural, agricultural, and conservation. Within the urban areas, county zoning regulations prevail. In effect, counties may (but do not have to) permit urban-type development in any area that the state designates as urban. In the rural and agricultural areas, land uses are controlled by the State Land Use Commission, a board set up when the system was created. In the conservation district, land use is controlled by the state's Board of Land and Natural Resources.

Perhaps it is no surprise that the first statewide system developed in Hawaii. A small, scenically beautiful state, subject to major growth pressures and having a limited supply of highly productive agricultural land, would appear to be an ideal candidate for such a system. The fact that much of the growth pressure came from outsiders, people from the U.S. mainland, may also have contributed to the passage of the act.

Partly as a result of the limitation on urban growth Hawaii is characterized by very high housing prices. But is that bad? The person who already owns property in the state is likely to take a very different view than the person who lives on the mainland but thinks it would be nice to buy a condominium in Honolulu to which to some day retire. Again, we see that planning decisions, no matter how well intended, create winners and losers.

The state of Vermont instituted a land-use control system in 1970 for somewhat similar reasons. The state's scenic beauty; what many believe to be the best ski areas east of the Mississippi; and its proximity to population concentrations in the New York, Boston, and Montreal areas made it a major locus for second-home development in the 1960s. Concerned about the threat to its physical environment, the state enacted a system of land-use controls that survives to the present time with only minor modification. The entire state is divided into districts. Within each district, no land subdivision involving ten or more lots may be made without district commission approval. In addition, no land development plans at elevations of 2,500 feet or more, even if only involving a single lot, may proceed without commission approval. The elevation standard exists to protect environmentally fragile hillsides and ridges, which are also the areas most likely to be the sites of resort and second-home development.

To grant a permit, the commission must find that a wide range of planning considerations, both environmental and otherwise, are satisfied. These include absence of undue air and water pollution effects; availability of sufficient water; absence of significant erosion effect; absence of significant highway congestion or safety hazard; absence of excessive burden on the local educational system; absence of excessive burden on local government services; absence of undue effect on scenic values, historic sites, or rare or irreplaceable natural areas; conformity with statewide land-use plans; and conformity with local land-use plans.

In 1988 the state legislature took a major step forward by passing Act 200, a bill that set up a system of statewide planning. What had begun as growth management had metamorphosed into a full-blown planning effort. Given Vermont's rural and small town flavor and its desire not to follow the path of its more populous and urbanized neighbors, Connecticut, Massachusetts, and New York, there is little doubt that state planning efforts will have a very strong growth management emphasis.

The goals of the plan are embodied in a series of statements in the legislation. These address housing, transportation, the environment, and other issues. The act provides a structure to bring local and regional planning efforts into conformity with these broad goals. The same structure also provides a mechanism to bring town plans into conformity with the plans of adjacent towns and of the regional planning district (there are 12 in the state) in which the town is located. It also attempts to synchronize the plans of the 12 regions. At the top of the system is the Council of Regional Commissions. If a dispute arises between towns, between districts, or between a town and a district, the dispute goes to the council to be ajudicated. If one of the disputants is unsatisfied with the decision, the matter may be appealed to the Vermont Supreme Court.

A central requirement of Act 200 is that the actions of state agencies must also be consistent with the goals set forth in the plan. This is important because state actions, particularly capital investments, can have major effects on the pattern of development. In the event of disagreement over whether or not there is consistency, the dispute again goes to the Council of Regional Commissions. In this case, if one of the disputants is unsatisfied, the appeal does not go to the Vermont Supreme Court but to the state legislature for resolution.

It does not take much to bring an issue to the council. For example, any ten town residents or even one affected property owner can take a town's or an adjacent town's plan to the council with the complaint that it is inconsistent with other plans or with the state planning goals. When Act 200 was enacted it was feared that the ease of bringing complaints would bury the council in minor or frivolous issues, but this has not happened.

Vermont is a small state, lacks large metropolitan areas, and is probably more homogeneous in a cultural and ethnic sense than most states. It also has a very long tradition of direct, participatory democracy. In the majority of its towns, issues that would elsewhere be resolved by a vote of the town council are settled by a direct vote of the citizens at a meeting. The appeal mechanism, which appears to work well in Vermont, might be a disaster in another state.

Participation in the plan is voluntary. About two-thirds of Vermont's towns do participate. Of the third that have chosen not to participate, many are small, often with populations of only a few hundred. In small, rural communities the need for large-scale planning is not likely to seem as pressing. Then, too, a very conservative political temper and a very strong attachment to private property rights also argue against participating in the plan.

At this writing Act 200 is too new to be judged. It appears well suited to Vermont, and it may well serve as a model for other states seeking to develop a state planning system that is comprehensive and readily open to citizen participation.

Numerous other states have some statewide controls over land use. Frequently, the control does not extend to the entire state but rather to areas of special concern. For example, many states have permit requirements for coastal zones, in recognition of their fragility and ecological value. Beaches exist in an equilibrium between sand removal and sand deposition by currents and wave action. Development that changes this equilibrium can make major changes in the shape of the shoreline. Tidal areas are ecologically valuable because they form the breeding grounds of many species and because they often hold large quantities of nutrients on which many species depend. Many states also control development in wetlands. Freshwater wetlands, like saltwater marshes, are important as "nutrient traps" and as habitats and breeding grounds for many species. Development in wetlands may also increase flood hazards elsewhere by increasing the rate of storm water runoff. Many states also exercise some development controls over areas of particular scenic or historic value.

The state of Florida faces serious environmental problems in several regards. Its population growth has been extremely rapid in the last several decades and is likely to continue at a brisk pace for the foreseeable future. Its swampy areas are environmentally fragile, as is often the case with tropical soils. Its ground water supplies are readily threatened by saltwater intrusion because much of the state lies very close to sea level.[13]

In 1972, after considerable lobbying by environmental groups, the state legislature passed the Environmental Land and Water Management Act, as well as several ancillary pieces of legislation. In "areas of critical state concern" and on "developments of regional impact" the state can overrule local land-use decisions if they fail to take into account effects that extend beyond the locality's boundaries.[14] DeGrove quotes the key language of the legislation defining areas of critical state concern as

1. An area containing, or having significant impact upon, environmental, historical, natural, or archeological resources of statewide importance

2. An area significantly affected by, or having significant effect upon, an existing or proposed major public facility or other area of major public investment
3. A proposed area of major development potential, which may include a proposed site of a new community, designated in a state land development plan

The "new community" provision is particularly germane to Florida because much of its population has been accommodated in major new developments, frequently carved out of environmentally sensitive former wilderness. Developments of regional impact are defined as projects that "because of [their] character, magnitude or location, would have a substantial effect on the health, safety or welfare of the citizens of more than one county." Thus, for example, a regional shopping center that would affect the pattern of vehicular traffic in adjacent counties could be classified as being of regional impact. So, too, could a power plant or industrial facility whose emissions could have measurable effects on the air quality in adjacent counties.

The legislation thus gives the state broad powers to impose regulation and control when statewide interests are at stake. State controls are not likely to require localities to permit that which they do not wish to permit. Rather, they will from time to time prevent or modify that which localities would be inclined to permit. In that sense they add a layer of control rather than substitute for local controls. As is true of all land-use controls, the ultimate arbiters of exactly what the words in the legislation mean in regard to specific cases are the courts.

GROWTH MANAGEMENT—PRO OR CON?

One cannot make a blanket judgment about growth management. Like any planning technique it is subject to use and misuse. At its best, it can be used to step into the future in a planned manner and emerge with good results—with a sensible and attractive pattern of development, with the public treasury in good shape, with community services adequate to the tasks demanded of them, and with the natural environment disrupted to a minimal degree. At worst, growth management techniques can be used to block legitimate growth, to defend the privileges of those already privileged, and to displace the inevitable costs of development to other jurisdictions.

Quite probably, the best results will be obtained when the government doing the managing corresponds in size to a natural labor market or housing market. If the primary purpose of the growth management system is environmental, it seems likely that all other things being equal, the best results will be obtained if there is a correspondence between the physical jurisdiction of the managing unit and the realities of the environmental processes. In this case the displacement effects of growth management decisions will be taken account of to a substantial degree. On the other hand, if the jurisdiction is small with regard to the economic, social, or physical effects resulting from its actions, the temptation to consider only parochial interests and to ignore the numerous effects of local decisions on outsiders may be hard to resist.

SUMMARY

Growth management is often defined as the regulation of the amount, timing, location, and character of development. Growth management programs generally use techniques that are common to much of planning. Thus such plans are distinguished from more traditional plans by their intent and scope rather than by the implementing techniques they use.

Growth management programs became widespread in the 1960s as a result of reaction to the rapid suburbanization of the postwar period and the growth of environmental consciousness and concern. Such programs raise a variety of equity issues, for controlling the rate and character of growth inevitably produces a variety of winners and losers, a point discussed in some detail in the chapter.

One of the earlier and best-known growth management plans was that adopted by Ramapo, New York. The town used a point system covering such items as sewers, drainage, roads, and public facilities to determine when a building permit might be granted. The stated goal was to limit the pace of development to match the provision of public infrastructure. The ordinance was challenged in court but ultimately sustained. A number of subsequent growth management plans have been instituted in various parts of the country. Some, such as Boulder's or Davis's, attempt to place a cap on growth or to hold growth to some predetermined annual percentage rate. Others, such as Fort Collins's, seek to shape the pattern of growth without attempting to limit the rate.

Many states have instituted growth management programs, beginning with Hawaii in the early 1960s. In general, state growth management programs cover only parts of the state, frequently for environmental reasons. State controls on development usually do not supersede local controls. Rather, they constitute an additional level of control intended to see that larger-than-local issues are given adequate weight in the making of development decisions.

NOTES

1. Randall W. Scott et al., eds., *Management and Control of Growth*, Urban Land Institute, Washington, D.C., 1975. Three volumes appeared in 1975; two more have since appeared.
2. See articles by Wilbur Thompson and Willard R. Johnson in vol. I, ibid.
3. One might ask what sources of air pollution purely residential development involves. According to EPA estimates, about one-half of U.S. air pollution comes from motor vehicle exhausts. Thus the vehicular traffic associated with residential development is a major source of air pollution. Smaller amounts of air pollution may come from home heating systems. In some areas of the country, for example, Denver, Colorado, emissions from wood-burning stoves have been a major source of air pollution.
4. William Alonso, "Urban Zero Population Growth," *Daedalus*, vol. 102, no. 4, Fall 1973, pp. 191–206. The article is reprinted in Scott, op. cit., vol. I, chap. 5.
5. Ernest F. Schumacher, *Small Is Beautiful: A Study of Economics as if People Mattered*, Harper & Row, New York, 1975. (Previously published in Great Britain.)
6. The plan was enacted because of strong growth pressures in the New York region during the 1950s and 1960s. At the end of the 1960s regional growth slowed and growth pressures abated, greatly reducing the

need for growth management. In the early 1980s, believing that it had sufficient other land-use control mechanisms, the town rescinded the ordinance.

7. For background and details of the plan, see Israel Stollman, "Ramapo: An Editorial and Ordinance as Amended," Scott, op. cit., vol. 2, pp. 5-14.
8. David W. Silverman, "A Return to Walled Cities: Ramapo as an Imperium in Imperio," Scott, op. cit., vol. 2, pp. 52–61. See also *Golden* v *Planning Board of Ramapo*, 285 N.E. 2d 291 (1972); quoted in Scott, op. cit., pp. 14–25.
9. For a case history of the effects of land-use controls on housing markets, see David. E. Dowall, *The Suburban Squeeze: Land Conversion and Regulation in the San Francisco Bay Area*, University of California Press, Berkeley, 1984.
10. In regard to the class aspects of environmental conflict, the reader might want to look into the concept of the "new class." For a set of essays on the subject, see R. Bruce-Briggs, ed., *The New Class*, Transaction Books, New York, 1979. For a presentation of the view that environmental controls have been used to defend privilege, see Bernard J. Frieden, *The Environmental Protection Hustle*, MIT Press, Cambridge, MA, 1979.
11. The reader interested in the shifting of costs to parties other than those who pay them directly can pursue the matter in most introductory economics texts under the heading of "tax incidence."
12. Many counties in or near metropolitan areas use preferential tax treatment to keep land in agricultural use. In general, this means taxing it at a rate appropriate to its value in agricultural use, rather than its market value as sold for nonagricultural use, say, residential or commercial development.
13. In low-lying areas near the sea a drop in the water table, caused by excessive use of ground water or a reduction in surface water available for aquifer recharge, will cause salt water from the ocean to move in. This can cause changes in vegetation and wild life and also render ground water unfit for drinking.
14. For details see John M. DeGrove, *Land, Growth and Politics*, Planners Press, American Planning Association, Chicago, 1984, chap. 4.

SELECTED BIBLIOGRAPHY

BROWER, DAVID J., GODSCHALK, DAVID R., and PORTER, DOUGLAS R., *Understanding Growth Management*, Urban Land Institute, Washington, D.C., 1989.

BURROWS, LAWRENCE B., *Growth Management: Issues, Techniques and Policy Implications*. Rutgers University Center for Urban Policy Research, New Brunswick, NJ, 1978.

DEGROVE, JOHN M., *Land, Growth and Politics*, Planners Press, American Planning Association, Washington, D.C., 1984.

DEGROVE, JOHN M., ED., *Balanced Growth: A Planning Guide for Local Government*, International City Manager Association, Washington, D.C., 1991.

GODSCHALK, DAVID, R., *Constitutional Issues of Growth Management*, rev. ed., Planner Press, Washington, D.C., 1979.

PORTER, DOUGLAS, R., *Understanding Growth Management*, Urban Land Institute, Washington, D.C., 1989.

SCOTT, RANDALL W., BROWER, DAVID J., and MINER, DALLAS D., *Management and Control of Growth*, Urban Land Institute, Washington, D.C., 1975 and subsequent years.

CHAPTER 16

ENVIRONMENTAL AND ENERGY PLANNING

Environmental planning covers a wide range of concerns having to do, generally, with minimizing the damage that human activity does to the natural environment. The goals may pertain to any of the following:

Minimizing threats to human health and life, for example, by reducing the concentration of dangerous pollutants in the air or the water supply or by limiting development in hazardous areas like flood plains

Preserving resources for future use, for example, minimizing soil erosion

Achieving aesthetic and recreational goals such as preserving some areas in a pristine condition

Minimizing damage to the environment for its own sake rather than humanity's sake, for example, by preserving the habitat of a rare species that has no known or readily foreseeable use to us

Energy planning has a much simpler goal: the saving of nonrenewable energy resources. An example would be designing a subdivision so that all the houses have unobstructed southern exposures to facilitate solar heating. Often, energy conservation will help achieve environmental goals. For example, solar heating will conserve energy, but it may also reduce the degradation of air quality by reducing the amount of fuel burned for home heating.

THE ENVIRONMENTAL PLANNING PROBLEM

Environmental problems can be difficult to deal with for several reasons:

1. Environmental processes may be complex and not fully understood. For example, both the physical and chemical pathways a pollutant takes through the environment may not be fully understood, nor may its exact effects as it is dispersed and transformed.
2. Environmental problems are not respecters of political boundaries. Agricultural chemicals sprayed on fields in Kansas may find their way into tributaries of the Mississippi River and end up in the drinking water supplies of a Louisiana community a few months later. Sulphur dioxide from smokestacks in Ohio may come down as acid rain in Vermont. In 1985 the United States and Canada held talks on acid rain because acid rains in eastern Canada result in part from oxides of sulphur and nitrogen released in the American Midwest. The ultimate environmental problem may be the so-called "greenhouse effect" resulting from increased levels of carbon dioxide in the atmosphere.[1] Fossil fuel burned anywhere on the planet contributes to the problem, so that it can only be fully addressed at an international level.
3. The solution of one environmental problem may become the cause of another. For example, air quality regulations require "scrubbers," which remove a certain percentage of sulphur from the smokestacks of coal-fired electric generating facilities. However, the resulting accumulation of sulphur-containing sludge can prove to be a source of ground water pollution.
4. Environmental issues can arouse strong emotions and produce formidable political conflict because environmental decisions may deliver large gains and large losses to particular individuals and groups.

In general the approach to environmental problems has been piecemeal, one pollutant or one source of emissions or one land-use question at a time. This is not because of shortsightedness or lack of vision. The problem of achieving higher levels of environmental quality is simply so complicated that a unified approach in which all side effects are considered has yet to be devised.

ENVIRONMENTAL PROGRESS AT THE NATIONAL LEVEL

For the reasons suggested, much of the attack on environmental problems must be made at the federal level, and indeed, the federal government has been very active in this area.

The U.S. Commitment to environmental quality, as indicated by pollution control expenditures, has grown substantially since the passage of NEPA. For 1972 expenditures are estimated at $30 billion (in 1990 dollars) and 0.9 percent of that year's GNP. For 1990 they are estimated at $115 billion, of 2.1 percent of GNP.[2] The figures include both public funds and private expenditures required by environmental laws and regulations. These costs are paid by the taxpayer in the form of higher taxes and by the consumer in the form of higher prices. In that sense they represent a reduction in the U.S. standard of living, or a slower rate of growth in that standard. In another sense, however, they represent a contribution to the standard of living by improving the air we breathe, the water we drink, and the environment in which we live. There is no question that in a populous, industrialized society environmental quality does not come cheaply.

In spite of all the difficulties suggested earlier much progress has been made, particularly in air and water quality, since the passage of the National Environmental Policy Act (NEPA) in 1969. Figure 16-1 shows trends in the total emission of six major air pollutants from 1960 to 1990. In general, the chart shows substantial improvement from 1970 on. Note, also, that had no regulatory actions been taken the trend lines would have continued upward, for during the 1970 to 1990 period U.S. population grew by 22 percent and U.S. GNP, adjusted for inflation, by 72 percent.

For water quality the situation is more mixed. The Council for Environmental Quality notes that:

> Between the mid-1970s and mid-1980s, U.S. Geological Survey (USGS) monitoring stations recorded improvements for dissolved oxygen deficit, fecal bacteria, and phosphorus, all of which are attributable to improved wastewater treatment. The same network, however, recorded higher readings for nitrogen, chloride, and dissolved solids, which appear to be due to increased fertilizer applications, use of salt on highways, and other nonpoint sources.[3]

Most of the improvement in air quality since the 1970s has come about through controls on emissions, particularly automotive, industrial, and power generating. Improvements in water quality have resulted primarily from two causes; controls on discharges and the greatly increased provision of sewage treatment facilities. From 1970 to 1990 more than $75 billion in public funds have been spent on sewage treatment facilities. In the decade from 1972 to 1982 the number of people served by sewage treatment plants that provide secondary or better treatment rose from 85 million to 144 million. Typically, most of the funding for sewage treatment plants comes from the federal government, however, detailed planning as well as construction and operation have been local responsibilities.

In many cases, the imposition of uniform national standards is absolutely necessary. If different standards prevailed, polluting activities would simply be shifted from places with tight standards to places with loose standards.

Progress is often most rapid when there are a few sources that can be clearly identified and a substitute product or technology can be introduced. Note that the most striking reduction shown in Figure 16-1 is that for airborne lead, a pollutant that can contribute to, among other maladies, mental retardation and developmental problems in young children. The primary source was leaded gasoline. When automobile manufacturers were required to market only cars that ran on unleaded gasoline, the problem was on the way to an almost total solution.

When the pollutant has multiple sources, when substitute technology is

Figure 16–1 U.S. air pollution trends.

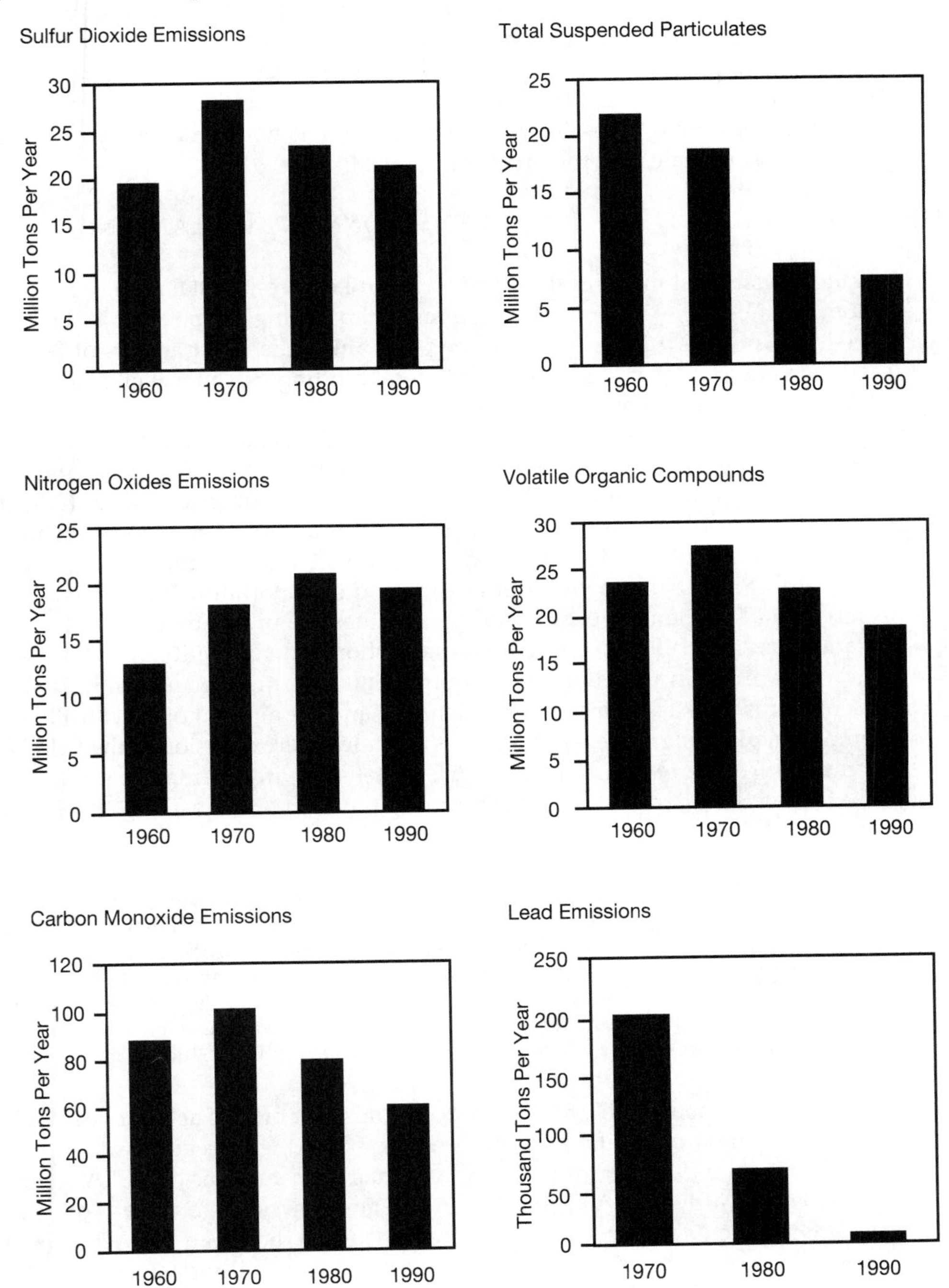

Source: *Environmental Quality: 22nd Annual Report of The Council on Environmental Quality*, U.S. Government Printing Office, Washington D.C., 1992, p. 11.

not available, or when the problem is global rather than local, solutions are much more difficult. The most serious pollutant—although we have only recently come to think of it as a pollutant—may be excess carbon dioxide because of its capacity to affect the global climate through the greenhouse effect. Its concentration in the atmosphere rises each year and so far shows no sign of slowing. Unlike airborne lead it has multiple sources, alternative technology is not immediately available on the necessary scale, and the problem is global.

THE INTERGOVERNMENT CONTEXT OF ENVIRONMENTAL PLANNING

Despite the fact that much of the effort to control environmental quality must be national, a substantial amount of environmental planning can be done at the local level. Much of it, as will be seen, is done pursuant to the requirements of federal legislation, and much of it is done with federal funding. Such local efforts are the substance of the remainder of this chapter.

In a sense, almost all physical planning can be considered to be environmental or energy planning since any decision about land use affects the environment and energy consumption. For example, the density of residential zoning affects how much of the site will be changed from a natural to a manufactured condition. The internal geometry of the development and the siting of houses will affect the amount of energy used for heating and transportation. Whether a community plans for a land-use pattern that facilitates the provision of public transportation may have effects on energy consumption and air quality.

However, in terms of legal requirements, the number of planners who think of themselves as environmental planners, and the amount of specifically environmental planning achieved, there was an enormous expansion of the field beginning in 1970. For reasons discussed in Chapter 4, environmental consciousness in the United States grew substantially during the 1960s. At the end of 1969 Congress passed the National Environmental Policy Act (NEPA).

> The Congress, recognizing the profound impact of man's activity on the interrelations of all components of the natural environment . . . declares that it is the continuing policy of the federal government, in cooperation with State and Local governments, and other concerned public and private organizations, to use all practicable means and measures, including financial and technical assistance, in a manner calculated to foster and promote the general welfare, to create and maintain conditions under which man and nature can exist in productive harmony.[4]

It was signed in 1970 as President Nixon's first official act that year. Subsequently, the Environmental Protection Agency (EPA) was created by executive action. During the 1970s many states enacted their own versions of NEPA, generally known as "little NEPA" acts. Within the next few years a variety of other major environmental acts became law. These included the Clean Air Act of 1970; the Clean Water Act of 1972; the Marine Protection, Control, and Sanctuaries Act of 1972; the Coastal Zone Management Act of 1972; the Safe Drinking Water Act of 1974; the Resource Conservation and Recovery Act of 1976; the Toxic Substances Control Act of 1976, and the Comprehensive Environmental Response, Compensation, and Liability Act (CERCLA) of 1980, more commonly known as "Superfund." More recent environmental legislation includes the 1990 ammendments to the Clean Air Act and the 1992 Energy Policy Act.

Environmental legislation vastly increased the amount of environmental planning in several ways. First, it mandated that environmental questions be addressed before federal funding could be received. In some cases federal legislation mandated that states design and implement environmental controls on their own. Funding for a variety of environmental studies and plans was provided. Finally, the passage of federal legislation served as a stimulus and model for the passage of analogous state legislation, as in the case of the "little NEPA" acts. As in other instances, the federal government, by providing a variety of carrots and sticks, as well as by its own example, brought about a substantial amount of local activity.

The provision of NEPA that did the most to bring the field of environmental planning into being was the requirement that environmental issues be considered in federal decisions that might have significant environmental impact. Thus all projects that used federal funding became subject to this requirement. The device that assured this consideration was the Environmental Impact Statement (EIS), a complex document that might run to many hundreds of pages and cost tens or even hundreds of thousands of dollars.

The NEPA Process

In brief, the NEPA process works like this.[5] The agency considering an action that might have significant environmental effects must prepare an Environmental Assessment (EA). This is a relatively brief document that describes the project in general and includes a "discussion of the need for the proposed action, the environmental impacts of the proposed action, and alternative actions, and a listing of the persons and agencies consulted." The EA either concludes that an EIS is necessary or that there is "no significant impact," in which case an EIS is not required. The EA is a public document, and it can be expected that if there is serious public concern with the issue it will be subject to considerable scrutiny. The process is designed for visibility and accountability. Thus an agency could not readily rule that an EIS was not necessary if, in fact, serious environmental effects could be demonstrated.

If an EIS is called for, a complex process begins. Notice of the agency's intent to prepare an EIS must be published in the *Federal Register*. This is a daily newsletter published by the federal government detailing regulations and a variety of other federal actions. The first step is a "scoping" process involving other federal agencies, lower levels of government, and the public. At this time, too, a lead agency, or agency having overall responsibility, is designated. Once the scope (hence the term *scoping*) of the work to be done has been determined, a draft EIS is prepared, either by the federal agency or an agency of a lower level of government or a party under contract to a body of government. The latter might be a consultant. The draft EIS includes

> a discussion of the purpose of and need for the proposed action, alternatives to the proposed action (for example, a highway EIS might include discussion of the merits of expanding mass transit instead), including a no action alternative, analysis of the affected environment and of the environmental consequences of the proposed action and alternatives, a list of persons who prepared the document, a list of agencies, organizations and persons to whom the document is being mailed.[6]

At this point the draft document is circulated for both official and public comment. The lead agency, after considering the comments, then produces the final EIS. There again ensues a comment period, and following this, the lead agency prepares a "record of decision." This is a summary of the agency's decision and indicates the basis for the decision, alternatives that were considered, and so on.

The process is an open one. The turn-of-the-century "muckrakers," who were fond of the expression "sunlight is the best disinfectant," would be quite pleased with the process. It prevents government from acting in secrecy, makes the process open to any concerned citizen, and makes it as practical as possible for interested parties to comment.

The EIS may be a long document, or in the case of a large project, a shelf of documents, often supported by large amounts of data. EIS requirements have brought a fair-sized consulting industry into being. EIS requirements have also provided an enormous amount of employment for attorneys. For the individual or group opposed to a particular project the most effective action often is to sue. A common basis for suing is to claim a procedural flaw in the environmental review process. The litigant does not necessarily have to show that the project is a bad plan. If it can be shown that there has been some fault in the process itself, that is, a violation of a law of regulation, the project can be stopped until that flaw has been remedied.

To take a well-known example, New York City's Westway project, a highway to be built on landfill along the Hudson shore of Manhattan, was killed by litigation. In the last chapter of this saga a federal judge found that state and federal officials had "colluded" in concealing information about the effect of the project on the Hudson River and, particularly, on striped bass in the river.

The project had already been entangled in litigation for a dozen years and the striped bass studies would have taken an additional two years. Thus shortly after this decision the city officially conceded defeat on Westway and filed an application with the Department of Transportation to have some of the funds that would have been spent on Westway diverted to mass transit. The project had been supported by every New York City mayor and every New York State governor in office while it was being considered, as well as by labor unions, most elected officials, and most planners. Approximately $200 million had been spent on land acquisition, design studies, and legal costs. But it was defeated in court.

Whether the litigants actually cared about the striped bass is a moot point. The complexity of the review process presents numerous opportunities for delaying actions, in this case sufficient delays to kill the project. Critics of the environmental review process have complained that it provides too many legal weapons for naysayers and that it permits small, determined groups to thwart the will of the majority. Defenders of the process argue that the law is meant to be obeyed and that if it has not been, the project should be delayed until it is.

Amendments to the Clean Air Act (CAA) of 1970 essentially brought air quality planning into being. The act required EPA to establish National Ambient Air Quality Standards (NAAQS) and required states to formulate State Implementation Plans (SIP) to achieve these standards. The CAA also required the EPA to set emission standards for new or substantially modified stationary sources (such as power-generating and production equipment, residential and commercial incinerators, materials-processing equipment, and the like), moving sources, and hazardous pollutants. For one particular moving source, the automobile, Congress itself set the emissions standards rather than delegating that task to the EPA. The emission control equipment on all new cars sold in the United States is there because of requirements that, although periodically modified, date from this time.

The Federal Water Pollution Control Act (FWPCA) brought into being state and local water quality planning efforts on a massive scale. Specifically, section 208 of the act required states to produce water quality plans, either directly or by delegating responsibility to substate governments. Accompanying the planning requirements were substantial sums of grant money to fund the work. The Coastal Zone Management Act imposed coastal zone planning requirements on the states. We note that about half of the U.S. population lives in counties that border on a coast, that coastal areas are often ecologically fragile, and that for many reasons coastal areas can be extremely attractive for commercial and residential development.

ECONOMIC AND POLITICAL ISSUES IN ENVIRONMENTAL PLANNING

To an economist the ultimate issue in environmental planning is to determine the efficient tradeoff between environmental goals and other goals. We all might like to see our society achieve as much as it can in the way of economic goals and also do so with a minimum of environmental damage. However, that is inherently impossible because there is an economic price to be paid for environmental quality. Clean processes generally cost more than dirty processes. If we say that we wish to minimize acid rain, this means that we need to invest more in scrubbers and other technology that removes sulphur from the smokestacks of coal-fired plants. That cost has to be paid by someone, whether it be the consumer, the producer, the taxpayer, or some combination.

The economist would say that the point at which we stop investing in pollution control should be the point at which the gain to society from an additional increment of pollution abatement just equals the cost of achieving that abatement. As it generally turns out, placing a cost figure on pollution damage is extraordinarily difficult.[7] Thus finding the right point is more easily said than done.

Beyond the questions of cost are questions of equity or fairness. Suppose we say that a certain coastline should be protected from excessive residential development. Upon further examination we determine that the acceptable upper limit of development is not much above the actual present development. If we freeze development, perhaps through large-lot zoning or perhaps through a permit process, we have delivered gains t to those who now own homes there. Simply by blocking the building of additional homes we are likely to cause the market value of existing homes to rise. By the same token we are imposing losses on those who would like to own homes there.

Comparable comments can be made with regard to business activity. In many coastal areas it is becoming increasingly difficult to open a marina because of environmental regulations. And this may be as it should be, for marinas necessarily involve disturbance of the coastal ecology—damage associated with construction, damage caused by oil leaks and engine exhaust, and damage caused by dredging operations required to keep channels open. But so protecting the environment does produce winners and losers. If you already own a marina the law is now protecting your business from new competitors. Of course, if you want to open a marina, the situation is not so nice. If you are a boat owner you will pay for environmental quality through higher docking or mooring fees because the law is limiting the number of places that provide such services.

On a larger scale, environmental planning decisions can involve more serious issues for individuals. For example, the level of emissions control required of an industry affects the cost at which it can produce. That, in turn, affects the amount of product it can sell. Thus there is a real connection between environmental control and employment. Perhaps if our environmental regulations are stringent enough, no domestic producer will be able to compete with overseas producers and the United States will lose the industry entirely.[8] Thus, beyond the overall issue of how much we as a society spend for environmental quality, there are equally vexing issues of who, specifically, in our society will pay what price.

LOCAL ENVIRONMENTAL PLANNING

Planning at the local level can make a contribution to the quest for environmental quality in several ways, including the following. (They are discussed in detail in subsequent sections of this chapter.)

1. Control of the intensity of development
2. Control of the type of development
3. Control of the location of development
4. Public capital investment
5. Control of operation once development is complete

Analyzing the Physical Environment

Several general approaches for looking at the physical environment for purposes of land-use planning have been suggested. They vary substantially in comprehensiveness.

The least comprehensive approach is simply to deal with each land-use issue as it arises. If major development is proposed, if citizens are complaining because the city water has acquired a slight odor, or if the fish are becoming less plentiful in a particular stream, the issue can be dealt with as a problem on its own. This approach may be likened to the physician "treating the disease and not the patient" and criticized on the grounds that it may give less than optimal results because it ignores the larger picture. Thus displacement effects, as we noted in Chapter 15 on growth management, may be ignored. Yet the case-by-case approach may still produce useful results. Many a patient has been cured by a physician who did, indeed, treat the disease and not the patient. The case-by-case approach is very common. Local governments tend to act most vigorously when their citizens put pressure on them. And that pressure is often strongest over a very specific issue.

A more comprehensive approach is *land capability analysis*. Here, the planner looks at all the land in a planning area, or at least all the land not now committed to a particular use, in terms of development cost. The technique makes use of geologic, hydrologic, soil, and other physical data to estimate the costs these physical conditions will impose on various types of development: residential, commercial, industrial, and agricultural. The sorts of physical conditions that enter into the calculation are items like slope, drainage conditions, settlement potential, shrink-swell potential, flood hazard, earthquake hazard, and the like.[9] For discrete risks (an event that either will or will not occur, such as a flood) the amount of damage likely to be done if the event occurs is multiplied by the possibility that the event will occur, to get what statisticians refer to as "the value of the expectation." For example, if it is estimated that there is 1 chance in 20 that a flood will occur in the time period under consideration and that such a flood would cause $15 million in damage, the value of the expectation is $750,000 ($15 million x. 05). That value is the figure entered into the cost calculation. Essentially, the area is mapped in terms of development cost for each type of land use. Thus for a given development type, say, residential, any point on the map would fall in some cost zone, expressed in dollars per acre.

The technique is obviously limited in that it does not take into account social, aesthetic, and other considerations. Thus there may be occasions when it is used in combination with other techniques. But even if land capability analysis is used alone, it will probably still help avoid some environmental mistakes simply because steep slopes, wetlands, flood hazard areas, and the like, which should be treated with care for other reasons, will show up as high-cost areas.

A somewhat more comprehensive approach has been developed by landscape architect Ian McHarg. He takes the view that to design well the designer must design with nature rather than impose his or her will on nature. McHarg has been a crusader for this particular viewpoint and, among landscape architects, has become something of a cult figure. Behind his work there is a strong feeling about nature and our proper relationship to it—about, in his words, turning from an attitude that is "exploitive and destructive" to one that is "deferential and creative." [10] The technique he advocates involves detailed study of the natural features of an area, followed by a graphic analysis that shows least and most desirable areas for the particular land use in question.

In connection with the Richmond Parkway (in the borough of Richmond, a part of New York City also called Staten Island) location study McHarg considered the following: slope, surface drainage, soil drainage, bedrock foundation, soil foundation, susceptibility to erosion, land values, tidal inundation, historic values, water values (lakes, ponds, streams, etc.), scenic values, forest values, recreation values, wildlife values, residential values, and institutional values. Each of these characteristics was mapped on a transparent sheet with three different tones, the darkest for the greatest value or cost.

> Let us map physiographic factors so that the darker the tone, the greater the cost. Let us similarly map social values so that the darker the tone, the higher the value. Let us make the maps transparent. When these are superimposed, the least-cost areas are revealed by the lightest tone.[11]

The optimal location is then revealed when all of the transparencies are overlaid in a single stack. McHarg does not try to rank some values more highly than others. In fact, he asserts that it is impossible to do so meaningfully. Rather, he states that his technique shows us the "maximum concurrence of either high or low social values." Note the difference between McHarg's approach and benefit/cost analysis discussed in Chapter 13.

> By abandoning absolute economic values . . . and employing a relative system of most to least, it is possible to include all of the important factors that defy pricing by economists. While this denies an illusory precision of cost-benefit economics, it does show the relative concurrence of positive factors and their relative absence. Although we are unable to fix precise money values on these, it is safe to assume that, in the absence of any supervening value, the concurrence of the majority of positive factors in any one location does indicate its intrinsic suitability for the land use in question.[12]

In the case of the Richmond Parkway there was already a great deal of development in place. Thus a large number of social values were considered. In doing a comparable study for an undeveloped area, some of the social values would be absent. For example, the "residential values" item, an overlay that simply reflects the market value of housing, would be absent. So, too, might be the "historic values."

McHarg's approach is considerably more comprehensive than land-capability analysis. Yet it, too, leaves much unaccounted for. For example, it largely ignores fiscal considerations. "What a crass and philistine matter to raise," a McHargian purist might object. Yet municipal funds might be used for environmentally virtuous purposes such as open space acquisition, sewage treatment, or planting grass and trees to stem erosion on publicly owned beaches. More generally, a purely McHargian approach neglects many social and economic issues. To some extent, it also neglects some large-scale planning questions. For example, suppose an overlay analysis suggests a land-use pattern that does not make sense in terms of, say, the regional transportation network. What is the comprehensive planner to do? A fully comprehensive land-use planning approach has yet to be devised.

TWO EXAMPLES OF ENVIRONMENTAL PLANNING

In this section we present examples of two types of environmental planning, one for water quality and one for solid waste disposal. Both are heavily conditioned by federal law and regulation. Both, also, can have significant effects on the health and welfare of individuals. Both, but particularly solid waste disposal, have potential for creating conflict within and between communities.

Water Quality Planning

In 1972 amendments to the federal Water Pollution Control Act set the national stage for water quality planning. Specifically, section 208 of the amendments required the states to initiate a comprehensive process for waste treatment and management. The states were permitted either to prepare plans themselves or to delegate the process to lower levels of government. Funds were provided for getting the work done. In the plans, regardless of what level they were prepared for, four main elements were to be included:

1. Water treatment facilities
2. Regulatory programs
3. Processes for identifying and controlling nonpoint sources
4. Identification of management agencies

The provision for nonpoint sources in item 3 opens up a wide range of planning possibilities and obligations. A point source might be a factory, an incinerator, or any identifiable pollution source. A nonpoint source is a source that cannot be specifically located or identified in order to be regulated individually. For example, in this usage, agriculture is a nonpoint source, for the runoff of fertilizer and pesticides from fields constitutes a source of water pollution. Housing is nonpoint source; household wastes have the potential for polluting ground and surface water. So, too, are automobiles; lead from their exhausts can be deposited on the roads and subsequently washed into streams by rain.

Nonpoint sources can to some extent be controlled by regulation—for example, rules regarding acceptable and unacceptable types of pesticides or rules regarding the lead content of motor fuels. But nonpoint source pollution can also be controlled through land-use planning: what activities are permitted and their extent and intensity. Section 208 specifically directs that "nonstructural" pollution control alternatives be considered. Basically, that means land-use planning.

Assume that the state has delegated to a county planning agency the task of doing its own 208 water quality planning. The work to be done is funded by the federal government and, in most cases, would be done by a combination of the county's planning agency and consultants. The latter are particularly likely to be hired for scientific and technical tasks for which the county agency is unlikely to have the necessary expertise. The following work elements are likely to be included in the planning effort:

1. *Inventory of existing discharges and present state of water quality.* This is a task of description and measurement. It is likely to involve direct measurements of water quality like pH, dissolved oxygen, and the presence of various pollutants. It may also involve some indirect investigation, for example, taking an inventory of the commercial activity in the area and collecting statements on what is produced and what is discharged. It might also involve judgmental matters such as characterizing the streams and lakes in the area in terms of their recreational potential.
2. *Projections of population, employment, and land use over the term of the study.* This will generally involve projecting population and employment first and then estimating land use from these figures; so many households per acre, so many employees per acre, and so on. In general, projections are made on some basis that is specifically relevant to water quality planning. For example, in one study, population for a large county was projected by county agency personnel on a municipality basis. These estimates were then delivered to the county's planning consultant, who apportioned them to each of the several dozen drainage basins into which the county was divided. As noted earlier the relationship between plans and projections is a two-way street. The projections constitute one of the bases on which planning is done. Yet the plans that are made affect the magnitudes (like population or employment) that are being projected.
3. *Projections of waste load.* These figures come directly out of the projections in the preceding phase: so much waste per capita, so much discharge per employee, and so on.
4. *Determination of effects on water quality.* This is essentially a modeling exercise. Generally, the first step is to assume the existing system of water treatment infrastructure and then estimate changes in water quality based on changed figures for population and economic activity.
5. *Determination of necessary wasteload reduction.* In this step the figures from the previous step are laid off against standards established by federal, state, and local laws to estimate the wasteload reduction required.
6. *Development of alternative wasteload reduction strategies.* Wasteloads can be reduced by two major approaches: (1) reduction in the wasteload generated in the first instance or (2) increases in the amount of wasteload eliminated by treatment. Approach 1 clearly ties wasteload reduction to land-use planning.

Land-Use Planning Approaches to Water Quality Land-use planning might be used to reduce wasteload generation in the following ways:

1. *Limiting the overall growth of population or economic activity.* This will prevent human activity from overloading the "carrying capacity" of natural systems. For example, a body of water can accept organic matter up to a certain level of biological oxygen demand (BOD) without being damaged. But beyond that a process of eutrophication occurs, in which fish die and the water becomes undrinkable and foul smelling.
2. *Limiting the growth of specific types of economic activity.* Particular types of manufacturing, commercial, or agricultural activities that generate a

heavy wasteload per dollar of value added or per worker might be banned or curtailed.

3. *Maximizing the natural degradation of pollutants and minimizing the amount of damage done to water sources.* For example, different types of soil have different capacities to accept and biodegrade septic fluids. Residential development in areas not to be served by sewers might be limited in intensity by the capacity of the soil to handle septic discharge without permitting appreciable pollution of surface or ground waters. In fact, this is not a new idea. A great many suburban land-use plans and zoning ordinances do reflect exactly such considerations in their lot-size requirements. McHarg suggests mapping aquifer recharge areas and considering them as one point against permitting development.[13]
4. *Controlling the quality or process of development.* For example, if flooding is a problem there might be a requirement that in specified areas certain types of developments must make provision for the temporary impoundment of storm water. Storm water is then discharged after the event at a controlled rate to prevent downstream flooding. Site development practices may be regulated to prevent water quality damage, for example, by mandating site development and construction practices that reduce silt runoff.
5. *Banning development from certain types of land such as flood plains and steep slopes.* In the former case development puts both structures and populations at risk but also may increase flooding by reducing the water-carrying capacity of the channel. In the latter case, steep slopes are generally more prone to erosion than flatter areas. The erosion may appear as siltation downstream.
6. *Minimizing the cost of active or "structural" approaches to reducing wasteload.* To some degree this point overlaps the preceding points. However, there may be more specific connections. For example, residential uses may be channeled into corridors for which public water and sewer lines can be supplied at lesser cost than would be the case with scattered development.

Solid Waste Management Planning

The issue of what to do about solid waste has bedeviled many communities. Typically solid waste just from households averages several pounds per person per day. To this is added solid waste from manufacturing, commerce, and the like. Basically, it can be disposed of in landfills, burned, or dumped (though ocean dumping is being phased out under pressure of federal legislation). In general, landfills are not popular with people who have to live near them. Such sites involve truck traffic and may be unsightly or odiferous. Beyond these essentially aesthetic issues they can often engender real fear in nearby populations. If solid waste is buried in landfills there is fear of ground water contamination because acids in surface or rain water dissolve pollutants in the waste and carry them into the ground water. Fears, quite obviously, are even greater if the landfill is to contain toxic wastes. Siting landfills is often more difficult as a political problem than as a technical problem.

Incineration causes fears regarding air quality. Reassurances from experts often do not carry much weight with nearby residents. For one thing, it takes a certain amount of technical background to interpret figures cast in terms like "parts per million" or "micrograms per liter." Then, too, there may be some fundam.ntal distrust of the expert. If the town government hires a consultant who tells the citizenry that the planned incinerator poses no threat to their health, there is always the suspicion that he or she is singing the song that those who pay the consulting fee wish to hear.

Having admitted that the decision on how to dispose of solid waste is politically sensitive, let us look at how the more technical side of the process might be carried out. Very often, a community is propelled into solid waste planning when the present system begins to look as though its days are numbered. If the community is now using landfill disposal, it may be that the landfill area is now nearly filled to capacity. It may be that the community is shipping its solid waste to a landfill in another municipality, which has indicated that when this waste disposal contract expires it will not be renewed. Or, perhaps, the cost of upgrading the municipal incinerator to meet air quality standards appears to be more than the community can manage.

A planning approach might be as follows:

1. *The dimensions of the problem are established.* Population and employment projections are used to estimate the probable load of solid waste that must be handled. The present disposal system is examined to see how long it can be expected to function adequately. For example, pounds of solid waste would be converted into cubic yards and that figure laid off against the remaining capacity of the community's landfill.
2. *A preliminary reconnaissance of alternative disposal methods might be undertaken.* These are likely to include landfill, incineration, and rail haul. The latter essentially means shipment out of the area to someone else's landfill or incinerator. This alternative is becoming less available as the cry of "NIMBY," an acronym for "not in my backyard," becomes more common. Within the incineration alternative there are several possibilities. Incineration may be combined with power generation. The heat might be used for generation of electric power or simply to produce steam for heating. In both cases a big question is whether there is a good market for the energy. In the case of steam, the market has to be close by because generally it is not practical to pipe steam for more than 1,000 yards or so. After incineration various material recovery schemes might be considered. For example, magnetic separation might be used to extract ferrous residues. Other systems might be used for glass and nonferrous metals. Some schemes for disposal of the residue after separation need to be considered. The residue might be buried in landfills. It might be disposed of at sea, though, as noted, this alternative is becoming less widely available. It may be possible to process the unburned residue into a useful product such as construction aggregate if a user who will enter into a long-term contract can be found.

   At this stage a final selection cannot usually be made because the costs and risks of each alternative may not be fully known. However, it may be possible to eliminate some possibilities and find some other possibilities that look promising. Consider, for example, the landfill alternative. A common way to approach it would be to make a list of criteria and then find all the sites in the jurisdiction that qualify. Such a list might include minimum site size; minimum distance from residential population; minimum distance from schools, hospitals, or other institutions; minimum distance from streams and aquifer recharge areas; minimum distance from wetlands; area outside of 100-year flood plain, maximum distance from main road; acceptable site geology; and soil characteristics.

3. *Cost estimates are developed*. For example, site acquisition costs might be estimated by examination of assessed values of land and consultations with assessors, appraisers, or real estate brokers. Operating costs on the site itself might be estimated by obtaining figures from presently operating sites. Transportation of solid waste to landfills can be a major cost, so this too might be estimated. Recent experience from the municipality itself or nearby communities could be used to obtain an average ton/mile figure. The community can be divided into a number of "wastesheds," and the distance from the center of each wasteshed to a given site measured. The population and commercial activity are then estimated and hence the ton/miles estimated.
4. *Site selection is made*. A common way to approach this final step is with some sort of scoring system. A system might assign so many points for cost, so many points for environmental impact, so many points for traffic impact, and so on. Thus potential sites identified in step 3 could be ranked from most to least acceptable. Such scoring systems are not entirely objective, for the matter of what weight one assigns to each consideration is necessarily judgmental. Nonetheless, a point system is a step in the direction of rationality. Then, too, the person who chooses to call its results into question has to state what attributes he or she thinks have been weighted incorrectly. That act in itself forces the participants in the process to be explicit and thus helps clarify discussion of the issue.

These steps are a fairly straightforward technical process. The next step—actually designating a site—is often the most difficult. Even if one site is clearly superior, the process of site selection is far from over and the choice of site not necessarily determined. In general, opposition from nearby residents can be expected. The opposition may take the form of political and public relations activity—neighborhood organization, protest meetings, letters to newspapers and legislators, and the like. It may also take the form of litigation. The state has an environmental permit system and groups opposed to the plan may mount legal challenges either on procedural or substantive grounds.

In practice, the location of such sites is often determined by a political process that bears some resemblance to a game of hot potato. In a multijurisdictional body—for example, a county made up of a number of municipalities—such a site may end up in that municipality that is least able to resist it.

Public participation in such a decision is likely to be substantial. State legislation pertaining to the granting of permits for such facilities is likely to require that plans be made public, that hearings or public meetings be held, and that the public be given an opportunity to comment. But even in the absence of any such legal requirements, public participation is likely to be high simply because of a high degree of interest and concern. In recent years many states have passed so called "sunshine laws," which make many government meetings and internal documents open to the public. Thus, as a practical matter, most local governments could not go very far in siting such a facility without the process becoming public knowledge. In many cases, the best policy for a local government seeking to choose a site may be to conduct the entire procedure in a very open way. That will not prevent conflict or even feelings of victimization on the part of the "losers," but it will at least protect the government against charges of secrecy and impropriety. A basic rule of politics is that no one likes surprises.

The reader might well ask why go through the procedure outlined if politics is likely to figure so heavily in the outcome? One answer is that the process, though not entirely rational, is not totally irrational either. One role for the planner—and not just in this situation—is to lay out options clearly and accurately in order to move the decision-making process in the direction of rationality as much as possible. In a democratic society the planner is only advisory to the elected political body, and it is unrealistic of the planner to expect that his or her advice will necessarily be followed as given. At a very practical level, if the actions of local government are challenged in court, there is no better defense than a well-documented, well-researched, systematically arrived at position.

ENERGY PLANNING

The field of energy planning emerged quite abruptly at the end of 1973. It resulted from the energy price increases and shortages that followed the Arab oil embargo at the time of the Arab-Israeli War in October of that year. Interest in energy planning was further increased by the second round of oil price rises in 1979–1980 occasioned by the Iranian revolution. Subsequently oil prices declined considerably, reducing national concern with energy conservation. Nonetheless, should the energy "glut" of the late 1980s and early 1990s be replaced by price rises or shortages, interest in energy conservation might again grow rapidly.

Many facets of energy conservation are best handled nationally, for example, mileage requirements imposed on automobile manufacturers. Funding research on new energy sources like hydrogen fusion also makes most sense if done nationally—or, perhaps, internationally. How energy is priced will affect how it is used. Thus energy pricing could be considered a form of energy planning. Clearly, steps like increased taxes on gasoline are best considered at a national level. However, a number of steps can and have been taken at the local level.

Steps that a municipality can take to conserve energy can be divided into four general categories.

1. Land-use planning
2. Changes in building characteristics
3. Changes in transportation
4. Community energy sources

Land-use planning can be used to reduce energy consumption in a variety of ways, the most obvious by minimizing transportation requirements. One way to do this is by favoring development that reduces the average distance between origin of a trip and the destination. However, the long-term trend in the United States, as noted in Chapter 1, has been to lower urban densities. An alternate, and probably more feasible approach, is to encourage mixed-use development. For example, mixing commercial and retailing uses with residential uses may permit shorter average commuting and shopping trips than would be the case if the three uses were strictly separated.

Another way that land-use planning can encourage energy efficiency is by making nonautomotive modes convenient. This might mean providing separate bus lanes along major thoroughfares.[14] In a major metropolitan area it might mean designating major highways with a median that would be suitable for future installation of rail lines. For example, Route I 66, which extends westward from Washington, D.C., was laid out in this way. In the mid-1980s the Washington Metro was extended into adjacent parts of northern Virginia along that routing. In a smaller community planning for energy efficiency might mean providing bikeways to separate bicycle from automotive traffic thus eliminating a major discouragement to bicycle use. The community in the United States best known for this plan is Davis, California. There, approximately 25 percent of all passenger miles, as opposed to about 2 percent statewide, are made by bicycle. In general, land-use planning can facilitate the development of public transportation by arranging residential and nonresidential uses to reduce the "collection" and "distribution" problems noted in Chapter 13.

Building characteristics can be altered to produce very sizable reductions in energy expenditures. In some cases these changes are closely linked to land-use planning decisions; in other cases they can be effectuated independently. A land-use plan might encourage row housing as opposed to free-standing single-family units. This need not mean higher density in the development but might, for example, mean clustering, with the provision of common open space. Row or attached housing, in general, reduces energy used in heating because it reduces the amount of building surface exposed to the elements. To see this just imagine two free-standing units moved into a side-by-side position. The side walls, which have been brought together, become interior walls and can no longer conduct heat to the outside.

Siting buildings with regard to the sun will affect the ease with which sunlight can be used to supply part of the energy used for heating. Streets that run east-west facilitate placing houses so that they face south for maximum solar exposure. A number of communities have adopted solar access zoning, which prevents structures or trees from being placed in such a position that they block the direct access of other buildings to the sun.

There are also building-related steps that are unrelated to overall land-use planning. A number of communities impose minimum insulation requirements on new houses. Some municipalities have implemented programs designed to encourage property owners to retrofit old buildings. These may be limited to giving technical advice or may also include low-interest loans and other financial incentives. A few communities require that before a house can be resold it must be brought up to some minimum standard of insulation, a technique that gradually forces a retrofitting of the existing housing stock.

To a large extent community efforts in transportation must be coordinated with the community's land-use planning, as noted. To a limited extent, however, a community might decrease the use of private automobiles by greater expenditures for public transportation, setting up new initiatives in public transportation such as van pooling and dial-a-ride systems, and encouraging car pooling.

A number of communities have begun community energy production systems. In a sense these do not represent energy conservation, but by their nature they tend to, and are intended to, conserve traditional energy sources. Many communities have developed or are developing so-called "low head" hydroelectric systems, for example, using a source that was used for power but subsequently abandoned when relatively low-cost power from central sources became available. One factor that makes such development practical is state laws that require utilities to buy power from small-scale generators and thus create a market for the output of such facilities. New England, with a large number of dams dating from the period when many mills and factories ran on water power, is the national center for such activity.

In many communities solid waste, which was once disposed of in landfills or burned in incinerators, is now used as the fuel for power generation. The power is either used locally or sold back to the area utility and distributed through the utility's transmission grid. A number of municipalities have looked at the possibility of cogeneration, a system in which waste heat from one process is put to a second use rather than simply discharged into the atmosphere. For example, waste heat from a municipal power generating facility might be converted to steam and used to supply heat for municipal or other buildings.

An Energy Planning Process

Given that a community wishes to reduce energy use, how does the planning process proceed? In some cases the approach may be very limited. A single type of conservation, say, reduction in energy use in home heating, is selected, as is a program(s) designed to achieve it. In other communities a more comprehensive approach, which resembles the making of a comprehensive plan, is used. One such planning approach—developed by Hittman Associates of Columbia, Maryland, and used by a number of communities—is broken into four phases:

1. *Energy audit.* In this phase the energy used in major categories of activity such as home heating, transportation, commercial activity, and the like is estimated.
2. *Objectives formulation.* The main objectives of the program are established.
3. *Examination of alternative strategies.*
4. *Implementation.* The particular programs and activities to be used are selected and designed.

The whole process takes two years or so and has an average cost of approximately $200,000. Both the expense and the time involved make it an approach only for the community that is serious about energy planning. For any community wishing to go beyond a single-purpose program, it is important that energy planning be integrated with the community's comprehensive planning because the land-use pattern has very strong implications for the use of energy in transportation and also significant, if not quite as powerful, implications for residential energy use.

The Political Context of Energy Planning To be successful, energy planning efforts need a considerable amount of public consensus. The communities in which energy planning efforts have been most impressive generally are those where there is high public consciousness of energy issues and a feeling that conservation has virtues beyond dollar savings. The community that is environmentally conscious is likely to support an energy planning effort because environmental and energy issues are related. To the extent that an energy planning effort may involve interference with the workings of the marketplace, a strongly conservative political temper will militate against energy planning. A number of well-known energy planning efforts like those of Davis have occurred in California, where environmental consciousness is strong. University towns, like Davis again, seem to be good candidates for such programs.

The decline in energy prices in the 1980s generally weakened the drive behind energy planning. As of 1993 the real cost (price adjusted for inflation) of gasoline was no higher than it had been before the Arab Oil Embargo of 1973–74. Environmentalists have long favored a tax on energy to encourage more efficient use. This idea, perhaps unfortunately, has never found much political support. In the 1992 presidential campaign Ross Perot suggested a tax on gasoline, but more for deficit reduction than for conservation purposes.

Both then President Bush and and his challenger, Bill Clinton, opposed the tax. After his election President Clinton reversed his position and favored a modest energy tax, the so called BTU (for British Thermal Unit) tax. The tax bill passed in the summer of 1993 contains a very small increase in the tax on gasoline and no across the board BTU taxes.

FEDERAL ENVIRONMENTAL POLICY DURING THE BUSH ADMINISTRATION

During the 1988 presidential campaign George Bush stated that he intended to be the "environmental president." Environmental issues had been low on his predecessor, Ronald Reagan's, agenda and environmentalists almost universally condemned Reagan's environmental record. By the end of the Bush administration most environmentalists concluded that Bush had not become "the environmental president" but they ranked him as considerably better than his predecessor.The Bush administration was marked by two important pieces of environmental legislation as well as considerable controversy over environmental policy. The Clean Air Act passed in November of 1990 placed stricter limits on the emission of sulfur dioxide, a primary component of acid rain. By the year 2000 tightened requirements on emissions from power plants are expected to have reduced emissions by about 10 million tons per year. (Emissions in 1990 were about 22 million tons.) The act also included an innovation that many economists have long advocated. It permitted a market in pollution abatement. The act allowed producers who "overcomplied" to sell the overage to other producers who undercomplied. Thus the burden of a given amount of total abatement would be met by that combination of producers that could do it at lowest cost.[15]

The act also required the phasing out of chloroflourocarbons (CFCs), widely used as a refrigerant, and carbon tetrachloride and methyl chloride, believed to be the main causes of ozone depletion. The deadline was originally set for the year 2000 but the Bush administration subsequently moved the deadline up to 1995. Finally, the act identified 84 metropolitan areas as failing to meet previously established air quality standards. It ordered that automobiles and light trucks undergo stringent emissions tests and subsequent repairs if necessary to bring them up to standard. Garages doing inspections will have to install treadmills equipped with computerized emissions measuring devices and costing an estimated $150,000 apiece. It is estimated that millions of vehicles that now pass inspection will fail, and have to be brought up to standard. It is calculated that this will reduce smog by about 30 percent and carbon monoxide by about 50 percent in many urban areas.

In October, 1992 Congress passed a wide-ranging energy bill. The legislation contained provisions to both reduce the use of nonrenewable energy sources (fossil fuels) and to reduce pollution from energy use. The bill requires that small energy producers be allowed to make use of the transmission lines of electric utility companies. In effect, this permits the small producer to sell power to the utility company and thus it is hoped will create a market for small-scale wind- and hydro-generated power. The bill will simplify licensing requirements for nuclear-generated power, making it easier to bring new plants on line and thus reducing dependence on fossil fuels that contribute to the greenhouse effect. The bill mandates efficiency standards for light bulbs and home heating systems. The latter is not a trivial item. About one third of all U.S. energy use is for space heating and a large part of that is residential. Finally, the bill authorizes the Department of Energy (DOE) to enter into agreements with companies to market electric vehicles. Note that this step may not reduce dependence on fossil fuels or total energy consumption if the vehicle's batteries are charged by electricity generated by burning coal or oil. However, air quality in the area where the vehicle is driven will be improved. The bill also contains provisions to encourage the use of cleaner burning alternative fuels such as alcohol and natural gas. Again, there may be no net energy saving but air quality, particularly in large metropolitan areas, will benefit. The bill also provided for the "environmentally sound use of our nation's abundant coal resources through research and development of advanced coal technologies . . ."[16]

But despite these two major pieces of legislation most environmentalists were not happy with the record of "the environmental president." One source of dissatisfaction was that higher Corporate Average Fuel Efficiency (CAFE) standards had been stripped from the energy bill. These, by mandating higher average vehicle mileage for the total of all passenger vehicles sold by each manufacturer, would have forced the production of more efficient automobiles even when fuel prices were low.

The provisions on cleaner coal in the energy bill looked like a mixed blessing to many environmentalists. They might improve air quality, but they would do nothing to slow the coming of the greenhouse effect. In fact, they might accelerate it for producing a given amount of energy from coal generates more CO_2 than does the equivalent amount of energy from a fuel with a higher hydrogen content, such as oil or natural gas. Altogether, environmentalists felt that the Bush administration had put too much emphasis on energy production and not enough on energy conservation.

Environmentalists were extremely unhappy with the actions of the president's Competitiveness Council chaired by Vice President Daniel Quayle. The mission of the council was a reasonable one, to prevent federal regulations from imposing undue burdens on industry. But environmentalists felt that the council almost always sided with industry and undermined the intent of the Congress and federal agencies such as the Environmental Protection Agency. The perception that the Bush administration was hostile to environmental concerns was, no doubt, heightened during the 1992 presidential campaign by Bush rhetoric about "the spotted owl crowd" and his reference to Albert Gore as "the ozone man."

The International Earth Summit Conference held in June, 1992 in Rio De Janeiro was another occasion for the environmentalists dissatisfaction. The Bush administration refused to sign an agreement to attempt to limit the reduction in biodiversity. The aim of the agreement was impossible to argue with. However, the agreement contained a provision that would have required the sharing, without cost, of newly developed findings in biotechnology, a field in which the U.S. is the world leader. The Bush administration took the view that this would mean throwing away billions of dollars in potential patent rights and licensing fees and giving up our lead in a major emerging industry. On June 15, the day after the conference ended, Bush stated in an interview on Cable News Network (CNN) "I did manage to protect the American taxpayer a little bit, and hopefully, stopped short of accepting things that would throw more Americans out of work."

The Bush administration also refused to join in agreements supported by western European nations that would have agreed to cap greenhouse gas emissions and roll them back to 1990 levels. It argued that the economic costs of such actions were not justified in view of the lack of certainty in the results of global climate models and disagreements among climatologists. This view within the administration had been strongly reinforced by the position of Bush's former Whitehouse Chief of Staff, John Sununu. Sununu was highly skeptical of the results of climate modelling and, as a former professor of engineering at MIT, felt that he understood the hazards of mathematical modelling and was competent to reject the views of the majority of climatologists.

SUMMARY

Much environmental planning and regulation must be done at the national level because of the scale of the problems and the great distances pollutants can travel through the environment. Local environmental planning often takes place within a framework of federal grants and regulations. Concern with environmental problems grew rapidly in the United States during the 1960s, culminating in the passage of the National Environmental Policy Act (NEPA) in 1969, the creation of the Environmental Protection Agency (EPA) in 1970, and the passage of a number of other major pieces of national environmental legislation in the 1970s. The passage of NEPA produced a massive increase in the number of planners and firms specializing in environmental planning because of its requirements for Environmental Impact Statements (EIS) as a prerequisite for the federal funding of large projects.

At the national level, environmental planning involves the establishment of standards and the funding of such activities as the construction of wastewater treatment facilities. At the local level, much activity is related to federal legislation and funding, for example, EISs, or to planning for projects that involve joint local and federal funding, such as wastewater treatment. However, much to enhance environmental quality can also be done at the purely local level, including controls on the intensity of development, and the type of development, the matching of development to the physiographic character of the area, the pattern of public capital investment, and regulation of the character of development and operation. There are various ways of thinking about environmental issues, from a purely case-by-case approach to the fairly comprehensive techniques advocated by Ian McHarg. The water quality planning process and a solid waste disposal site location process discussed in the chapter are examples of how environmental planning questions might be approached by a municipality.

Energy planning arose with the oil price increases that followed the 1973 Arab-Israeli war. The concern of the energy planner is the conservation of nonrenewable energy sources, that is, fossil fuels such as petroleum. At the local level, reductions in consumption of nonrenewable energy may be achieved by urban design, which reduces trip lengths and facilitates public transportation or the use of nonautomotive modes (foot or bicycle). Energy savings can also be affected by site design and land-use control ordinances, which facilitate the use of solar energy, and by regulations that mandate minimum insulation standards. During much of the 1980s interest in energy planning declined somewhat with the fall in energy prices but picked up subsequently as concern over the greenhouse effect and global warming mounted.

NOTES

1. This is the possibility that increases in atmospheric carbon dioxide will reduce the amount of heat the earth can radiate back into space, with the result that world climate may warm significantly, with changes in rainfall pattern, flooding of low-lying coastal regions, and other major environmental consequences. Numerous references to this possibility can be found in the general and scientific literature under the heading "greenhouse effect." See, for example, Stephen J. Schneider, *Global Warming*, Sierra Club Books, San Francisco, 1989.
2. *Environmental Quality: 22nd Annual Report of the Council on Environmental Quality*, U.S. Government Printing Office, Washington, D.C., 1992, p. 58.
3. *Environmental Quality*, p. 187.
4. From Title I of the National Environmental Policy Act (NEPA) of 1969, PL 90–190.
5. For an account of this process see *Environmental Quality*, 1983, pp. 253ff.
6. Ibid.

7. For an account of the economist's view of the environmental problem and the difficulties of assigning costs to environmental damage, see David Conn,"The Economics of Urban Environmental Quality," in John M. Levy, *Urban and Metropolitan Economics*, McGraw-Hill, New York, 1985.
8. Some writers have referred to "the export of pollution." The phrase refers to a process in which more prosperous nations enact such stringent controls that certain polluting operations are no longer economically feasible. The operations will then move to poorer nations, which are willing to tolerate a higher level of pollution for the jobs and income that the polluting activity will bring. This point was raised during the 1992 presidential campaign in connection with the North American Free Trade Agreement (NAFTA) that had been negotiated by the Bush administration but not yet approved by the Congress. Those opposed to the agreement and those who wanted it modified argued that one reason that U.S. manufacturers were locating plants in Mexico just south of the Rio Grande was that Mexican environmental standards were much lower than those of the U.S. and that, therefore, the cost of complying with them was much lower.
9. For an account of some of the conditions considered and some types of simple calculations that can be done regarding land suitability, see John H. Baldwin, *Environmental Planning and Management*, Westview Press, Boulder, CO, 1985, chap. 3.
10. For a presentation of McHarg's design philosophy, see Ian McHarg, *Design with Nature*, Natural History Press, Doubleday & Co., Inc., New York, 1969.
11. Ibid., p. 34.
12. Ibid., p. 115.
13. An aquifer recharge area occurs where surface water such as a stream, lake, or wetland overlies an underground layer of gravel or porous rock, permitting recharge of the underground from the surface source or, in dry periods, the reverse.
14. In general, bus transportation is more energy efficient than automobile transportation. "Big Wheels: How Dreams of Clean Air Get Stuck in Traffic," *The New York Times*, March 11, 1990, sect. 4, p. 4, gave the following average energy use for moving a person 1 mile. All are expressed in calories: bicycle, 35; walking, 100 ; rail transit, 885; bus transit, 920; single-occupant automobile, 1,860.
15. News Release (L-92-043), Department of Energy, Washington, D.C., October 24, 1992.
16. "A New Geography for the Coal Industry," *The New York Times*, November 25, 1990, Sec. 3, p. 5.

SELECTED BIBLIOGRAPHY

BALDWIN, JOHN H., *Environmental Planning and Management*, Westview Press, Boulder, Co, 1985.

COUNCIL ON ENVIRONMENTAL QUALITY, *Annual Report*,, Washington, D.C. (This series begins in 1970.)

KAMIENIECKI, SHELDON, O'BRIEN, ROBERT, and CLARKE, MICHAEL, EDS., *Controversies in Environmental Policy*, State University of New York Press, Albany, NY, 1986.

MCHARG, IAN, *Design with Nature*, Natural History Press, Doubleday & Co., Inc., New York, 1969. Second edition, 1992.

MORRIS, DAVID, *Self-Reliant Cities: Energy and the Transformation of American Cities*, Sierra Club Books, San Francisco, 1982.

SCHNEIDER, STEPHEN J., *Global Warming*, Sierra Club Books, San Francisco, 1989.

CHAPTER 17

PLANNING FOR METROPOLITAN REGIONS

C. David Loeks

In this chapter we sketch out briefly the scope of planning for metropolitan regions in the United States. By a metropolitan area we generally mean a central city, its suburbs, and perhaps some of the surrounding rural hinterland. In some cases, such as the St. Paul-Minneapolis area, to be discussed later, there may be more than one central city for the region. Where the metropolitan area extends across state lines, metropolitan area planning assumes an interstate dimension. The Washington, D.C., metropolitan area includes not only the District of Columbia but also counties in Maryland and Virginia. The Chicago metropolitan area includes portions of northwestern Indiana as well as Illinois.

As we saw in Chapter 3 the need for planning at a scale larger than the individual municipality was recognized early in this century. Important regional elements appeared in the 1909 Plan for Chicago. In the 1920s the post-World War I suburban housing boom and the explosive growth in automobile ownership resulted in metropolitan areas whose economic and social realities dwarfed the boundary lines of the municipalities of which they were composed. One response was the creation of regional planning organizations, usually under private sponsorship. The best known of these is the Regional Plan Association (RPA) of New York, which sought to plan for a three-state area around New York City. Other organizations were set up for the Philadelphia, Cleveland, Detroit, Chicago, St. Louis, and Minneapolis-St. Paul regions, among others.

THE EVOLUTION OF URBAN REGIONAL PLANNING

Since the 1920s four distinct types of regional planning organizations have appeared on the metropolitan scene.

1. Private citizen-supported efforts
2. Metropolitan planning commissions
3. Councils of local government
4. Regional councils

In the 1920s, the period when regional planning became widespread, the predominant type of regional planning agency was the private citizen group. These efforts were funded by private subscription and generally focused on a few major issues such as open space, transportation, recreation, and housing. As the interdependencies among these issues came to be better understood, many such organizations gradually shifted their focus to preparing comprehensive plans for the development of the region as a whole. (See the RPA of New York in Chapter 3.)

Because such efforts were private and limited to generating advice, the need for publicly chartered regional planning efforts with official status became evident. Sometimes publicly chartered efforts replaced the private planning bodies. In other cases the two functioned in tandem.

In the 1950s the emergence of federally sponsored programs in transportation, housing, and community facilities gave publicly chartered regional planning efforts a major push. The federal government first encouraged and then demanded official regional planning as a basis for federal grants for urban programs. And as we have seen, the carrot of generous funding can be a poweful shaper of local planning practice. Initially, such federal assistance programs focused on metropolitan areas. Then as the federal establishment became more involved in funding efforts in a variety of areas, programs for small cities and rural communities also evolved. This result probably could have been predicted from the legislative mechanics involved. Members of Congress from rural districts and small towns would be unlikely to vote billions for urban projects without some benefits to their own constituents. By the late 1970s, there were 39 federal programs that supported substate regional planning activities of one kind or another. Of these, 23 were available to all communities throughout the nation. The remaining 16 percent focused on a limited number of substate regions and dealt with problems such as rural poverty or coastal zone management or airport planning.[1]

A few regional planning bodies, such as the Twin Cities Metropolitan Planning Commission in Minnesota and the Atlanta Regional Planning Commission in Georgia, were created directly by the state legislatures. However, many more were created by intergovernment agreement, pursuant to state enabling legislation, in the form of regional councils of local governments. This preference came about because local government officials naturally favored a mechanism that was closely tied to the existing structure of local government, both for reasons of effectiveness and because politicians, like most other people, do not voluntarily relinquish power and prerogatives. By the early 1970s it became a matter of federal policy to encourage regional planning organizations made up primarily of local officials. By 1977, 26 percent of metropolitan regional councils had memberships totally composed of elected officials and 90 percent had a majority of such members.[2]

In addition to the growth of regional councils, the 1960s and 1970s saw a proliferation of single-purpose substate regional organizations to administer federal aid programs in the areas of aging, health, criminal justice, and poverty. By 1977 there were over 1,200 such organizations. Unlike the multipurpose regional councils, 80 percent were organized as nonprofit corporations and 62 percent of their governing boards were made up of private citizens representing the target groups being served.[3] By 1977 approximately 76 percent of all the funds for substate regional councils and 92 percent of the funds for special purpose substate regional organizations were from federal programs.

THE BASIC FUNCTIONS OF REGIONAL PLANNING AGENCIES

Essentially, regional planning agencies perform the following functions, although not all agencies perform all of them:

1. *Comprehensive planning*. This means doing for the region work that is similar to, though generally less detailed than, the comprehensive planning done by municipalities. Ideally, other planning by the agency would be guided by and in conformance with the comprehensive plan. As the municipality takes its citizens into the comprehensive planning process, a regional planning agency would take its local governments into the process. Given the limited powers of regional agencies, there is little hope that a regional plan will be carried out unless it has widespread support from local governments.
2. *Planning for specific functions*. These commonly include transportation, water supply, sewage treatment, and recreation. Often it is easier to get consensus for these specific issues than for comprehensive planning because the need for them is easier to see. Traffic congestion or an inability to provide sewer connections for new subdivisions are clear and unarguable reasons for collective action. In many cases a regional agency builds its skills and credibility on single functions like transportation and then edges into more comprehensive regional planning.
3. *Technical assistance and advice to member governments*. This is directly useful to local governments and also builds the credibility of the regional agency. It may also produce some automatic coordinating effects on the planning efforts of numerous municipalities simply by getting them to use a common set of numbers and assumptions. For example, the Washington, D.C., Council of Governments furnishes population and traffic forecasts to its member governments.
4. *Coordination in policy formulation and plan implementation* . The agency can engage itself in both the formulation of overall regional goals and the plans or strategies to move toward them. For example, if the goal were to

increase residents' access to outdoor recreation, the agency would also address land planning and budgeting issues related to parkland acquisition and development.

5. *Review of resource allocations to various programs affecting the region.* This function often developed as a response to federal funding requirements. Before certain types of federal grants can go to a locality, the regional agency may be required to certify that the project to be funded will be consistent with regional plans or regional development goals.

Implementing the Regional Plan

Even though the regional planning agency may have some legal powers granted to it by the state legislature, the mass of political power resides with the municipalities. Thus the implementation of regional planning must rely on the ability of the agency to persuade others to act. Some basic strategies for implementation follow.

1. *Implementation by constituent units of government.* First, this means assigning planning implementation roles to existing units of government. For example, county governments within the region might be asked to make plans for the provision of a certain number of units of low- or moderate-cost housing as part of the regionwide housing plan. Or local governments might be requested to plan for the development of a certain acreage of industrial and commercial sites as part of a regional economic development plan.

   A state legislature might also create new units of government such as special purpose authorities. The Port Authority of New York and New Jersey, which has had a major effect in shaping the transportation system of the New York region, was created by acts of the New York and New Jersey state legislatures. The agency has built and operated airports, tunnels, bus terminals, and harbor facilities. Its decision to build Port Newark (a major shipping facility on Newark bay below the confluence of the Hackensack and Passaic Rivers) shaped the pattern of ocean freight handling in the port of New York for decades to come. Thus major regional planning decisions may be made by such special purpose authorities.

   The existing government structure can be adjusted by annexation and mergers as well as the redistribution of powers and resources among governments serving the region. Such redistribution might occur as a result of voluntary intergovernment decision, court decision, or act of the state legislature.
2. *Advice and persuasion to influence the behavior and decisions of others.* Examples of such activities are project review, special studies, technical assistance, intergovernment liaison and coordination, and facilitation of intergovernment bargaining and conflict mediation.
3. *Policy-oriented efforts to influence key decisions concerning the region's structuring facilities* such as the timing and location of highways, sewer and water facilities, major urban space, shopping centers, and major industry.
4. *Direct efforts to mobilize public and political support for the policies and pro-*

grams. Such efforts concentrate on fostering a sense of regional identity, interaction, and interdependence and on creating political support for regional planning and development. These efforts have included meetings, forums, publicity in the print and electronic media, providing speakers for civic and other groups, setting up citizen's advisory boards, and so on. As noted earlier, the idea of going to the public for political support is an old one, reaching back at least as far as the 1909 Plan for Chicago.

The path to regional cooperation is not generally smooth. Inevitably, there will be tensions between local self-interest and that of the region as a whole. A new general aviation airport might do fine things for the economy of the region, but these regional considerations may weigh lightly in community X, located at the end of the proposed airport's main runway.

Traditionally Americans value highly the concept of home rule: the right of each local government to make decisions independently of higher levels of government. Thus the success of efforts to plan at the regional scale depends on the ability of the regional planning agency to persuade local governments that the course of action advocated on behalf of the region is also in their particular interest.

However, the distribution of the costs and benefits resulting from regional planning initiatives may fall unevenly. An economic development plan that proposed to concentrate development-related public expenditures on a few sites with the most potential for attracting industry might make sense in regional terms. But the plan would be hard to sell to those municipalities that did not contain the sites and therefore would not collect any of the new property taxes. Thus considerable effort is spent on intergovernmental bargaining to even things out. In the Twin Cities metropolitan area, the Minnesota state legislature provided that the revenues from regional activities such as shopping centers, major industries, and power plants is to be distributed to all of the communities in the region on the basis of the individual municipality's position above or below the region's average property tax-paying ability (assessed value per capita). This provision eliminates some intermunicipal competition over attractive "ratables" and thus promotes more rational decisions about land use. Another example of efforts to reduce disparities in fiscal impacts is the use of in-lieu tax payments by regional authorities to the local governments who play host to major regional facilities such as airports or military installations.[4] Thus the local government is compensated for such costs as traffic control and fire and police protection that the facility imposes on it.

In general, the most successful regional planning agencies are those that local governments see as being essential to their interests. Regional planning efforts either prosper or suffer in direct proportion to the extent to which they serve the interests of local governments.

REGIONAL PLANNING IN PRACTICE—A TALE OF TWO CITIES

One part of the country in which the state of regional planning is relatively advanced is the St. Paul-Minneapolis Twin Cities area. At the turn of the century this region had a population of about 460,000, which by the 1950s had grown to about 1.2 million. The two cities, once separate entities, had coalesced into "siamese twins," both of which were suburbanizing as did many U.S. cities after World War II.[5]

The problems associated with rapid suburban expansion coupled with a need for rebuilding the centers of the two core cities focused the attention of civic and government leadership on how to guide this rapid growth. The problem was brought to a head by problems connected with the expansion of the metropolitan sewer system and by the advent of the interstate highway system. These events forced the people of the region to recognize that they had problems that could not be solved by the efforts of local governments alone. The sewer problem required joint action if there were not to be wasteful duplication of facilities and if the efforts of one community to solve its sewage treatment problem were not to cause problems for another community. It is hardly an optimal arrangement if one community discharges its sewage upstream from another community's water intake. Such situations can be avoided only if the communities involved seek a joint solution. Similarly, a highway system that serves the residents of the region well is best designed if the region is viewed as a whole.

Citizens' groups such as the Citizens League of Minneapolis and Hennipin County undertook major studies of the region's problems. These efforts were paralleled by the government sector under the aegis of the League of Minnesota Municipalities, which convened the area's municipal governments to discuss and define the issues. The consensus of these discussions was embodied in a bill presented to the legislature under the governor's sponsorship. It called for the creation of a metropolitan planning commission to serve the five-county district comprising the Twin City metropolitan area. After two tries in the legislature and much bargaining and compromise, the bill was passed into law and the Metropolitan Planning Commission (MPC) was created in 1957.

The Rise of the Twin Cities Metropolitan Planning Commission

The law creating the MPC provided for a 28-member body. Twenty-one members reflected the existing government structure of the area, representing the central city mayors, the central city councils, the suburban municipal representatives, townships, school districts, county boards, and special districts. The remaining seven were appointed by the governor to represent civic, business, and community interests in the region. The law made it clear that the commission's powers were limited to conducting studies and providing advice. Decisions concerning what to do about this advice were left in the hands of the local governments and the state legislature. However, the legislature provided an important qualification to this advisory character. It gave the commission limited taxing authority to ensure it the resources necessary to do its job.

Shortly after its inception the commission hired a professional staff and developed and adopted a long-term work program to guide its future operations. This program was broken down into three basic phases:

1. *Problem identification*. Analyzing and developing a sense of regional identity and a commitment to act based on a shared perception of common problems

2. *Plan making.* Achieving consensus on essential regional goals, policies, and implementing programs
3. *Implementation.* Achieving the organizational structure to execute the required programs and putting the programs themselves in place

Planning for Planning Early on, it was realized that the commission was geared to undertake phases 1 and 2, but phase 3, *implementation,* would require a new organization with stronger powers to coordinate decision making affecting the region as a whole. It was estimated that phases 1 and 2 could take up to ten years before sufficient political consensus could be achieved to set up an organization that could implement a regional plan. As events worked out, it took exactly ten years. Let us now examine the activities of the MPC that played a decisive role in establishing the preconditions for the creation of the current Metropolitan Council by the state legislature in 1967. Phase 1 on the commission's work program focused on seven basic activities.

1. *The organization of the commission and staff.* This required development of procedures and bylaws and staff recruitment and establishment of a basic operational philosophy and work program.
2. *Fostering public understanding of the commission and its purposes.* Since the organization exerted its major effect by influencing others rather than through direct exercise of its limited powers, public visibility was vital.
3. *Monitoring and assessing significant conditions and trends and the analysis of specific high-priority metropolitan problems.* Trends typically monitored by a large regional planning effort include such items as population, employment, housing starts, vehicular traffic, and land use. Problems examined include the adequacy of public infrastructure (such as roads, sewer and water facilities), housing problems, regional land-use pattern, and the like.
4. *Fostering a sense of regional identity and interdependence.*
5. *Raising public perception and willingness to act on regional problems.*
6. *Establishing mechanisms for public involvement and intergovernment cooperation.*
7. *Direct efforts to influence decisions by developing and advocating goals, policies, and specific courses of action.*

During this period the commission moved vigorously on all of these activities through an intensive public information program, meetings and conferences, news releases, speeches before civic organizations, advice and assistance on specific planning issues, and the development of specific proposals for regional improvement. By 1962 the commission had published ten major reports and a variety of monographs on such subjects as organizing for intergovernment cooperation and planning, water supply, land use, recreation and open space, the economy, sewage, transportation, and population. In addition, it actively advocated action by the Minnesota legislature on such matters as the creation of a metropolitan sewer district and open space initiatives.

The result of this activity was a remarkable increase in public understanding of and concern with regional issues. The nonauthoritarian nature of the commission's mission became clear to the majority of people, and this engendered mixed feelings. Some, who had seen the commission as the camel's nose under the tent of local government and were concerned by the erosion of home rule, felt relieved. Others perceived the commission as a toothless tiger that could not implement its recommendations. The middle ground was held by those who maintained an open mind about subsequent steps but who saw the commission as a logical first step.

Developing a Regional Plan Having obtained a grip on basic regional issues and having built a base of public support, the next step was to develop a comprehensive regional plan. This effort was shaped by the interest of the federal government in assuring that huge federal expenditures then being made in housing, urban renewal, and highways would be used effectively.

There is a two-way relationship between land use and highway building. Land uses shape the demand for roads and highways. However, the building of roads is a powerful shaper of land use. Staff discussions between the MPC, Minnesota's State Highway Department, and the Federal Department of Transportation pushed this idea to its logical conclusion. Why not develop a comprehensive land-use plan and then adjust the scale, timing, and location of investment in transportation as well as in other region-structuring facilities such as sewer and water to facilitate its implementation?

The commission's staff engaged the governments in the region as well as state and federal agencies in a formal intergovernment cooperation agreement called the Joint Program for Land Use and Transportation. The prospectus described the effort as follows:

> A continuing planning program for the Twin Cities Metropolitan area undertaken collaboratively by existing public agencies. The objective of the program is to encourage development decisions that will enhance both the livability and efficiency of the metropolitan environment. The basic instrument for achieving this objective will be the comprehensive metropolitan plan for the seven county area to be completed in 1965 which will integrate transportation systems and the urban activities they serve.

The effort included the MPC, the cities of St. Paul and Minneapolis, seven counties in the region, the Minnesota Department of Highways, the federal government's Housing and Home Finance Agency, and the Bureau of Public Roads. The three-year program produced a regional development plan.

As a result of this planning effort, a number of things became clear to the region's leadership as well as to the general public. One realization was that there were bona fide alternatives simply to predicting or extrapolating present trends and then endeavoring to cooperate with them. Choices could be made among alternative patterns and could make a significant difference in the quality of life of the region. To many this issue was sharpened by the insight that the least viable alternative might be the continuation of present trends because the central cities were being built at densities that demanded a high level of public transit to provide effective transportation, whereas the outlying suburban areas were being developed at densities that could not generate sufficient ridership to support public transit and therefore absolutely required reliance on the private car. It seemed clear from the analysis the planners had undertaken that basic conflicts implicit in this kind of urban schizophrenia must inevitably produce a deflection from this pattern. Either the region would move toward greater *centralization* and concentration of activity to permit the use of more efficient modes of transportation, or it would move toward *greater dispersal* to loosen things up so that the private car could operate without excessive traffic congestion.

Another realization was that there are a few strategic "levers," which if wielded effectively could guide future development along lines that would implement the plan. The shape, pattern, and timing of urban development could be influenced by decisions concerning sewers, water, open space, and transportation. Furthermore, this could be done without dismantling the existing pattern of local government if tax effects were adjusted to minimize the fiscal disparities that would result from the distribution of benefits and costs among localities (the tax-sharing mechanisms noted earlier).

The plan itself opted for a development policy that would minimize sprawl and concentrate urban development in the two central cities and a series of large-scale self-contained satellite communities. These would be separated by open space and farmland but linked by the metropolitan transportation system. It would be an overstatement to imply that the plan met with universal approbation and instant commitment. It did, however, create a cadre of civic and government leaders who understood the magnitude and seriousness of the problem of serving a rapidly expanding metropolis.

Enter the Twin Cities Metropolitan Council

By 1966 as the work on the Joint Program for Land Use and Transportation was nearing completion, a lively debate had emerged among the members of the MPC, the Citizens League, and other civic interests. It concerned the question of what institutional arrangements would be required to translate the goals and policies of the plan into action. It was agreed that the Metropolitan Planning Commission (MPC) would not be adequate to the task.

Several different viewpoints on what the nature of the implementing agency should be quickly became apparent. A number of state legislators favored a model in which the organization would essentially be advisory to the legislature. Clearly, this would keep control of events in the hands of the legislature and would prevent the development of a "state within a state." That possibility did not seem altogether farfetched since the region contained or soon would contain a majority of the state's population and economic activity.

A contrasting approach was the model advocated by the Citizens' League. It featured a policy board that operated metropolitan services as what might be regarded as "wholly owned subsidiaries." The intent was to avoid the common situation in which ad hoc special purpose agencies functioned independently of one another with no mechanism for lateral coordination to achieve the region's interests. But this model was not acceptable to many legislators for the state-within-a-state reason already noted.

The conflict over these two alternative models was, at base, an example of the classic tension between urban and rural interests that has been with us since the founding of the Republic. The result was a compromise. In 1967 the legislature created a Metropolitan Council made up of some 16 representatives appointed by the governor with the advice and consent of the senate. The council comprised members from the legislative districts that made up the metropolitan area, plus a chairperson at large appointed by the governor. The council was charged to undertake studies and research on metropolitan problems and to prepare and recommend legislation for submission to the legislature. The council's first and primary charge was to study the sewer issue and to prepare legislation and report to the next session of the legislature. Advocates of a strong regional policy and operating body were disappointed, to say the least. Ten years of effort had resulted in what was perceived to be another legislative study commission to provide staff services and member advice to the legislature. However, those who felt that the game was up reckoned without the resourcefulness of the new council.

In 1969, at the council's urging the legislature passed a far-reaching law that gave the council policy supervision over a variety of legislatively mandated metropolitan functions. Over the next few years the list was expanded to include items such as sewers, open space, waste management, sports facilities, transit, and highways. Some, like the sewer function, were structured with close policy supervision by the council. Others, not integrated as closely, such as the existing airport commission, were required to submit their programs and budgets for commission approval. The commission also was charged with the duty to prepare and adopt a metropolitan development guide, which would set forth the essential regional development policies. By 1971 the guide was in place and an act was passed that redistributed property tax revenues from metropolitan-wide facilities, as noted earlier. In 1975 a "metropolitan framework" law was enacted that set forth the essential procedures under which the commission would try to fit the individual pieces together in terms of the metropolitan pattern. It provided that the commission would establish urban service areas within which subdivisions would be concentrated, commercial/agriculture areas that would not allow freestanding subdivisions, and rural development zones that would not provide urban services except around existing communities and centers. The pattern for this was set forth in the guide, which called for some ten additional "major diversified centers" in addition to the six that the commission had identified. In addition to doing this state-mandated work, the commission functioned as the management agency for a variety of federally mandated programs in criminal justice, health care, arts, and aging.

By the mid-1970s the council had come of age and emerged as a powerful instrument for defining and resolving metropolitan problems and for supervising the operations of the various service agencies that were created to address these problems.

What Has Been Accomplished?

What has been accomplished? The council, by itself, does not literally put bricks on mortar. But it has over the years created a framework in which regional planning takes place and in which public decisions are made with regional considerations in mind. The resident of the region benefits from a better system of transportation, a well-planned system of regional open space, and perhaps a generally higher level of environmental quality.

There are also some economic benefits. The region has benefited greatly from investment by such organizations as the 3M (Minnesota Mining and Manufacturing) Corp. The corporation's willingness to commit itself to the region stems, in part, from its understanding that regional problems that affect its own operations and the lives of its employees will be effectively addressed. The revitalization of downtowns in the Twin Cities has taken place partly because investors knew that the region could deal with its transportation and other problems and thus that investment in the region was a sound move.

More generally, the Twin Cities area is widely regarded as having a high quality of life as measured by public services, employment, education, and a wide variety of recreational and cultural amenities. There is a widespread "pride of place," which emanates from a raised regional consciousness and a sense of national leadership in urban planning, development, and governance. Some features of the region in which residents can take pride are an array of colleges and universities, rebuilt and functioning downtowns, stable and rehabilitated residential areas, a first-rate park and open space system, and first-class medical facilities, among others. To a considerable degree, these are the result of strong regional consciousness and energetic regional leadership.

A LOOK AHEAD

Regional planning as we know it today is largely a post-World War II product. Specifically, much of what we have discussed developed in the 1950s and 1960s. This was a period when population growth was more rapid than today, when economic growth was very rapid, and when the nation was making up for things not done during the Great Depression and war years. Thus much of the thrust of regional planning was growth management. Today growth is slower simply because the "baby boom" of the late 1940s to mid-1960s is over. National population growth, which once approached 2 percent a year, is now under 1 percent a year. The gross national product continues to grow, but it does so more slowly than in the 1950s or 1960s.

Thus the need for growth management is lessening. However, other issues are emerging. Much of the infrastructure, such as the highway systems built a few decades ago, is approaching middle age and work needs to be done on maintenance and modification. At one time regional efforts floated along on a tide of federal funding. The tide greatly diminished during the Reagan and Bush administrations. The need to deal with the federal deficit makes it unlikely that federal aid to localities, perhaps other than for infrastructure, will increase greatly under President Clinton. Thus, regional planners may be spending much more of their time on fiscal issues than previously. As noted in Chapter 14, competition with overseas producers has gotten much tougher in the last decade or so. Thus we are likely to see much greater focus on helping industry within the region remain competitive. The focus of regional planning may change, but the need for it is not likely to diminish.

SUMMARY

Many problems relating to transportation, water supply, sewage disposal, and economic development transcend municipal boundaries and hence are best dealt with on a regional level. Planning at the metropolitan level was clearly evident in the 1909 Plan for Chicago, but it was not until the 1920s that regional planning became widespread. The rapid suburbanization and growth in automobile ownership that followed World War I were key factors in creating obvious needs for regional planning. At first, most metropolitan-level planning organizations were citizens' groups with no official standing. But these gradually came to be supplanted by organizations that were created either by state legislatures or by agreements between substate units of government.

Since regional agencies have very little power relative to that of local governments, and since attachment to the "home rule" principle is very strong in the United States, regional agencies succeed to the extent that they have the support of local governments. Thus the process of building an effective regional agency involves creating an understanding of regional problems, building a constituency interested in those problems, and convincing local governments that the regional agency can help them rather than compete with them.

The Twin Cities case is an example of a successful regional planning approach. The Metropolitan Planning Commission, a purely advisory organization, spent a decade in information gathering, consensus building, and planning before the time was ripe for the legislature to set up a council of governments, which would actually begin to implement the plan. The regional planning process began when a particular problem, sewage treatment, made it clear that some regional planning effort was necessary. As is often the case, regional planning began over a single, clear-cut, and pressing problem and then gradually expanded to a more comprehensive effort, in which a vision of the future pattern of development was enunciated and planned for, came after a consensus for such planning was built over simpler issues. The federal government plays a key role in bringing regional planning efforts into being through the mechanism of demanding them as a condition for the receipt of federal funds.

NOTES

1. Frank S. So, Irving Hand, and Bruce D. McDowell, eds., *The Practice of State and Regional Planning*, American Planning Association, Chicago, 1986, p. 148.
2. Ibid., p. 141.
3. *1977 Consensus of Governments, Topical Studies, Vol 6., No 6., Regional Organizations*, Bureau of the Census, Washington, D.C., 1978.

4. *In lieu* in this context means "in place of." Real property owned by public bodies is exempt from property taxation. Thus in-lieu payments in place of the taxes that would be paid were the property not in public ownership.
5. Twin Cities Metropolitan Planning Commission, *The Challenge of Metropolitan Growth,* Report no. 1, St. Paul, MN, 1958.

SELECTED BIBLIOGRAPHY

SO, FRANK S., HAND, IRVING, and MCDOWELL, BRUCE D., eds., *The Practice of State and Regional Planning,* American Planning Association, Chicago, 1986.

CHAPTER 18

NATIONAL PLANNING IN THE UNITED STATES

IS THERE NATIONAL PLANNING?

Is there national planning in the U.S.? In one sense the answer is no, for there is no person or organization charged with drawing up a physical plan for the nation. There is no national master plan corresponding to the master plan that a city or town or county might have. In fact, when Congress terminated the National Resources Planning Board (NRPB) in 1943 it expressly prohibited any other agency in the federal government from assuming the board's national planning functions. No national planning agency comparable to NRPB has ever been set up since then.

One reason that we do not have a national plan is simply ideological. A national masterplan sounds like socialism and for most of our history that has not been a welcome sound. Another reason may be the formidableness of the task. A national land-use plan for a small country is feasible. The Dutch engage in national land-use planning and, in the view of this writer, do it very well. But the Netherlands has a land area of a little more than 13,000 square miles, not much bigger than the state of Maryland. That is quite different from the 3 million square miles of the "lower forty-eight."

Finally, and perhaps most important, we have a federal system of government in which a great deal of power resides with the states' congressional delegations. That dispersion of power makes the formation of a unified national plan extremely difficult. The sort of top-down planning that the Dutch do is simply not possible in the U.S. political environment. Note that this is not a matter of democracy versus autocracy, for the Netherlands is just as much a democracy as is the U.S. Rather, it is a matter of the degree of centralization of political power within a framework of representative government.

While there is not now nor has there ever been a master plan for the settlement pattern of the U.S., there is no question that the federal government has engaged in a number of acts that have had a major effect upon the pattern of development in the U.S. Thus while there has been no national plan there have been a number of major acts of national planning. This chapter briefly describes some of these acts which, to an extent, constitute *de facto* national planning.

All of these acts do not fit together neatly as parts of a single grand design. But although there is no grand design, there are some commonalities.The federal style, in most cases, has not been to command but to permit and to encourage. In most cases there has been more carrot than stick, the carrot being federal money or federal land. The general direction is set by a system of federal guidelines and incentives, but the details are decided at the state or substate level. Where the federal government is the actor that actually does the work as in an Army Corps of Engineers' project much of the initiative is local. In general, the federal hand in shaping the pattern of development in the U.S. looms larger as one moves west. Federal ownership of land necessarily made the federal government a major player in determining the pattern of land development. And it was in the west that the federal government became the major land owner. In the immediate postrevolutionary period most of the land east of the Mississippi was claimed by the thirteen colonies, though much of that land came into the union as other states. However, west of the Mississippi the Louisiana Purchase, lands obtained from Mexico after the Mexican War, lands ceded by Great Britain in the Oregon Compromise, the Gadsden Purchase and the Alaska purchase made the federal government a land owner on a huge scale. Climate has also favored a larger federal role in the west. In most of the U.S. west of the 100th meridian rainfall is generally under 20 inches a year and is not sufficiently reliable to support agriculture other than grazing.[1] Thus agriculture in most of the western half of the country is dependent on irrigation. That dependency makes federal water policy a key shaper of the development of the region.

THE PATTERN OF LAND SETTLEMENT

The ordinance of 1785, passed by the Continental Congress under the Articles of Confederation, laid out the basic pattern of land ownership in what was then the Northwest Territory, a tract extending from the western border of Pennsylvania westward to the Mississippi, bounded on the south by the Ohio River and on the north by the Great Lakes. The act established the six mile by six mile square township and the one square mile section as the basic units for land division. In the original plan land was to be auctioned off in blocks of one square mile (640 acres) at a minimum price of $1 per acre. The money was to provide the Congress with revenue and the process of auctioning land in relatively small pieces would people this vast area with small, independent farmers. When the $1 per acre price proved to be too high Congress backed away from the plan to some extent by selling off large blocks of land to investors and speculators at a much lower price. The area then developed in a manner largely determined by the rate at which these buyers could create new settlements and resell land to individual holders. The effect of the act was to permit the rapid peopling of the area and to lay down a basic grid pattern that is still readily seen on the map of Ohio, Indiana, and in other parts of the upper midwest. The decision to sell farm-sized plots of land to individuals reinforced the rural American pattern of scattered farmsteads as opposed to a pattern commonly seen in Europe in which a rural population lives in hamlets or villages surrounded by the fields farmed by its residents.

In the latter half of the nineteenth century the settlement of the west was very much influenced by a few key decisions of the federal government. The Homestead Act of 1862 permitted settlers to claim 160 acre blocks of public land at essentially no cost if they would reside on the land for five continuous years.[2] Ultimately, about 80 million acres, roughly 125,000 square miles were homesteaded. Most homesteading occured west of the Mississippi and much of it in areas that did not have adequate and predictable rainfall sufficient to support agriculture. This situation, some decades later, helped to propel the federal government into taking a major role in water development throughout the west.

In the same year Congress passed the Morrill Land Grant Act which granted each state 30,000 acres of federally owned land for each member of the state's congressional delegation. The states were to use the monies from the sale of these lands to establish at least one college that would have as its primary role the teaching of "agriculture and the mechanic arts." A great many of the state universities in the U.S. today are land grant colleges. The suffix A&M in a university's name dates from the act. In the case of many other schools the A&M has subsequently been lost. A major intention of the act was to ensure the teaching of practical arts to support agriculture. And in this regard it was extremely successful. Again, the federal government's actions were all carrot and no stick. No state was required to create an A&M college nor told where such a college should be located. The states were simply offered an attractive option and most of them made use of it. The scattering of major state universities in small towns across the U.S. is, in part, a legacy of the Morrill Act.

ESTABLISHING THE RAIL NETWORK

The railroad network that facilitated and shaped the rapid development of the U.S. during the nineteenth century was, itself, shaped and its construction greatly accelerated by the actions of Congress. In 1850 there was no national network of railroads. There were under 10,000 miles of track in the eastern United States, mostly connected to large cities but not forming a unified system. For example, the furthest west one could continuously travel by train from New York City was to Buffalo. Other than along the east coast there were no major north-south links. Yet by 1860 national rail mileage had tripled and most of the major cities east of the Mississippi were tied together in a network so that people or goods could travel between any two major cities entirely by rail.

A major factor in this expansion was federal land grants to railroad companies. The grants provided the right of way plus large amounts of land adjoining the right of way that the company could sell or use as collateral against which to issue bonds to pay for construction. The first such grant, totalling 3,736,000 acres (5,837 square miles), was to build a continuous link from Chicago to Mobile, Alabama. By 1860 Congress had granted a total of 18 million acres for railroad construction.[3] That area, about 28,000 square miles, is roughly the area of Vermont, New Hampshire, and Massachusetts combined.

With the rail system of the East relatively complete the next obvious task was to span the continent with railroads. The First Pacific Railway Act of 1862 provided both the authorization and the financial incentives for a transcontinental railway.[4] The act authorized the Union Pacific Railroad to build westward from St. Joseph, Missouri and the Central Pacific Railroad to build eastward from Sacramento, California. The act granted the railroads a 400-foot right of way and five alternate square miles of land for each mile of track built (a figure that was doubled by Congress two years later). In addition the federal government issued bonds to provide construction funds. Thus investors in the project bore relatively little of the total risk. The building of the lines was accompanied by considerable corruption and malfeasance. Exactly how much corruption will probably never be known.

> Their bookkeeping was, to say the least, primitive, and such records as existed, were destroyed, possibly by design, in a fire in 1873. But there can be little doubt that the profits were enormous. [5]

Construction proceeded rapidly over formidable obstacles and the two lines met at Promontory Point near Ogden, Utah in 1869 making coast to coast rail travel possible.

Within a decade or so other lines crossed the continent, both north and south of the Union Pacific route. Here, too, congressional aid played a major role. In 1863 Congress granted the Atchison, Topeka and Santa Fe ten square miles of land for every mile of route constructed and in 1864 the Northern Pacific was given lands that totaled more than the entire area of the New England states.[6]

Grants of public lands to railroads continued until 1873 by which time approximately 160 million acres of land had been given to railroads either directly by the federal government or indirectly by the federal government through the states.[7] It is hard to imagine a more powerful stimulus to railroad building. The grants provided a clear and uncontested title to the route and the potential sale of land to settlers and speculators made the financial prospects very attractive. U.S. rail mileage grew from about 30,000 miles in 1860 to about 200,000 in 1900 by which time the rail network as we now know it was essentially complete.[8] A key element in this spectacular accomplishment was the role of the federal government sketched out above.

WATER AND THE WEST

The combination of the Homestead Act and the spanning of the continent by railroads greatly accelerated the peopling of the western states and this brings us to the question of water. In the eastern U.S. rainfall is generally adequate to support farming. Water policy is rarely the most important public issue. In much of the West, water policy is an absolutely vital issue. In the years immediately after the Civil War the populations of the plains states grew very rapidly for reasons noted. These years were wetter than usual and if many western farmers did not thrive, they at least survived. The favorable weather, in fact, caused some to believe that the very act of cultivating large areas of land would cause rainfall, a notion then expressed in the phrase "rain follows the plough."

In the 1880s the weather turned drier and it became apparent that rain did not follow the plough. In a number of plains states both the farm population and the total population fell sharply as farmers abandoned their barren lands. By the end of the nineteenth century of somewhat over 1 million families that had tried homesteading only about 400,000 had made a go of it.[9]

The failure of rain-fed agriculture in the western half of the nation did not cause the U.S. to give up on western agriculture, but rather promoted a great interest in irrigation to "reclaim" the desert lands for agriculture. But private irrigation efforts, by and large, were not very successful. Inadequate technical knowledge, undercapitalization and, in many cases fraud and chicanery doomed a majority of private irrigation projects. Pressure mounted for federal action.

The Reclamation Act of 1902 established the Reclamation Service (which became the Bureau of Reclamation in 1923). Under the act funds from the sale of public lands were to be used to pay for irrigation projects and the investment repaid (without interest) by the parties using the water. At first the repayment period was to be 10 years, then 20 years with a five-year grace period and subsequently was extended even further.[10] The principle of federal subsidization of water development thus became firmly established. From the act's passage to well into the 1920s the federal role in providing water in the west was relatively modest. In fact, there was much criticism in Congress of federal investment in reclamation projects because many projects showed a relatively low return on the dollar. But in the late 1920s a combination of events propelled the nation into almost a half century of dam building and water projects that shaped much of the modern west.

In the period around World War I people in the rapidly growing Los Angeles region recognized that growth would be brought to a halt by water shortages if a new source were not found. The nearest major source was the Colorado River which begins in central Colorado more than two miles above sea level and follows a tumultous southwesterly course ending in the Gulf of California between Baja, California and the main land mass of Mexico. But the river does not flow through California itself and thus California could not make a direct claim on it. The Californians took the initiative and after much negotiation the Colorado River Compact to divide the waters of the Colorado was signed by the seven states of California, Arizona, New Mexico, Colorado, Nevada, Utah, and

Wyoming. In1928 Congress authorized the construction of Boulder Dam (subsequently renamed Hoover Dam), smaller dams downstream, and the All-American Canal. The latter was to run westward from a lower point on the river, Lake Havasu to be formed by Parker Dam, to Los Angeles. The centerpiece of the project was Boulder Dam on which construction began in 1931 under the auspices of the Bureau of Reclamation. Completed in 1936 the dam was a massive testimony to the civil engineer's art. It was 726 feet high, almost a quarter of a mile across the crest, contained 66 million tons of concrete and was altogether an impressive if not amazing accomplishment. A system of canals and aqueducts and canals was then constructed to carry the waters of the Colorado across the width of California to serve the city of Los Angeles. Further south, the All-American canal carried the Colorado's waters westward just north of the California-Mexico border and turned the desert of California's Imperial Valley into one of the nation's most productive agricultural areas.

The dam was a spectacular demonstration of what could be done both to supply huge quantities of water and to produce enormous amounts of cheap hydroelectric power. At the same time the Great Depression had left a quarter of the nation's labor force unemployed and federal job creation looked like the best way to deal with the problem. Dam building and associated reclamation projects were one way to soak up unemployed labor and produce a useful product. The dust bowl of the early 1930s (a result of dry weather and overcultivation) was driving hundreds of thousands of farmers off their land in states like Oklahoma (hence the term "Okies") and sending them westward toward California. Another use, then, for funding reclamation work would be to open lands for farmers displaced by the storms of the dust bowl. For these various reasons a great era of dam building was soon underway. The prime agency for this work was the Bureau of Reclamation though some dams were also built by the Army Corps of Engineers. Figure 18–1 shows 105 Bureau of Reclamation dams all having a height of 150 feet or more. As the map indicates, virtually every major river in the west has been dammed and controlled.

In connection with the dam building and associated construction done in on Colorado one writer states:

> If the Colorado River suddenly stopped flowing, you would have two years of carryover capacity in the reservoirs before you had to evacuate most of Southern California and Arizona and a good portion of Colorado, New Mexico, Utah and Wyoming. The river system provides over half the water of greater Los Angeles, San Diego and Phoenix; it grows much of America's domestic production of fresh winter vegetables; it illumines the neon city of Las Vegas . . . whose annual income is one-fourth the gross national product of Egypt—the only other place on earth where so many people are so helplessly dependent on one river's flow. . . . [11]

What was done on the Colorado was not unique, but only a harbinger of what was soon to be done elsewhere. By the start of World War II Grand Coulee and Bonneville (built by the Army Corps of Engineers) Dams had been completed on the Columbia River and Shasta Dam on the Sacramento River in Northern California had been completed. The process of damming and controlling the rivers of

WASHINGTON
OREGON
IDAHO
MONTANA
WYOMING
NORTH DAKOTA
SOUTH DAKOTA
NEBRASKA
MINNESOTA
WISCONSIN
IOWA
ILLINOIS
KANSAS
MISSOURI
OKLAHOMA
ARKANSAS
TEXAS
LOUISIANA
MISSISSIPPI
NEVADA
UTAH
COLORADO
CALIFORNIA
ARIZONA
NEW MEXICO
Salt Lake
6. Grand Coulee 1942
83. Cle Elum 1933
23. Tieton 1925
103. Scoggins 1975
64. O'Sullivan 1949
5. Hungry Horse 1953
66. Gibson 1929
53. Canyon Ferry 1951
87. McKay 1927
78. Mason 1968
43. Aurthur Bowman 1961
85. Deadwood 1931
12. Owyhee 1932
16. Arrowrock 1915
11. Anderson Ranch 1950
38. Palisades 1957
8. Yellowtail 1966
18. Buffalo Bill 1910
59. Anchor 1960
81. Keyhole 1952
54. Boysen 1952
49. Pactola 1956
69. Angostura 1949
7. Trinity 1962
4. Shasta 1954
68. Spring Debris 1963
98. Keswick 1850
32. Whiskeytown 1963
89. Prosser Creek 1963
3. Auburn Bridge
47. Stampede 1970
61. Sugar Pine 1982
71. Sly Park 1955
93. Lahontan 1915
25. Monticello 1957
15. San Luis 1957
22. Fiant 1942
82. Los Banos 1965
102. Little Panoche 1966
45. Twitchel 1958
34. Bradbury 1953
17. Casitas 1959
1. Hoover 1936
65. Davis 1950
21. Parker 1938
30. Bartlett 1939
33. Theodore Roosevelt 1911
2. Glen Canyon 1964
42. Lost Creek 1966
97. Echo 1931
56. Causey 1966
77. Wanship 1977
39. Alcova 1938
58. Pathfinder 1909
44. Kortes 1951
28. Seminoe 1939
72. Glendo 1958
73. Meeks Cabin 1971
100. Horsetooth 1949
55. Spring Canyon 1949
52. Soldier Canyon 1949
9. Flaming Gorge 1964
40. East Canyon 1966
48. Deer Creek 1941
75. Redfleet 1980
91. Steinaker 1961
63. Starvation 1970
37. Soldier Creek 1973
76. Currant Creek 1982
70. Joes Valley 1966
46. Dixie Canyon 1949
57. Carter Lake No.1 1952
27. Granby 1950
90. Sugar Loaf 1968
41. Pueblo 1975
84. Medicine Creek 1949
80. Kirwin 1955
96. Bonny 1951
101. Webster 1956
62. Cedar Bluff 1951
94. Vallecito 1941
29. McPhee 1987
86. Platora 1951
104. Nambe Falls 1976
31. Lemon 1963
74. Jackson Gulch 1949
13. Navajo 1963
36. Heron 1971
50. Sanford 1965
105. Arbuckle 1966
88. Sumner 1937
26. Elephant Butte 1916
35. Marshall Ford 1942
Inset area
10. Morrow Point 1968
14. Blue Mesa 1966
19. Crystal 1978
20. Ruedi 1968
24. Green Mountain 1943
51. Ridgeway 1986
60. Taylor Lake 1937
67. Paonia 1962
79. Silver Jack 1971
92. Vega 1959
95. Crawford 1962
99. Rifle Gap 1967
0 250 500 Miles
0 300 600 Kilometers

the West continued with great speed after World War II. By 1971, according to a Bureau of Reclamation tabulation Hoover Dam ranked only forty-seventh in size among dams built or under construction by the Bureau.[12] The largest of these, the earth-filled San Luis Dam in California had an interior volume of over 77 million cubic yards, more than 30 times that of Hoover Dam.

Construction of water projects peaked in the 1960s with the addition of about 29 million acre feet of storage per year and then slowed in the 1970s. It has since come to an almost complete stop. What happened? First, most of the best damsites had been developed.

> In the 1920s, a cubic yard of dam produced 10.4 acre feet in reservoir capacity. The average declined in each decade, and by the 1960s only .29 acre feet of storage was produced per cubic yard of dam.[13]

Thus newer projects showed lower benefit/cost ratios than older ones and it became increasingly difficult to justify large federal expenditures for them.

Then, too, our notions of conservation have changed. Consider the idea of "reclaiming" the desert. To Theodore Roosevelt, the greatest turn-of-the-century conservationist, the idea of reclaiming the desert and making it bloom made perfect sense. The conservationist of today might ask why we thought it was ours to "reclaim" and what prior claim were we "reclaiming." He or she might ask why not just "let it be." We have come to question how much sense it makes to deliver water to the farmer at 10 cents on the dollar in a nation that uses billions of federal dollars to buy up farm surpluses and pay farmers elsewhere to take land out of cultivation. Does it really make sense to grow rice, as is actually done, in the California desert? Then, too, it has become apparent that the great Bureau of Reclamation and Corps of Engineer's projects of the past make both friends and enemies. Farmers and the industrial users of hydropower love them. But environmentalists become concerned about converting wetlands into reservoirs, for wetlands serve as breeding areas, as sources of biodiversity, and as stopping areas for migrating birds. They are concerned that changing the flow of a river by damming it changes the life within it and may drive some species to extinction. Fly fishermen, canoeists, and kayakers who use rivers for recreation often want them left in their natural state. Archeologists do not want to see historic sites submerged forever. In short, the growing strength of the environmental movement thus helped to bring the era of great water projects to an end.

In 1986 Congress passed the Water Resources Development Act (WRDA). The law mandated much higher local contributions to federal water projects and higher user fees for federal water projects. By shifting a substantial part of the cost downward it ended the era when state and local governments would lobby for inefficient projects simply because the project would bring them some benefits while imposing no costs on them.[14] The law applied to the Corps of Engineers and not to the Bureau of Reclamation, but it affected the Bureau nonetheless. At present both the Bureau and the Corps are much more attuned to issues of conservation and efficient use of resources rather than massive new projects. In the West the key issue in regard to water will not be that of making more available but of making the best use of the amount that is now available. The big conflict and decision making is likely to be over questions of water rights and water pricing and of balancing the needs of growing urban and suburban populations with the prior claims of agriculture. In the west water rights have generally been determined on the basis of "prior appropriation," meaning on the basis of who first claimed the right and used the source.[15] Agriculture, which employes a very small part of the total population of the region, uses a very large share of its total water supply. It has a grip on this supply because of the doctorine of "prior appropriation." Should water be allocated on a more economic basis, whether it be competitive bidding or simply pricing water at its true cost of delivery that change will favor urban and industrial users over agricultural users.[16] Decisions on this apparently technical issue of how to price water will have a major effect on the future development of the West and one can foresee that the matter will not be decided without considerable contention.

Western Water Policy in Retrospect

Looking back on the era of reclamation what is one to make of it? Some, like Marc Reisner, the author of *Cadillac Desert* cited earlier, regard much of the damming and reclamation work in the west as a giant combination of hubris, delusion, and scandal. But millions of westerners who like their region and the life they lead in it take a very different view. They will tell you that even if mistakes were made along the way they are, by and large, pleased with what was done and what it has made possible. Some of them might also tell you that it is not right to judge actions in the past by the sensibilities of today. One should not condemn those who dammed the Colorado and the Columbia in the 1930s because they lacked the particular sensibilities of the Sierra Club member of the 1990s. The outsider who neither disparages nor approves uncritically, but simply contemplates what was done with a vast region whose climate was fundamentally hostile to development cannot help but be impressed.

Projects, some by the Bureau of Reclamation, some by the Army Corps of Engineers, and some by state or municipal public authorities, made the modern U.S. West vastly different than it otherwise would have been. Dams, aqueducts,and canals provided the water for vast metropolitan areas like Los Angeles. Hydroelectric power at a fraction of the cost of fossil fuel-generated power in the East provided a basis for western industry. Western agriculture is largely a product of public water policy. In 1990 the total value of farm products produced in California was $18.7 billion ranking California first among the 50 states in value of farm output.[17] In California's Imperial Valley, one of the most productive agricultural areas in the U.S., rainfall averages 2–3 inches a year. Without the waters of the Colorado it would be as dry as the Sahara.

Were it not for the great water projects the population of the American west would be much smaller than it is and it would be strung out along the region's rivers. Los Angeles could not exist at anything close to its present scale. Reno and Los Vegas would, at best, be small towns depending upon whatever water could be brought up from the wells. The West would be a food importing rather than a food exporting region and its industrial base far smaller than it currently is. People would not be able to waterski on manmade lakes in the desert.

The rest of the nation would be somewhat different too. The population of the eastern United States would be substantially larger than it is today and the centroid of U.S. population would be further east than it now is, for there would have been much less east to west migration of population.[18] The eastern United States would have considerably less forest than it now does for without so much food production in the West there would necessarily be much more land cultivated in the East.

How much of this development can we consider to be national planning? Certainly projects involving the damming of rivers, the generation of vast amounts of low-cost hydroelectric power, creation of huge artificial lakes, and the transportion of water over hundreds of miles were major acts of planning. In some cases the impetus for the project came from local politicians, local commercial interests, or the area's congressional delegation. In other cases the idea for the project originated in a federal agency. But there was no single plan for water development in the West. There was, in a very general way, a policy expressed in a multitude of appropriations bills to develop the water resources of the west using billions of federal dollars. Beyond that, there was a decision to develop western agriculture with irrigation water that, in many cases, cost the farmer only a few cents per dollar of actual cost. One might then say that there was no overall plan but there was an overall policy and, under that, numerous separate plans.

SYSTEMATIC REGIONAL PLANNING

The sort of systematic planning for an entire region that one might think of as typifying national planning has been done only once. That project was the work of the Tennessee Valley Authority (TVA). The Tennessee River originates in the Cumberland Mountains of the eastern part of Tennessee, flows westward then turns southward into northern Alabama and then swings north emptying into the Ohio at Paducah, Kentucky, a few miles upstream from the confluence of the Ohio and the Mississippi. Over half of its drainage basin is in Tennessee but the basin also includes parts of Virginia, North Carolina, Georgia, Alabama, Mississippi, and Kentucky.

> The natural regime of the Tennessee River is characterized by large spring flows that produce destructive floods and low summer flows that inhibit navigation. The intensity and frequency of these events discouraged development and contributed to persistent poverty in the valley.[19]

The idea for integrated development of the valley originated shortly after World War I and was persistently and skillfully backed by Senator George Norris of Nebraska. One selling point for a project on the Tennessee, aside from the poverty of the region, was that there already was some federal investment in the valley. Toward the end of World War I the federal government had started to build a dam at Muscle Shoals on the Tennessee River to generate hydroelectric power and an industrial facility to use that power to make nitrates for explosives. The nitrate plant was tested and then "mothballed" in 1919. The dam was completed in 1925. The presence of that wartime investment provided a rationale for more development to properly utilize the original public investment. The nitrates that would have been used for explosives in wartime would be used for fertilizer production in peacetime. In 1928 Congress passed legislation that would have created an organization similar to TVA but it was vetoed by President Coolidge.

The coming of the Great Depression changed the political equation. In April, 1933 President Roosevelt requested passage of legislation creating an authority and Congress quickly complied.[20] Both job creation and alleviating the persistent poverty in the region were motivations. The act created a single authority to deal with all aspects of water development and policy within the region.

The river was dammed at a number of points to control flooding and the same dams used to produce hydroelectric power. The hydropower made possible electrification and furnished power for industry. In time the economic growth of the region raised the demand for electricity beyond what could be produced from the river and in the years after World War II TVA branched out into fossil fuel and nuclear-generated power as well. The building of locks rendered the river navigable from Knoxville, Tennessee to the Missouri thence to the Mississippi thus contributing to the commercial growth of the region. Lakes created by the water projects provided recreation for the residents and also contributed to the economic development of the region by bringing in income from tourism.

As a project and as an experiment the TVA has its critics and its admirers. From the political right it has been criticized as socialistic and as permitting government to compete unfairly with private power companies. In fact, early in its history electric power companies brought suit to enjoin it from selling electric power. The appeal went to the Supreme Court which upheld the right of governmental body to produce and sell electric power. TVA has been criticized from the left for being too cautious and sticking to an excessively narrow agenda. The agency has concentrated on a few areas—flood control, navigation, and power and has eschewed a more comprehensive planning and social engineering role. Its admirers will argue that the agency performed yeoman service for the region by ending flooding, rendering the Tennessee River navigable (over a 652-mile stretch from Paducah to Knoxville) and providing the region with low-cost power. It let the region compete rather than languish in a state of underdevelopment.

Regardless of the agency's success or failures, Congress has never duplicated the TVA, though many "little TVAs" have been proposed. One reason clearly is ideological. One writer who worked for TVA for some years suggests that another reason is bureaucratic rivalry.[21] In the TVA various functions are all the responsibility of a single commission. Thus, she asserts, "little TVA" proposals have been opposed by the Corps of Engineers, the Bureau of Reclamation, and other agencies because they would take functions out of the hands of those agencies. Although the TVA experiment has never been duplicated in the U.S. the project has been the object of study for planners, economists, and administrators from developing nations all over the world as an example of how to do regional development.

THE INTERSTATE HIGHWAY SYSTEM

The design and construction of the Interstate Highway System represents a major act of national planning. In physical magnitudes like cubic yards of earth moved or cubic yards of concrete poured the system, taken as a whole, may well be the largest construction project in human history. The construction of coordinated system of highways all built to the same standards and linking every major city and more than 90 percent of all cities down to a population of 50,000 or more residents across a land of area of about 3 million square miles was a major act of planning. It was done as a cooperative venture between the federal government and 49 states.[22]

The federal presence in highway construction began with the Federal Aid Road Act of 1916. This act provided federal funds to assist states in the construction of intercity highways. It established a basic pattern of shared funding responsibility and local consent to and participation in highway planning that persists to the present time.

In the 1920s and 1930s the increase in the number of automobiles and the dispersal of population, largely because of widespread automobile ownership, tended to outpace the rate at which the states and municipalities built roads. Traffic congestion and inadequate highway connections between cities were a continuing fact of American life. In 1934 federal aid legislation authorized funds for state highway planning in addition to supplementing the state's construction expenditures. This set in motion a variety of traffic studies and placed the idea of a national highway grid on the national political agenda.

In 1938 Congress requested the Bureau of Public Roads (BPR, a federal agency that subsequently became the Federal Highway Administration) to study a proposal for a system of six superhighway toll roads, three to cross the country from east to west and three from north to south. Toll roads were suggested because the federal government and the states were starved for revenues during the Great Depression and tolls appeared to be a way to make the highways self-financing. BPR studied the matter and decided that this proposed 14,000 mile system would not be able to generate enough toll revenues to be self-financing. Instead, in 1939 BPR came back with a proposal that recommended a national highway system of 26,700 miles. A succession of planning studies over the next decade and a half produced a vision of a national highway system of roughly 40,000 miles.[23] The system would be jointly planned by the federal government and the states, would be built to the same design standards across the nation, and would be a system of limited access roadways. Limited access was necessary to maintain a smooth, high-speed flow. The concept had been proven on a very small number of parkways beginning with the Bronx River Parkway in the late 1920s (see Chapter 2).

Although the vision of a single, integrated, limited access system was compelling, the passage of legislation that would bring it into being was stalled by the problem of how to finance it. Studies indicated that that tolls, despite their financial success on a few roads such as the Pennsylvania Turnpike, could not generate the revenue required to build and maintain a national system. Both Congress and the Truman and Eisenhower administrations were concerned about keeping the federal budget in approximate balance and did not favor massive highway funding from general revenues, nor were the states willing or able to finance the major share of the proposed system. A variety of interests including the trucking industry, motor vehicle manufacturers, and the American Automobile Association resisted increases on taxes on new vehicles and fuel. It thus took a decade after the end of the Second World War before a compromise solution could be reached.

In 1956, at the urging of the Eisenhower administration, Congress passed the Federal Aid Highway Act of 1956. Title I of the act called for uniform design standards across the nation, established methods for apportioning highway funding among the states, and dealt with questions of procedure and administration. But the crucial part of the act was title II which provided for a mechanism that would deliver massive funding for highway construction. The act set up the Highway Trust Fund which would receive money from excise taxes on new vehicles and sales taxes on motor fuel. These funds would be dedicated, meaning that they could be used only for highway construction. In the years since the passage of the act, motor vehicle ownership, miles driven, and fuel consumed have risen very rapidly thus providing a large and growing tax base to sustain highway construction. For 1992 Highway Trust Fund revenues were about $19 billion.[24]

The design of the system was a joint effort between the Federal Highway Administration and state officials. The overall plan of the system was worked out by the federal people but the exact routing within the states was largely determined by state officials. Design standards were uniform. There were four 12-foot lanes to be separated by a median and provided with shoulders at least 10 feet wide. The highways were designed for maximum speeds of 50, 60, or 70 mph depending upon topography. Early on it was decided not to permit any services on the highways themselves, in contrast to the practice on toll roads. The argument given for this was to preserve competition and avoid the granting of "monopoly positions." But one might speculate that this decision had the fortuitous effect of increasing support from local businessmen who would see the highway as a source of additional customers, rather than as a source of additional competition.[25]

The system, at this writing, covers about 42,500 miles and is virtually complete. The total cost of the system is estimated at about $129 billion. In the sense that the entire system is a single entity built to a single set of standards providing high quality connections between virtually all of the major urban centers in the U.S., it is a huge act of planning. And there is no question that it has shaped the development of the nation to an enormous degree. But it must be said that many of the system's effects were unanticipated and that in at least one way the building of the system has had an effect opposite to that intended.

From the beginning it was recognized that there would be a choice between whether the interstates would go through cities or would bypass them with a circumferential road. It was understood that this would have important urban design consequences and the 1956 legislation provided that where such a decision was to be made a public hearing would be required. Within a few years enormous

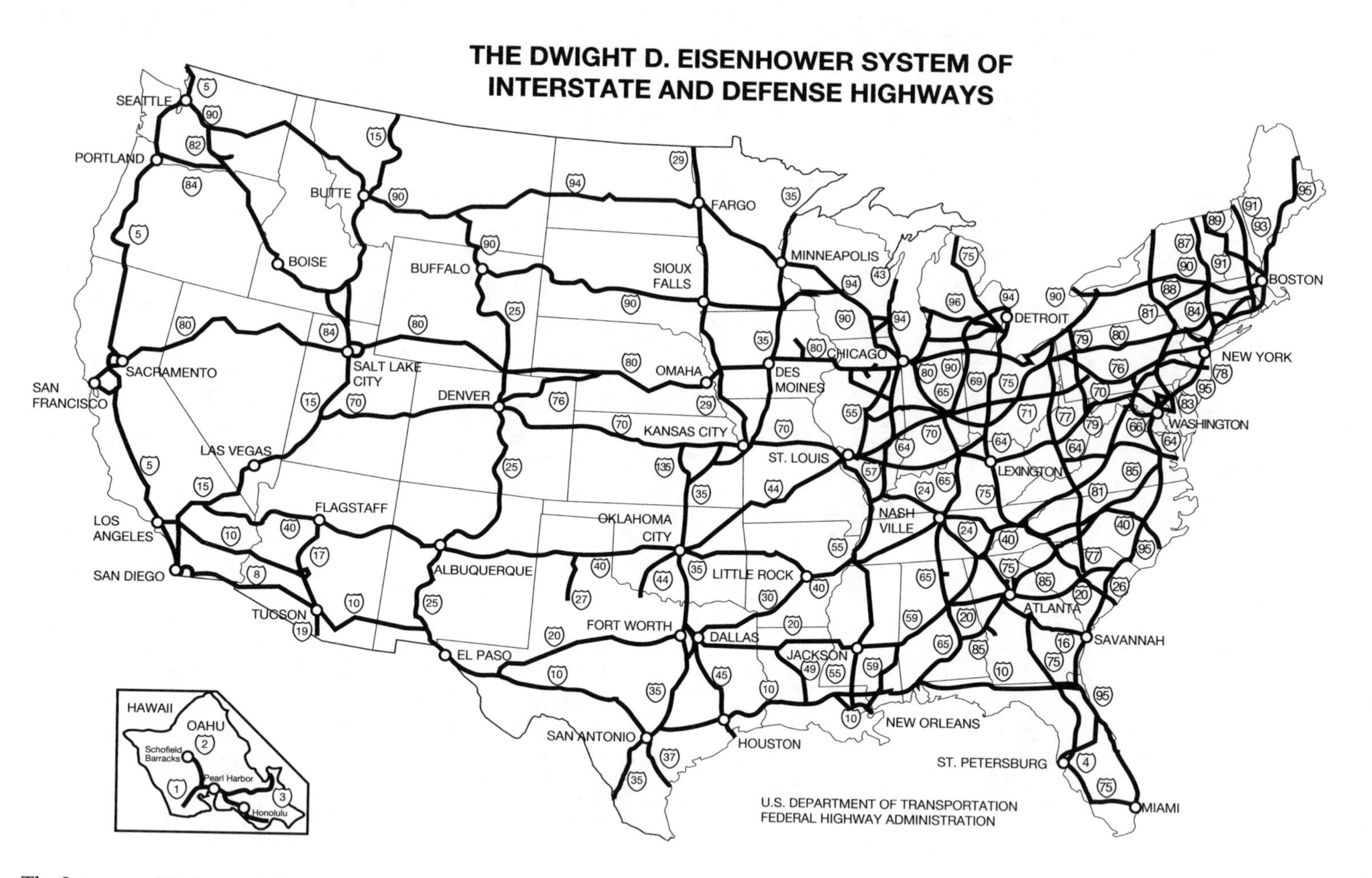

The Interstate Highway System as completed. Note that the figure does not show the beltways discussed in the text.

public opposition to cutting interstates through cities developed and the decision was almost always to bypass. The citizens had earlier learned how to organize to stop the "federal bulldozer" (in connection with Urban Renewal) and they applied that knowledge with considerable effect to highway proposals.

The decision to bypass brought into being the familiar beltway pattern that we see about most major cities. And that is a profoundly deurbanizing design. The beltway (not shown in the figure on the preceding page) creates a major locus for economic activity around the city. People who work for businesses on the beltway no longer need to live within commuting range of downtown. The beltway, in effect, becomes the new downtown. The "edge city" of which Joel Garreaux writes is made possible by the beltway design.

Proponents of the interstate highway system believed that it would strengthen the economy of the city by providing better access to the city's central business districts both from other cities and from the city's hinterland. But it was not foreseen that this effect would be swamped by the larger effect of creating huge masses of highly accessible commercial space outside of the central business district and outside of the city itself.

In the cases of the largest metropolitan areas, congestion on the beltway and the areas around it, in time, create demand for a second beltway. The New York metropolitan area has, in effect, a double beltway system though it has breaks in it because of topographic considerations and bodies of water (Long Island Sound and the lower reaches of New York harbor). In the Washington D.C. metropolitan area the beltway and environs are heavily congested and real estate prices in the D.C. suburbs are extremely high as a result of the competition for land. There is now much discussion of a second beltway 10 or 15 miles further out. This would spread the region further and bring many hundreds of square miles of exurbia into the metropolitan area. To some extent the racial and class separation of America might be attributed to the system because it was such a powerful suburbanizing force.

The building of the interstate highway system accelerated the shift of U.S. manufacturing from rail-borne to truck-borne freight by providing a road network that greatly increased the efficiency of trucking. That, of course, was also a decentralizing force. It probably also accelerated the growth of the Sunbelt relative to the rest of the country by tying formerly remote rural southern areas into a single, highly efficient national highway system.

One might wonder how different America would look if instead of taking the path we did we had attempted to keep cities compact and spent much of the money devoted to interstates on a high quality, heavily subsidized rail system—in other words followed a path similar to many European nations. But although one may wonder about this, there was no real possibility for such a choice. The American love affair with the automobile and the process of suburbanization were well underway by the time the interstate system was begun. The rail served, compact city configuration has its appeal and it certainly can make a claim for environmental virtue. But it never had the mass support that might have made it a real possibility.

The system accomplishes what it was intended to do. It provides rapid, safe, high-quality automotive transportation between cities and between cities and nonurban hinterland. It also, as suggested above, accomplished a great deal that was not intended.

FINANCING THE SUBURBS

Few acts of the federal government have had more effect upon the physical form of American metropolitan areas than legislation concerning the financing and taxation of housing. Prior to 1935 mortgage lending was very different than it is today. To protect themselves from losses when the borrower defaulted on a mortgage loan, banks required very large downpayments. That, by itself, prevented many people from becoming homeowners. There were other barriers as well.

> Lenders considered a ten year mortgage to be long term. Many mortgages ran only one, two or three years, with most of the loan amount due in one large payment at the end of the short term. At the end of this short period, the home purchaser faced great uncertainties. Could he persuade the lender to renew his mortgage? At what interest rate? If he failed to get a renewal, he often lost his home. The standard plots in melodramas of the time [the villain about to foreclose on the hapless widow] were not entirely fiction. . . . [26]

This situation was radically changed by a single act of the federal government. In 1935 the Federal Housing Administration (FHA), which had been created the previous year, began to offer mortgage insurance. The insurance fund consisted of a small fee paid by each borrower (the buyer of the house). The fund reimbursed banks should the borrower default on the mortgage. Federal mortgage insurance effectively eliminated the risk of default and thus made banks willing to lend for 25 or 30 years and with little downpayment. Shortly thereafter the federal government created the Federal National Mortgage Association (FNMA, often referred to as Fannie Mae) to buy mortgages from banks. The bank could sell the mortgage to FNMA thus converting the mortgage into cash. The home buyer would continue to make mortgage payments, but they would go to FNMA with the bank acting as intermediary. By creating a secondary market for mortgages the federal government further increased the willingness of banks to issue mortgages because the bank could now get out of the commitment if and when it saw a more profitable use for its funds. In other words, the operations of FNMA removed much of the "opportunity cost" risks of mortgage lending.[27] After World War II the Veterans Administration further encouraged home buying by insuring veterans' mortgages that carried little or no downpayment.

Congressional intent in passing the required legislation was primarily to increase homeownership, something that is generally considered to be a central element of "the American dream." Another goal during the Great Depression was to reduce unemployment by stimulating residential construction. The stimulating effect during the Great Depression was not very large. But the effect on both construction and homeownership in the prosperous years that followed World War II was enormous. So far as is known there was no spatial intent behind Congress' actions. In fact, there is no evidence that congressmen were aware early on that the above actions would have any spatial effect. But the effect of making homeownership more accessible was to promote rapid and extensive suburbanization, for the suburbs rather than the cities were where the mass of land available for building single-family houses was located.

Suburbanization and Tax Policy

The federal government has also contributed to suburbanization through tax policy. If you own a house you can deduct from your taxable income both interest on the mortgage and property taxes on the house and the lot. If one rents a house or an apartment one implicity pays mortgage insurance and property taxes because the landlord must cover these taxes through the rent. However, you cannot deduct these expenses from your taxable income. This favorable treatment of the owner *vis à vis* the renter creates a powerful push toward homeownership.[28] The larger the house and property and the higher one's tax bracket the more powerful the push. A few years ago when marginal tax brackets extended up 70 percent the push was almost irresistable for the very wealthy, for it meant that at that margin the federal government was reimbursing the homeowner for 70 cents of every dollar that he or she paid in mortgage interest and property taxes.

Again, there is no explict spatial dimension to this favorable tax treatment, nor was any spatial effect ever intended. One can take advantage of the tax treatment just as well by buying an apartment in a high-rise condominium or cooperative in midtown Manhattan as one can in the suburbs or in rural America. But because in most metropolitan areas most of the land available for new construction is located in the suburbs and exurbs the net effect is deurbanizing.

One should not underestimate the force of this favorable tax treatment acting year after year. For 1993 the federal government's Office of Management and the Budget estimates the value of the favorable treatment of mortgage interest on owner occupied property at $42.9 billion and the favorable tax treatment of property taxes on owner occupied housing at another $12.6 billion.[29] That sum, $55.5 billion, dwarfs any other federal housing or urban program.

But Is It Planning?

The question is whether one should to refer to the federal government's actions described above as "planning." In the matter of restructuring mortgage lending there was, in a loose sense, a plan. The goal of the plan was to promote homeownership. And there is no doubt that the federal government was highly successful in this regard.

The issue is less clear with regard to tax treatment. Provisions exempting interest and local taxes have been part of the IRS code since its inception. The Tax Reform Act of 1986 took away the exemption on most other local taxes and most other types of interest payments (for example, interest on a credit card or a car loan is not tax exempt). But Congress left the homeowner treatment untouched. One reason was obviously that trying to eliminate it or scale it back would have provoked a political firestorm, for about 64 percent of all occupied housing units in the United States are owner occupied. Whether or not there was also widespread feeling in Congress that homeownership was an important national goal to be pursued through continued favorable tax treatment is harder to discern.

OTHER AREAS

The previous material sketches a few areas in which we have experienced a form of national planning adapted to our federal poltical structure and the size and physical diversity of the nation. Most of the examples discussed were those that appeared to have a major effect upon the pattern of settlement. But the reader should be aware that this chapter is far from complete.

The Urban Renewal program, discussed in Chapter 12, shaped the cores of hundreds of cities. Army Corps of Engineers' projects have had a major effect on the development of many parts of the nation through flood control and navigation projects and by the generation of hydroelectric power.

The federal government is involved in land management on a grand scale. As of 1989 the federal government owned 662,158,000 acres, about 1.035 million square miles of the U.S., the vast bulk of it west of the Mississippi.[30] The Bureau of Land Management (BLM) manages hundreds of millions of acres. Much of the land that it manages is low value land for reasons of low rainfall, poor access, or the like. Its role is, therefore, more one of stewardship than of planning for development.

In the U.S. 231 million acres (about 361 thousand square miles) are designated as National Forest, of which almost 83 percent is actually owned by the federal government. Again, the role of the federal government is largely one of stewardship. Shaping the pattern of settlement in the nation is not a primary intent. Nonetheless, decisions about how much development to permit in national forests and about where to permit the cutting of timber have economic consequences that exert some influence on the pattern of settlement. And, of course, in the long term decisions by the Bureau of Land Management and the Forest Service about how hundreds of millions of acres are to be used cannot help but have an effect on the environmental quality of vast areas. The National Park system, often considered to have begun with the setting aside of Yellowstone National Park in 1872, is a series of acts of national planning now covering an area of about 119 thousand square miles.

SUMMARY

The United States has never had a national plan nor, since the termination of the National Resources Planning Board in 1943, a national planning agency. However, the federal government has, through a variety programs and policies over the last two centuries, played a major role in shaping the pattern of settlement in the United States. In general, the federal style has been to provide guidelines and funding and to let the states, localities, and private parties fill in the details. The federal actions and legislation discussed in this chapter were: The Ordinance of 1785, the Homestead Act, the Morrill Land Grant Act, land grants to railroads, the work of the Bureau of Reclamation, the Tennessee Valley Authority, the building of the Interstate Highway System, and federal mortgage insurance and the tax treatment of owner-occupied housing. It was also noted briefly that today the federal government owns and manages somewhat over one million square miles of the U.S., primarily west of the Mississippi River.

NOTES

1. The 100th meridian passes through North Dakota about one third of the way west from the eastern border of the state, passes through South Dakota, Nebraska, Kansas, Oklahoma and then forms the eastern edge of the Texas panhandle. The exceptions to this generalization about rainfall are the northwest coastal region about as far south as San Francisco and a few scattered areas in the northwest quarter of the region.
2. In some western states where the dry climate made it impossible for 160 acres to support a farm family larger homesteads were permitted.
3. Richard Hofstadter, William Miller, and Daniel Aaron, *The American Republic, 2nd. ed.*, Vol.. 1, Prentice Hall, Inc., Englewood Cliffs, N.J., 1970, p. 545.
4. The fact that several of the pieces of legislation mentioned in the chapter were passed in 1862 is not a coincidence. Both the opening up of western lands for settlement and the choice of transcontinental rail routes had important implications for the balance of power between free and slave states. Thus prior to the Civil War Congressional agreement had not been possible. But with southern representatives out of the Congress in 1862 agreement was easily reached.
5. Dexter Perkins and Glyndon G. Van Deusen, *The United States of America: A History*, The Macmillan Co., New York., 2nd ed., 1968, p. 73. The interested reader can look up further details under the heading "Credit Mobilier" in numerous U.S. history texts.
6. Ibid., p. 73.
7. Hofstadter, Miller, and Aaron, op. cit. p. 683.
8. Perkins and Van Deusen, op. cit., p. 69.
9. Marc Reisner, *Cadillac Desert: the American West and its Disappearing Water*, Viking, New York, 1986, p. 111.
10. On a long-term loan the sum of the interest payments can be significantly greater than the principal. Thus interest forgiveness of these loans represented a very substantial subsidy. In point of fact the actual subsidy was even greater than that would suggest because the Bureau would not (or politically could not) force the farmer who became delinquent off his land. For a brief account of the early years of the Bureau of Reclamation see Kenneth D. Frederick "Water Resources: Increasing Demand and Scarce Supply," in Kenneth D. Frederick and Roger A. Sedjo, eds., *America's Renewable Resources: Historical Trends and Current Challenges*, Resources for the future, Washington, D.C., 1991. For a more detailed presentation see Richard W. Wahi, *Markets for Federal Water*, Resources for the Future, Washington, D.C., 1989.
11. Reisner, op. cit., p. 127.
12. *Major Dams, Reservoirs, and Hydroelectric Plants, Worldwide and Bureau of Reclamation*, release by U.S. Department of the Interior, Bureau of Reclamation, Denver, CO, undated.
13. Frederick, op. cit, p. 49.
14. For a detailed account of the events leading to the passage of the act see Martin Reuss, *Reshaping National Water Politics: : The Emergence of the Water Resources Development Act*. IWR Policy Study 91-PS-1, U.S. Army Corps of Engineers, 1991.
15. In the East the law has generally relied on riparian rights, a concept derived from English Common Law, that assigns rights on the basis of immediate proximity to the water source. This worked reasonably well in the East but was not practical in the water-short West.
16. Robert Reinhold, "New Age for Western Water Policy: Less for the Farm, More for the City," *The New York Times*, October 11, 1992, sect. 1, p. 18.
17. Statistical Abstract of the United States, 112th edition, U.S. Department of Commerce, Economics and Statistics Administration, Bureau of the Census, Washington, D.C., 1992, Table 1,096. Texas ranked second, also largely on the strength of irrigated land. In the case of Texas, however, irrigation waters largely come from wells in the great Ogallala aquifer. Unlike surface waters which are renewable, "mining" the Ogallala is a one-time event, for the aquifer's recharge rate is only a miniscule fraction of the rate of current withdrawals. At the present rate of withdrawal much of the aquifer's water will be gone in half a century or less.

18. The centroid is a calculated point "at which an imaginary flat, weightless and rigid map of the United States would balance if weights of identical value were placed on it so that each weight represented the location of one person on the date of the census." In 1990 the centroid was located a few miles southwest of St. Louis See Ibid., Table 3.
19. Frederick, op. cit., p 37.
20. For an account of the legislative history see Marguerite Owen, *The Tennessee Valley Authority*, Praeger, New York, 1973.
21. Ibid., p. 235.
22. There is no interstate mileage in Alaska.
23. This account is drawn from *America's Highways 1776/1976: A History of the Federal Aid Program*, U.S. Department of Transportation, Federal Highway Administration, Washington, D.C. undated.
24. *Statistical Abstract of the United States*, op. cit., Table 493.
25. For a detailed account of the politics of the interstate highway system see Mark H. Rose, *Interstate Express Highway Politics*, revised edition, University of Tennessee Press, Knoxville, 1990.
26. Carter M. McFarland, *The Federal Government and Urban Problems*, Westview, Boulder, CO, 1978, p. 117.
27. For further details see an urban economics text such as James Heilbrun, *Urban Economics and Public Policy*, 3rd. ed., St. Martins Press, New York, 1987; McFarland, Ibid.; Henry Aaron, *Shelter and Subsidies*, The Brookings Institution Washington, D.C., 1972; or a text on real estate finance such as William Brueggeman and Leo D. Stone, *Real Estate Investment*, 8th ed., Richard D. Irwin, Homewood, IL, 1989.
28. It has been suggested many times that balance could be achieved by extending the same favorable tax treatment to renters but Congress has never shown much interest in the idea nor has the idea ever gathered much grass roots support.
29. *Statistical Abstract of the United States*, op. cit., Table 497.
30. *Statistical Abstract of the United States*, op. cit., Table 343.

SELECTED BIBLIOGRAPHY

FREDERICK, KENNETH D., and SEDJO, ROGER A., EDS., *America's Renewable Resources*, Resources for the Future, Washington, D.C., 1991.

OWEN, MARGUERITE, *The Tennessee Valley Authority*, Praeger, New York, 1973.

ROSE, MARK H., *Interstate Express Highway Politics*, revised edition, University of Tennessee Press, Knoxville, 1990.

WAHL, RICHARD W., *Markets for Federal Water: Subsidies, Property Rights, and the Bureau of Reclamation*, Resources for the Future, Washington, D.C., 1989.

Note: Detailed information about the work of federal agencies such as the Bureau of Reclamation, the Department of Transportation, or the Army Corps of Engineers can be obtained by writing or calling them directly. A number of federal agencies employ a department historian, an especially good source for the student or scholar.

CHAPTER 19

PLANNING THEORY

In this chapter we discuss planning theory from two perspectives: (1) theories of planning as a process, both how it ought to be done and how it is done, and (2) some ideological issues. But first, a legitimate question to ask is this: Is planning theory necessary? Cannot the planner simply apply his or her intelligence to a particular situation and proceed without theory?

IS THEORY NECESSARY?

The question of whether theory is not simply a waste of time or a diversion is the question with which the "practical" person or the "man of action" derides the philosopher. But theory cannot be avoided. We all possess theories and they form the basis on which we act. Everyone has ideas about how things are and how the world works. One difference between the "practical" person and the "theorist" is that the former takes these ideas for granted and the latter thinks about them consciously and makes them explicit. But when one acts, regardless of how much contempt one might have for theory or theorists, one inevitably acts on the basis of some theory about how things work. On what other basis can one act?

In 1936 John Maynard Keynes, whom many regard as the greatest economist of this century, wrote,

> . . . ideas of economists and political philosophers, both when they are right and when they are wrong, are more powerful than is commonly understood. Indeed, the world is ruled by little else. Practical men, who believe themselves to be quite exempt from intellectual influences, are usually the slave of some defunct economist. Madmen in authority, who hear voices in the air, are distilling their frenzy from some academic scribbler of a few years back.[1]

Keynes's reference to "madmen in authority" has particular reference to Europe of the 1930's, but the point that even the most powerful are themselves ruled by the ideas they hold is as valid today as then.

We noted in Chapter 6 several alternative roles the planner might play. How is a person to decide whether he or she favors an advocacy position or a neutral civil servant position, without some theories of how society works, how decisions are made, and what constitutes right and wrong? At a more concrete level, assume the city is beset with housing problems. The planner is asked to comment on whether a rent control ordinance would be a good idea. How can he or she even begin to think about the issues without some theory of how housing markets work? To the extent that controls would deliver benefits to some individuals and losses to others, how can we decide whether these effects would be good or bad unless we have some theory of what constitutes social justice?

If the planner is asked to set up some process by which the community can consider an issue, say, whether to acquire an additional 100 acres of parkland with public funds, the planner must have some theories of how groups work and some theories about how communities govern themselves in order to think about how the process should be structured. If theory is inescapable, perhaps it is best to make it as explicit as possible.

It is common to make a distinction between theory and practice, and it is easy to exaggerate this difference. To a large extent theory is developed and tested on the basis of the experience acquired in practice. As stated, every practitioner is, to some extent, a theoretician. And, conversely, the experience of practice is likely to make the theoretician better at his or her chosen work. The theoretician who has had no contact with practice has not subjected his or her theorizing to the test and has little basis to assert its validity. Without the experience of practice, it is hard to separate good theory from bad theory and useful theory from useless theory.

A DISTINCTION BETWEEN PUBLIC AND PRIVATE PLANNING

It is true that public planning and nonpublic planning, such as that done by corporations, have much in common. However, there is at least one important difference. Public planning is often more difficult than private planning and, for a very simple reason, its results may sometimes appear to be less rational: Public planning must usually satisfy many different ends, some of which may be in conflict with one another. Private planning, very often, is directed toward satisfying a single or a very small number of ends. It thus often admits of more coherent solutions.

Consider the builder formulating plans to build an apartment house. He or she is likely to have one major goal, profit.[2] No one reasonably expects a builder to consider the effect of his or her building on the city as a whole. Society has formulated a variety of rules regarding zoning, construction standards, taxation, and the like. Within these rules the builder is free to follow his or her own interests.

Now consider a public body that is building housing. It has cost and revenue estimates to make, as does the private builder. But it has numerous goals to consider that the private builder does not. How does the project affect community goals regarding integration? How will the project affect the process of gentrification? If the project involves demolition, where will the residents of the soon-to-be-demolished housing live? How does the rent structure of the project square with what is known about the income distribution of the city's population? And so on.

The public body operates in the open and is accountable to the entire body politic of the city—voters, labor unions, neighborhood groups, civic groups, tenant organizations, landlord organizations, ad infinitum. The plan it finally settles on must satisfy many of these groups. The plan does not literally have to have something for everybody, but it must have something for a number of parties if it is to have any chance of survival. For all of these reasons the public planner's task is often more frustrating and difficult than that of the private planner.

THE PROCESS OF PLANNING

Sometimes a distinction is made between "substantive" theory and "procedural" theory. Substantive theory in this usage is theory *in* planning, for example, the gravity model mentioned in connection with transportation planning. Procedural theory is theory *about* the act of planning. The various theories of planning to be discussed fall under the heading of procedural theory. Note, however, that the two types of theory are related. We have to have substantive ideas (ideas about how the world works) to form procedural theories.

Here, we address three approaches to the process of planning:

The rational model
Incrementalism
Middle-range models

The Rational Model

The rational model has been prevalent for several decades and might be considered the orthodox view.[3] It is the philosophy reflected in the comprehensive plan. Though its proponents will readily admit that in the real world it cannot be carried out precisely as described, many would argue that it still constitutes a kind of holy grail to be approached as closely as possible. The idea behind the model, as its name suggests, is to make the planning process as rational and systematic as possible. A listing of steps in the model follows. Not every writer might list exactly this sequence, but the general idea would be the same.

1. *Define the problem.* Obviously if more than one party is involved, this means reaching agreement.
2. *Clarify values.* Suppose the problem is stated as an inadequate housing stock. Before we can formulate policy we have to agree on how highly we value certain conditions. How important is the physical condition of housing? Is physical condition more or less important than the cost of housing? How important is it that housing be racially integrated? How important is good traffic circulation in residential areas? How important is growth in the number of housing units? Often, we will find that an action that takes us toward one goal takes us away from another. Tearing down substandard units will certainly improve housing quality. But by reducing the number of units on the market, demolition will push up rents. Should we do it? We cannot answer that question unless we have some idea of how important quality is relative to price.
3. *Select goals.* Having gone through steps 1 and 2, we are now presumably in a position to choose one or more goals relative to the problem.
4. *Formulate alternative plans or programs..*
5. *Forecast the consequences of the alternatives developed in the previous step.*
6. *Evaluate and select one or more courses of action (alternatives).*
7. *Develop detailed plans for implementing the alternatives selected.*
8. *Review and evaluate.* Once implementation has begun it is necessary periodically to review the process and results to date with a view to deciding whether the original plan should still be followed or whether—as is usually the case—changes and adjustments are necessary.

Although the steps are presented in sequence, there is a great deal of going back and forth between them. For example, if step 4 suggests that a certain goal selected in step 3 cannot be reached or can only be reached at an exorbitant price, the planners may go back to step 3 to select an alternative goal. Obviously, defining the problem and clarifying values are closely intertwined. Very often, we do not know how much we value something until we learn its price and then have to decide whether to pay it. In that case, the insights that come out of the latter steps will often carry us back to the first three steps.

Criticisms of the Rational Model Although the rational model seems eminently sensible, it has been subject to a great deal of criticism. Some critics assert that the steps described are simply not how things are actually planned. If the model does not describe reality at least very roughly, what good is it?

Consider the first four steps. Few real problems can be approached as if there were a clean slate in front of the planner. Legal, political, and other constraints eliminate some possibilities and necessitate others. In fact, it has been argued that the mandatory requirements and limitations that legislative bodies impose on boards, commissions, local governments, and so on are intended precisely to constrain those organizations. They are there to prevent them from going back to square one and rethinking and hence resolving the problem from the beginning.

Critics also argue that value clarification sounds logical but often cannot be done. If agreement is necessary for action and the various parties have different values, making value clarification a requisite for the next step would make further progress impossible. During World War II the United States, Great Britain, and the USSR agreed on the necessity of cooperating to defeat Germany. But their values and goals were radically different. Cooperation was achieved only by suppressing, ignoring, or denying these very deep differences. Had honest value clarification been required as a first part of the planning process, no progress would have been made. To make extended value clarification a prerequisite to further planning steps when the parties have substantially different interests and views is simply an invitation to hypocrisy.

The critic of the model might also argue that the later steps in the process do not describe reality very well. The laying out and studying of a number of alternatives is often simply not possible because of time or resources. In many cases the planner(s) arrives at a very short list of alternatives very quickly and then focuses on implementation. The look-at-everything-so-as-to-make-the-optimum-choice approach is not possible.

A final point critics make is that the goal of the rational model is optimization—making the best choice from a substantial array of possibilities. These possibilities have themselves been developed by a systematic and—as far as is possible—all-inclusive process. It has been said that in most situations organizations do not optimize but rather they "satisfice," meaning that they strive for solutions that are satisfactory or adequate.[4] Optimization is simply too difficult.

So far the arguments against the rational model are essentially arguments from practicality—matters of time, cost, complexity, or inability to reach agreement on values and goals. But one writer, Charles Lindblom, has suggested that even in the ideal, the rational model may not be best. He notes that it presumes that the participants in the planning process each consider the totality of goals and objectives and think of which courses of action produce the greatest good. The idea that the various parties go into the planning process guided only by notions of what will be optimum for society as a whole is just unrealistic. Let us admit that we live in a world of partisanship, constituencies, and special interests and not expect the participants to act like candidates for sainthood. May we not, then, get a better result?

The argument Lindblom makes is quite simple. Assume that the participants come into the planning process from various vantage points and that they, to some extent, represent special interests (as opposed to the public interest as a whole). Then it is doubtful that the interests of any major group in the public will be ignored.

> The virtue of such hypothetical division of labor is that every important interest or value has its watchdog. . . . In a society like that of the United States in which individuals are free to combine to pursue almost any possible common interest they might have and in which government agencies are sensitive to the pressures of these groups, the system is approximated. Almost every interest has its watchdog. Without claiming that every interest has a sufficiently powerful watchdog, it can be argued that our system often can assure a more comprehensive regard for

> the values of the whole society than any attempt at intellectual comprehensiveness.[5]

In support of the "watchdog" argument, we note that it has been demonstrated beyond doubt that well-intentioned members of the majority often do not know what is important to members of minorities or how strongly members of minorities may feel. In the 1950s how many whites knew quite how anguished blacks were about the constraints society placed on them? More recently we might ask how many men understood how angry many women were about their limited job opportunities. How many heterosexuals perceived how frustrated gays felt about their second-class status? One can make a credible argument that no group's interests and concerns can be completely understood or advocated by anyone other than members of the group itself. If so, this is a powerful argument that an adversarial and pluralistic planning process may give better results than a unified and nonadversarial one, no matter how well intentioned. And, of course, the phrase *well intentioned* carries a heavy burden of assumption.

Lindblom's argument for an adversarial process is quite consistent with the U.S.'s Anglo-Saxon judicial and political tradition. Our courts function on an adversarial basis. We expect each party's attorney not to attempt to present the facts objectively but within the constraints of the law, to present the strongest possible case for his or her client. We assume that truth will best emerge from this clash of adversaries and we are extremely suspicious of judicial systems in which the roles of judge, prosecution, and defense are combined in a single individual.

Party politics as practiced in the United States and other Western democracies are clearly adversarial. We are highly dubious of any political system in which there is no real clash of adversaries, for we suspect that the outward harmony is a mask for oppression.

In Defense of the Rational Model The defender of the rational model, and there are many among practicing planners and planning educators, might answer some of these points as follows.

Of course values cannot always be clarified fully. But to the extent that they can be clarified, it is wise to do so. Not all parties will always be willing to reveal their real goals in the planning process, but again to the extent that goals can be clearly formulated, it is wise that this be done. We have no shortage of public programs with contradictory and unstated goals and purposes. Perhaps conscientious resort to the rational model might help.[6]

He or she might argue that the point about going back to square one is not such a damning criticism after all. In considering any problem other than the creation of the universe, we must always take some things for granted. How far back we go depends on the importance of the problem, the time and resources available, and other practical considerations. The rational model simply suggests going as far back to square one *as is practical* in a given situation.

The argument regarding the watchdog effect of an adversarial process is not easily countered. However, the defender of the rational process might argue that the need for representation of conflicting views can, in some measure, be accommodated by requiring adequate diversity of interests in the body that does the planning. Given that the planning body is ultimately selected and empowered by the political structure of the community, that responsibility lies with the executive and legislative branches.

Disjointed Incrementalism

Having expressed strong doubts about the rational model, both in terms of feasibility and of underlying theory, its critics have suggested an alternative view of the planning process. The terms *disjointed incrementalism, muddling through,* and *successive limited comparisons* have been used for an alternative approach, of which Lindblom has been the most prominent advocate.[7]

Lindblom believes that value clarification at the outset, though it sounds attractive in principle, is usually not practical. Rather, what counts is achieving agreement on goals. He suggests that the range of possible courses of action not be the very comprehensive one suggested by the rational model. Rather, he argues, the planners should quickly come down to a short list of serious possibilities and focus their efforts on these. He argues that planners and policymakers should be strongly influenced by precedent and by experience and that they should recognize the advantages, in many cases, of policy options that represent marginal or incremental changes from previous policies. The argument for an emphasis on marginal change is twofold. First, a policy that is simply an adjustment or fine-tuning of a previous policy is much more likely to gain acceptance than one that is a radical departure. Second, marginal or incremental adjustments require less knowledge and theory. Even if we do not really know why a policy or a program functions as it does, we can often see that if we adjusted it this way or that it is likely to function better. In Lindblom's phrase the rational model is "greedy for facts."

> . . . it can be constructed only through a great collection of facts. . . . In contrast, the comparative [incremental] method both economizes on the need for facts and directs the analyst's attention to just those facts which are relevant to the fine choices faced by the decision-maker.

The greed for facts is not a small point. Gathering facts takes time and costs money, and sometimes the facts cannot be had no matter how much effort is expended. Similar observations can be made regarding theory. Building theory takes time and money, and sometimes when all is said and done alternate theories will prove equally plausible. What is one to rely on then? Perhaps it is best to rely on the fine-tuning of disjointed incrementalism.

The arguments for the incremental or muddling-through approach are powerful, and even most advocates of the rational model will admit that there are times when incrementalism is the most practical route. But it must be said that there is one important situation in which the incremental approach is no good—the situation in which a decision to move in a new direction must be made. If the problem is new, it is hard to see how an incremental approach can work. In the

1960s the United States began to confront the problem of nuclear waste disposal. There simply was no existing program that could be incrementally adjusted to deal with a problem that had not existed a decade earlier. The proponent of the rational model might argue that the reason we have hundreds of thousands of "hot" fuel rods in temporary storage at dozens of sites around the country is precisely because we took the incremental approach.

The critic of the incremental model might also argue that excessive reliance on the incremental approach can make one excessively dependent on precedent and past experience and thus blind to worthwhile new ideas. Thus heavy reliance on incrementalism can lead one into excessive caution and missed opportunities.

The incrementalist-rational model argument surfaces quite often, though not always in those terms. For example, the U.S. Constitution has a built-in amendment process, and the document has been substantially changed in the last two centuries. Clearly constitutional amendment is an incremental approach. The focus is on that aspect of the Constitution to be changed, not on the document as a whole. In the mid-1980s there was some discussion about a constitutional convention, which would have had the option of a major redrafting (the rational model approach). Those who favored a convention in effect were asserting the view that looking at "the big picture" might lead to major improvement. Those who feared and opposed a convention in effect took the incremental view. They were asserting that the document had served us well so far, that improvements can always be made through the amendment process, and that the risks of a wholesale rewriting were not worth the possible gains. Even though the rational model-incrementalist vocabulary was not invoked, that was the real subject of the argument.

To some extent the choice between the rational model and incremental model may be an expression of one's willingness to take risks. The rational model may hold out the hope of big gains because going back to the beginning may yield a new and much superior approach. But if one goes back to the beginning and gets things all wrong, there is the possibility of big losses. The incremental approach, by holding fast to the handrail of experience and precedent, tends to reduce the chances both of big gains and big losses. Table 19-1 summarizes the circumstances in which one might favor either the rational model or the incremental approach.

Middle-Range Models

The rational model and disjointed incrementalism represent opposite poles. Various intermediate approaches have also been proposed, perhaps the best known of which is "mixed scanning" by sociologist Amitai Etzioni.[8]

The idea is quite simple. Etzioni advocates a two-step process. In the first step a general scanning process is conducted to get the overall picture and to decide which elements merit more detailed examination. Etzioni uses the analogy of a weather monitoring system using space satellites.

TABLE 19–1 Which Model to Use

Favors Rational Model	*Favors Incremental Model*
Adequate theory available	Adequate theory lacking
New question	Modification of old question
Resources generous	Resources limited
Substantial time for study	Limited time for study
Numerous relations to other policy issues	Few relations to other policy issues
Wide range of policies might be politically acceptable	Policy options highly limited by political realities

> The rationalistic approach [rational model] would seek an exhaustive survey of weather conditions . . . by scheduling reviews of the entire sky as often as possible. This would yield an avalanche of details, costly to analyze and likely to overwhelm our action capabilities.

He then goes on to contrast the rational model approach with his mixed scanning approach.

> A mixed scanning strategy would include elements of both approaches . . . a broad angle camera that would cover all parts of the sky but not in great detail and a second one which would zero in on those areas revealed by the first camera to require more examination. While mixed scanning might miss areas in which a detailed camera could reveal trouble, it is less likely than incrementalism to miss obvious trouble spots in unfamiliar areas.

Etzioni elaborates on his model by pointing out that the scanning process might actually have more than one stage. We might scan a large field quickly and then, depending on what we had learned, scan a smaller field somewhat more thoroughly. But the basic idea is unchanged. We scan to find those areas that are then suitable for more detailed analysis. When we have located the area that deserves fine scrutiny, a systematic approach such as that of the rational model is appropriate.

Etzioni argues that his model avoids the excessive commitment to precedent and past experience inherent in the incremental model. At the same time, it is far more feasible than a doctrinaire rational model approach: "The strategy [mixed scanning] combines a detailed ('rationalistic') examination of some sectors—which, unlike the detailed examination of the entire area, is feasible—with a 'truncated' review of other sectors."

Etzioni's mixed scanning has generally received a favorable response from planners interested in the how-to-plan or what-is-planning questions. For one thing, it seems to describe a fair amount of what planners actually do. The working planner is likely to spend a little time looking around very broadly, narrow his or her options very quickly, and focus intently on a small range of possibilities. Then, too, both the rational model and the incremental model have obvious strengths and obvious weaknesses. Etzioni's synthesis appears to allow the user the strengths of both models while minimizing their weaknesses.

If we wanted to criticize mixed scanning we might say that perhaps it is little more than what sensible and nondogmatic people do anyway. Most working planners cannot afford to take either the rational model or the incremental model as gospel and will necessarily use some synthesis of the two. Etzioni has simply formalized and made explicit that synthesis.

PLANNING AND IDEOLOGY

In this section we discuss ideologically based criticisms of planning—both the idea of planning and planning as actually practiced. The reader will note that there is a certain amount of national or systemwide material in this section, which may seem puzzling in view of the fact that the focus of this book is at the municipal level. But this larger focus is necessary because much of the ideological debate about planning, even as practiced in small jurisdictions, is based on different views of the nation's political and economic system.

The right-wing criticism that falls on city, town or regional planning does so largely because planning in that particular sense happens to be in the general target area. Specifically, almost any sort of public planning requires some replacement of signals from the marketplace with the calculations of planners, technicians, bureaucrats, and others. For example, we noted earlier how zoning may interfere with the workings of the market by preventing those uses that, in a pure market situation, the property owner would choose on the basis of profitability. The person of the right, almost by definition, is one who is convinced of the wisdom of markets and of the efficacy of Adam Smith's "invisible hand." He or she is likely to see the inefficiency and loss of personal freedom in centrally planned economies not as accidents but as inevitable concomitants of excessive central control and of insufficient reliance on markets. With such a general world view, one is likely to view specific instances of planning with a certain degree of suspicion.

The criticism from the left, in contrast, has not been directed at planning in general. By and large, the replacement of market decision making by political decision making is part of the agenda of the left. In fact, a preference for planning as opposed to markets is one of the left's defining characteristics. Rather, the left's criticism has often been directed quite specifically at municipal planning as currently practiced.

There is also another difference in the attacks from the right and the left. The criticism from the right, by and large, comes from people who are not trained as planners and who have not practiced as planners. This is hardly surprising, for if one disdains the idea of planning, one is not likely to acquire formal training in it nor seek employment in it. On the other hand, much of the criticism from the left comes from within the profession, not so much from practitioners but from planning educators—people who are trained in planning and in a number of cases who also have some experience as practitioners.

The View from the Right

The right-wing criticism makes two main points. First, it is argued that the marketplace does a better job of allocating resources than does planning. A modern economy involves thousands of different intermediate and final goods and, every day, millions of transactions. For this vast activity to be planned would require a degree of competence and foresight that it is unrealistic to expect from any organization. Then, too, it can be argued that performing this great task of planning would, beyond the issue of technical competence, make the virtually impossible demand that the planners know the preferences and interests of all those for whom they plan. The opponent of planning will argue that the market, because it is decentralized, requires no such knowledge of either objective facts or personal preferences. He or she would also argue that the decentralization of the marketplace permits more rapid adjustment to changes than does a centralized system. Surpluses and shortages, price rises and falls, send quick and unambiguous signals to suppliers of goods and services. Can anything unplanned provide both stability and easy adjustment to changed conditions? The free market proponent would answer yes and might ask the doubter to consider an ecosystem such as a forest. No one planned it, yet it displays great stability over time, and should some external condition, say, the amount of rainfall, change, the ecosystem will change smoothly and quickly.

These arguments might be supplemented by comments on the administrative costs of central planning and the general slowness of bureaucratic decision making. Finally, the opponent of planning (the term here is used in its generic sense) might ask those who doubt his or her argument to consider the real world. Which economies seem to function smoothly and which seem bedeviled with shortages and dislocations?

Perhaps more important to the proponent of the free market than efficiency is the view that economic and political freedom are inseparable. The conservative economist and Nobel Prize winner, Milton Friedman, argues,

> The kind of economic organization that provides economic freedom directly, namely, competitive capitalism, also promotes political freedom because it separates economic power from political power and in this way enables one to offset the other.
>
> Historical evidence speaks with a single voice on the relation between political freedom and a free market. I know of no example in time or place of a society that has been marked by a large measure of political freedom, and that has not also used something comparable to a free market to organize the bulk of economic activity.[9]

Note that Friedman's claim is a limited one. Although he states that the marketplace is necessary for political freedom, he does not state that it guarantees freedom—only that its absence guarantees the absence of freedom. Note, also, the phrase *bulk of economic activity*. He does not argue that all economic activity must be in the market sector for political freedom to prevail.

How might the planner of centrist political persuasion respond? One line of argument would be to grant the generality of the argument but point to two very important caveats.

1. *Public goods.* Some goods and services must be provided outside the market because it is either impractical or impossible to create markets for them. National defense cannot be provided through market mechanisms because either everyone is defended or no one is defended. Therefore the nonpayer or "free rider" is as well served as the individual who pays. The lighthouse is often cited as a good that must be provided publicly because one is equally able to see the light whether one pays or does not pay. Since a market cannot be created, the good or service is either provided publicly or not at all. Other goods, such as city streets could, in principle, be provided through market mechanisms. But the difficulty of doing so renders the idea impractical.
2. *Externalities* or *spillovers.* If the good or service in question visits substantial effects on parties who are not represented in the transaction, the market, even though it produces optimal results when we consider only the interests of buyer and seller, will produce suboptimal results for society as a whole. As noted earlier, third-party effects related to land use are one of the principal justifications for zoning.

These ideas about public goods and externalities or spillovers are hardly radical. They can be found in any standard economics text. They suggest that the market necessarily has its limits and thus that some degree of planning is inevitable. The issue then is not whether to plan or not to plan but rather about how and how much to plan.

The planner might push the point further and argue that the conservative ought to favor timely public planning efforts on the grounds that dealing with problems early will alleviate the pressure for radical change later.[10] As we shall see, some radicals have castigated planners for performing exactly that function.

With regard to the issue of political freedom, the centrist might also grant the basic conservative argument but still raise an important caveat. He or she might argue that the sort of planning described in this book is hardly comparable with the sort of centralized planning that was practiced in the former Soviet Union. The difference in degree, it might be argued, is so great as to constitute a real difference in kind. The word *planning* is applied to both but we should not be misled by that semantic similarity.

The hand of the planner is far more evident in the Netherlands than it is in the United States and there is far more public control there over the use of privately owned land. The results that the traveler sees in both city and country-side are often quite admirable. It is hard to name another place in the world where land is better and more efficiently used. Yet the Netherlands is just as much a functioning democracy as is the United States.

In summary, the centrist could argue that he or she can agree with the right in its general view of central planning and the relationship between economic and political freedom. Yet he or she can still argue that in a capitalist democracy like the United States, planning is a necessary and useful activity to which the enlightened conservative should not object.

The View from the Left

In the 1970s the planning profession and planning as practiced began to come under heavy criticism from the political far left. Much of the attack came from what might loosely be called neo-Marxism. Marxist theories made a comeback in academe during the 1970s and 1980s. The radical might argue that this was due to their inherent virtue. The skeptic might respond that the cause was historical, namely, the radicalizing effect of the Vietnam War. How much deradicalizing effect, the collapse of Socialism in Eastern Europe and the former Soviet Union will have remains to be seen.

The radical position is not a majority position among planning educators but it is much more common among planning educators than among planning practitioners. One reason is that in a great many planning jobs, although not all, radicals would feel uncomfortable because they would be cooperating with a system that they did not respect and achieving ends to which they could not feel fully committed. That sort of psychological dissonance is not easy to live with over the long term.

What is the radical view? America's liberal capitalism, or welfare capitalism as it has been called, is regarded rather dimly (though many radicals will concede it to be more humane than the capitalism of earlier years). It is seen as still containing vast and inexcusable extremes of wealth and poverty and as largely dominated by and therefore run for the benefit of the capitalist class (bourgeoisie). It is also believed that the working class or the "masses" accept the system largely because they have been prevented from seeing the truth by those who control the flow of information and ideas. In this view the media and the educational system disguise reality and convey a picture that is favorable to the interests of the capitalists because they are owned or controlled by or in some way beholden to the capitalists. It is thus a view that is profoundly cynical about the system as it now exists.

Fainstein and Fainstein, two planning educators, set forth the radical view as five propositions:[11]

1. The capitalists organize the state to serve their own interests. They quote Marx and Engels: "The state is nothing more than the form of organization the bourgeoisie necessarily adopt for internal and external purposes." In this view the state is simply the agent or "executive committee" of those who own capital.
2. "Planning is necessary to the ruling class in order to facilitate accumulation and maintain social control." The "ruling class" through its creature, the state, uses planners both to facilitate economic activity and growth and to deal with problems that, if left untended, might cause social instability, which would threaten the wealth and security of the capitalists.
3. Planners are agents of the state. Either they are directly employed by the state or if not, as in the case of consultants and the like, they still dance to a tune called by the state. (They bid for contracts let by the state, they prepare plans needed by the state, etc.)

4. "Urban planners specialize in managing the contradictions of capitalism." The term *contradiction* here does not have the meaning it has in logic, that is, a situation in which both of two statements cannot be true. Rather it is used in the Marxian sense of conflict. If *monopoly capitalism*, to use a term that appears frequently in Marxist literature, necessitates that some low-income housing needs to be leveled to make way for industrial or commercial development, the planner will help deal with the consequences for the poor and thus deflect some of their anger. This is the social control concept noted in proposition 2.
5. "Planners depoliticize." That is, they state in technical terms issues that would otherwise be cast in political terms. By so doing they tend to legitimize much that the radical thinks is not legitimate. They wrap exploitation of one sort or another in a disguise of technical language and mathematics. For example, suppose the issue at hand is whether to spend a given sum of money available for local economic development on subsidizing the training of poor residents of a community in basic job skills or subsidizing the building of an office for a major industrial conglomerate. To the radical this looks like an issue of class conflict. The planner is likely to convert the issue to statements about numbers: so many jobs, so many tax dollars, and the like.

For the radical who sees the situation in these terms, the question is "What is a planner to do?" He or she might subscribe to the view that worse is better—the idea that the worse things are, the more chance there is for radical change. In that case there is little room for cooperation with the system. Fainstein and Fainstein take a more moderate stance, perhaps partly because of their view that the short-term prospects for radical change in the United States are extremely small. They take a "better is better" position, asserting that the radical planner can in good conscience cooperate with the system on projects that in some way help the working class even if only in small ways. They also take the view that "expansion of the state is more likely to mark a transition to socialism than its alternative." On that basis alone they tend to favor courses of action that expand the role of planned activity relative to market activity.

Like Marxism itself, the radical critics of planning have devoted more effort to discussion of the existing system than to suggesting the details of alternative policies.[12] In general, radicals would assign a much larger role to the public sector and a correspondingly smaller role to the private sector. Issues such as where industrial plants are to be located would be decided in some collective manner rather than simply by managers and stockholders. Most radicals would favor a more equal distribution of income and wealth than now exists. Many radicals would favor a considerable public role in the setting of prices, profits, and wages. Many radicals would transfer political power downward toward neighborhoods and small groups to counterbalance the power of capital. But many others would not, for "power to the people," if that means small groups and local groups, is antithetical to the idea of planning on a large scale. In general, and with some exceptions, the radical critique is more an attack on the present than a roadmap to the future.

How might the nonradical respond? He or she might begin simply by questioning the most basic assumptions of the critique. For example the nonradical might assert the basic goodness rather than badness of the system, perhaps by comparing it with other systems. He or she might argue that the amenability of the system to a long series of reforms and ameliorative measures, from the abolition of child labor to food stamps for the poor—says something very positive about the system. If one finds the system to be good, on balance, then one should have no overarching problems of conscience in cooperating with it. Beyond this overall judgment, the nonradical might attack the radical critique by asserting the pluralism of society. Although admitting that capitalists do indeed exercise much influence over the state, the nonradical might note that other groups, including labor, academe, federal and local government workers, and so on, also exercise major influence over the actions of the state.[13] He or she might thus deny the basic Marxist postulate that the state is the "executive committee" of the bourgeoisie. If it is true that the state, by virtue of this pluralism, does not confine its services in the main to a single small class, there is little reason to be troubled about serving it.

Finally, the centrist might argue that the radical critique regarding the planner as a co-opter or a disarmer of discontent is not a very strong argument. Rather, it is an obviously true statement cast in a negative way. If one satisfies grievances, whether they be about poverty, housing, or some much smaller matter such as street noise or the need for a new stoplight at the corner, of course one is reducing discontent and the possibility of disorder. But what is wrong with that? Should we deny food to the hungry lest when their stomachs are full they will lose their righteous anger about being hungry?

The centrist might also agree with the radical that the planner does indeed depoliticize and cast what could be political issues in technical terms. But does not reducing the political heat and introducing some facts and numbers increase the chances of harmonious and rational solutions? In short, is not depoliticizing a good thing to do?

Finally, the centrist might suggest that the radical academic who takes the planning profession to task for not waging the fight for radical change is asking the working planner to take risks that he or she is not required to take. As the planning educator Michael Brooks has said,

> Certainly the progressive spirit thrives more readily in the halls of academe—where there is virtually no risk attached to its espousal—than it does in the nation's city halls.[14]

The radical critique has unsettled many planners, for many people go into the profession out of idealism. Thus a critique that accuses the profession of allowing itself to be used as the tool of an unjust system tends to cause some soul searching and psychic pain. To the extent that such pain causes productive introspection by the profession it is useful. To the extent that it demoralizes it is not so useful. As suggested, how seriously one takes the radical critique depends on what basic assumptions one holds about the U.S. political and economic system—

whether or not one holds it to be basically good and whether or not one sees it as dominated by a single class.

SUMMARY

Approaches to the act of planning are (1) the rational model, (2) incrementalism, and (3) a mid-level approach as exemplified by "mixed scanning."

The rational model prescribes a comprehensive-approach, which begins with problem definition and proceeds through value clarification to selection of goals, formulation of alternative possible actions, forecasting the consequences of those actions, selection of a course of action, detailed plan formulation, and evaluation and modification. The model is comprehensive and systematic. It is designed to begin at square one and proceed to an optimum choice of actions. The model can be regarded as the orthodox view. It has been subjected to a variety of criticisms. Some have asserted that it is unrealistic and may ignore valid interests and considerations that would be taken into account in a planning process that placed less emphasis on system and optimization and more on reaching agreement among disparate and contending parties.

The incremental approach, of which Charles Lindblom is the best-known proponent, stresses reaching agreement, making incremental adjustments, and relying on precedent. For reasons discussed at length, he suggests that the use of the rational model is often neither possible nor wise.

The mixed scanning introduced by Amitai Etzioni is essentially a synthesis of these two approaches. It involves a less than complete scan of the situation followed by the application of a comprehensive approach to only parts of the total problem. It has been generally well received by planners, in part because it appears to describe a process that many planners actually follow.

Criticism of planning from the right has generally been based on a view that market mechanisms are more efficient allocators of resources than are administrative decisions. Some antipathy on the right also comes from the view that political freedom is most likely to flourish in an environment in which decisions about the allocation of resources are made privately rather than collectively.

Criticism of planning from the left has not been directed at planning as an idea but rather at the manner in which planning is perceived to be done in the United States. Specifically, radicals have claimed that planning as practiced supports the interest of the capitalist class (which the left sees as the dominant class) and that it papers over major injustices and disparities in wealth and power with minor reforms and palliatives.

The chapter suggested the manner in which the planner of a more or less centrist ideological persuasion might respond to criticisms from right and left. How one views planning cannot be separated from one's overall political and ideological position.

NOTES

1. John Maynard Keynes, *The General Theory of Employment, Interest and Money*, first published in 1936. The quote is from the last page of the final chapter.

2. This example is taken, with some modification, from Edward C. Banfield, "Ends and Means in Planning," in *A Reader in Planning Theory*, Andreas Faludi, ed., Pergamon Press, New York, 1973.
3. For a description of the rational model, see Martin Meyerson and Edward C. Banfield, "Supplement: Note on Conceptual Scheme," *Politics, Planning and the Public Interest*, The Free Press, Glencoe, IL, 1955, pp. 314ff.
4. The term was invented by Herbert Simon. See his *Administrative Behavior*, Macmillan & Co., New York, 1955.
5. Charles E. Lindblom, "The Science of Muddling Through," *Public Administration Review*, Spring 1959. Reprinted in *A Reader in Planning Theory*, 1st ed., Andreas Faludi, ed., Pergamon Press, 1973, p. 163.
6. A commonly cited example of this sort of contradiction is federal housing policy. We have, over the years, spent many billions of federal funds through Urban Renewal, Community Development, Urban Development Action Grants, housing subsidies, and the like to restore the economic vitality of central cities. We also have a federal tax code that provides very powerful incentives to the construction of suburban housing. To some degree the contradictions may exist because we do not have a unified planning process for federal urban policy. The committees that write the tax law, for example, are not the same as the committees that write the housing and economic development legislation, nor is there any statutory requirement that they consult each other.
7. Lindblom, op. cit.
8. "Mixed Scanning: A 'Third' Approach to Decision Making," in Faludi, ed., op. cit., pp. 217–30.
9. Milton Friedman, *Capitalism and Freedom*, University of Chicago Press, Chicago, 1962.
10. For example, it has often been suggested that the reformist initiatives such as unemployment insurance, the right to collective bargaining, and the Social Security system during the Great Depression of the 1930s may well have prevented radical social change in the United States.
11. Norman I. Fainstein and Susan S. Fainstein, "New Debates in Urban Planning: The Impact of Marxist Theory Within the U.S.," *International Journal of Urban and Regional Research*, vol. 3, no. 3, 1979, pp. 381–402. Reprinted in *Critical Readings in Planning Theory*, Chris Paris, ed., Pergamon, Press, New York, 1982, pp. 147–74.
12. For essays on what a left-wing political and social agenda might be, see Martin Carnoy and Derek Shearer, *Economic Democracy*, M. E. Sharpe, Inc., Armonk, NY, 1980. See also works by Michael Harrington, Barry Bluestone, Bennett Harrison, and David M. Gordon.
13. For essays that discuss the rise of other centers of power in society, particularly academe and bureaucracy, see R. Bruce-Briggs, ed., *The New Class*, Transaction Books, New Brunswick, NJ, 1979.
14. Michael Brooks, "Four Critical Junctures in the History of The Urban Planning Profession," *Journal of the American Planning Association*, Spring, 1988, pp. 241–8.

SELECTED BIBLIOGRAPHY

FALUDI, ANDREAS, ED., *A Reader in Planning Theory*, Pergamon Press, New York, 1973.

FRIEDMAN, JOHN, *Planning in the Public Domain*, Princeton University Press, Princeton, NJ, 1987.

MEYERSON, MARTIN, and BANFIELD, EDWARD C., *Politics, Planning and the Public Interest*, The Free Press, Glencoe, IL, 1955.

INDEX

Abandonment of housing, 24
Abrams, Charles, 182
Acid rain, 243, 249
Advocacy planning, 83
Agriculture, production in, 9, 22
Air quality, trends in, 244
Albuquerque, 204
Alonso, William, 226
Altschuler, Alan, 82
American Institute of Architects (AIA), 89
American League for Civic Improvement (National League of Improvement Associations prior to 1900), 35
American Public Transport Association, 208
Anderson, Martin, 181
Appalachian region, 211
Aquifer recharge area, 255, 257
Architectural Board of Review, 128
"Arcology," 157
Arcosanti, 157
Army Corps of Engineers, 285, 286, 296
Assessment of real property, 116, 132
Atlanta Regional Planning Commission, 267
Austin, TX, 214
Automobile ownership, 18, 40, 196, 259

Babbitt, Bruce, Secretary of Interior, 74
Baldwin, John H., 251, 265
Baltimore:
  Inner Harbour, 183
  Urban Homesteading and, 186
Banfield, Edward C., 82, 86, 87, 315
Barret, Jonathan, 158
Bassett, Edward M., 41, 66
Battery Park City, N.Y., 137–42
Bauman, Gus, 125
Beckman, Norman, 86
Benefit/cost analysis, 202, 219, 252
Benevolo, Leonardo, 158
Berman vs. *Parker*, 179
Bluestone, Barry, 222, 312
Bonds (financing), 167–170
  Industrial Revenue Bonds (IRBs) and Industrial Development Bonds (IDBs), 212, 223
Bork, Robert H., 53
Bosselman, Frederick, 129, 136
Boston, 13, 24, 65, 128, 204
  Metropolitan Planning Commission, 44
  Waterfront, 182
Boulder, CO, 232
Brambilla, R., 158
Branch, Melville C., 106
Broad Acre City, 154
Bronx River Parkway, 16, 290
Brown, A. Theodore, 29
Brown vs. *Board of Education*, Supreme Court Decision, 1954, 90
Bruce-Briggs, R., 313
Buck, Peter L., 76
Bucks County, Penn., 232
Burchell, Robert W., 97
Bureau of Land Management (BLM), 296
Bureau of Public Roads, 290
Bureau of Reclamation, 285, 286
Burnham, Daniel, 37, 38
Burrows, Lawrence B., 241
Bush, George H.W., Pres.:
  environmental policy, 261
  housing policy, 189
  tax policy, 74
  transportation policy, 207

Callies, David, 129
Callow, Alexander B., 26
Capital budget, Capital expenditure. *See* Public capital investment
Capital facility planning, 159–75
Carnoy, Martin, 312
Carson, Rachel, 57
Catanese, Anthony J., 82, 87
Central city:
  accessibility, 108
  decline, 24
  population trends, 7, 15
  poverty, 21–23
Centralized planning, 310
Centrally planned economy, 55
Central Park, New York, 32
Centroid, 288
Chapin, F. Stuart, 100, 106
Chicago, 36, 266
  Plan of 1909, 38, 79
Chicago Area Transportation Study (CATS), 57, 200
Christenson, James A., 194
Circulation system, 97, 101, 141, 197
Citizen participation, 79, 85
City Beautiful movement, 36–38
City Realty Corporations, 179
Ciucci, Dal Co, 158
Civic art, 35
Clarke, Michael, 265
Clean Air Act, 58
  amendments, 74, 246, 249
Clean Water Act of 1972, 246
Cleveland, 23
Climate. *See* "Greenhouse effect"
Clinton, William, Pres., 189, 213, 261, 277
Coastal Zone Management Act, 249
Cohort survival method, 99, 161
Colorado River Basin Compact, 55, 284
Columbia, Tenn., 214
Columbian Exposition, Chicago, 1893, 36–37
Coolidge, Calvin, President, 289
Commoner, Barry, 57
Community Development, 176–93
Community Development Block Grants (CDBG), 185
Competitiveness Council, Bush administration and, 263
Comprehensive Environmental Response, Compensation and Liability Act (CERCLA), also known as "Superfund," 247
Comprehensive plan, 96–106, 159, *See also* Master plan.
Computer:
  in capital facilities planning, 162, 164–65
  in transportation planning, 198–202

Congress of United States:
  on Area Redevelopment Administration(ARA), 211
  on community development, 183
  on Economic Development Administration, 211
  on National Defense Highway Act, 198
  on National Environmental Policy Act (NEPA), 244
  Research Service, 177
  on Urban Development Action Grants (UDAG), 186, 212
  on Urban Renewal, 177
Conn, David, 249
Constitutional framework (U.S.), 62, 306
Corporate Average Fuel Efficiency (CAFE) standards, 75
Council on Environmental Quality, 244
Council of Governments (COGs), 267

Davidoff, Paul, 83
Davis, Calif., 232, 259
Debt limits, municipal, 24
Decentralization:
  employment, 21
  manufacturing, 16
  population, 14
"Defense of privilege," 231
DeGrove, John M., 241
Denver, 240
Depression. *See* Great Depression
Development agreements, 127
Dickey, John W., 208
Dillon, John F., 62
Dinkins, David, Mayor, 23
Down, Anthony, 202–204
Duany, Andres, 150, 154

Easement, 113
Easley, Gail, 127
Eastern Europe, events in, 52
Economic base studies, 101
Economic Development Administration (EDA), 211
Economic development agencies, 213–15
"Edge City," 293
Ehrlich, Paul, 59
Eichner, Alfred, 210
Emergency Financial Control Board (EFCB), 23
Eminent domain, 63, 113, 145, 179, 217
Energy planning, 58, 258–61
Energy bill of 1992, 262
Environmental Impact Statement (EIS), 58, 247–49
Environmental Land and Water Management Act, 1972, 238
Environmental planning, 57–58, 242–65
Environmental Protection Agency (EPA), 58, 246, 249
Environmental quality, trends in, 244–45
Equalization rate, 132, 175
Equity-efficiency trade-off, 212
Erie Canal, 209
Etzioni, Amitai, 306–308
Euclid vs. *Ambler*, 67
Eutrophication, 253–55
Evans, James H., 170
Exactions, 127
Exhaust emissions, monitoring of, 262
Externalities, 130, 133, 310

Fainstein, Norman I. and Susan S., 311
Fairfax County, Va., 112, 234–35
Fairfield County, Conn., 130, 223
Faludi, Andreas, 87, 315
Fannie Mae, 294
Farley, Josh, 214
Federal Aid Highway Act of 1956, 291
Federal Aid Road Act of 1916, 290
"Federal bulldozer" re: Urban Renewal, 77, 180, 293
Federal grants, political ideology and, 73
Federal Housing Administration (FHA), 17, 294
Federal ownership of land, 280
Federal Water Pollution Control Act (FWPCA), 249
Fifth Amendment, 63
Financial stake in planning (vested interest), 78
First Pacific Railway Act of 1862, 282
Fiscal impact analysis, 115, 219
Fiscal problems, local, 23–24, 97, 170, 230
Fiscal zoning, 97
Floor Area Ratio (FAR), 111, 126
Flory, Charles F., 66
Ford, Henry, 15
Ford, James, 13
Fort Collins, Colo., 235–36
Frederick, Kenneth D., and Roger A. Sedjo, 298
"Freeway revolt," 203
Frieden, Bernard J., 231
Friedman, Milton, 309
Frost Belt, 19–20
Fuller, R. Buckminister, 154

Galleria, White Plains, N.Y., 109
Gans, Herbert J., 82
Garreaux, Joel, 293
General Motors, Saturn plant location, 214
General Revenue Sharing, 73
Gentrification, 182, 192
Geographic Information Systems (GIS), 100
Giarranti, Frank, 20
Gist, John, 73
Glabb, Charles N., 26, 29
Glenpoint development, Teaneck, N.J., 125
Glickman, Norman J., 214
Godschalk, David R., 241
Gordon, David M., 312
Gore, Albert, Vice President, 263
Gramm-Rudman Amendment, 186
Grants, federal, 71–73
Gravity model, 201
Great Depression, 15–18, 47–52, 276, 289, 290, 294, 315
"Greenhouse effect," 243, 263
Greer, Guy, 54, 178
Gridiron, street pattern, 30, 182
Ground water, contamination of, 254
Group homes, 89
Growth management, defined, 224
Growth management planning, 224–41

Hadachek vs. *Sebastian*, 65
Hand, Irving, 267
Hansen, Alvin W., 54, 178
Harr, Charles, 133
Harrigan, John J., 87
Harrington, Michael, 312
Harris, Jack C., 64
Harrison, Bennett, 222, 312
Harrison, N.Y., 116, 130–31
Hartford, Conn., 128
Hatry, Harry P., 170
Hausman, Baron von, 134
Health hazard, 96, 171
Hefland, Gary, 87
Highway Act of 1954, 198
Highway Trust Fund, 196
Historic preservation, 124, 129
Historical statistics of the United States, 7
Hofstadter, Richard, William Miller, and Daniel Aaron, 282
Homestead Act of 1862, 281
Honolulu, 236
Hoover Dam, 285, 286
Hoover, Edgar M., 20
Hoover, Herbert: Model state zoning ordinance, 41
Housing, 11–12, 179–93, 220, 229–30
  public, 54, 301
Housing Act of 1949, 54, 56, 178, 192
Housing Action Plan (HAP), 185, 190
Housing and Community Development Act, 1974, 185
Housing reform, 33
Housing and Urban Development (HUD), 4, 90, 189, 190
Howard, Ebenezer, 46–49

"Ice Tea"; *see* Intermodal Surface Transportation Efficiency Act of 1991
Ickes, Harold, 53
Impact analysis, 103
Incrementalism, 301, 305–306
Incubation of industries, 181, 193
Induced demand, 203
Industrial parks, 217–20
"Industrial Policy," 213
Industrial Revolution, 9, 143
Infrastructure, 100, 160, 218, 228, 235
Intergovernmental aid, 71–73
Intermodal Surface Transportation Efficiency Act (ISTEA) of 1991, 205–207
International Earth Summit of 1992, 263
Interstate Commerce Clause, 222
Interstate Highway System, 18, 54, 131, 197, 205, 290–94

Jacobs, Allan, 87
Jacobs, Jane, 122, 148
Johnson, Willard R., 225
Johnston, Robert A., 125

Kahn, Anna Reines, 125
Kain, John F., 22
Kaiser, Edward J., 99, 133
Kamieniecki, Sheldon, 265
Kemp, Jack, 189
Kent, T.J., 106
Keynes, John Maynard, 299
Krueckeberg, Donald A.,
Krumholtz, Norman, 93, 98

Land capability analysis, 251
Landfills, 255–58
Land use:
  controls on, 78, 103, 107, 110–30, 145
  economic development and, 217–18
  energy planning and, 258–60
  growth management and, 224, 226–30, 232–39
  holding zones and, 232
  inventory of, 100
  pattern of, 3, 98, 186–87, 196–99
  regional planning and, 2, 196–99, 275–76
  transportation and, 196, 197–98
  water quality and, 253–55
Land values, 108–109, 177
Largo, Fla., 126
Larsen, Wendy U., 119
Le Corbusier, 154, 157–58
L'Enfant, Washington D.C., 30
Letchworth Garden City, 49
Leuchtenberg, William, 53
Lincoln Center, New York, 182
Lindblom, Charles, 303–304
Listokin, David, 97
Local Public Agencies (LPAs) re: Urban Renewal, 179–80
London, 144
Long Island, N.Y., 113
Los Angeles, Calif., 44, 65
Lucas vs. *South Carolina Coastal Council*, 121
Lynch, Kevin, 140

Mandelkar, Daniel R., 65, 76
Manhattan, 66, 108, 139–43, 182
Maniere-Elia, Tafurri, 158
Marxist view of planning, 83, 311–14
Mass transit system, 108
  planning for, 204
Master plan, 43–44, 88–94, 218, 233, 235, 236. *See also* Comprehensive Plan
McDowell, Bruce D., 267
McFarland, Carter M., 18, 294
McHarg, Ian, 251–52, 265
McKelvey, Blake, 26, 34, 79
McKenzie, Richard B., 222
Metropolitan areas, population of, 17
Meyerson, Martin, 82, 87, 301, 315
Microelectronics and Computer Corp., 214
Millar, Annie, 170
Mills, Edwin, 14
Minneapolis, 148
Minneapolis-St. Paul, 266, 270–76
Mixed scanning, 306–308
Mobile homes, 119
"Model" (mathematical), 162–65, 198–202
Moore, James D., 125
Moore, William Douglas, 64
Moriarty, Brian J., 223
Morrill Land Grant Act, 281
Morris, A.E.J., 158
Morris, David, 265
Mortgage insurance, 17–18, 294
"Mother-in-law" apartments, 90
Mount Laurel I, II, and III, 119–20
Mugler vs. *Kansas*, 65
Mumford, Lewis, 47, 134
Municipal Art Movement, 35

National Air Quality Standards (NAAQS), 249
National Association for the Advancement of Colored People (NAACP), 90, 118
National Defense Highway Act of 1956, 18, 54, 57, 198
National Environmental Protection Act of 1969 (NEPA), 58, 145, 244, 246
National Resources Planning Board (NRPB), 55, 279, 296
Neighbourhood, concept of, 148, 149–50
"neotraditional" planning, 152
Netherlands, planning in, 279
Newark, Port of, 269
"New Class" in environmental conflict, 231
New England Regional Commission, 55
New Federalism of Reagan administration, 74, 102
Newman, Oscar, 97
New towns, 42, 54
New York City, 7, 19, 23, 33, 40, 42, 44, 122, 123, 139, 266
  port of, 269
  metropolitan area, 293
  Regional Plan Association, 44, 266
  regional transportation system, 44
  subway system, 205
  Tenement Housing Act of 1901, 33
  Westway, 203, 248
  zoning ordinance, 40, 66, 68
Nolen, John, 44
Nonmetropolitan growth, 25
Nonpoint sources, pollution, 253
Norris, George, Senator, 288

O'Brien, Robert, 265
Oglethorpe, James, 28–29
Olmstead, Frederick Law, 32–33
Olmstead, Frederick Law, Jr., 37
Open space, 29, 30, 143, 252
Options on land purchase, 114, 217
Ordinance of 1785, 280
Osborn, F.J., 49
Owner occupied housing, tax treatment of, 295
Overcrowding of housing, 11, 190–91

Pacific Northwest Regional Planning Commission, 55
Paris, 134–35, 155
Parking facilities, 109
Parks, 34–35, 143, 150
Parkways, 16
Pasadena growth moratorium, 233–34
Pedestrian-friendly streets, 153
Penn, William, Philadelphia, 28, 30
Perkins, Dexter and Glyndon G. Van Deusen, 282
Perry, Clarence, 149
Peterson, John A., 31
Phalen, Tam, 127

Philadelphia 30, 28, 232
Pierce, Samuel J., 189
Planned communities, 42, 146–47
Planned unit development (PUD), 125–26, 145, 235
Planner,
as advocate, 83
as agent of radical change, 83
background of, 4
as builder of community consensus, 82
education of, 4
as entrepreneur, 82
as neutral public servant, 82
Planning:
goals of, 3, 97–98
and politics, 77–86
Pre-revolutionary, 27–29
Planning agency, structure of, 84–85
Planning enabling legislation, 69–71
Planning process, 79–81, 82–84, 98–104, 139–44, 301–308
Plous, F.K., Jr., 205
Police power, 64, 110, 228
Pollution. *See also* Solid waste management; Ground Water, contamination of
and economic considerations, 249–50
export of, 265
legislation pertaining to, 246–48
nonpoint sources of, 253
political concern with, 58
progress in control of, 243, 244
Population:
change by region, 20
control, 58, 226
decline of urban, 19
density, 10–12, 14, 32
forecast (projection), 99, 160, 161, 195, 254, 256
Port Authority of New York and New Jersey, 269
Pred, Alan, 10, 209
Preferential tax, 232
Pre-Revolutionary planning in America, 27–29
Preservation, 187
historic, 124, 187
"prior appropriation," doctrine of, 287
Private property, public control of, 64–68, 107–108
"Proffers," 234
Property rights, 80
Property tax, 78, 97, 116–17, 163, 188, 192, 215, 218, 228, 270. *See also* Assessment
Proposition 13, California, 60, 101, 163
Prospect Park, Brooklyn, N.Y., 32
Pruitt-Igoe, St. Louis, 89
Public capital investment, 107–109, 114, 145, 159, 177, 185, 216–17, 228, 250, 255, 270
Public finance. *See also* Capital investment; Grants; Property taxes; Subsidies
debt limitations, 23
tax limitations, 23
Public goods, 310
Public health and safety, 96–97, 171
Public interest, 83
Public utilities. *See* Capital investment
Public welfare, 64, 96–97, 119
Pushkarev, Boris, 158

Quayle, Daniel, Vice Pres., 263

Rubushka, Alvin, 163
Radburn, N.J., 42–43
Railroads, land grants for, 281–82
Ramapo, N.Y., 226–30
Rational model, 301–305
Raymond, George M., 124
Reagan, Ronald, President
and cutbacks in local funding, 59
environmental policy of, 261
housing policy of, 189
and UDAG program, 186
"reclaiming" the desert, 286
Reclamation Act of 1902, 284
Regional Planning, 42–48, 55, 229
metropolitan, 266–78
Regional Planning Association, 44, 158, 266
Regional Planning Commissions:
Atlanta region, 267
Colorado River Basin, 55
metropolitan, 267
New England Regional Commission, 55
Pacific Northwest, 55
Twin Cities, Minn., 267, 270–73
Regional transportation system (network), 45, 108, 199
Reich, Robert, Secretary of Labor, 213
Reilly model, 201
Reiner, Thomas A., 83
Reinhold, Robert, 287
Reisner, Marc, 284, 285
Rent control, 190
Reps, John W., 29, 61
Resettlement Administration, 54
Residual value of land, 178
Reston, Va., 147
Revitalization, 177
of downtown, 187–88
Richmond Parkway, N.Y.C., 251–52
Rio Conference, *See* International Earth Summit
Riis, Jacob, 33
Riverside, Ill., 33
Roanoke, Va., 187
Robinson, Charles Mulford, 35
Robinson, Jerry W., 194
Roehampton, Great Britain, 155
Roosevelt, Franklin D., President, 53
Rose, Mark H., 298
Russell Sage Foundation, 44
Ryan, Pauline, 163

Sand, Judge Leonard B., 91
St. Louis, highway map of, 199
St.Paul-Minneapolis region, 270
San Francisco, 128, 137
Embarcadero Freeway, 203
Sanitary reform, 31–32
Sanitary survey, 31
Santa Monica, Calif., 127
Savannah, Ga., 30
Schlesinger, Arthur M., 53
Schumacher, Ernest F., 226
Schumpeter, Joseph, 182
Schwartz, Seymour I., 125
Scott, Claudia D., 164
Scott, Mel, 40, 41, 43, 61
Scott, Randall W., 225
Sears Roebuck, location and subsidies, 214
Separation of powers, 80
Sewers:
development and, 227, 232
"water carriage," 31
Shearer, Derek, 312
Shopping center, location of, 109
Sierra Club, 81, 231
Silverman, David W., 228
Simon, Herbert, 303
Single-parent family, 90
Site plan review, 121–22
Slum clearance, 56, 179–81
Smith, Adam, 308
So, Frank, S., 11
Soil characteristics, 101
Solar heating, 242, 259
Soleri, Paolo, 154, 156
Solid waste management, 255–57
Southern Burlington County NAACP vs. *Township of Mt. Laurel*, 118
Soviet Union, 52

Stamford, Conn., 184
Standard Metropolitan Statistical Area (SMSA), 16
State Implementation Plans (SIP), 74, 249
State planning, 46, 56, 59, 74
  Florida, 238
  Hawaii, 236
  Vermont, 237
Steam engine, 11
Sternlieb, George, 14, 21, 115
Stockbridge, Mass., 34
Stollman, Isreal, 110
Strict constructionism, 53
Structural unemployment, 59, 210
Subdivision regulations, 110
Subsidies for economic development, 212–13
Suburbanization, 16, 18–19, 195
Suburban planning, 150–51
Summers, Gene, 218
Sunbelt, 19
"Superfund," 247
Sununu, John, 263
Supreme Court:
  housing integration, 90–91
  public housing, 54
Suskind, Lawrence, 82

"Taking" power, 65
Tamany Hall, N.Y., 79
Tax base, 110, 117, 160, 163, 180, 215, 218, 230
Tax incidence, 241
Tax Reform Act of 1986, 295
Taylor, Barbara, 125
Tenement Housing Act of 1901, New York City, 34
Tenements, 10–11
Tennessee Valley Authority (TVA), 55, 288
Thompson, James J., Gov., 214
Thompson, Wilbur, 181, 225
Toxic Substance Control Act, 58
Trancik, Roger, 158
Transfer of development rights (TDR), 124
Transportation:
  air, 220
  auto, 197–208
  bicycle, 259
  cost of, in nineteenth century, 10
  gravity model, 201
  induced demand, 203
  planning, 204–208
  public, 97, 196, 204, 246, 259
  railroad, 210
  study, 101
  subway, 108, 205
  system, 136, 197–200
Transportation Management Systems (TMS), 205–206
Tugwell, Rexford, 55
Twin Cities Metropolitan Planning Commission, 267–75

Union Pacific Railroad, 282
Urban concentration, 10–13
Urban design, 122, 125, 134–58, 176
Urban Development Action Grant (UDAG), 186, 212
Urban growth, 9
Urban homesteading, 186
Urban Mass Transit Acts (UMTA), 204
Urban political reform movement, 79
Urban Renewal, 54, 56, 77, 82–83, 136, 177–85, 293, 296
Urban sprawl, 14
Urban "underclass," 89
Utilities, 217, 228–30

Vaux, Calvin, 32
Vermont Plan, 231
Village of Euclid vs. *Ambler Realty Co.*, 67
Ville Radieuse (Radiant City), 154
"Voisin" plan, Paris, 155

Wallace, Henry, 53
Wall Street, 66
Warner, Sam Bass, 13
Washington, D.C., 30, 38, 65, 108, 293
  highway map of, 199
  metro, 205, 259
Water policy, 284–87
Water Pollution Control Act of 1972, 253
Water quality planning, 253–55
Water Resources Development Act (WRDA), 286
Weber, Adna, 9, 11, 26
Wells, H.G., 13
Western water policy in retrospect, 287–88
Westchester County, N.Y., 44, 130
West Village, of Manhattan's Greenwich Village, 122
White Plains, N.Y., 109, 130
Whyte, William, 148
Williams, Serena, 125
Wilson, James Q., 193
Wilson, William J., 89
Wood, Robert, 46
Wright, Frank Lloyd, 154
Wrigley, Robert L., Jr., 37, 39

Yearwood, Richard, 110
Yellowstone National Park, 296
Yonkers housing controversy, 90–92

Zero-population growth (ZPG), 59, 226
Ziggurat design, in high-rise buildings, 66
Zoning, 110–28
  Board of Appeals, 111
  bonus/incentive, 123
  capital gains from change of, 114
  cluster, 126
  development agreements and, 127
  early developments, 39–41
  exclusionary, 118–21
  fiscal, 97
  inclusionary, 125
  laws, 110–11
  legal basis of, 64–68, 116–21
  model state ordinance, 41
  new trends in, 121–28
  New York City ordinance of 1916, 67–68
  performance, 126, 232
  relation to property tax, 116–17
  saturation studies, 122
  solar access, 258
Zupan, J., 158